Jewish Concepts of Scripture

Jewish Concepts
of Scripture

A Comparative Introduction

EDITED BY

Benjamin D. Sommer

New York University Press
NEW YORK AND LONDON

NEW YORK UNIVERSITY PRESS
New York and London
www.nyupress.org

© 2012 by New York University
All rights reserved

References to Internet websites (URLs) were accurate at the time of writing.
Neither the author nor New York University Press is responsible for URLs
that may have expired or changed since the manuscript was prepared.

Library of Congress Cataloging-in-Publication Data
Jewish concepts of Scripture : a comparative introduction /
edited by Benjamin D. Sommer.
p. cm.
Includes bibliographical references and index.
ISBN 978-0-8147-4062-0 (cl : alk. paper)
ISBN 978-0-8147-6002-4 (pb : alk. paper)
ISBN 978-0-8147-2479-8 (ebook)
ISBN 978-0-8147-2460-6 (ebook)
1. Bible. O.T.—Criticism, interpretation, etc., Jewish.
I. Sommer, Benjamin D., 1964–
BS1186.J474 2012
221.1—dc23   2012015882

New York University Press books are printed on acid-free paper,
and their binding materials are chosen for strength and durability.
We strive to use environmentally responsible suppliers and materials
to the greatest extent possible in publishing our books.

Manufactured in the United States of America

c 10 9 8 7 6 5 4 3 2 1
p 10 9 8 7 6 5 4 3 2 1

שָׁם, מֵעֵבֶר לַבַּיִת,
בָּאֹפֶק,
חַיִּים אֶת חַיֵּיהֶם הָאִלְּמִים
הֶהָרִים הַנִּשָּׂפִים, הָעוֹטִים
אֶת סוֹדָם בִּצְעִיף אָפֹר,
וּמִתַּחַת לְרִצְפַּת הַבַּיִת
חַי אֶת חַיָּיו הַטְּמִירִים,
אֶת חַיָּיו הַמְיֻחָדִים,
הֶעָפָר,
וְכָל מַה שֶּׁטָּמוּן בְּתוֹכוֹ
זְרָעִים, שָׁרָשִׁים, מַעְיָנוֹת . . .
. . . .
אֲרֶשֶׁת שֶׁל סְתָמִיּוּת שְׁפוּכָה
עַל פְּנֵי אֲבָנָיו הַכֵּהוֹת —
וַהֲרֵי זֶה כִּמְעַט בִּטָּחוֹן.
—זלדה, "הבית הישן"

There, beyond the house,
on the horizon,
the lofty mountains, wearing
their secret as a gray veil,
live their mute lives,
and beneath the floor of the house
the dust
lives its hidden life,
its unique and solitary life,
along with all that is hidden in it—
seeds, roots, springs . . .

. . . .

An expression—uncertainty, just so—is poured
over the surface of its dark stones—
and after all, that is almost faith.

—Zeldah, "The Old House," in *Shirei Zeldah*
(Tel Aviv: Haqqibbutz Hame'uchad, 1985), 9
Translation by Benjamin D. Sommer

Contents

	Acknowledgments	ix
1	Introduction: Scriptures in Jewish Tradition, and Traditions as Jewish Scripture *Benjamin D. Sommer*	1
2	Concepts of Scripture in the Synagogue Service *Elsie Stern*	15
3	Concepts of Scripture in Rabbinic Judaism: Oral Torah and Written Torah *Steven D. Fraade*	31
4	Concepts of Scripture in the Schools of Rabbi Akiva and Rabbi Ishmael *Azzan Yadin-Israel*	47
5	Concepts of Scriptural Language in Midrash *Benjamin D. Sommer*	64
6	Concepts of Scripture among the Jews of the Medieval Islamic World *Meira Polliack*	80
7	Concepts of Scripture in the School of Rashi *Robert A. Harris*	102
8	Concepts of Scripture in Maimonides *James A. Diamond*	123
9	Concepts of Scripture in Nahmanides *Aaron W. Hughes*	139
10	Concepts of Scripture in Jewish Mysticism *Moshe Idel*	157

11	Concepts of Scripture in Martin Buber and Franz Rosenzweig *Jonathan Cohen*	179
12	The Pentateuch as Scripture and the Challenge of Biblical Criticism: Responses among Modern Jewish Thinkers and Scholars *Baruch J. Schwartz*	203
13	Concepts of Scripture in Yehezkel Kaufmann *Job Y. Jindo*	230
14	Concepts of Scripture in Moshe Greenberg *Marc Zvi Brettler*	247
15	Concepts of Scripture in Mordechai Breuer *Shalom Carmy*	267
16	Scripture and Modern Israeli Literature *Yael S. Feldman*	280
17	Scripture and Israeli Secular Culture *Yair Zakovitch*	299

Glossary   317
About the Contributors   321
Index   325

Acknowledgments

I am grateful to Jennifer Hammer from New York University Press for suggesting that I edit this volume and for her patience. I worked on the volume during sabbaticals at the Shalom Hartman Institute in Jerusalem, the Hebrew University of Jerusalem, and the Tikvah Center for Law and Jewish Civilization at New York University School of Law and also while serving as a faculty member at Northwestern University and the Jewish Theological Seminary. All these places provide settings that nurture rigorous and engaged scholarship, and I am privileged to be associated with each of them. Funding for producing the indices and proofreading was provided by the Lucius N. Littauer Foundation. I am, always, very grateful to their support for research in Jewish Studies. My friend Richard Tupper gave me consistently excellent advice on matters of writing, conceptualization, and style. Andrew Katz did a fine job of editing the manuscript and preparing it for publication. Leslie Rubin did a masterful job preparing the index and aiding me with the proofs. It was a pleasure working with her. My family —Jennifer, Avraham Ayyal, Sarah Gilah, and Eliana Shlomit—create the perfect mix of respect and love, sometimes letting me sit in my office to study and work, and sometimes coming in and thus reminding me it's time to play. יעמדו כלם על הברכה.

Benjamin D. Sommer
ערב יום כפור תשע״ב
October 7, 2011
Teaneck, NJ

Chapter 1

Introduction
Scriptures in Jewish Tradition, and Traditions as Jewish Scripture

Benjamin D. Sommer

On one level, there is a simple answer to the question "What is scripture for the Jews?" For roughly the past two thousand years, Jews have had a canon of twenty-four books that form the Jewish Bible,[1] starting with Genesis and ending with Chronicles.[2] Some Jewish groups up until about two thousand years ago accepted additional books as scripture, but by the end of the first century CE the canon used by Jews today was more or less universally accepted by all Jews. In this respect, Jews differ from Christians, since to this day there are books regarded by Orthodox Christians and Catholics as scripture that Protestants either reject or regard as less than fully scriptural.[3] The anthology containing these twenty-four books is known to Jews by several names: *Kitvei Ha-qodesh* ("sacred texts"), *Miqra* ("Reading"), and *Tanakh* (an acronym for the three sections of the Jewish canon: *Torah*, *Nevi'im*, and *Ketuvim*).[4]

On a deeper level, however, Jews of different times, places, and sects would answer the question "What is scripture?" in profoundly different ways. However much they agree on what books and even what precise words, consonants, and vowels constitute scripture, they have a wide range of views regarding the nature and purpose of these texts. The chapters in this volume attempt to answer the questions: How have various Jewish thinkers and movements conceptualized scripture? What is scripture for? What type of information does one get from it—historical, scientific, theological, moral, or something else? Is one primarily supposed to get information or guidance from it, or does it have some other purpose altogether?

For example, are copying it, decorating it, or marching around a sacred space with it commendable ways to show reverence to God? By chanting it, can one acquire merit or perhaps alter the Godhead or even perform magic? Answering these questions involves not so much studying how various Jews have read scripture (that is, examining the interpretive methods Jews have used to derive meaning from it) but asking prior questions: Why do they read it, or perform rituals with it, in the first place? For what reasons have Jews turned to this anthology?

The varied answers to these questions in the chapters that follow will speak for themselves. Before turning to them, however, it is useful to consider an overview of certain core ideas regarding scripture that almost all Jewish groups have assumed for the past two thousand years. We will see that these ideas differentiate Jewish conceptions of scripture from Christian ones in fundamental ways. To be sure, all twenty-four books of Jewish scripture are part of the Christian Bible in its various forms. Nonetheless, in many respects these texts function so differently in the two traditions that one can rightly say that the books in question are not the same books at all but entirely different works that happen to have the same words.

The Primacy of Torah

We should begin by noting that the twenty-four books of the Jewish canon are not all equal. The first five books (Genesis, Exodus, Leviticus, Numbers, and Deuteronomy, often referred to in Hebrew as the Torah or the *Ḥumash* and in English as the Five Books of Moses or the Pentateuch) are by far the most important, the most authoritative, and the most familiar to Jews. The remaining books are traditionally divided into two groups, the *Nevi'im*, or Prophets (a category that includes not only prophetic books such as Isaiah and Jeremiah but historical works such as 1–2 Samuel), and the *Ketuvim*, or Writings (sometimes called the Hagiographa). On a practical level, however, it would be more helpful to say that the Jewish Bible has two parts: First and foremost, there is the Torah—the *T* in the acronym *Tanakh*. Also, there is the rest of the Bible—the *Nakh* of the acronym; in fact, one does sometimes hear the term *Nakh* used among Jews to refer to "the part of the Bible coming after the Torah." Only the Torah is chanted in its entirety in the course of synagogue worship (usually, over the course of a year); only a fraction of the remaining material is chanted in the synagogue. Jewish schools tend to give much more attention to the Torah than they give to the

Nakh. While Jewish beliefs flow from and to some degree claim to be based on the whole Tanakh, Jewish law—the core of Jewish practice and identity—claims to be based on the Torah alone.

Scripture and Tradition

One can justly wonder whether it is accurate to equate "scripture" in Judaism solely with the Tanakh. The historian of religion William Graham writes in his very useful article on scripture in *The Encyclopedia of Religion* that the term "scripture" designates "texts that are revered as especially sacred and authoritative in . . . religious traditions," and he goes on to describe a number of characteristic roles and attributes of scriptures in religious traditions from around the world.[5] As one thinks about Graham's definition from the point of view of Judaism, one quickly realizes (as Graham himself notes)[6] that the classical works of rabbinic literature—that is, the Mishnah, the Talmuds, and the midrashim[7]—fit the definition almost as well as the Bible, and in some ways even better. For example, Graham writes that "the written scriptural text symbolizes or embodies religious authority in many traditions (often replacing the living authority of a religious founder such as Muhammad or the Buddha)."[8] This sentence applies to both the Bible and rabbinic literature in Judaism; more specifically, we might say that the Bible *symbolizes* religious authority, while rabbinic literature *embodies* it, for on a practical level Jewish religious authorities seeking directives regarding Jewish law and ritual turn not to the Bible but to rabbinic texts. Similarly, Graham points to the importance of scripture both in public ritual (where it may be recited aloud or it may serve as a ritual object) and in private study (which shapes devotional and spiritual life). It is true that the Torah and, to a lesser degree, passages from the Prophets and the Writings play roles in public ritual in a way that rabbinic texts do not: they are chanted in synagogue worship according to highly formalized rules, for instance—and in this respect, the Bible is more typically scriptural than rabbinic literature is. Nonetheless, in many forms of Judaism (especially in the culture of ultra-Orthodoxy), studying as a devotional act focuses on the Talmud and not on the Bible[9]—and in this respect, the Talmud is more scriptural for many Jews than the Bible is. "Every text that achieves scriptural status in a religious community elicits extensive popular and scholarly exegesis and study of its contents," Graham points out, and this exegesis tends to stress what Graham calls the "unicity" of the scripture, its wholeness and its lack of self-contradiction.[10] Here again, rabbinic literature fits the description just as much as the Bible does; whole literatures emerged in medieval and modern Judaism that comment on the Bible and the Talmud, and these literatures often stress the unity of the texts they interpret, focusing on harmonizing what appear to be contradictions between different parts of the biblical or talmudic whole. In the case of the Babylonian Talmud, a whole literature of commentaries, known as *Tosafot*, arose whose main concern is to emphasize this harmony of the whole talmudic corpus. Graham asserts that "a text is only 'scripture' insofar as a group of persons perceives it to be sacred or holy, powerful and meaningful, possessed of an exalted authority, and in some fashion transcendent of, and hence distinct from, other speech and writing."[11] This sentence fits the Mishnah and also, for many Jews, the Zohar, the central work of Jewish mysticism; but it is even truer of the Tanakh, or at least of the Torah (indeed, the Zohar itself makes claims about the exalted, transcendent, and ontologically distinct nature of the Torah that it does not make about itself).

One senses, then, that in Judaism scripture is not an either/or category. Biblical books and some postbiblical texts are scriptural, but in different ways and to different extents. Within the Tanakh, the Torah is more scriptural than the Prophets and Writings are. Within rabbinic literature, the Babylonian Talmud is more scriptural than the Jerusalem Talmud is, and some, but not all, Jews accept the Zohar as having what Graham identifies as scriptural attributes. One can even argue—and some classical Jewish thinkers have argued—that in many ways some works of rabbinic literature are more canonical than the biblical Prophets and Writings are.[12] Thus, for Judaism, the whole category of scripture is more fluid than it is in Christianity (especially in Protestant Christianity). In this regard, Judaism has much more in common with, say, Hinduism or Buddhism. In a magisterial work titled *What Is Scripture?* (whose probing analyses underlie the whole project of the book you are now reading), the historian of religions Wilfred Cantwell Smith shows that a "theoretically somewhat informal scripture" exists in Hinduism, an amorphous or polymorphous set of texts that are variously sacred, authoritative, transcendent, and/or influential.[13] Much the same can be said of the manifold scriptures of Mahayana Buddhism and even of the more restricted, but still polymorphous, scriptures of Theravada Buddhism.[14] Precisely the same situation exists in Judaism. Pausing to examine the ways that several types of literature (biblical, rabbinic, and otherwise) are variously sacred, authoritative, transcendent, and/or influential will be worth our while.

The modern Jewish thinker Moshe Halbertal distinguishes between two types of canon, which he calls *normative* and *formative*. Texts that are canonical in the *normative* sense are obeyed and followed; they provide the group loyal to the text with guides to behavior and belief. Texts that are canonical in the *formative* sense are "taught, read, transmitted and interpreted. . . . They provide a society or a profession with a shared vocabulary."[15] For Jews, both the Bible and rabbinic literature function as canon in the formative sense. Both are studied, taught, transmitted, and interpreted, and consequently both help to form Jewish identity.[16] Halbertal suggests in passing that the Bible is canonical in the normative sense, but I think that in practice this is not the case. In Judaism, the Bible is taught and read, transmitted and interpreted, but it is not the location of legal norms that are followed on a practical level. When one wants to know whether a pot is kosher or whether a business transaction is acceptable or what time the Passover Seder must begin, one does not open up a Bible. One turns instead to works of rabbinic literature. Crucial beliefs regarding messianism, resurrection, and the nature of God are also articulated in rabbinic and postrabbinic texts rather than in the Bible.[17] Judaism's normative canon is found primarily within rabbinic literature rather than in the Bible.

In short, one can make a very strong argument that the religious category "scripture" applies in Judaism to both the Bible and rabbinic literature, even though the latter has usually been thought of as belonging in the extrascriptural category that theologians and scholars of religion refer to as "tradition." For Jews, however, the categories of "scripture" and "tradition" overlap; the very distinction between them is a Protestant one, and its application to Judaism can lead to misunderstanding.[18] Many Jewish texts apply the Hebrew term *torah* to both the Bible and rabbinic literature. As Steven Fraade explains in his chapter in this volume, rabbinic texts use the term "Written Torah" to refer to the Bible and "Oral Torah" to refer to works of rabbinic literature. Both, according to classical rabbinic thought, were revealed at Sinai.[19] The classical rabbis often stress the unity of these two Torahs, effectively denying that there is an ontologically significant difference between them at all.[20]

All this raises the question: if this volume is concerned with Jewish conceptions of scripture, should it limit itself to describing how various Jewish thinkers and movements view the Bible? Perhaps in our discussions we should include rabbinic literature under the rubric "scripture"; some works of Jewish philosophy and mysticism might come under this rubric as well. A strong argument can be made that in focusing on the Bible, this volume imports a Protestant Christian notion of scripture into Judaism and thus misrepresents the tradition it is attempting to explicate.

Nonetheless, several arguments, both theoretical and practical, support the decision to limit this volume's discussion to Jewish conceptions of what might—without redundancy—be termed "biblical scripture." First, for all the emphasis in some rabbinic texts on the close relationship and underlying unity of the Written Torah and the Oral Torah, Jewish tradition does distinguish between them. As a ritual object, the Written Torah has a status that the Oral Torah lacks. Scrolls of Written Torah used in synagogue worship (especially scrolls of the Pentateuch, but also of the book of Esther and in some synagogues of other works from the Writings and the Prophets as well) serve as rule-bound loci of holiness in a way that editions of rabbinic texts do not. Jewish law regulates and ritualizes the chanting of biblical texts in liturgy, but it does not do so for rabbinic texts. (Here we should recall that Judaism is a religion of law, and thus the highest honor Judaism bestows on a person or thing is to subject it to rules. That biblical texts are rule bound to a far greater degree than rabbinic ones is therefore significant.) On a more theoretical level, Jewish thinkers and movements have invested considerable time and effort into conceptualizing both the Written Torah and the Oral Torah, but they do so in different ways; and thus it makes sense to focus our discussions on one or the other. A book that attempted to treat conceptions of the Bible as scripture as well as conceptions of rabbinic literature as scripture would either be too long or too shallow. The chapters that follow focus therefore on the Bible, but the reader will always need to keep in mind the scriptural characteristics of some postbiblical teachings in traditional Judaism.[21]

The Term "Scripture"

The English term "scripture" is misleading in a discussion of Judaism for two reasons. First, this term focuses our attention on the Bible as a written document and may lead us to forget that the Bible was both a written and an oral/aural text for most of Jewish history.[22] To be sure, the Bible is known in rabbinic literature as the Written Torah, and rabbis often cite biblical verses with the phrase *kakatuv*, "as it is written." But one of the most common terms for the Bible in Hebrew, *miqra*, comes from the verb *qara*, which means not only "read" but "read aloud, call"; similarly, biblical verses in rabbinic literature are often cited with the phrase *sheneʾemar*, "as it is said." For centuries, most Jews knew the Bible primarily from hearing it chanted. Many Jews memorized large parts of it (and here it is useful to recall that the Hebrew word for memorizing "by heart," *'al peh*, literally means memorizing "by mouth"). The technology through which one comes to know information shapes how we use that information, and thus it is important to recall the extent to which the Bible was as much an aural/oral document for Jews throughout the ages as a written one. When scripture was mostly memorized, recited, and chanted, it functioned in one set of ways, and people searched it for certain types of information or guidance. When it became more widely available in handwritten copies and, ultimately, in printed editions, changes occurred in the ways it was interpreted and the sorts of information people tried to get from it.[23] The chapters in this volume by Sommer and Harris describe a move from an ancient approach to the Bible as a collection of verses to medieval and modern views of the Bible as a collection of stories, poems, and legal corpora; the rabbis of the ancient period read the Bible atomistically, while later scholars tended to read it more holistically. Many factors contributed to this change, but the greater availability of written texts played a particularly important role.

The term "scripture" is misleading in another way: for much of Jewish history, the plural form "scriptures" would be more appropriate than the singular.[24] In the modern West, we tend to think of the Bible as a single entity. Typically, one owns a Bible in one volume. But in antiquity, this was not the case; individual biblical books were written on individual scrolls. Thus, the conceptual category of a unified scripture was less prominent. (This situation probably played some role in engendering Judaism's two-tiered conception of the Tanakh, in which Torah is most sacred and Nakh less so.) One might have expected this situation to change with the invention in the first century CE of the codex, a one-volume format that could contain the whole Bible, or with the rise of printing in Europe in the fifteenth century. Even then, however, the situation stayed largely the same. Jews continued to use individual scrolls of the Pentateuch for liturgical purposes; indeed, Jews still use these scrolls for liturgical reading in synagogue. For study, they used multivolume editions that usually included only part of the Bible, along with rabbinic commentaries; many Jews use these volumes for study to this day. In the majority of cases, these editions contained the Pentateuch or, somewhat less frequently, the Pentateuch along with those selections from the Prophets used in synagogue lectionary.[25] These simple facts had profound effects on the way Jews conceptualized the Bible until fairly recently. For contemporary Jews, the idea that one might have a conception of "the Bible" seems natural: "the Bible" is a category we think with, since "the Bible" is a volume many of us own. But religious Jews prior to the twentieth century rarely owned *a* Bible. Rather, they owned multi-volume collections that contained both biblical texts and rabbinic commentary; or they did not own any books at all but heard selections from the Bible chanted from scrolls and explicated by preachers at a synagogue. Thus, they were less inclined to think of "the Bible" as a category, though they were not entirely unfamiliar with it either.

Several factors fortified the notion of the Bible (as opposed to "scriptures") as an important category for modern Jews. These included, first of all, the rise of Zionism, which emphasized the Bible instead of the Talmud as the central text of the Jewish people.[26] Thus, for example, Israeli schoolchildren and new recruits to the Israeli military are normally given a small, one-volume Tanakh—an important cultural artifact that conveys certain values even if the student or soldier rarely opens it. Another factor, at least for central European and North American Jews (and Jews elsewhere influenced by them), was greater contact with Protestants, for whom scripture was a central category of religious thought. We should recall that the increasing prevalence of the one-volume Bible and, with it, the greater prominence of the concept of "scripture" as opposed to "scriptures" in Judaism are very recent developments in Jewish history.

Theologies of Scripture versus Conceptions of Scripture

This book is meant to complement another volume published by NYU Press, *Christian Theologies of Scripture: A Comparative Introduction*, edited by Justin Holcomb. The differences between the books, which begin with the title, are instructive, because they reflect some essential differences between Judaism and Christianity. First, Judaism is not only a religion but in wider senses a culture, and the Jews are not only a faith community but an ethnicity.[27] One can be a Jew and an atheist in a way that one cannot be a Christian and an atheist. (Jewish law, especially as established by Maimonides, regards an atheistic Jew as a sinner, but in Jewish law such a Jew remains a Jew.) As a result, this volume cannot limit itself to discussions of *theologies* of scripture. The Bible plays roles not only in Jewish religious thought and practice but throughout all realms of Jewish culture. Secular Jews (and especially secular Zionists) have found the Bible more useful, more relevant, more malleable, and more interesting than they have found rabbinic literature and other Jewish religious writings. On a practical level, the Bible has an even more important place in secular Judaism than it has in religious Judaism—hence the need for chapters by Yair Zakovitch and Yael Feldman on the place of the Bible in Israeli culture and Israeli literature. (Had space permitted, chapters on the Bible in Yiddish literature and in American Jewish culture would have been appropriate additions to this volume. Given Feldman's focus on Israeli fiction, a separate chapter on the fascinating roles the Bible plays in Israeli poetry might have been written as well, but space did not allow this.)[28]

Second, the discipline of theology does not have the same place in Judaism that it has in Christianity, while the genre of commentary does not have the same importance in Christianity that it has in Judaism. Both types of literature are known in each religion, but commentators play for Jews the central role that theologians play for Christians. Jewish children start learning Rashi—not Maimonides—as early as third grade; adults, laypeople and scholars alike, study both, but they are rather more likely to study the commentaries penned by the former than the philosophical works of the latter. When religious Jews do study Maimonides, they are more likely to study his legal works, which points to another central literature in Judaism: halakhic texts, including both legal codes and responses to specific questions addressed to legal authorities over the centuries. Thus, my statement regarding the role of theologians might be rephrased: for Jewish communities, commentators and legal authorities play a central role that theologians rarely achieve. We saw previously that the Jewish thinker Moshe Halbertal discusses "formative canon"—that is, the curricula that shape Jewish lives not only within the walls of educational institutions but far beyond them as well.[29] The formative canon of Jews for the past two thousand years has involved commentaries on the Bible and on rabbinic literature; it has involved legal texts; but to the extent that it has included theological and philosophical works, their influence has been more mediated, and their place in curricula has been less robust.

Consequently, unlike the volume that Holcomb edited, this volume does not limit itself to theologians. It attends to biblical scholars and interpreters, ancient, medieval, and modern: Azzan Yadin-Israel discusses the interpretive schools of Rabbi Akiva and Rabbi Yishmael; Meira Polliack and Robert Harris discuss medieval commentators; Baruch Schwartz, Job Jindo, and Marc Brettler discuss various modern Jewish biblical scholars. (In Schwartz's case, the discussion of how Jewish scholars in the past two centuries responded to modern theories about the Pentateuch not only lays out several schools of modern Jewish thought but clarifies core attitudes to the Pentateuch among premodern Jews as well.) This volume does include discussions of some theologians, but it is noteworthy that most of them were biblical commentators and/or translators as well. This is the case for Nahmanides, whom Aaron Hughes discusses, for Martin Buber and Franz Rosenzweig, whom Jonathan Cohen examines, and for Mordechai Breuer, whom Shalom Carmy analyzes; this also applies to some of the mystics whom Moshe Idel discusses in his chapter. (Similarly, Yehezkel Kaufmann, whom Jindo discusses, might be considered a Jewish thinker or theologian as much as a biblical critic.) Maimonides, the subject of James Diamond's chapter, is the only thinker who could not in some sense be considered a biblical commentator. Yet even Maimonides devotes close to a third of his philosophical magnum opus, *The Guide of the Perplexed*, to explaining the nature of biblical language and metaphor. Mindful of W. C. Smith's thesis that scripture is a human activity, often manifesting itself through ritual,[30] I also commissioned Elsie Stern's chapter on the conception of scripture that emerges from the Jewish lectionary cycle (a conception, Stern reminds us, that has enjoyed the most widespread purchase among actual Jews throughout history). Some ritual uses of scripture are also discussed in Idel's chapter.

The list of topics that appeared in the preceding two paragraphs will raise a question among many readers: why these thinkers and movements and not other, equally important and influential ones? There is no doubt that this volume is impoverished by its many absences. There are dozens of commentators, ancient, medieval, and modern, to whom space might have been devoted. Among the philosophers and theologians, many of great interest are missing: Saadia Gaon on one end of the historical spectrum, Abraham Joshua Heschel and Emmanuel Levinas on the other. Conceptions of scripture in nonrabbinic forms of ancient Judaism, such as the community responsible for the Dead Sea Scrolls, were vastly different from what has been surveyed here, and their absence is keenly felt. Several modern biblical scholars[31] have taught us that scripture existed before Scripture, torah before the Torah: already in the biblical period itself, long before the Bible was canonized and indeed before many biblical books had been edited into the forms in which we know them, some texts were already regarded as sacred and authoritative. These included, for example, sayings of the prophets that were later edited into the prophetic books we know and law codes attributed to Moses that later became parts of the Pentateuch. Thus, even before there was a Bible, there was scripture in ancient Israel; one might say that texts regarded as holy in the preexilic biblical period gradually became the Bible in the postexilic biblical period and the early postbiblical period. Consequently, chapters on ancient Israelite conceptions of scripture would have added much to this volume. Had we but space enough, and time, we could have added more chapters, but the resulting volume would have been impossible to publish. So this smaller volume will have to suffice. Turning its pages, readers will not find everything in it; but the fact that finishing its work is impossible should not dissuade one from beginning it.

NOTES

1. To count twenty-four books, one needs to recall that Jewish tradition regards twelve short prophetic books (beginning with Hosea and ending with Malachi) as a single unit, known as *Trei Asar* (the Twelve); so, too, Ezra-Nehemiah are a single book, as are First and Second Samuel, First and Second Kings, and First and Second Chronicles.

2. In a few manuscripts, the order of these books differs slightly; for example, in the oldest manuscript of the Masoretic text, the Aleppo Codex, Chronicles appears before Psalms rather than at the end of the canon. This fact hardly overturns my observation that there has been unanimity among Jews regarding the canon's contents over the past two millennia.

3. Specifically, most Protestants do not accept certain Jewish books from the late Second Temple period as part of their scripture; they often term these books "the Apocrypha." Catholics and Orthodox Christians, however, do accept these books as scriptural (and thus do not traditionally refer to them as Apocrypha). These books have not been part of Jewish scripture for around two thousand years, but many of them were probably regarded as scriptural by some Jewish groups in the late Second Temple period.

4. In English, Jews generally refer to the anthology as "the Bible." Contrary to what some people assume, they do not typically refer to it as "the Hebrew Bible"; that term is a neutral, nondenominational one used in academic settings to refer to the anthology in question, instead of using the specifically Christian term "the Old Testament" or the specifically Jewish term "the Bible."

5. William Graham, "Scripture," in *Encyclopedia of Religion*, 16 vols., ed. Mircea Eliade and Charles Adams (New York: Macmillan, 1987), 13:133b–45b; the definition is from 133b.

6. See ibid., 134a–b, and cf. 141b. See also the discussion of Talmud as "parascripture" in Wilfred Cantwell Smith, *What Is Scripture? A Comparative Approach* (Minneapolis: Fortress, 1993), 204–6.

7. For brief definitions of these terms (and of similar terms that occur throughout this volume), see the Glossary at the end of the book.

8. Graham, "Scripture," 138a–140b.

9. On the relative place of Bible and Talmud in Jewish curricula through the ages, see the helpful summary in Moshe Halbertal, *People of the Book: Canon, Meaning, and Authority* (Cambridge: Harvard University Press, 1997), 98–100, with extensive references to primary and secondary sources. This book is crucial reading for anyone interested in Jewish conceptions of scripture.

10. Graham, "Scripture," 141b, 143a.

11. Ibid., 134b.

12. For references to such thinkers, see Menahem Kasher, *Torah Shelemah*, 48 vols., in Hebrew (Jerusalem: Beit Torah Shelemah, 1979), 19.277 §108. See further my discussion of this issue in "Unity and Plurality in Jewish Canons: The Case of the Oral and Written Torahs," in *One Scripture or Many? Perspectives Historical, Theological and Philosophical*, ed. Christine Helmer and Christof Landmesser (New York: Oxford University Press, 2004), 119–20.

13. Smith, *What Is Scripture?*, 126–27, 299n. 3; see also Graham, "Scripture," 134a–b, 141b.

14. See Smith, *What Is Scripture?*, 146–75, esp. 150–53

15. Halbertal, *People of the Book*, 3.

16. Some groups focus more on one, and some more on others. The Bible is a much more important part of the formative canon for secular Israeli Jews; rabbinic literature, and especially the Babylonian Talmud, is a more important part of the formative canon for ultra-Orthodox Jews.

17. To be sure, traditional Jewish thinkers have linked these beliefs and practices to the Bible through exegesis, but one would not be able to note their presence there without the rabbinic commentaries.

18. In many ways, "scripture" in Judaism (and in Catholicism) is a subset of the larger category of "tradition," or in any event tradition is conceptually and historically prior to scripture rather than, as many people assume, vice versa. See my remarks in "Unity and Plurality," 109–11, esp. n. 3, and 124–25, esp. n. 46.

19. Note that at this point we have seen three distinct uses of the term "Torah" in this chapter, all of them frequently found in Jewish literature:
- "Torah" (especially, "*the* Torah") can refer to the first and most important part of the Jewish Bible, the Five Books of Moses.
- The "Written Torah" refers to all twenty-four books of the Jewish Bible.
- "Oral Torah" refers to works of rabbinic literature. The boundaries of this sort of Torah are fluid and ever expanding; clearly, the Mishnah and

Talmuds and classical midrashim are part of it, but so are some (though not all) comments made by both students and teachers during classes held at a yeshiva or a synagogue just yesterday, and today, and tomorrow.
A fourth use, also common in Jewish circles, should also be noted:
- "Torah" (but not "*the* Torah") can mean all Jewish learning in all times, whether written down or not.

It is worth pausing to ask which meaning a classical Jewish text intends when it uses the term "Torah." In some cases, the answer to this question is not entirely clear—a circumstance which further supports the notion that Jewish scriptures represent the sort of polymorphous, theoretically informal scripture that W. C. Smith describes in Hinduism.

20. See Sommer, "Unity and Plurality," 121–27.

21. There are exceptions to what I have said here about the scriptural nature of rabbinic tradition in Judaism, especially in the Judaism of the Sadducees, the Karaites, and perhaps also the Dead Sea Scrolls. On the Karaites, see chapter 6 in this volume by Meira Polliack.

22. On the importance of recalling the oral/aural aspect of scripture not only in Judaism but in religious traditions around the world, see Smith, *What Is Scripture?*, 7–9 and 376, s.v. "Oral/aural," as well as Graham, "Scripture," 137b–39a. Graham has devoted an entire volume to this crucial issue: William A. Graham, *Beyond the Written Word: Oral Aspects of Scripture in the History of Religion* (Cambridge: Cambridge University Press, 1987).

23. The invention of the printing press (a relatively recent event, from the point of view of Judaism's long history) had a profound effect on the ways people related to the Bible and conceptualized it. The availability of the Bible in easily searched and retrieved digital formats today is likely to have a significant effect on Jewish and Christian notions of scripture in the future, indeed in the very near future.

24. Smith, *What Is Scripture?*, 13–14, 53–56, 126–27.

25. See Herbert Zafren, "Bible Editions, Bible Study and the Early History of Hebrew Printing," *Eretz Israel* 16 (1982): 240–51. Zafren's listing of early printed editions shows that only about 15 of the 142 Hebrew editions of biblical texts and commentaries printed between 1469 and 1528 contained the full Tanakh. The way these early Hebrew printers responded to the market's demand shows that above all, Jews wanted editions of the Pentateuch and Pentateuchal commentaries; to a lesser extent, they wanted other biblical texts chanted in synagogue; and to some degree they also wanted copies of the Psalter. Printings of all other biblical texts seem to have been the early equivalent of hardcover books purveyed by a European academic press. Zafren's study covers the first century of printed Bibles; my impression is that similar tendencies endured until the twentieth century, when Zionism and other factors encouraged the proliferation of small one-volume editions of the whole Tanakh—though a visit to a traditional Hebrew bookstore will show

that to this day multivolume editions with commentary, most often consisting of the Pentateuch alone (or Pentateuch with prophetic lectionaries), remain exceedingly common.

26. See chapter 16 by Yael Feldman and chapter 17 by Yair Zakovitch in this volume on the centrality of the Bible in Zionist and Israeli identity.

27. To be sure, all religions are in some sense cultures, but in the case of Judaism, nonreligious aspects of the culture are unusually prominent.

28. For such a discussion, see Chana Kronfeld, *On the Margins of Modernism: Decentering Literary Dynamics* (Berkeley: University of California Press, 1996), 114–40 (originally published in *Prooftexts* 5 [1985]: 129–40), as well as Ruth Kartun-Blum, *Profane Scriptures: Reflections on the Dialogue with the Bible in Modern Hebrew Poetry* (Cincinnati: Hebrew Union College Press, 1999).

29. See note 15.

30. Smith, *What Is Scripture?*, 18 and passim.

31. I think of James Barr, John Barton, Alexander Rofé, Yair Zakovitch, Avigdor Shinan, and Michael Fishbane. These scholars followed up insights from their predecessors, especially Yehezkel Kaufmann and Isac Leo Seeligmann.

Chapter 2

Concepts of Scripture in the Synagogue Service

Elsie Stern

For most contemporary Jews, the "Jewish Bible" is a single volume containing the twenty-four books of the Tanakh, which is readily available and accessible through the process of reading. While totally familiar to us, these paired phenomena—the Bible as a book and reading as the primary means of accessing it—are relatively new developments in the history of Jewish encounters with scripture. Until the onset of printing, most Jews would never have encountered a "Bible." They might have encountered a Torah scroll in the synagogue or scrolls or volumes containing selections from other parts of the canon. However, manuscripts of the entire biblical corpus, bound together in a single volume, would have been quite rare. In addition, while it is difficult to gauge past rates of literacy with any precision, it is likely that most premodern Jews would not have "read" the Bible.[1] Rather, they would have heard texts contained in the Bible either recited or retold in various settings. Of these settings, the synagogue was, by far, the most common. Since as early as the first century CE, the synagogue has been a site for the encounter between Jews and Torah.[2] By the mid-third century, the authors of the Mishnah were already advocating the regular recitation of biblical texts in the synagogue.[3] The rudimentary practices outlined in the Mishnah became the foundation for a lectionary practice that continued to grow and develop throughout the medieval period and continues to be a central part of synagogue practice today.[4] While there have always been opportunities for more educated Jews to encounter texts of scripture in school settings, since the earliest days of Judaism, the majority of Jews have encountered scripture primarily in synagogue.

This sociological reality has important implications for our understanding of Jewish scripture. In theory, the entire contents of the Tanakh are invested with scriptural status and wield the communal authority that this status brings. However, most Jews would never have encountered texts that were not recited in the synagogue. For example, many Jews would never have encountered the books of Chronicles or Ezra-Nehemiah as well as vast swathes of the prophetic literature. They might have been entirely ignorant of the contents of these books and, in some cases, might not have known the books even existed. While these texts had scriptural status and authority, this status and authority remained theoretical because the books were not deployed as authoritative texts in communal settings. If we are interested in scripture as a category of text which helps to shape a community's self-understanding and worldview, then the short list of texts which most Jews actually encountered in synagogue is particularly important. In this chapter, I will outline the contours of this synagogue Bible.

Even though the synagogue Bible, or lectionary, is composed solely of biblical texts, it differs in a variety of ways from the canonical Tanakh: its scope is smaller, its contents are arranged differently, and, most importantly, it is a strikingly bicultural text. The contents of the lectionary are all drawn from the canonical Tanakh and, as such, articulate the perspective of the ancient Israelite authors. At the same time, the rabbinic creators of the lectionary cycle deployed strategies of selection and arrangement to shape a synagogue scripture that articulates central rabbinic ideologies. In what follows, I will focus on material from the rabbinic (third to sixth centuries CE) and early medieval periods (seventh to tenth centuries CE) since these were the foundational eras for the development of the lectionary and the rituals for its recitation. While contemporary synagogue rituals for the reading of scripture vary widely from one another and, at times, from the rituals described here, the ritual and lectionary developments of the rabbinic period remain foundational for the ideological construction of the synagogue Bible.

The Contents of the Lectionary

Since the rabbinic period, the recitation of scriptural texts has been a central part of Jewish communal worship. Scripture readings are a core element of Sabbath and festival services and are also included in the morning services on Mondays and Thursdays. On Sabbaths and festivals, the scripture reading consists of a reading from the Pentateuch (hereafter, *parashah*, pl. *parshiyot*) and a reading from the prophetic literature (hereafter, *haftarah*, pl. *haftarot*). The weekly parshiyot follow the order of the canonical Torah: each successive parashah picks up where the previous one left off. The weekly haftarot, however are not arranged sequentially. Instead, they are excerpts from the prophetic corpus that have a thematic or verbal link to either the parashah or, in the case of festivals and special Sabbaths, to the occasion on which they are read. On festivals, the Torah portion also corresponds to the festival itself rather than following the sequence of weekly readings. For example, the Torah reading for the festival of Rosh Hashanah comes from the book of Genesis even though the surrounding Sabbaths will have readings of sequential selections from Deuteronomy. On Mondays and Thursdays, there is no haftarah, and the reading from the Torah anticipates the opening part of the subsequent Sabbath's reading.[5] In addition to the recitation of the entire Pentateuch and the haftarot, the five scrolls (Ecclesiastes, Esther, Song of Songs, Ruth, and Lamentations) are also part of the lectionary: each scroll is recited on a particular festival over the course of the year.

As is the case with most Jewish liturgical practice, the lectionary was quite fluid in the rabbinic period. The Mishnah (third century CE) mandates the recitation of parshiyot and haftarot and specifies the parshiyot for holidays and special sabbaths (m. Meg. 4:4–6). The Tosefta, a collection containing materials roughly contemporaneous with the Mishnah, designates haftarot for four special Sabbaths (t. Meg. 4:2), while a tradition cited in the Babylonian Talmud (b. Meg. 31a–b) designates haftarot for holidays and other special Sabbaths. The first complete extant lectionary lists date from the medieval period. These lists demonstrate that while individual communities had standardized lectionaries, there was still variation from community to community with regard to the parameters of the parshiyot and the texts selected as haftarot. By the modern period, two major lectionary traditions came to dominate: the Ashkenazic tradition and the Sephardic tradition. While some communities still follow other more local traditions, these two are the most common and are followed by the majority of synagogues today. By the modern period, all the lectionary traditions had become quite similar to one another. For example, in the Ashkenazic and Sephardic traditions, as well as the Yemenite tradition, which is the largest of the remaining local rites, the parshiyot are identical, and the haftarot only differ from rite to rite in a minority of cases. In all modern traditions, the entire Torah is recited over the course of a year, yielding fifty-four parshiyot of about three chapters each.⁶ Including the haftarot for festivals and special Sabbaths, there are eighty-three haftarot ranging in length from about ten to forty verses.⁷ These texts then, along with the five scrolls which are recited on festivals, compose the synagogue Bible.

When we compare the contents of this synagogue Bible to those of the canonical Tanakh, striking differences emerge. First, the synagogue Bible is much shorter than the canonical Tanakh. If, for simplicity's sake, we were to say that each haftarah was about a chapter long, we would find that the synagogue Bible consists of the Pentateuch and five scrolls plus eighty chapters of prophetic material, whereas the canonical Tanakh consists of the Torah and the Five Scrolls plus 990 chapters of additional material: If we exclude the Pentateuch and scrolls that are already a part of the lectionary, the haftarot include only approximately 10 percent of the remaining canonical material. If we consider only the prophetic books (Joshua–Malachi in a canonical Tanakh), then the haftarot overlap with 20 percent of this canonical material.

Second, the haftarot are not representative of the diversity of the prophetic canon. Whereas in the canonical Bible, the former prophets constitute a large part of the prophetic corpus, few texts from this extended narrative are recited as haftarot. A person who reads the canonical Bible "cover to cover" spends a lot of time engaging with the tribal prehistory and political pasts of the kingdoms of Israel and Judah. In contrast, a Jew whose Bible is the synagogue Bible only engages systematically with the accounts of Israel's past contained in the Pentateuch. This discrepancy has a significant impact on the portrait of Israel encountered by these two hypothetical readers/hearers. The reader of the former prophets encounters a tribal Israel who conquers the land of Canaan and ultimately establishes two kingdoms there, organized around the political structures of kingship and kingdom. He or she is immersed in extended narratives of political intrigue marked by international pressures and internal discord set in a theological framework and sporadically inflected with explicitly theological ideologies. In contrast, the recipient of the synagogue Bible only engages comprehensively with the narratives of Israel's preconquest, premonarchic mythic past. The Israel of the synagogue Bible is a collective that emerges as a people outside of the land of Israel and remains there for the duration of the sequential recited story. It is a people whose formal organization is based on kinship and on obedience to human authorities (Moses, the priests) who receive their authority from God, not by merit of their role as kings. In contrast to the narratives contained in the former prophets, the narratives of the Pentateuch are intensely theological. The relationship between God and Israel is the primary factor that determines the fate of the people.

The latter prophets are also represented disproportionately. Of the classical prophets, Isaiah, especially Deutero-Isaiah, is the most heavily represented. The lectionary does include selected Jeremiads and prophecies of rebuke and doom. However, the rabbinic and medieval framers of the various lectionary traditions gave more air time to depictions of YHWH as a loving, comforting, and compassionate God than they did to depictions of the deity as an angry and punishing God. This tendency is underscored by the addition of final verses of consolation to haftarot of rebuke or doom. Even in cases where the body of the haftarah articulates a harsh theology, the final verse always underscores the loving and compassionate nature of God and God's plans for the people of Israel.

Last, and perhaps most important, is the pride of place granted to the Torah, in its entirety. Whereas Christian lectionaries largely bypass the legal codes of the Pentateuch, the Jewish lectionary mandates the reading of the entire canonical Torah, including those cultic laws which had become obsolete before the sequential reading of the Torah was institutionalized.[8] By putting the recitation of the Pentateuch, cultic laws and all, at the center of the lectionary, the rabbinic framers of the synagogue Bible asserted the ongoing relevance of the functionally obsolete laws. This choice set the stage for the ongoing process of seeking contemporary relevance in the legal material that is one of the hallmarks of Jewish interpretive practice to this day.

The difference in content between the canonical Tanakh and the synagogue Bible, then, undergirds three thematic trends that distinguish the two corpora. These thematic trends are also central pillars of rabbinic theology and ideology. The inclusion of the entire Pentateuch coupled with the relative lack of attention paid to the history found in Joshua–Kings enables the elevation of the portrait of Israel as a people who lack sovereignty but have a distinct national identity. This Israel's identity and destiny are defined by its relationship with God rather than by the vicissitudes of domestic and international politics. This national portrait resonates strongly with the communal self-portrait asserted throughout the rabbinic literature.

Like the canonical corpus of prophetic texts, the haftarot include texts of rebuke and punishment along with texts of consolation and redemption. Both corpora, in their entirety, portray God as an agent of both punishment and redemption. Both corpora also include texts that portray the relationship between God and Israel as one that is marked by conflict and reconciliation. However, unlike the canonical prophetic corpus, the collection of haftarot emphasizes the gentler and more redemptive aspects of the divine character, thereby constructing a divine portrait that is kinder and gentler than its canonical counterpart. This characterization of God is also typical of a prominent strand of rabbinic theology that is articulated in both the liturgy and the midrashic literature.[9] In each of these cases, then, the creators of the lectionary selected texts from the diverse biblical canon that resonated most closely with central rabbinic ideologies.

The second major difference between the synagogue Bible and the canonical Tanakh is the order and arrangement of their material. For readers of biblical books, the beginnings and ends of episodes are determined by literary features embedded by the redactors of the biblical books as well as by punctuation, paragraph markers, and chapter divisions added by later editors. For Jews who receive the synagogue Bible, the boundaries of episodes or texts are determined by the framers of the lectionary, who were responsible for designating where parshiyot and haftarot would begin and end. Readers of biblical books encounter their contents sequentially according to the order of the material in the book. Thus, their understanding of any individual unit, be it a verse, chapter, or episode, is informed most immediately by the surrounding context within the book itself. In contrast, audiences of the synagogue Bible encounter the contents of that Bible in minianthologies of parashah and haftarah. As a result, the parashah and the haftarah for any given week provide the most immediate and most influential context for understanding the other half of the lectionary pair. While at first glance, the determination of textual boundaries and context might not seem particularly significant in determining the meaning of texts, in practice, these are quite powerful redactional strategies.[10]

The parashah *Lech Lecha* that begins in Genesis 12:1 provides an example of how the designation of textual boundaries can be a powerful tool for articulating meanings that might not emerge from the texts in their canonical contexts. Within the book of Genesis, the first mention of Abram/Abraham occurs in the genealogy of his father Terah.

> Now these are the descendants of Terah. Terah was the father of Abram, Nahor, and Haran; and Haran was the father of Lot. Haran died before his father Terah in the land of his birth, in Ur of the Chaldeans. (Genesis 11:27–28)[11]

Immediately after this genealogical notice, Abram begins to function as a character who acts in the narrative.

> Abram and Nahor took wives; the name of Abram's wife was Sarai, and the name of Nahor's wife was Milcah. She was the daughter of Haran the father of Milcah and Iscah.
> Now Sarai was barren; she had no child. Terah took his son Abram and his grandson Lot son of Haran, and his daughter-in-law Sarai, his son Abram's wife, and they went out together from Ur of the Chaldeans to go into the land of Canaan; but when they came to Haran, they settled there. The days of Terah were two hundred five years; and Terah died in Haran. (Genesis 11:29–32)

After the report of Terah's death, the text continues:

> Now the LORD said to Abram, "Go from your country and your kindred and your father's house to the land that I will show you. I will make of you a great nation, and I will bless you, and make your name great, so that you will be a blessing. I will bless those who bless you, and the one who curses you I will curse; and in you all the families of the earth shall be blessed." So Abram went, as the LORD had told him; and Lot went with him. Abram was seventy-five years old when he departed from Haran. (Genesis 12:1–4)

Within the canonical context of the book of Genesis, then, God's command to Abram to go to Canaan is a continuation of the story that began in 11:31. Terah and his family had set out to emigrate to Canaan but had settled en route in Haran. In Genesis 12:1, God is telling Abram to continue the interrupted journey. Abram's subsequent journey to Canaan is certainly a sign of his obedience to God's command; however, since God is telling Abram to do exactly what he had been doing in the first place, this act of obedience is not particularly radical or indicative of intense commitment to this heretofore unknown deity. In the synagogue Bible, however, Genesis 12:1 begins a new parashah. For the audience of this parashah, God's command to go to Canaan is experienced not as the middle of a story but rather as the beginning of one. When the story begins in Genesis 12:1, there is no context for God's command. Rather, it is a stark mandate issued by an unknown deity. In this context, Abram's willingness to obey the command is more surprising and functions as a sign of his extraordinarily high degree of commitment to YHWH. While there are certainly rabbinic texts that comment on moments in the Abraham story when the protagonist seems lacking in absolute confidence in God, overall, the portrait of Abraham constructed in the rabbinic literature is one of radical faith in and obedience to YHWH. By beginning the parashah in Genesis 12:1, the creators of the lectionary cycle shape Abraham's journey to Canaan in ways that conform to, and support, this rabbinic portrait.

The parashah and haftarah pair for the morning of Yom Kippur (Day of Atonement) provides an example of the power of the lectionary pairing to shape the meaning of its constituent texts. The Torah reading for Yom Kippur morning is Leviticus 16:1–34 and Numbers 29:7–11. The first of these describes the prescribed priestly ritual for the Day of Atonement. It includes the purification of the innermost, holiest parts of the shrine and describes the scapegoat ritual in which a goat, which was ritually loaded with the outstanding sins of the Israelites, would be sent over a cliff into the wilderness. The unit also includes the commandment to practice self-denial and cessation from all work. The unit concludes by reiterating the purpose of these yearly rituals:

> This shall be a statute to you forever: In the seventh month, on the tenth day of the month, you shall deny yourselves, and shall do no work, neither the citizen nor the alien who resides among you. For on this day atonement shall be made for you, to cleanse you; from all your sins you shall be clean before the LORD. It is a sabbath of complete rest to you, and you shall deny yourselves; it is a statute forever. The priest who is anointed and consecrated as priest in his father's place shall make atonement, wearing the linen vestments, the holy vestments. He shall make atonement for the sanctuary, and he shall make atonement for the tent of meeting and for the altar, and he shall make atonement for the priests and for all the people of the assembly. This shall be an everlasting statute for you, to make atonement for the people of Israel once in the year for all their sins. And Moses did as the LORD had commanded him. (Leviticus 16:29–34)

The reading from Numbers reiterates the commands to practice self-denial and cessation from all work and also enumerates the sacrificial offerings particular to the day. It is clear why the framers of the lectionary designated these readings for Yom Kippur: they are the pentateuchal texts that describe the rituals mandated for the holiday by the priestly authors in ancient Israelite times. Even though the sacrificial rituals became obsolete in the post–Second Temple period, the mandates regarding self-denial (interpreted as fasting from food and drink in addition to other abstentions) and the cessation of work were maintained as central elements of Yom Kippur practice. The haftarah for Yom Kippur, however, is more surprising. It is Isaiah 57:14–58:14. This text is a critique of fasting and penitential rituals which are not accompanied by a cessation of unjust actions on the part of the penitents and by active work to alleviate social and economic suffering and injustice. Isaiah 58:5–9 states,

> Is such the fast that I choose, a day to humble oneself? Is it to bow down the head like a bulrush, and to lie in sackcloth and ashes? Will you call this a fast, a day acceptable to the LORD? Is not this the fast that I choose: to loose the bonds of injustice, to undo the thongs of the yoke, to let the oppressed go free, and to break every yoke? Is it not to share your bread with the hungry, and bring the homeless poor into your house; when you see the naked, to cover them, and not to hide yourself from your own kin? Then your light shall break forth like the dawn, and your healing shall spring up quickly; your vindicator shall go before you, the glory of the LORD shall be your rear guard. Then you shall call, and the LORD will answer; you shall cry for help, and he will say, Here I am. (Isaiah 58:5–9)

The combination of parashah and haftarah here serves to shape the hearer's experience of both texts and, perhaps as importantly, to articulate a particular and distinctly rabbinic position regarding effective penance and atonement. On its own, the parashah states that ritual actions will effectively cleanse outstanding sins. In their context in Leviticus, the rituals of the Day of Atonement are presented as self-sufficient and effective. If they are performed, the shrine will be cleansed of impurity caused by sin, and the divine presence will be able to remain there. On its own, the Isaiah text articulates a powerful critique of ritual penance unaccompanied by moral action and argues that alleviation of oppression and injustice are the effective means to gaining divine favor and protection. In isolation, then, these two texts offer very different advice for communities seeking to gain divine favor and protection through acts of penance. However, when combined, they articulate a perspective that embraces both ritual and moral activity. The centrality of the Torah portion validates the importance of ritual action, whereas the inclusion of the haftarah serves to recast the ritual approach as only a part of effective penance. One cannot only practice self-denial; one also has to work for justice. In addition, the two texts serve as elements in a theological system of checks and balances. Whereas the recitation of the haftarah provides a bulwark against complete reliance on ritual, the recitation of the Leviticus text asserts that ritual actions are still necessary, even if not sufficient. Not surprisingly, the perspective on atonement articulated by the lectionary unit as a whole resonates strongly with perspectives articulated and developed elsewhere in the rabbinic literature that argue that effective atonement includes both ritual and moral action.[12]

While the haftarah seems quite vituperative, it also plays a consolatory role in the lectionary context. Within the canonical context, proper performance of the ritual described in Leviticus 16 is crucial to the ongoing maintenance of the relationship with God. However, during the period of the development of the lectionary, this ritual could not be performed because the Temple had been destroyed centuries before. The assertion of the ritual's necessity combined with its impossibility would certainly have been anxiety provoking for post–Second Temple Jews. Isaiah's assertion that God will protect Israel if its members work to alleviate injustice and oppression gives post–Second Temple Jews another means to maintain the relationship with God even in the absence of the Temple and its cult. Thus, through the strategic conjunction of texts and occasion, the framers of the lectionary are able to make the biblical texts speak a message which is not articulated fully in either text in its canonical context but is appropriate to the historical reality of its audience and resonant with the ideology of its rabbinic creators.

The sequence of haftarot for the weeks following the holiday of Tisha b'Av provide another example of the way in which the creators of the lectionary use biblical texts, strategically selected and arranged, to articulate theological messages that are not articulated by the texts in their canonical contexts. The holiday of Tisha b'Av is a day of mourning that in the rabbinic and early medieval periods commemorated the destructions of the First and Second Temples.[13] While throughout most of the year, the haftarot correspond to the parshiyot, in the three weeks prior to Tisha b'Av and the seven weeks between the holiday and the festival of Rosh Hashanah (the new year), the haftarot are linked sequentially to one another, not to their corresponding parshiyot. In the three weeks leading up to the holiday, the designated haftarot are texts of rebuke in which the prophets scold Israel for its sins and prophesy the disasters that will occur as a result of them. On Tisha b'Av itself, the book of Lamentations is read, and for seven weeks after the holiday, texts of consolation selected from Isaiah 40–66 are recited. As a whole, the ten-week sequence articulates a narrative of sin followed by punishment, penitence, and eventual consolation and reconciliation.[14] Within this sequence, the haftarot of consolation articulate a discrete narrative of consolation in which God repeatedly tries to console the people of Israel, who remain resistant to consolation until the very last week of the sequence. The fourteenth-century Spanish commentator Abudarham paraphrases the sequence, using citations of the first verse of each haftarah, as follows:

> It says in the midrash, in high language, that they decided to begin the haftarot of consolation with *Comfort, comfort my people* (Isaiah 40:1), which is to say that the Holy One Blessed be He says to the prophets, *Comfort, comfort my people*. The congregation of Israel responds to this, *And Zion says YHWH has abandoned me* (Isaiah 49:14). Which is to say, "I am not appeased by the consolations of the prophets." And he says, *Arise, arise, don strength, arm of YHWH. Arise as in days of old* (Isaiah 51:9). And in the places where they recite *Unhappy, storm-tossed one, uncomforted* (Isaiah 54:11) instead of this haftarah, this is to say that the prophets respond and say before the Holy One Blessed be He, "Behold the congregation of Israel is not pacified by our consolations."
>
> To this the Holy One Blessed be He replies *I, I am he who comforts you* (Isaiah 51:12). And he says further, *Rejoice, barren one who has not given birth* (Isaiah 54:1) and he says, *Arise, shine for your light comes* (Isaiah 60:1). To this the congregation of Israel responds, *I will greatly rejoice in YHWH* (Isaiah 61:10) which is to say, "Now I have reason to rejoice and be happy. My soul rejoices in God because he clothed me in garments of salvation." (Isaiah 62:10)[15]

As Abudarham's summary demonstrates, the haftarot of consolation create a dialogue between God and Israel in which Israel refuses to be consoled by prophetic agents. It will only accept consolation directly from God. Through the selection of the haftarot, the creators of the lectionary cycle construct a divine portrait in which God is remarkably persistent in the divine attempts at consolation. While there are certainly moments of divine consolation in Isaiah 40–66, this coherent portrait of God as Israel's comforter is a rabbinic creation, not an Isaianic one. In addition, the haftarot of consolation include a high concentration of texts that represent the relationship between God and Israel in emotional and romantic terms. These romantic metaphors are paired with references to God's saving power. Through the strategic conjunction of these texts, the creators of this lectionary sequence are able to articulate a theology of consolation that asserts that because God loves Israel and because God is the master of history, God will necessarily use God's power to save Israel sometime in the future. In the meantime, though, the sequence asserts that the love relationship between God and Israel endures. As was the case with the lectionary texts for Yom Kippur, the constituent parts of this theology of consolation are certainly present in the biblical texts. The authors of Isaiah 40–66 deploy romantic metaphors and use these romantic metaphors as a rationale for his prophecies of redemption and restoration. "For your Maker is your husband, the LORD of hosts is his name; the Holy One of Israel is your Redeemer, the God of the whole earth he is called" (Isaiah 54:5). In addition, this Isaianic corpus certainly includes references to Israel's ongoing misery and its resistance to consolation (Isaiah 49:14, Isaiah 54:11). However, the creators of the lectionary concentrate and crystallize these themes and tropes to a degree that is not expressed by the texts in their canonical context. Through the strategies of selection and arrangement, the shapers of the lectionary transform the biblical texts into texts that are culturally bilingual. While the lectionary texts are still verbatim biblical texts, they are shaped by strategies of selection and arrangement to articulate or at least to resonate with central rabbinic ideologies that are not always prominent in the biblical texts themselves.

Thus far, I have discussed the synagogue Bible as a text that differs in its content and arrangement from the canonical Tanakh. In the final section of this chapter, I discuss how the discursive boundaries of synagogue scripture distinguish it from scripture in other contexts. In Judaism (as well as in Christianity and Islam), scripture is characterized by two different, and somewhat contrastive, ideological convictions. On the one hand, scripture is identified as a discrete body of revealed discourse. At some point in the history of each of these traditions, the canon of scripture was delineated, and, as a consequence, it was possible to identify which instances of discourse were scripture and which were not. At the same time, each of these traditions asserts, both explicitly and implicitly, that the words of scripture do not fully express the totality of the revelation that they encode. If they did, interpretation and commentary would be unnecessary. The rabbinic doctrine of the dual Torah expresses this dynamic succinctly.[16] The totality of the revealed torah consists of two parts: the Written Torah (scripture) and the Oral Torah (the authoritative teachings of the rabbinic sages, which are now also preserved and transmitted in writing). Within the doctrine of the dual torah, the Written Torah (scripture) is not the whole torah, yet it is a discrete and defined element of it. In settings where scripture is encountered as a written text, the first tendency, that which asserts its discrete and distinctive identity, is often paramount. The most basic Bibles contain (after the front matter) only the words of scripture. If a Bible contains commentary, typographical elements such as typeface, font size, and placement on the page strongly delineate between the words of scripture and the more expansive discourse that accompanies them. While both sets of discourse, the scripture and the commentary, might ultimately contribute to the reader's understanding of the text, many elements of the textual encounter facilitate the distinction between scripture and commentary.

In the synagogue setting, various elements of the lectionary ritual support both convictions. Ultimately, though, the synagogue ritual creates an experience in which the performed Torah consists of both scriptural and nonscriptural discourse and the boundaries between the two discourses are quite porous, and diffuse. The Torah performance ritual articulated in the Mishnah provides an example: M. Megillah 4:4 mandates a bilingual, dialogic performance of the parashah and the haftarah. In the case of the parashah, the Torah reciter reads aloud a verse from a Torah scroll. He then pauses to allow the translator (*meturgeman*) to recite an Aramaic translation (*targum*) of the verse. According to the Mishnah, the Torah reader and the translator must be different people, and unlike the Torah reader, who must recite from a scroll, the translator must offer his translation without reference to a written text. In the case of the haftarah, the reader of the prophetic text can read up to three verses before pausing for translation. This mode of performance clearly enacts the distinction between the words of scripture and their accompanying discourse. The two are uttered by different people in different languages, and one of them is visibly derived from a text, while the other is not. At the same time, though, the actual "script" received by the audience is a thorough hybrid of scripture and nonscripture. The audience of this ritual never receives continuous scripture. Rather, they only receive a discourse in which scripture and its nonscriptural explanation are consistently interwoven.

While the Mishnah gives a clear picture of what this intralinear, bilingual performance should have looked like, it is impossible to reconstruct the actual content that any given audience in late antiquity would have received. While there are extant Aramaic translations of scripture dating from the rabbinic period, it is impossible to know to what degree the orally performed translations would have conformed to these extant written texts.[17] It is also difficult to know to what degree late-antique Palestinian audiences would have relied on the Aramaic translation for their understanding of the text. Even with these uncertainties about actual lectionary performances in late antiquity, it is clear from the Mishnah's mandates that the authors envisioned the torah received by the synagogue audience as a hybrid of scriptural and nonscriptural discourse.

While the Mishnah only discusses the *targum*, later rabbinic and medieval evidence bears witness to the performance of other forms of nonscriptural torah discourse in the ancient synagogue. The Talmud testifies to the performance of homilies by rabbinic sages, and scholars have hypothesized that at least some of the material preserved in the extant midrashim might have corresponded to material preached in synagogues.[18] Even if we cannot determine with certainty the content of any given sermon, it is probable that the content of the sermons was an influential component of the audience's understanding of the scripture. One need only think of the impact that contemporary preachers have on their congregations' understanding of biblical texts to appreciate this point. In addition to the midrashic literature, there are extant hundreds of liturgical poems that are undoubtedly relics of actual synagogue practice. These poems (*piyyutim*) are highly stylized compositions that blur the boundary between the lectionary service and the statutory liturgy. The poems correspond to the main prayers of the Sabbath liturgy and, in some contexts, may have been performed as, or instead of, the statutory prayers. While their structure is determined by the liturgy, their content is deeply saturated with biblical language, allusions, and litanies of biblical verses. If, in fact, these *piyyutim* were performed instead of the statutory prayers, then the synagogue congregation would not have experienced the Torah service as their sole encounter with the week's lectionary texts. Rather, the surrounding prayer experience would also have been saturated with the language and themes of the week's readings. The *piyyutim* especially are another example of the diffusion of scripture in the synagogue setting. Through the *piyyutim*, the statutory liturgy became saturated not only with biblical language and allusion but often specifically with correspondences to the weekly readings. The existence of these performance genres—intralinear translation, homily, and liturgical poetry—demonstrate that the scripture that was performed in the synagogue was, from its inception, not a discrete and highly demarcated corpus that corresponded precisely to the canonical Tanakh. Rather the synagogue performance of torah was a hybrid discourse which contained both scriptural and nonscriptural elements. The boundaries between these elements were porous, as the three genres that interweave biblical citation and extrabiblical discourse demonstrate. In addition, while the actual recitation of the parashah and the haftarah represented the most concentrated presence of scripture in the service, the genres of homily and *piyyut* extended the footprint of the weekly lectionary beyond the boundaries of the recitation itself into liturgical and pedagogical discourses as well.

NOTES

1. The combined factors of restricted literacy, scarcity of texts, and limited understanding of Hebrew would have significantly limited the number of Jews who encountered biblical texts, in their original language, through reading. While educated men would have had the necessary literacy, Hebrew fluency, and access to allow them to read biblical texts, most women and many men would not.

2. Josephus, *Against Apion*, 2.2.17; Acts 15:21.

3. M. Meg. 3:4–4:10.

4. For a detailed description of the development of the ritual, see Ismar Elbogen, *Jewish Liturgy: A Comprehensive History*, trans. R. Scheindlin (Philadelphia: Jewish Publication Society, 1993), 129–64.

5. T. Meg. 3:10 mandates an alternative system in which each reading, including the weekday readings, picks up where the previous one left off.

6. In late antiquity, there were two systems for reading the Torah. In the system that was dominant in Palestine, the entire Torah was read over the course of about three and a half years. In Babylonia, the entire Torah was recited in the course of a single year. Some contemporary, non-Orthodox communities have revived a variation of this tradition.

7. For a more detailed history of the development of the lectionary cycle, see Elbogen, *Jewish Liturgy*, 129–51.

8. By the time the Mishnah was redacted, the Jewish temples in Jerusalem had been destroyed. The destruction of the Second Temple in 70 CE marked the end of the sacrificial cult and also made obsolete most of the laws of purity that constitute much of Leviticus. In addition, the other legal material in the Torah was largely obsolete because rabbinic law primarily follows the Mishnah and the Talmuds, not the biblical sources.

9. The blessing that immediately precedes the recitation of the shema in the statutory liturgy and the rabbinic interpretations of the Song of Songs contained in Song of Songs Rabbah provide examples of this tendency.

10. For a more detailed discussion of these strategies, see Elsie Stern, *From Rebuke to Consolation : Exegesis and Theology in the Liturgical Anthology of the Ninth of Av Season* (Providence, RI: Brown Judaic Studies, 2004), 24–28. For analyses of the way these strategies function in any given week of the lectionary, see Michael Fishbane, *The JPS Bible Commentary: Haftarot* (Philadelphia: Jewish Publication Society, 2002).

11. All English translations are from the *New Revised Standard Version* (1989).

12. See m. Yoma 8:9 for an early rabbinic expression of this idea.

13. In later historical periods, other tragedies were also added to the list of events commemorated on the day.

14. For a detailed analysis of this sequence, see Elsie Stern, "Transforming Comfort: Hermeneutics and Theology in the Haftarot of Consolation," *Prooftexts* 23 (2003): 150–81.

15. *The Complete Abudarham* (Jerusalem: Usha, 1958), 203 (in Hebrew; translation mine).

16. See chapter 3 by Steven Fraade in this volume.

17. Contemporary communities that follow Yemenite tradition still perform an intralinear Hebrew-Aramaic reading. In these communities, the Aramaic translation is Targum Onkelos, a translation that was current in the rabbinic period.

18. See, for example, Rachel Anisfeld, *Sustain Me with Raisin-Cakes: Pesikta deRav Kahana and the Popularization of Rabbinic Judaism* (Leiden, Netherlands: Brill, 2009), 16–19.

Chapter 3

Concepts of Scripture in Rabbinic Judaism
Oral Torah and Written Torah

Steven D. Fraade

Introduction

If at the center of Judaism is "the book," meaning the Hebrew/Jewish Bible (TaNaKh),[1] at the core of the Jewish Bible is the Torah, the Five Books of Moses (Pentateuch/Ḥumash), traditionally thought to have been revealed by God via Moses to the Israelites standing at the foot of Mt. Sinai. However, from the perspective of the ancient rabbis (ca. 70–500 CE, in the Land of Israel and in Babylonia), who came to define, even more than did the Hebrew Bible, the practice and meaning of Judaism in all of its subsequent varieties, Judaism is less based on the written biblical record of revelation than by an accompanying oral human elaboration, with the latter constituting as much "words of Torah" as the former. The former is referred to as "Torah that is in writing" (*torah she-bikhtav*), while the latter is known as "Torah that is by the mouth" (*torah she-beʿal peh*), or, alternatively, as denoted by their modes of performance, that which is read from a written text (*miqraʾ*/Scripture) and that which is recited or repeated without recourse to a written text (*mishnah*). The former consists of a fixed, closed text, the latter of fluid oral transmission and expansion. The former is the record of divinely revealed laws, the sacred history of ancient Israel, and the utterances of divinely inspired prophets and teachers of wisdom. The latter is the multitude of collections of rabbinic rules and legal debates, stories, and interpretations of Scripture, whose origins are traced ultimately back to Moses at Sinai. At the very least, the Written Torah (traditionally understood to encompass Torah, Prophets, and Writings), though the center of ritual attention in its own right in the synagogue liturgy, cannot be apprehended except in tandem with and as interpreted by its accompanying Oral Torah.

Eventually (when exactly is itself a matter of scholarly debate), the Oral Torah of the ancient rabbis (like that of their successors) was committed to writing, presumably so as to be more surely preserved, first as scrolls and eventually as books. However, even when recorded in writing, it remained ever expanding and fluid (compared to the Written Torah) and retained qualities of oral expression, for example, in its constant dialogue and debate, often unresolved, between rabbis of differing opinions across the generations.

The "books" of the Oral Torah began as being of two types: (1) *Midrash* (literally, "seeking" [of meaning], or explication): commentaries on books of the Hebrew Bible or their liturgical cycles of reading, whether their contents be mainly law (*halakhah*; literally, "the way to go") or narrative ('*aggadah*; literally, "narration"), in some cases more exegetical and in others more homiletical; and (2) *Mishnah*: topically grouped lists of rabbinic laws (*halakhot*), with only minimal reference to their biblical sources, in some cases practically applicable (e.g., specific kinds of work prohibited on the Sabbath), in some cases theoretical (e.g., procedures for offering sacrifices in the Jerusalem temple, which had been destroyed by the Romans in 70 CE). Today we have one such authoritative collection, the Mishnah of Rabbi Judah the Patriarch (ca. 200 CE), but with remnants of mishnaic rules that did not make it into this collection, preserved in other sources. In turn, the Mishnah demanded its own commentary, largely due to its concise, elliptical style (possibly designed so as to facilitate its being memorized), which resulted in the Talmud (literally, "study"), comprising both the Mishnah and its expansive elucidation, the Gemarah (from a verb meaning "to complete" or "learn"). There are two such talmuds (*talmudim*), one produced by the rabbinic sages of the Land of Israel (the Palestinian or Jerusalem Talmud, the *Yerushalmi*) and the other, more expansive and authoritative, produced by the rabbinic sages of Babylonia (the Babylonian Talmud, the *Bavli*). The subsequent development of the Oral Torah, through medieval and modern times, follows the same basic divisions: biblical commentaries, collections (or codes) of laws, and commentaries on those laws or supercommentaries on preceding commentaries on either Scripture or collections of laws, without end.

Returning to the "two Torahs," how they are related to each other—in origin, status, authority, contents, forms, mode of study, and transmission—cannot be stated in simple or absolute terms, given the variety of expressions within rabbinic literature (that is, Oral Torah) as it evolved in anonymously edited anthologies over the centuries. Although strictly differentiated from each other in mode of transmission and performance, they deeply intersect with each other. Nor is it clear what the relation might have been between what became the rabbinic Oral Torah and the plethora of prerabbinic extra- (or para-) scriptural laws, narratives, and forms of scriptural interpretation now known (most recently, thanks to the discovery of the Dead Sea Scrolls) but excluded from the Hebrew biblical canon.

At issue, it should be stressed, is not the existence of an "oral tradition" (or "unwritten law"), common to all literate cultures, but the attribution of *revealed* status and authority to the specifically rabbinic Oral Torah. The classical rabbis used their interpretive methods to deduce this Oral Torah, both in its parts and as a whole, from the Written Torah, thus claiming that the Oral Torah was contained within the Written. But they do not understand Oral Torah's status and authority to be secondarily derived from the Written Torah. Rather, as traditions revealed at Sinai, Oral Torah in their eyes has legal authority in its own right. While several prerabbinic (Second Temple period) bodies of literature adduce dual aspects of revelation —for example, literal and allegorical, exoteric (available to all) and esoteric (revealed only to a few and concealed from the rest)—none of them differentiates between the two in terms of their modes of transmission or performance as "written" and "oral," mutually distinguishable thereby from each other. The closest possible antecedent is found in an ambiguous comment by the first-century CE Jewish historian Josephus with respect to the Second Temple group known as the Pharisees (thought to be the closest antecedent to the rabbis), that they

> had passed on to the people certain regulations handed down by former generations and not recorded in the Law of Moses, for which reason they are rejected by the Sadducaean group, who hold that only those regulations should be considered valid which were written down (in Scripture), and that those which had been handed down by former generations need not be observed.[2]

All we can surmise for certain is that the Pharisees attributed (divine) authority to ancestral laws not written in the Torah, but not necessarily that they preserved or transmitted these laws orally, and even less that they claimed an ultimate Sinaitic origin for them.

How are we to understand, therefore, both historically and functionally, the rabbinic emphasis on the orality of rabbinic discourse, in contrast to the writtenness of Scripture? We shall examine noteworthy passages from classical rabbinic literature (Oral Torah) that thematize (and in some cases problematize) the nature of that Torah, especially in relation to its written sibling, as well as to the social, pedagogical context of their dual recitals. Contrary to my usual practice of working through such sources from earliest to latest in chronological sequence, so as to discern historical development, I shall begin with later, more conceptually developed traditions and work my way back to the earliest textual expressions. Given the limits of space, my aim is to highlight some salient aspects of the rabbinic concept of Written and Oral Torahs, and thereby rabbinic conceptions of Scripture and revelation.

A Late Story of Rabbinic Origins

Although it is impossible to determine with any certainty whether the "myth" of the Oral Torah goes back to prerabbinic (Pharisaic) times, the following story (which in its extant form dates to a late period in the rabbinic era) from the *Fathers According to Rabbi Nathan* is a good indication of how foundational that idea was to become:[3]

> What was the impatience of Shammai the Elder? They said: A story [is told] about a certain man who stood before Shammai, saying to him, "My master, how many Torahs do you [plural] have?"[4] [Shammai] said to him, "Two, one written and one oral." [The man] said to him, "With respect to the written one I believe you, but with respect to the oral one I do not believe you." [Shammai] rebuked him and angrily removed him.
>
> He came before Hillel, saying to him, "My master, how many Torahs were given?" [Hillel] said to him, "Two, one written and one oral." [The man] said to him, "With respect to the written one I believe you, but with respect to the oral one I do not believe you." [Hillel] said to him, "My son, have a seat."
>
> He wrote out for him the alphabet. [Pointing to the first letter,] he said to him, "What is this?" [The man] said to him, "It is an *aleph*." [Hillel] said to him, "This is not an *aleph* but a *bet*." [Pointing to the second letter,] he said to him, "What is this?" [The man] said, "It is a *bet*." "This is not a *bet*," said [Hillel], "but a *gimmel*." [Hillel] said to him, "How do you know that this is an *aleph*, and this is a *bet*, and this is a *gimmel*? Only because our earliest ancestors have passed it on to us that this is an *aleph*, and this is

a *bet*, and this is a *gimmel*. Just as you have accepted [received] this [the alphabet] on faith, so too accept the other [the two Torahs] on faith.[5]

Although the ostensible purpose of the story in its present setting is to contrast the impatience of Shammai with the patience of Hillel, two protorabbinic teachers of early-first-century CE Jerusalem, for our purposes the story is remarkable in several other respects. First, it presumes that whatever their differences in patience or teaching style, Hillel and Shammai, the last of the Second Temple proto-rabbinic teachers and, implicitly, the ones whose differences of opinion set the initial agenda for rabbinic study, are indistinguishable from each other as to their "curriculum" of Written and Oral Torahs. Second, the prospective student (or convert) presumably reflects a widespread Jewish acceptance of the Written Torah as being divinely revealed/authoritative, but not the Oral one. Thus, from the perspective of our story, the "doctrine" (if we may call it that) of the Written and Oral Torahs at once defined rabbinic Judaism already at its origins, notwithstanding its many internal disagreements, and differentiated it from much (if not all) of nonrabbinic Judaism of its time.

Most significant, it seems to me, is the argument that Hillel employs to gain the confidence of the prospective student, according to which belief in two Torahs is as fundamental to rabbinic teaching as are the most elementary building blocks of language (and hence all learning) itself. What Hillel, according to this story, does *not* do (which we will see in other rabbinic passages later, beginning in the earliest strata of rabbinic literature) is try to convince the man of this idea through the exegetical reading of biblical verses, that is, to prove the existence (or status) of the Oral Torah from prooftexts drawn from the Written Torah, whose authority is already accepted by the man, as indicated by his ready acceptance of the Written Torah.

Rather, Hillel argues by way of an epistemological analogy, entirely free of scriptural proof: All systems of knowledge and communication rest on foundational postulates that cannot be proven but must be accepted ("on faith") in order for the system's foundations to be constructed. Thus, without a collective, societal understanding of the identity of the letters or the sounds they represent, reading (e.g., of written scriptures) cannot occur. After all, what is the Written Torah if not, at the most basic level, an assembly of letters to be read? Similarly, rabbinic learning cannot progress without a shared acceptance of the existence (and shared status) of two Torahs, Written and Oral. Just as the one (the alphabet) must be accepted as received, so too the other (two Torahs). Of course, one need not accept this postulate, but without doing so, it would be impossible to learn from Hillel and Shammai or their rabbinic successors. Implicit in this comparison (although not admitted by the story) is the arbitrariness of a culture's assignment of names (that is, sounds and meanings) to the letters, which arbitrariness Hillel displays to the consternation of the prospective student, wherein lies the rhetorical force of his argument: Why presume the one (alphabet) as being self-evident and not the other (two Torahs)?

However, the story is even more subtly profound, in that Hillel's analogical argument itself instantiates its very point. While the man is prepared to accept the Written Torah but not the Oral Torah, his apprehension of the written word (or letter) is itself deeply dependent on his acceptance of received (oral) tradition/transmission. Whether Hillel's argument would convince anyone not already committed to the rabbinic conception of revelation and study of a dual Torah, it would bolster the attachment of rabbinic sages and disciples to the revelatory and authoritative status of Oral Torah as being as pedagogically "natural" as the acceptance of *aleph* as *aleph* and *bet* as *bet*.

The Linked but Differentiated Performances of Written and Oral Torahs

The rabbinic claim to be in possession of two revealed Torahs, Written and Oral, was not just of epistemological (how do we know this?) or ontological (what is the nature of each?) significance but of performative importance for how the two bodies of tradition were recited and studied, that is, ritually enacted, in relation to each other. In this regard, the following passage from the Palestinian ("Jerusalem") Talmud is particularly interesting for its concern with the practice of rendering the Hebrew text of Scripture into the Aramaic translations known as *targum*, since *targum* resides along the liminal borderline between written Scripture and oral teaching, partaking of each (although the rabbis defined *targum* as part of the latter):

> [A] R. Samuel bar R. Isaac [ca. 280 CE] once entered a synagogue. A man was standing and translating [the lection] while leaning against a pillar. He said to him: "You are forbidden to do so [translate while leaning]! Just as it [the Torah] was given in reverence and fear, so too must we relate to it in reverence and fear."

[B] R. Ḥaggai [ca. 350 CE] said: R. Samuel bar R. Isaac once entered a synagogue. He saw the sexton (*ḥazzan*) standing and translating without having appointed someone else under him [to translate].[6] He said to him: "You are forbidden to do so! Just as it was given by way of a middleman, so too we must relate to it by way of a middleman."

[C] R. Judah [bar R. Simeon] bar Pazzi [ca. 300 CE] entered and provided a biblical prooftext: "I [Moses] stood between God and you [Israel] at that time to declare to you the word of the Lord" (Deut. 5:5).

[D] R. Ḥaggai said: R. Samuel bar R. Isaac once entered a synagogue where he saw a teacher drawing the targum out of a [Hebrew] scroll.[7] He said to him: "You are forbidden to do so! Teachings which were said [revealed] orally [must be presented] orally and teachings which were said [revealed] in writing [must be presented] in writing."[8]

We have here accounts of three instances in which the same rabbinic sage upon entering a synagogue objects to the manner of the public translation of Scripture. These stories presume rabbinic rules for the synagogue reading of Scripture and its interlinear accompaniment by targum translation, according to which the two are to be separate and distinct, the former read from a written scroll and the latter recited orally (whether extemporaneously or from memory), with the former performed by a person of higher status than that of the latter.

The first incident (A) stresses that the practice of translation, as a crucial part of the Torah's public reception, is to be conducted in a manner consistent with the awe-inspiring manner of the Torah's original revelation, for which Moses and the Israelites stood in rapt attention. Whereas the translator might view his translation as an ancillary service to the central ritual of the Torah reading, R. Samuel conceives of the translation as constituting a part of both the medium and the message of that mythic reenactment. The second incident (B–C), while building on the analogy between synagogue lection and original revelation, conversely stresses the need to *differentiate* between Torah reading/reader and translation/translator. Just as the Torah was revealed by God but *mediated* to the people by Moses (C), so too the weekly reenactment of that event is performed by a reader through the mediation of the translator, the two needing to remain distinct from each other. The reception of written Scripture is orally mediated in the synagogue as it was at Sinai (there was *sola scriptura*, "Scripture alone," at neither).[9] If the second incident stresses the need to have two different people play the roles of reader/reveler and translator/transmitter, the third incident (in paragraph D) stresses the difference between the ways in which the two recite their "lines," the first from a fixed written text, the second according to a rule-governed but fluid oral tradition. Notwithstanding this distinction, this incident stresses, as did the first and second (with C), that *both* types of revelatory communication (written and oral) originated at Mt. Sinai and are reenacted as revelation in the synagogue ritual.

As this section of the Palestinian Talmud continues, it has much more to say about the relation between Written and Oral Torahs, once again employing words of the former to argue for the status of the latter:

> [E] R. Ḥaggai (ca. 350 CE) in the name of R. Samuel bar Naḥman (ca. 300 CE): Some teachings were said [revealed] orally and some teachings were said [revealed] in writing. We do not know which of them is more beloved, except from that which is written, "For in accordance with (*'al pi*: "by the mouth of") these things I make a covenant with you and with Israel" (Exod. 34:27), which is to say that those that are transmitted orally [literally, "by the mouth"] are more beloved.
>
> [F] R. Yoḥanan (ca. 250) and R. Judah b. R. Simeon (ca. 350). One said: If you keep what is oral and what is written, I [God] will make a covenant with you, but if not, I will not make a covenant with you. The other said: If you keep what is oral and what is written, you will receive reward, but if not, you will not receive reward.
>
> [G] [With respect to Deut. 9:10, in which Moses says, "The Lord gave me the two tablets of stone, written by the finger of God, and on them were (something) like all the words which the Lord spoke to you on the mountain from the midst of the fire on the day of assembly"], R. Joshua b. Levi (ca. 225 CE) said: "On them," "*and* on them"; "words," "*the* words"; "all," "*like* all": [this expansive language includes] written teaching [*miqra'*], oral teaching [*mishnah*], dialectical argument [*talmud*], and narrative ['*aggadah*].[10] And even that which an experienced disciple will one day teach before his master was already said to Moses at Sinai.
>
> [H] This is related to what is written, "Sometimes there is a phenomenon of which one might say, 'Look, this one is new!,'" to which his fellow responds to him, "It occurred long ago, in ages that went by before us." (Koh. 1:10)

Were we to think of Oral Torah as being derivative from Written Torah, or of less direct revelatory authority, we might suppose that the answer to R. Ḥaggai's implied question (E) would be that the Written Torah is the more beloved of the two. Playing on the phrase '*al pi* with respect to revelation and covenant in Exod. 34:27, the midrash avers that it is the Oral Torah that is the more beloved (by God? by Israel? presumably by both). Although the Written Torah, as a physical object, has greater iconic significance (e.g., in the way it is produced, handled, and read in synagogue), Jewish (especially halakhic) life is much more based on the Oral Law than on the Written Law. Even though the laws of the Written Torah are considered to have stronger divine backing, it is precisely the weaker authority and grounding of the laws of the Oral Torah that require their being paid greater attention and being accorded greater protection from violation. Furthermore, because the Pentateuch formed a part of the Christian (and Jewish-Christian) scriptures at this time, the rabbis regarded the Oral Torah as defining Jewish identity more distinctly. This rendered the Oral Torah more beloved as the *exclusive* possession of Jewish people.

We find this idea most clearly expressed in the following late midrash. After stating that the synagogue Torah reader cannot read from memory but must be looking at the Torah scroll, it adds that the person reciting the targum cannot look at a text, whether the targum or the Torah scroll (R. Judah b. Pazzi derives both rules from Exod. 34:27). The midrash continues:

> R. Judah b. R. Shalom (ca. 375) said: Moses requested [of God] that the oral teaching [*mishnah*] be written. The Holy One, blessed be he, foresaw that in the future the nations would translate the Torah and read from it in Greek and say, "They are not Israel." The Holy One, blessed be he, said to him, "O Moses! In the future the nations will say, 'We are Israel; we are the children of the Lord.' And Israel will say, 'We are the children of the Lord.' Now, the scales would appear to be balanced [between the two claims]." The Holy One, blessed be he, would say to the nations, "What are you saying that you are my children? I only recognize as my son one in whose hand are my 'mysteries.'" They would say to him, "And what are your 'mysteries'?" He would say to them, "the oral teaching [*mishnah*]." . . . Said the Holy One, blessed be he, to Moses, "What are you requesting, that the oral teaching be written? What then would be the difference between Israel and the nations?" Thus, it says, "Were I to write for him [Israel] the fullness of my teaching [*torah*]"; if so, "they (Israel) would have been considered as strangers" (Hos. 8:12).[11]

Returning to the Palestinian Talmud, the statements attributed to R. Yoḥanan and R. Judah b. R. Simeon (F) would seem, in contrast to what precedes them, to stress the *equal* importance of the Oral and Written Torahs (although note the order), whether for establishing the covenant or receiving its rewards. The difference between the two sages is whether observance of the commandments is a precondition for establishing the covenant or the condition for receiving its rewards. Implicitly, one might ask whether Israel's failure to preserve the Oral and Written Torahs would risk nullifying the covenant (and Israel's special relationship with God) or simply deny them the rewards *within* the covenantal relationship. This question was, in the aftermath of the destruction of the Second Temple and the continuing dispersion and subjugation to foreign rule, not merely an academic one.

Next (G) R. Joshua b. Levi provides scriptural proof for the claim that all branches of Torah teaching, both written (*miqra'*) and oral (*mishnah*), and all forms of the latter, were revealed to Moses at Sinai. This is a claim not just for the comprehensive scope and diversity of *past*, received revelation but for its continuation in the *present* and well into the *future*, all of which were anticipated and authorized at Sinai. Implicit in this interpretation is not just the variety of *forms* of rabbinic oral teaching but the variegation of its *contents*. We might not yet know what a future disciple will someday expound before his master, or that it will not differ from what will be taught by another disciple, but we are assured that whatever it will be, it was already contained within "*all* the words" communicated by God to Moses (and by Moses to the Israelites). The expansive language of the fixed verse of Written Torah suggests that teachings of the inexhaustibly fluid Oral Torah are ever expanding, in both form and content. Lest this claim be thought to be overly daring, an anonymous voice, itself anticipated by the words of the biblical book of Kohelet (Ecclesiastes), concludes, what appears to be new and novel was there from the revelatory beginning (i.e., do not take credit for intellectual innovation).[12]

Written and Oral Torahs in Pedagogical Tandem

Several rabbinic passages suggest ways in which Written and Oral Torahs were not only experienced in tandem as part of the synagogue service on Sabbaths and festivals but also in the central ritual of study. According to Deut. 17:19, the Israelite king is obligated to keep by his side a "copy of this Teaching [*mishneh torah*]," followed by a sequence of verbs: "It shall be with him, and he shall read [from the root *qr'*] *it all the days* of his life, in order that he may learn [root *lmd*] to fear [*yr'*] the Lord his God, to keep all the words of this Teaching [*torah*], and to perform [*'sh*] these laws." The midrashic commentary of *Sifre Deuteronomy* (itself part of the Oral Torah) interprets the verse as follows: "This teaches that the sight [*r'h*] [of it] leads to reading [*miqra'*, from the root *qr'*], *reading leads to translation* [*targum*], translation leads to oral teaching [*mishnah*], oral teaching leads to dialectical study [*talmud*, from the root *lmd*], *dialectical study leads to performance* [*'sh*], and performance leads to fear of God [*yr'*]."[13] The scriptural verb *yilmad* (learn/study) is unpacked so as to comprise three branches and consecutive stages of the *rabbinic* study curriculum—*targum*, *mishnah*, and *talmud*—which are interposed between the king's reading of the Torah and his fear of God, with his practice of the commandments being inserted from the end of the verse as the immediate consequence of his study. From the rabbinic perspective, mere reading of the Written Torah alone is insufficient to bring the king to proper practice and fear of God. It is by dynamically engaging words of Torah, both Written and Oral—through rabbinic-style study—that the king joins the people in submission to God, thereby rendering himself worthy of the people's submission to him.[14]

The commentary's envisioning of the king's practice of Torah "reading" as leading to dialectical study is modeled after the rabbinic curriculum of study of Written and Oral Torahs, precisely the kind of engaged, dialectical study in which the rabbinic student of the *Sifre*'s text would be presently engaged. Note, in particular, the transitional role of scriptural translation (into Jewish Aramaic, itself a hybrid language) as a bridge between the reading of written Scripture and the interpretive dialectics of oral study. This probably reflects the sequence of rabbinic study.

For another look at the rabbinic curriculum of combined study of Written (*miqra'*) and Oral (*mishnah*) Torah, we will look at *Sifre Deuteronomy*'s commentary on Deut. 32:2, in which Moses employs the metaphor of rain to describe how he wishes his "discourse" to fall upon and penetrate the Israelites:

> "May my discourse come down as rain" (Deut. 32:2): Just as rain falls on trees and infuses each type with its distinctive flavor—the grapevine with its flavor, the olive tree with its flavor, the fig tree with its flavor—so too words of Torah are all one, but they comprise written teaching [*miqra'*] and oral teaching [*mishnah*]: [the latter including] exegesis [*midrash*], laws [*halakhot*], and narratives [*'aggadot*]. . . .

> Another interpretation: Just as with rain, you cannot see [anticipate] it until it arrives, as it says, "And after a while the sky grew black with clouds and there was wind and a heavy downpour" (1 Kings 18:45),[15] so too with respect to a disciple of the sages, you do not know what he is until he teaches [*yishneh*] oral teaching [*mishnah*]: exegesis [*midrash*], laws [*halakhot*] and narratives [*'aggadot*]; or until he is appointed provider [*parnas*] over the community.[16]

Of particular significance is the way, once again, in which Moses's teaching is understood to contain already the diverse forms of rabbinic Oral Torah, which despite their distinctive "tastes" "are all one," that is, derive from a single divine source and revelatory event. However, of even greater interest is the metaphoric slippage whereby the rain, having at first signified the diverse forms of rabbinic *teaching*, comes to signify the rabbinic *teacher* (disciple of the sages) of these very same forms of oral learning. His active engagement with and production of rabbinic words of Torah, rather than passive reading of the Written Torah, accomplished to no small measure by memorization, ensures that the sage not only exemplifies the Oral Torah but embodies it, in all its branches, as he learns it and teaches it.

In many areas of rabbinic thought and practice (as in the priestly stratum of the Hebrew Bible), division and differentiation (*havdalah*) of seeming opposites (e.g., light and dark, holy and profane) is a necessary precondition to their intersection and ultimate integration. Similarly, the following passage from the *Fathers According to Rabbi Nathan* exemplifies the performative differentiation between Oral and Written Torahs, as among the subdivisions of the latter (e.g., between law and narrative, *halakhah* and *'aggadah*), and their ultimate integration in the idealized master of all the curricular divisions:

> "Provide yourself with a [single] teacher" (*m. 'Abot* 1:6): How so? This teaches that one should provide himself with a regular teacher and study with him written teaching [*miqra'*] and oral teaching [*mishnah*]—exegesis [*midrash*], laws [*halakhot*], and narratives [*'aggadot*]. Then the meaning which the teacher neglected to tell him in the study of *miqra'* he will eventually tell him in the study of *mishnah*; the meaning which he neglected to tell him in the study of *mishnah* he will eventually tell him in the study of *midrash*; the meaning which he neglected to tell him in the study of *midrash* he will eventually tell him in the study of *halakhot*; the meaning which he neglected to tell him in the study of *halakhot* he will eventually

tell him in the study of *'aggadah*. Thus, that man remains in one place and is filled with good and blessing. R. Me'ir used to say: He who studies Torah with a single teacher, to what may he be likened? To one who had a single field, part of which he sowed with wheat and part with barley, and planted part with olives and part with oak trees. Now that man is full of good and blessing. But one who studies with two or three teachers is like a man who has many fields: one he sows with wheat and one he sows with barley, and plants one with olives and one with oak trees. Now this man is scattered among many pieces of land, without good or blessing.[17]

Just as the diversity of forms of rabbinic oral teaching, in hermeneutical tandem with written Scripture, are said to derive ultimately from a single God, the same diversity is integrated, ideally at least, within the teaching of a single rabbinic sage. However, we must assume that this emphasis on unity gives indirect expression to its very opposite: the tendency, known to all scholars, to master one subject well, and for the student who seeks a comprehensive education to study from a wide range of such specialized teachers, moving from one to the next. Such specialization, and its attendant competition, among the rabbinic masters of the Oral Torah is well evidenced in rabbinic literature.

Conclusion

The rabbinic conception of a revelatory and pedagogical curriculum of written Scripture and oral teaching is without antecedent or parallel in the ancient world. While the idea of a twofold Torah, differentiated as Written and Oral, was not without its opponents and detractors, it became a fundamental part of rabbinic theology and self-understanding. The rabbis viewed themselves as the receivers, transmitters, and masters of an ever growing and diversifying corpus of interpretations, laws, and narratives. They understood this corpus to constitute a chain of tradition originating as divine revelation through Moses to the people of Israel at Mt. Sinai. It would not be an exaggeration to say that the dialogical pairing of a *fixed* scriptural text with a *fluid* oral complement enabled rabbinic society, and eventually broader Jewish society, to survive the many vicissitudes of history by striking a delicate balance between cultural permanence and plasticity. Even today, the idea that the foundational, divinely revealed scriptures of a religion cannot be understood or applied aside from the accompanying tradition of their continual and variegated human interpretation remains a radical one—especially because the human interpretation in Oral Torah is as determinative in practice as the revealed scripture is. This "humanizing" of scriptural transmission and interpretation would appear to run counter to an emphasis on the primacy of Scripture alone (*sola scriptura*) in other scriptural religions, as in some streams of Judaism.

The rabbinic "movement" (if we can call it that) began as one of many marginal Jewish groups at a time of great social, political, and religious upheaval in the early centuries CE. This is the context in which the rabbinic teachings that we have examined took form and need to be understood. One of the great mysteries of ancient and late-antique Jewish history is the ability of this relatively small and marginal group of scholars to eventually, sometime in the mid- to late first millennium, redefine the very nature of Judaism as both practice and belief around the central obligation and ritual of textual study. While an important part of any explanation thereto must be sought at the *outer* plane of historical transformation and cultural realignment (whether identified with Greco-Roman paganism, Christianity, or Islam), a major aspect of the transformation of Judaism and Jewish society must be understood as having occurred at the *inner* plane of Jewish history, as shaped by the rhetorical power of rabbinic discourse in its exegetical (*midrash*), legal (*halakhah*), and narrative (*'aggadah*) modes of expression, whether directed to the people as a whole or mastered by a scholastic elite (or the two in tandem). The discursive world that these distinctive forms of *torah* constructed and inhabited, and from which vantage the surrounding world was increasingly viewed and understood, is a phenomenon yet to be adequately apprehended and appreciated. Central to the lasting and renewing vitality of the rabbinic "conception of Scripture" is its pedagogical pairing of the closed and open, fixed and fluid, the timeless and the timely, of the Written and the Oral (even long after the latter was consigned to writing), by which Jewish society and culture were to understand themselves along the continuum of reenacted revelation and awaited redemption.

NOTES

1. *TaNaKh* stands for the three components, in sequence, of the canonical Hebrew Bible: *Torah* (Pentateuch), *Nevi'im* (Prophets), *Ketuvim* (Writings).

2. *Jewish Antiquities* 13.297 (trans. Ralph Marcus; LCL 7:376–77).

3. For the two earliest rabbinic statements that "Two Torahs were given to Israel (at Mt. Sinai): one written and one oral," see *Sifre Deut.* 351 (ed. Louis Finkelstein, 408), commenting on Deut. 33:10, where the order of "written" and "oral" is reversed; and *Sifra Beḥuqqotay pereq* 8:12 (ed. Isaac Weiss, 112c).

4. In a parallel version in *b. Shabb*at 31a, the man is a non-Jew, a prospective convert.

5. *'Abot deRabbi Natan* A15 (ed. Solomon Schechter, 61; trans. Judah Goldin, 80). Cf. *'Abot deRabbi Natan* B29 (ed. Solomon Schechter, 61–62; trans. Anthony Saldarini, 174–75).

6. The sexton usually assigns the Torah lection to someone else. See *t. Meg.* 3(4):21. Presumably, on the present occasion, the sexton was acting both as reader and as translator, thereby failing to differentiate performatively between written Scripture and its oral translation.

7. The reference here is either to a text of targum, which had been inserted within the Hebrew text or scroll of the Torah, or to the rendering ("drawing" here intended not in a physical sense) of the targum from the written Hebrew text, with the translator looking at the Hebrew text for guidance, thereby giving the impression that the targum itself is written in that text.

8. *P. Megillah* 4:1, 74d (ed. Academy of the Hebrew Language, 768).

9. Nor was there *sola scriptura* in Ezra's mediated public reading of the Torah according to Neh. 8:8.

10. The word *miqra'* denotes that which is read (literally, "called out") from a written text, whereas *mishnah* denotes that which is recited from memory, or through repetition. The former appears first in this sense of "reading" in Neh. 8:8, with respect to Ezra's public reading of the Torah. The two nouns are used in the present sense of written and oral teaching for the first time in tannaitic rabbinic literature.

11. *Pesiqta Rabbati* 5 (ed. Meir Friedmann, 14b; trans. William Braude, 93; ed. Rivka Ulmer, 51–52).

12. See especially *Kohelet Rabbah* 1:29(9): "Similarly, if you have heard Torah from the mouth of a scholar, let it be in your estimation as if your ears had heard it from Mount Sinai. That is what the prophet rebukes the people for when he tells them, 'Draw near to me and hear this: From the beginning, I did speak in secret; from the time anything existed, I was there' (Isa. 48:16 NJPS). They said to him, '[If you were present at the revelation] why have you not told us [this teaching before]?' He replied to them, 'Because chambers [for the reception of prophecy] had not been created within me, but now that they have been created within me, "And now the Lord God has sent me, endowed with his spirit"' (ibid.)."

13. *Sifre Deut.* 161 (ed. Louis Finkelstein, 212). My translation follows Finkelstein's edition, with the exception that "sight" renders *hammar'eh* found in the better witnesses.

14. Note that our text begins with *mar'eh* ("sight, vision," from the root *r'h*)

and ends with *yir'ah* ("fear, awe," from the root *yr'*), creating an *inclusio* based on a word play.

15. The prophet Elijah sends his servant seven times to look for signs of rain until on the seventh try he spots a small cloud in the distance. The rain storm then comes suddenly.

16. *Sifre Deut.* 306 (ed. Finkelstein, 339). I translate the text according to MS London.

17. *'Abot deRabbi Natan* A8 (ed. Schechter, 35–36; trans. Goldin, 49–50).

Chapter 4

Concepts of Scripture in the Schools of Rabbi Akiva and Rabbi Ishmael

Azzan Yadin-Israel

Once a year, Israel celebrates "Book Week," a holiday devoted to the written word, consisting of book fairs in city centers, deep discounts on books, and various interviews and panels of authors, critics, and other literary figures. Alongside the mainstream celebrations, there is also "Torah Book Week," during which ultraorthodox book vendors sell religious texts and artifacts. Years ago, I was perusing the booths of a "Torah Book Week" exhibitor, looking for rabbinic Torah commentaries, when I spotted a series of illustrated children's books—age-appropriate retellings of Bible stories for young ultraorthodox readers. Curious, I leafed through the first volume, which recounted the life of Abraham. The book was a heavily bowdlerized mixture of biblical and midrashic narratives: the story of Abraham destroying the idols in his father's house (which occurs in midrashic texts but not in Genesis itself) was included, but Sarai/Sarah's visits to the harems of the Egyptian pharaoh and Melchizedek (Genesis 12 and 14) were not—which was all to be expected. I was, however, taken aback by the illustrations. The landscape of ancient Mesopotamia was typical: palm trees, the Tigris or Euphrates flowing in the background, the desert sun a constant presence, and camels meandering throughout. Abraham is in many ways integrated into these scenes, wandering from Ur to Canaan on foot, doing battle with the northern kings on camel, greeting angels by his tent, and almost sacrificing his son on a simple altar of stones. But one detail stood out. Through it all, Abraham is dressed in the long black frock coat and tall fur hat, and sports the long, curly sidelocks, of the ultraorthodox community that produced the book series.

One of the challenges facing historically conscious collectives is how to assert their identities over time—that is, to recognize the passage of time and ensuing change in circumstances, while maintaining some common elements that anchor the group's sense of self. The publishers of the Abraham book do this by collapsing the historical distance between the present-day readers and the historical forefathers. Abraham may have lived many centuries ago, ridden camels,[1] and fought with a sword, but he was fundamentally identical with his 20th- and 21st-century readers—a Hasidic Jew. Though this is an extreme example, the tendency to retroject present ideas and assumptions onto the past is strong and can easily pass undetected, and it is probably nowhere more persistently manifested than in areas considered canonical and therefore constitutive of a community's identity. One of the virtues of a collection such as the present one is that it highlights the rich variety of ideas and practices that have grown out of the Jewish engagement of the Hebrew Bible. Even so, and even among critically informed readers, some assumptions remain largely unexamined. The present chapter represents an attempt to address one such assumption, namely, that the early rabbis were unproblematically committed to the authority of Scripture.

Legal Midrash

The literature of the early rabbis, or Tannaim (roughly 70–220 CE), consists of two genres: legal decisions presented as received tradition, with only minimal reference to Scripture, and legal decisions presented as the result of sustained interpretation of Scripture, known as legal midrash. This distinction is addressed elsewhere in this collection[2] and is here mentioned solely to clarify the scope of this chapter, which deals with the legal midrashim and not the "received" legal codices (the Mishnah and the Tosefta). My claim is that even within early rabbinic legal midrash, it is possible to discern different conceptions and valorizations of Scripture.

The texts in question are preserved in a number of collections, each devoted to a different book of the Bible. The most important are the Mekhilta of Rabbi Ishmael and the Mekhilta of Rabbi Shimon bar Yohai, both commenting on the book of Exodus; the Sifra, on Leviticus; the Sifre to the book of Numbers; and the Sifre to Deuteronomy.[3] Since the late 19th century, scholars have recognized that these midrashic works or, to use the Hebrew plural form, midrashim, make up two groups: the Mekhilta of

Rabbi Ishmael and the Sifre Numbers belong to one group, associated with the figure of Rabbi Ishmael, while the Mekhilta of Rabbi Shimon bar Yohai, the Sifra, and Sifre Deuteronomy make up another, associated with that of Rabbi Akiva. This view has been adopted by broad swaths of the scholarly community, most notably the mid-20th-century Israeli scholar Jacob Epstein and his students (and their students), and has recently found expression in an authoritative survey of the legal midrashim.[4] This division, however, has generally been understood as one of style—the terminology and the hermeneutic canons employed—while in fact it reflects profound differences in the conceptualization and valorization of Scripture.

The School of Rabbi Ishmael

One of the accomplishments of the study of midrash in recent decades has been to recognize the extent to which rabbinic interpretation maintains a dialogue with the biblical text, often responding to its "gaps and indeterminacies."[5] Though these claims are often formulated in the context of nonlegal midrash (Aggadah), they are no less evident in the Rabbi Ishmael midrashim,[6] which employ a series of formulas that cast the rabbinic interpreters' intervention as a response to a difficulty arising from the Scripture itself. These formulas typically point to an apparent ambiguity in the biblical text that is subsequently clarified. I refer to these textual ambiguities (some immediately evident in the plain sense of Scripture, others generated by the rabbinic interpretation) as *hermeneutic markers* since they mark the biblical text as requiring interpretation. The most common formulas in this context are *lammah ne'emar* (why was this stated?) and *mah talmud lomar* (what is the instruction?). Here is one example of the former, in a discussion of the laws for the daily burnt offering of ancient Israel's sacrificial worship:

> "The second lamb you shall offer at twilight" [Num. 28:8]: Why was this stated, because it says, "and all the assembled congregation of the Israelites shall slaughter it at twilight" [Exod. 12:6—a law concerning a similar but distinct burnt offering sacrificed on the eve of Passover]. I do not know which comes first, the daily burnt offering or the paschal offering, thus [Scripture] teaches, saying: "second," second to the daily burnt offering, not second to the paschal offering. (Sifre Numbers §143, p. 191)[7]

The question "Why was this stated?" is linked with the repetition of the phrase "the second lamb" in Numbers 28:4 and 28:8. The first occurrence establishes that one lamb is to be offered in the morning and a second at twilight. Why, then, does the Torah first discuss the meal offering and libation of the first offering and then repeat the command that the second lamb be offered at twilight? According to the Sifre, the second statement is necessary because it resolves a legal ambiguity. Exodus 12:6 commands the sacrifice of the paschal lamb at twilight, so the paschal lamb and the daily burnt offering are to be sacrificed at the same time, though the order of sacrifice is unclear. Is the paschal lamb sacrificed before the daily offering, or vice versa? Numbers 28:8 responds to this question: the repetition of "the second lamb" indicates that the daily twilight burnt offering remains the second sacrifice of the day at Passover; that is, it is not pushed down into the third position by the paschal offering.

Of course, we are not concerned here with the actual legal conclusions; what is important is that Sifre Numbers sets its conclusion up as a response to an ambiguity within Scripture. It is as though the rabbinic reader must be *invited* to intervene by Scripture. Though this may sound like an overstatement, there are, in fact, a number of passages that counsel the interpreter to refrain from interpreting until Scripture provides a definitive answer to the question:

> "He who insults his father and his mother shall be put to death" [Exod. 21:17]: I thus know only about one who curses both his father and his mother. How about one who curses only his father or only his mother? . . . Rabbi Yonathan says: It can mean both of them together and it can mean either of them until Scripture [*ha-katuv*] should expressly decide in favor of one of these. (Mekhilta Neziqin 5, pp. 267–68; Lauterbach 3:47)

The letter *vav* in the phrase "he who insults his father and [*vav*] his mother" is ambiguous: it may mean that one who insults *both* his father and his mother will be put to death, or it may mean that one who insults *either* his father or his mother shall be put to death. Rabbi Yonathan, a prominent member of the school of Rabbi Ishmael, recognizes that both readings are possible and does not essay a resolution. Instead, he suggests the ambiguity remain unresolved "until Scripture [*ha-katuv*] should expressly decide in favor of one of these." In terms of determining that an interpretive intervention is justified, Scripture plays an important and in some cases even a leading role.

But Scripture's active participation in interpretation extends beyond the initial engagement of the verse (i.e., of itself). Indeed, the Rabbi Ishmael midrashim attribute to Scripture a wide range of actions: "Scripture [*ha-katuv*] comes to teach," "Scripture draws an analogy," "Scripture prohibits," "Scripture singles out this case from a broader statement," and so on.[8] Strikingly, in some cases, Scripture teaches the reader how best to interpret, and it does this in two ways. In some passages, Scripture is represented as providing general hermeneutic rules.

> "When a man gives to another an ass, an ox, a sheep or all animals to guard . . ." [Exod. 22:9]: I thus know only about an ass, an ox, and a sheep. How about any other beast? [Scripture] teaches, saying: "Or all animals to guard." I read, then, "All animals to guard." What does it teach by saying, "an ass, an ox, a sheep"? Because if it had read only "all animals" I might have understood that the keeper is liable only if all beasts have been put in his care. Therefore it says, "an ass, an ox, a sheep," to declare him liable for each one by itself. And what does [Scripture] teach by saying, "all animals"? Scripture [*ha-katuv*] comes to teach you that a general statement that is added to a specific statement includes everything. (Mekhilta Neziqin 16, pp. 302–3; Lauterbach 3:121)

Exodus 22:9 contains an apparent redundancy. It lists the domestic animals that a person might lend his fellow—an ass, an ox, a sheep—and then states "or all animals." But initial impressions notwithstanding, the Mekhilta suggests that both phrases are necessary since the absence of either could lead to confusion: the general statement is necessary lest one think Exodus is referring only to the three animals listed, and the enumeration is necessary lest one think Exodus is referring only to cases when a person guards "*all* animals." This is all well and good, and one would think the issue has been resolved, but the derashah (midrashic interpretation) does not end here. Instead, it suggests that the entire passage has been doing double work—resolving the specific matter of the animals in Exodus 22:9 but also communicating a general interpretive conclusion: "Scripture [*ha-katuv*] comes to teach you that a general statement that is added to a specific statement includes everything." In resolving legal matters, Scripture employs interpretive practices, and these practices—and the principles that underlie them—become the ultimate content of its teaching.

The second way Scripture imparts the craft of proper interpretation is by setting interpretive precedent, that is, by functioning as an interpretive model. This function is most evident in passages that employ the phrase "Just as Scripture [*ha-katuv*] specifies . . . so too I specify."

> "An oath of YHWH shall be between the two of them" [Exod. 22:10]: An oath by the Tetragrammaton [the four-letter personal name of God]. From this you can conclude with regard to all the oaths in the Torah. Since all the oaths in the Torah were stated without specification and Scripture specifies for you with regard to one that it must be by the Tetragrammaton, so too I specify with regard to all the oaths in the Torah that they must be by the Tetragrammaton. (Mekhilta Neziqin 16, p. 303; Lauterbach 3:122–23)

Exodus 22:10 deals with a man who entrusts his possessions to another and they go inexplicably missing. Though the guardian claims that they were stolen, no thief is found, and so both must take an "oath of YHWH." This is the only verse that specifies the name of God employed in oaths, or, in the Mekhilta's description, *all* oaths are unspecified except for the *single* example at hand, a structure that is itself imbued with interpretive meaning. Namely, it allows the reader to extend the legal conclusion of the derashah—that the oath in Exodus 22:10 invokes the Tetragrammaton—to the other, unspecified oaths. The justification for this move is Scripture's precedent: "Scripture specifies . . . so too I specify."

Examining the interpretive practices of the Rabbi Ishmael midrashim, we find them determined by Scripture on both sides of the process. First, it is Scripture that determines whether a verse may be interpreted. It is only once Scripture signals to the reader that there is a difficulty to be resolved or misinterpretation to be avoided that it becomes legitimate to interpret.[9] Second, the rabbinic reader takes cues from Scripture throughout the interpretive process. Scripture provides specific legal conclusions (it "comes to teach" regarding various matters), as well as general hermeneutic principles, and serves as a model and a precedent for the attentive reader. The overall thrust of these midrashim, then, is to cast Scripture as orchestrating its own interpretation: providing clues and rules for the reader, who, like the reader of a detective novel, identifies the signs left for him or her by the author and ultimately reaches the correct solution.

Before turning to the Rabbi Akiva midrashim, it is worth noting that the Scripture-centered hermeneutic of the Rabbi Ishmael midrashim dovetails with a marginalization of extrascriptural traditions (the "Oral Law"). Legal rulings are not transmitted "in the name of" this or that sage; Rabbi

Ishmael seems not to be the disciple of any expert in Oral Law; and many of the interpretive principles these midrashim apply to Scripture are applied in the Mishnah to extrascriptural traditions. In one passage, Rabbi Ishmael apparently offers a minimalist understanding of extrascriptural tradition:

> "You shall take an awl" [Deut. 15:17]: This was the source of Rabbi Ishmael's saying: In three places extra-scriptural tradition [*halakhah*] circumvents Scripture: the Torah says, "he shall pour out its blood and cover it with earth" [Lev. 17:13] while the *halakhah* says, with anything that grows plants; the Torah says "He writes her a document of divorce" [Deut. 24:1] while the *halakhah* says, he may write on anything that was separated from the ground; the Torah says "with an awl." (Sifre Deuteronomy §122, Finkelstein, 180)

The point of this derashah is that there are *only* three *halakhot*—extrascriptural traditions—that circumvent Scripture.[10] This is significant because an extrascriptural tradition functions as an independent source of authority only inasmuch as it *does* bypass Scripture, that is, only inasmuch as it stands as an independent source of legal authority. By limiting the number of independent traditions to three, the derashah marginalizes the role of extrascriptural tradition, limiting it to a bare minimum of instances.

The School of Rabbi Akiva

I begin the discussion of Rabbi Akiva at the point with which Rabbi Ishmael concluded—extrascriptural traditions, since the contrast between the two is immediately apparent. Unlike the Rabbi Ishmael midrashim, those of Rabbi Akiva (here and throughout, my focus is on the outstanding representative of this school, the Sifra) regularly transmit legal rulings that are not scriptural, at times accompanied by the characteristic terminology of extrascriptural transmission, "in the name of" (*mishem*) a sage: "Rabbi Elazar says in the name of Rabbi Yose . . ." (Tzav pereq 13.6; Weiss, 37a; *TK*, 164);[11] "Rabbi Shimon ben Yehudah says in the name of Rabbi Shimon . . ." (Tazri'a Nega'im pereq 9.15; Weiss, 66b; *TK*, 475); "Rabbi Yehudah said in the name of Rabbi Elazar . . ." (Aḥarei Mot pereq 4.10; Weiss, 81b; *TK*, 347). Similarly, the Sifra speaks of the "testimony" of sages, a technical term for the transmission of *halakhot*: "Rabbi Zadoq testified that the brine of impure locust is pure" (Shemini pereq 5.10; Weiss, 51a; *TK*, 212); "This is the testimony Hezekiah the father of 'Aqesh bore before Rabban Gamliel, when he said in the name of Rabban Gamliel the Elder: Any earthen vessel that does not have an internal space [*tokh*], no regard is paid its external space [*aḥorayim*]" (Shemini parasha 7.4; Weiss, 53b; *TK*, 224); "Rabbi Yose ben Yoezer of Tzereda testified regarding the liquids of the house of slaughter that they are pure" (Shemini parasha 8.5; Weiss, 55a; *TK*, 230). In addition, the Sifra contains several statements as to the legitimacy and binding nature of nonscriptural traditions. For example, "If this is *halakhah* [extrascriptural tradition], we accept it but if it is a logical argument based on Scripture [*din*] rebuttal is possible" (Hova pereq 1.12; Weiss, 16b; *TK*, 71 [in the margins]). Another example is the set of statements in the Sifra that attribute a legal decision to a decree of the scribes (*soferim*), sometimes in explicit contrast to those derived from Torah: "Rabbi Yose says, The impurity of liquids in vessels is not from Torah but from the words of the scribes" (Shemini parashah 8.5; Weiss, 55a; *TK*, 229). Not surprisingly, the Sifra presents many legal rulings without reference to Scripture—a conspicuous tendency in a verse-by-verse interpretation of Leviticus.

But what of the Sifra's interpretive practices? Here too we find dramatic differences from those of the Rabbi Ishmael midrashim. For one thing, the Sifra is not committed to the idea of hermeneutic markers, at least not in the same manner and with the same consistency as the Rabbi Ishmael midrashim. Here is one example:

> "And if anyone ['*ish* '*ish*; literally, "person person"] of the house of Israel or of the alien who reside among them ingests any blood . . ." [Lev. 17:10]: . . . why is " '*ish* '*ish*" [person person] stated? Rabbi Eliezer the son of Shimon says, to include the offspring of an Israelite woman from a gentile or from a slave. (Aḥarei Mot parashah 8.1–2; Weiss, 84b; *TK*, 363)

I have omitted much of the derashah, to better focus on the point at hand that has to do with the Sifra's question "why is '*ish* '*ish* stated?" Clearly the Sifra presents '*ish* '*ish* as a redundancy[12] that hermeneutically marks the verse and invites the rabbinic reader to include elements not stated by Scripture. So far so good—the procedure appears quite similar to that of the Rabbi Ishmael midrashim. But just a few verses earlier we read,

> "If anyone ['*ish* '*ish*] of the house of Israel slaughters an ox or sheep or goat in the camp, or does so outside the camp . . ." [Lev. 17:3]: Might it be that

one who slaughters the purification offering in the south is liable? Scripture teaches, saying "outside the camp." (Aḥarei Mot parashah 6.3; Weiss, 83b; *TK*, 358)

Leviticus 17:3 introduces the prohibition against nonritual slaughter, and the Sifra addresses a certain aspect of the slaughter, namely, its location. For the question at hand, however, I am concerned with what goes unaddressed, namely, the repetition *'ish 'ish*. The phrase is also ignored in the Sifra's commentary to Leviticus 22:4 ("No man [*'ish 'ish*] of Aaron's offspring, who has an eruption or a discharge shall eat of the sacred donations . . .").[13] This is a critical issue, since couching midrash in terms of a response to a biblical irregularity shifts the agency of initiating interpretation to the text and away from the reader (who is now merely picking up on textual clues). But for this to work, the marker must be consistently recognized. Otherwise, the agency shifts back to the reader, who must decide arbitrarily whether, in this case, the repetition "*'ish 'ish*" counts as a marker (as in Leviticus 17:10) or not (as in Leviticus 17:3). An inconsistent marker is no marker at all.

Another perplexing aspect of the Sifra is the wide range of conclusions it can draw from the same biblical phrase. Repetitions such as *'ish 'ish* function in the Sifra as a *ribbui*, or inclusive argument; that is, they appear to legitimate the introduction of new elements not mentioned explicitly in the verse. Thus, in the commentary on Leviticus 17:10, *'ish 'ish* served to "include the offspring of an Israelite woman from a gentile or from a slave." This is not problematic in and of itself, but the procedure grows increasingly opaque as we examine additional verses that contain the phrase *'ish 'ish* and the additional elements that, according to the Sifra, they introduce:

- "YHWH spoke to Moses, saying . . . Whenever any person [*'ish 'ish*] from the house of Israel or from the aliens in Israel presents an offering . . ." [Lev. 22:17–20]: . . . why is *'ish 'ish* stated? To include the gentiles, that they be held accountable on matters of vows and freewill offerings like Israel. (Emor parashah 7.1; Weiss, 98a; *TK*, 434)
- "And if anyone [*'ish 'ish*] from among the Children of Israel or any alien who resides among them hunts down an animal or a bird that may be eaten, he shall pour out its blood and cover it with earth" [Lev. 17:13]: . . . why does it say *'ish 'ish*? Since it says "hunts." From this I know only regarding hunting. Whence do I learn regarding one who purchases,

inherits, or receives as a present? [Scripture] teaches saying *'ish 'ish*. (Aḥarei Mot pereq 11.1; Weiss, 84b; *TK*, 364)
- "When any man [*'ish 'ish*] has a discharge" [Lev. 15:2]: . . . From this I learn only regarding the man [*'ish*], whence do I include the woman and the minor? [Scripture] teaches saying, *'ish 'ish*. (Metzora Zavim parashah 1.1; Weiss, 74b; *TK*, 311)
- "If anyone [*'ish 'ish*] . . . offers up a burnt offering or a well-being offering . . ." [Lev. 17:8]: . . . why does [Scripture] state *'ish 'ish*? To include two individuals who offered an offering—the words of Rabbi Shimon. (Aḥarei Mot pereq 10.2; Weiss, 84a; *TK*, 361)
- "No one [*'ish 'ish*] shall approach anyone of his own flesh to uncover nakedness" [Lev. 18:6]: . . . why does [Scripture] state *'ish 'ish*? To include the gentiles, who are warned against sexual transgressions when among Israel. (Aḥarei Mot pereq 13.1; Weiss, 85b; *TK*, 370)

And there are more. As this list demonstrates, the elements "included" by *'ish 'ish* are a fairly arbitrary set. In some cases, they are discrete groups such as "the gentiles" or "women" or combinations of groups, for example, "women and minors." In other cases, they represent very specific legal scenarios, such as the case of an individual who receives or purchases an edible animal or bird rather than hunting it, as Leviticus 17:13 specifies. The list gathered here—representative but not exhaustive—points to the Sifra's tendency to juxtapose scriptural elements (here the repetition *'ish 'ish*) and legal conclusions without the slightest attempt at justification or explanation.

Finally, consider the terms *yekhol* and *minayin*. The former introduces interpretations that the Sifra ultimately rejects ("It could mean X, but this is not so . . ."); the role Scripture plays in these derashot is unclear and in any case minimal:

"And it shall be when he is guilty in any of these matters . . ." [Lev. 5:5]: It could be [*yekhol*] that in imparting impurity to the Temple and its holy vessels, a transgression punished by *karet*, that is, being cut off from the nation, one is liable for each and every action, but regarding transgressions related to hearing a statement regarding a public adjuration or the utterance of an oath—transgressions not punished by *karet*—perhaps one is liable only for one action. Scripture teaches, saying "in any," asserting liability for each and every action. It could be [*yekhol*] that concerning the Temple purity on its own and the purity of the Temple vessels on their own, even in cases of a single bout of forgetfulness, one is liable only for one, [Scripture] teaches saying, "in any," asserting liability for each and every action. (Hova pereq 14.2–3; Weiss, 23b)

This passage contains very little interpretation, as the Sifra anchors the exclusion of all these legal cases in a single scriptural element: Leviticus's statement that one is guilty "in any of these matters" is proof that the legal scenarios introduced by *yekhol* are incorrect. The Sifra does not introduce a second verse to clarify the matter (as the Rabbi Ishmael midrashim regularly do), which raises a difficulty: if the legal cases proposed by *yekhol* are rejected by the verse itself—that is, if the incorrectness of the interpretation is evident from the verse—why propose it in the first place? Unlike Rabbi Ishmael's *shomeaʿ 'ani* arguments, which introduce a plausible reading but reject it as untenable in light of another verse, *yekhol* introduces a slew of legal scenarios that are not connected with the verse in any immediately visible manner. Nor, for that matter, is any interpretive reason given to suggest that "in any of these matters" in Leviticus 5:5 aims specifically at the case of a public adjuration or of distinct oaths involving the temple and its sancta, and so forth.

The same disconnectedness from the verse is apparent in the many derashot that begin with *minayin*, "whence." Structurally, *minayin* derashot are the mirror image of *yekhol*: whereas *yekhol* introduces legal rulings to be rejected, *minayin* introduces rulings that will ultimately be accepted. For example,

"If his offering . . . is from the flock, of sheep or of goats" [Lev. 1:10]: . . . whence [*minayin*] to include the surplus of the purification offering and the surplus of guilt offerings, the surplus of the tenth of the *efah*, the surplus of the bird offerings of men suffering from genital discharge, the surplus of the bird offerings of women suffering from genital discharge, the surplus of the bird offerings of women who have given birth, the surplus of the offerings of the nazirite and the leper; and one who dedicates his property to the temple and they included things that are fit for sacrifice—wines and oils and birds—whence [*minayin*] that these should be sold and the funds used for burnt offerings? [Scripture] teaches, saying [both] "from the flock, of sheep or of goats," to include all these cases. (Nedava parashah 5.4, Weiss, 7b; *TK*, 27–28)

The Sifra here points to a typical hermeneutic marker, namely, the apparent redundancy of describing the offering as "from the flock" and then adding "of sheep or of goats." But how, precisely, does the arguably redundant addition of the phrase "of sheep or of goats" introduce the slew of sacrifices and legal cases cited by the Sifra? The problem is similar to the one we encountered in discussing *'ish 'ish*—how can a single phrase give rise to a variety of legal conclusions—but perhaps more visible here because the conclusions are introduced in a single derashah. Can Leviticus 1:10 be said to generate all the possibilities mentioned in the derashah? Unlikely. But more important, the Sifra does not appear to be making this claim. Nothing in the derashah just cited, or in countless derashot like it, suggests that the Sifra is attempting to bridge the gap between the biblical verse and the legal decisions it seeks to affirm or reject. Far from yielding a clear sense of the Sifra as an interpretive text, then, our discussion has laid out a series of difficulties that arise in the attempt to understand the midrashic practices of this text: the Sifra is often obscure regarding the precise scriptural elements that putatively give rise to its interpretation; even when these are explicitly specified, the Sifra does not engage the marked word or phrase regularly (as when instances of *'ish 'ish* do not elicit interpretation); the same biblical element can be used to introduce or reject a long list of different legal conclusions. Overall, the Sifra maintains a tenuous, at times even arbitrary, relationship with the biblical text.

What are we to make of such a midrash? To my mind, the most plausible explanation (already suggested by earlier scholars, albeit in too sweeping statements about "the rabbis") is that the Sifra is an ex post facto engagement of Scripture, a sustained attempt at finding biblical "hooks" on which to hang already existing extrascriptural traditions. This suggestion carries a certain risk since it may be born of nothing more than the modern interpreter's inability to uncover (and subsequent frustration with) the hermeneutic rules that underlie the Sifra's interpretation of Leviticus. However, this risk is mitigated by a series of derashot in the Sifra that deal explicitly with the relationship between midrash and extrascriptural traditions (*halakhot*) that consistently represent the former as handmaiden to the latter. The Sifra, in other words, lauds its interpreters for their ability to produce midrashic arguments that support existing *halakhot*.[14] Here is a brief synopsis of the passages in question. In the Sifra's interpretation of Leviticus 11:33, Rabbi Akiva offers an innovative reading of the verse, proving that a ritually impure loaf of bread transmits impurity to other objects. Upon hearing this interpretation, one of his teachers, Rabbi Yehoshua, states,

"Who will remove the earth from your eyes, Rabbi Yohanan ben Zakkai, for you used to say that a future generation will declare the third-level loaf clean since it is not scriptural—but your disciple Rabbi Akiva adduced a scriptural prooftext for its impurity" (Sifra Shemini, parashah 7.12; Weiss, 54a; *TK*, 226; parallel at Mishnah Sotah 5.2).[15] The critical point for our purposes is that, according to Rabbi Yehoshua, his teacher, Rabban Yohanan ben Zakkai, feared that a purity law will be forgotten or ignored by future generations since it "is not scriptural." Rabbi Akiva, however, is able to interpret Leviticus 11:33 so as to support this ruling and thus posthumously allay Rabbi Yohanan Ben Zakkai's fears. Rabbi Yehoshua states in no uncertain terms that Rabbi Akiva's midrash did not establish the ruling in question; it was authoritative to the previous generations of sages who knew nothing of his interpretation.

The idea that scriptural interpretation serves as ex post facto support for existing (nonscriptural) legal traditions is also expressed in a fascinating debate between Rabbi Akiva and Rabbi Tarfon, a senior contemporary, as to the proper understanding of Leviticus 1:5, "The offerer shall slaughter the bull before the Lord; and Aaron's sons, the priests, shall offer the blood, dashing the blood against all sides of the altar which is at the entrance of the Tent of Meeting."[16] The sacrificial details that animate the debate are not relevant to the question at hand. What is important is that Rabbi Akiva offers an interpretation that Rabbi Tarfon rejects out of hand: "Rabbi Tarfon said to him, Akiva, how much longer will you pile up [verses] against us? May I lose my sons if I did not hear a clear distinction between the collection of the blood and its dashing, but I cannot explain it." Rabbi Tarfon's language is important: he has *heard*—that is, he has received an extrascriptural, oral tradition—regarding the sacrificial procedures in question, and he disparages Rabbi Akiva's midrash: "how much longer will you pile up verses against us?" Rabbi Akiva, in response, does *not* insist that Scripture is the ultimate source of rabbinic authority; he *accepts* Rabbi Tarfon's scolding but points out that on his interpretation too there is a distinction between the procedures. His midrash, in other words, is not mutually exclusive of Rabbi Tarfon's *halakhah*. At this point, Rabbi Tarfon is swayed and exclaims, "May I lose my sons! You have not swerved to the right or the left. It was I who received the oral tradition but was unable to explain while you explicate [*doresh*] and agree with the oral tradition. Indeed, to depart from you is to depart from life itself." What a robust celebration of Rabbi Akiva's midrashic prowess! But what precisely is being celebrated? Contrary to the claims of some scholars,[17] it is Rabbi Akiva's ability to interpret Scripture in a way that accords with received extrascriptural tradition. Note further that Rabbi Tarfon's resistance is based on a vague recollection of a tradition he had heard but cannot fully recollect. It is Rabbi Akiva's midrash that helps recover the forgotten teaching, and this is precisely the point: Rabbi Akiva's interpretive genius is celebrated for its utility for extrascriptural tradition.

Conclusion

Stepping back and surveying the ground we have covered, we find that the Rabbi Ishmael midrashim marginalize extrascriptural tradition, producing a robust and articulated theory of scriptural interpretation that identifies Scripture itself as the most important agent in the process. Scripture first marks the verses to be interpreted; in some instances, it produces the requisite interpretation ("Scripture draws an analogy" and the like); in others, the rabbinic reader is charged with interpretation but does so having identified the general hermeneutic rules established by Scripture and the relevant precedents it has set. The Rabbi Akiva midrashim, in contrast, are much less committed to midrash, as such, and when they do interpret (this is true of many, though not all, passages), it is with a different intent—to provide support for existing *halakhot*, extrascriptural traditions—and a correspondingly different method, one much less determined by the precise language and meaning of Scripture.

The views I have outlined in this chapter—conflicting and perhaps antithetical—pose a number of challenges to generally accepted terminology. The most obvious term in urgent need of refinement is *midrash*, as it is not in the least clear that the Rabbi Ishmael midrashim and the Rabbi Akiva midrashim are engaged in the same activity. To be sure, scholars have long recognized that certain interpretations of Scripture claim to generate new laws, while others buttress existing traditions, and, consequently, they have dubbed the former "constitutive" and the latter "supporting" midrash (*midrash mekhonen* and *midrash somekh*), respectively. But this characterization glosses over a more profound difference—can supporting midrash be considered scriptural interpretation? For one thing, it is not clear to what extent it constitutes meaningful interpretation, since the legal conclusions are already known. No less important, the legal ruling precedes the midrash, and its authority is independent of it—and in fact we are dealing with two different models of authority, each of which generates a different ideal type. The ideal scholar to produce a constitutive midrash is one whose familiarity with the text of the Bible allows him or her to recognize patterns from which to derive scripturally sanctioned interpretive procedures and to recognize irregularities to which to apply them. The ideal scholar to produce a supporting midrash is not a midrashist at all but first and foremost the recipient of authorized extrascriptural traditions—a link in a long (idealized) chain of transmission that extends back to Moses himself. If a scholar is able to link these traditions with biblical verses, this may or may not be laudable,[18] but it does not affect the legal standing of his statement one way or another. Now, if a biblical interpretation is adduced not as the source of a legal practice, or even as a necessary authorizer of the practice, it is questionable whether it is functioning as *Scripture*. These are complex issues that cannot be addressed in the present study, but it is worth raising the following interrelated questions: Do the different halakhic midrashim reflect a similar or even mutually recognizable conception of Scripture? And if not, what does this mean for our ability to subsume the groups that produced them under the same heading of "rabbis"?

NOTES

1. In preparing this chapter for publication, Ben Sommer pointed out to me the anachronistic nature of the camels in Genesis itself. The biblical narrative situates Abraham in the middle or late Bronze Age, but camels were only introduced into the eastern Mediterranean in the later Iron Age, during which Genesis was written. (On the archaeological and textual evidence for camels in the ancient Near East, see Philip King and Lawrence Stager, *Life in Biblical Israel* [Louisville, KY: Westminster John Knox, 2001], 117.) Thus, in one sense, the anachronistic portrayal of Abraham by modern ultraorthodox writers follows a long tradition of anachronistic portrayals of this character, which (modern biblical critics show) occurs already in scripture itself.

2. See Steven Fraade's chapter 3 in this volume.

3. For a summary, see H. L. Strack and Günter Stemberger, *Introduction to Talmud and Midrash*, trans. Markus Bockmuehl (Minneapolis: Fortress, 1996), 247–51.

4. See M. Kahana, "The Halakhic Midrashim," in *The Literature of the Sages*, vol. 2, ed. S. Safrai, Z. Safrai, J. Schwartz, and P. Tomson (Assen, Netherlands: Royal Van Gorcum / Fortress, 2006), 3–105.

5. Daniel Boyarin, *Intertextuality and the Reading of Midrash* (Bloomington:

Indiana University Press, 1994), 27. It is no coincidence that this book, the most forceful and sophisticated statement of midrash as close reading, grew out of Boyarin's intensive engagement with the Mekhilta.

6. I discussed the legal hermeneutics of the Rabbi Ishmael midrashim at length in Azzan Yadin, *Scripture as Logos: Rabbi Ishmael and the Origins of Midrash* (Philadelphia: University of Pennsylvania Press, 2004).

7. The editions cited in this study are: *Sifre Numbers*, ed. H. S. Horovitz (Jerusalem: Shalem, 1992; repr. of Leipzig, 1917); *Mekhilta de-Rabbi Ishmael*, ed. H. S. Horovitz and I. Rabin (Jerusalem: Bamberger and Wahrman, 1960; repr. of Frankfurt, 1931); *Mekhilta de-Rabbi Ishmael*, ed. and trans. Jacob Z. Lauterbach (Philadelphia: Jewish Publication Society of America, 1933–36); H. Weiss, *Sifra: Commentar zu Leviticus* (Vienna: Schlossberg, 1862); *Siphre ad Deuteronomium*, ed. Louis Finkelstein (New York: Jewish Theological Seminary of America, 1993).

8. For a full list, citations, and analysis, see Yadin, *Scripture as Logos*, 26–33.

9. It is important to recognize that the legitimacy of interpretation is truly in question. There are derashot in which one interpreter thinks he has identified a hermeneutic marker, but that turns out not to be the case. The repetition of a word, for instance, is commonly accepted as legitimizing rabbinic interpretation; however, the Rabbi Ishmael midrashim explicitly reject the interpretation of the *first* instance of the word, since this marks the introduction of the matter and is thus not superfluous. Only from the *second* occurrence and on can one speak of redundancy. This rule is *'ein dorshin tehilot*, "first statements of a matter cannot be interpreted." Once a verse has been shown to be unmarked, no interpretation is proffered.

10. See Yadin, *Scripture as Logos*, 142–47.

11. Sifra citations are followed by page number to the H. Weiss edition (*Sifra: Commentar zu Leviticus* [Vienna: Schlossberg, 1862]) and to the facsimile edition of MS Assemani 66, published by L. Finkelstein (*Sifra or Torat Kohanim* [New York: Jewish Theological Seminary of America, 1956]).

12. In terms of biblical Hebrew grammar, however, the repetition produces a distributive sense ("every person"). For a discussion, see B. Waltke and M. O'Connor, *An Introduction to Biblical Hebrew Syntax* (Winona Lake, IN: Eisenbrauns, 1990), 7.2.3.

13. See Sifra Emor pereq 4.1; Weiss, 96b; *TK*, 427.

14. The Sifra's representation of Rabbi Akiva accords precisely with that of the Mishnah. See Yishai Rosen-Zvi, "Who Will Uncover the Dust from Your Eyes? Mishnah Sotah 5 and Rabbi Akiva's Midrash," *Tarbiz* 75 (2005–2006): 95–128.

15. For a fuller discussion, see Azzan Yadin, "Resistance to Midrash? Midrash and *Halakhah* in the Halakhic Midrashim," in *Current Trends in the Study of Midrash*, ed. Carol Bakhos (Leiden, Netherlands: Brill, 2006), 35–58, here page 54; and see Rosen-Zvi, "Who Will Uncover the Dust from Your Eyes," 96–101.

16. The debate is recorded in Sifra Vayiqra, parashah 4.5; Weiss, 6a.

17. Menachem Fisch, *Rational Rabbis: Science and Talmudic Culture* (Bloomington: Indiana University Press, 1997), 106.

18. For an example of a laudatory response to this enterprise, see Rabbi Tarfon's reaction, discussed earlier. For an example of a critical response, see my discussion of Rabbi Eleazar ben Azaria's response to Rabbi Akiva in Sifra Tzav pereq 11.4, in Yadin, "Resistance to Midrash," 54–57.

Chapter 5

Concepts of Scriptural Language in Midrash

Benjamin D. Sommer

Virtually all Jewish conceptions of scripture since late antiquity grow up in the shadow of the rabbinic interpretations known as midrash. Whether by incorporating them, adapting them, or reacting to them, postrabbinic Jewish thinkers who studied the Bible lived in a conceptual world shaped by the midrash. To this day, the interpretations of the weekly biblical reading one hears from a *darshan* (a rabbi, teacher, or preacher who gives the sermon) in the course of synagogue worship[1] is likely to consist of a paraphrase of a passage from a midrashic anthology that treats the weekly reading; alternatively (if the *darshan* is more ambitious), it may begin with a summary of a midrash and move on from there. Thus, one needs to acquire some appreciation for midrashic approaches to scripture not only to understand the Bible's role in the Judaism of the classical rabbis who produced the midrashim but also to understand the Bible's role in the Judaisms of all who came after them. In what follows, I provide a definition of the term, and I explain how the rabbis viewed the language of scripture, which, for them, differed in essential ways from all other uses of language on earth.[2]

Properly used, *midrash* refers to interpretations of scripture found in classical rabbinic texts—that is, the texts that were produced in the first millennium of the Common Era or shortly thereafter.[3] More specifically, the term *midrash* is used in several ways:

- Midrash can refer to the methods of reading that produce these interpretations. (Thus, a person might speak of midrash in contrast with some other mode of reading, such as the interpretive method of medieval or modern biblical exegetes.)

- A midrash (plural, midrashim) can be a particular interpretation of a passage or verse that uses one or more of these methods. ("Let me share with you a wonderful midrash on a verse from the Psalms that I just heard.")
- A midrash can refer to an anthology that collects these interpretations. ("I just bought a nice edition of a midrash on Exodus.")

Midrashim (in the second of these senses) are often found embedded in the Talmuds (one of which was edited in the Land of Israel around 400 CE, the other in Babylonia in the 500s and 600s). To be sure, neither Talmud is a commentary on the Bible; they are rather sets of discussions on the Mishna (the central text of rabbinic Judaism that lays out Jewish law in a more-or-less systematic manner, which was edited in the mid-third century CE). Nonetheless, the rabbis of the Talmud often strive to link the laws found in the Mishna back to the Bible, and thus they engage in scriptural interpretation or midrash in the course of their discussions. Further, they not infrequently digress into passages that involve midrashic interpretation of biblical passages unrelated to a strictly legal issue. Midrashim are also found in anthologies that collect rabbinic interpretations and homilies on a biblical book, several biblical books, or cycles of liturgical readings. Some of the earlier anthologies collect midrashim of the *tanna'im*, or rabbis from the period of the Mishna; these tannaitic anthologies, edited in the mid-first millennium, contain interpretation of both legal matter (Hebrew, *halakhah*) and of nonlegal matter (*aggadah*).[4] (There can be, and are, aggadic interpretations of *halakhic* passages from the Bible; these *aggadic* interpretations deduce moral, theological, or homiletic lessons from verses dealing with ritual, civil, or criminal law.) Many post-tannaitic anthologies also exist; edited in the last half of the first millennium CE and into the first few centuries of the second millennium CE, they contain some teachings that go back to the Mishnaic or tannaitic era, teachings of the rabbis of the Talmud, and some early post-Talmudic teachings, and they limit themselves to *aggadah*.[5] When one refers to a book of midrash, it is one of these tannaitic or post-tannaitic anthologies one has in mind. These anthologies are not quite commentaries on biblical books; rather, they are collections that string together multiple interpretations of various verses, often following the order of the biblical texts. But they typically include varying or even contradictory interpretations of many scholars on a given verse. They may focus on a few verses, only to skip large blocks of material. By the beginning of the second millennium, other methods of interpreting scripture were becoming common among Jews throughout the world, and the era in which specifically midrashic interpretations were produced came to an end.[6]

Four Characteristics of Biblical Language and Text

One of most important and distinctive characteristics of midrash is its view of scriptural language. Indeed, the midrashic conception of scriptural language is the most important engine that drives midrashic interpretation forward. In what follows, I sketch out this conception and give a few examples of the sort of interpretations it produces.[7] For midrashic interpreters, four characteristics of scripture, and especially of scriptural language, are of crucial importance.[8]

Characteristic 1. The classical rabbis believe that the Bible's language is divine language. The Torah is the word of God; the remaining books of the Bible are divinely inspired. Consequently, their language is different from human language, no matter how similar it seems on the surface. When a human being says something, she generally means one thing. Perhaps she is punning or telling a joke, in which case she means two different things in this one utterance; or perhaps she is a poet or a particularly fine novelist, in which case she might mean three or four things in a single utterance. But the general rule is that a human being puts a fairly limited number of meanings into an utterance: a human means one, two, maybe three, very rarely four things when she says or writes something. But God's language is different. God can pack huge amounts of meaning into an utterance. Scriptural language, on the surface, may seem similar to, say, Homer's *Odyssey* or Justinian's legal code, but in fact it is supercharged with meaning. The challenge, then, is to find keys to unlock some of the additional meanings that are not so obvious at first reading.[9] For example, a midrash might focus intensely on each word of a verse, presuming that each one contains a whole, complete thought that can be unpacked as its own sentence or clause. Further, the midrashic interpreters take advantage of the fact that Hebrew in their era was written without vowels, so that biblical texts contained only consonants.[10] They would at times propose a new (or, better, an additional) vocalization of a text, thus discovering two different meanings lurking in a verse or phrase.

Characteristic 2. The rabbis believe that the main unit of expression in the Bible is the verse or a group of two or three successive verses. They are not especially interested in larger literary units, such as a whole poem or a complete story, much less a whole biblical book.[11] Thus, as Robert Harris has emphasized to me, there is no conception of "The Binding of Isaac" among the classical midrashic interpreters. Only in the Middle Ages, when Jewish interpreters began thinking about longer textual units, does this concept (or this famous term) appear in Jewish literature.[12] For the rabbis, the Bible is not so much a collection of poems, laws, and narratives. It is a collection of verses.

Characteristic 3. The first two conceptions of biblical language and text work together to produce an especially crucial midrashic conception, which is worth exploring in some detail: the Bible is unity, a single document, but a unity of a unique kind. Stemming from the mind of God and not merely from the mind of human authors, the Bible is an infinitely complex unity, in which all parts are related to each other. Any verse in the Bible is potentially linked to any other verse, and not only to the verses right next to it. James Kugel sums up this aspect of midrashic exegesis especially well:

> Midrash is an exegesis of biblical verses, not of books.... There simply is no boundary encountered beyond that of the verse until one comes to the borders of the canon itself—a situation analogous to certain political organizations in which there are no separate states, provinces, or the like but only the village and the Empire. One of the things this means is that each verse of the Bible is in principle as connected to its most distant fellow as to the one next door.[13]

Thus, when discussing, say, Genesis 22:1, a midrashic interpreter may not be particularly interested in the relationship of this verse to Genesis 22:2 and Genesis 22:3. To be sure, 22:1 *is* related to those verses from the same local literary context, but it is just as closely related to verses found in Psalm 11 and Psalm 60, in Deuteronomy 6 and 16, in Isaiah 57 and Ecclesiastes 8. These seemingly more far-flung relationships interest the midrashic interpreter more than the rather obvious connections to other verses in Genesis 22. Indeed, in *Genesis Rabbah* §59, the interpreters of Genesis 22:1 do not for the most part contextualize this verse alongside other verses from Genesis 22; they do not examine Genesis 22:1 within what postmidrashic interpreters would call the story of the binding of Isaac. Instead, they attend to the verses I have just mentioned from Psalms, Deuteronomy, Isaiah, and Ecclesiastes, among others. When they do turn to a verse from Genesis, it is, tellingly, from Genesis 39. For the rabbis, any verse has significant connections to other verses *throughout* the canon, not just in the passage in which the verse is found, and those cross-canonical connections produce meaning. Of course, it is always possible that Genesis 22:1 is closely related to Genesis 22:3, so that Genesis 22:3 holds the key to unlocking something significant in 22:1. But it is just as possible that a distant verse such as Micah 6:6 or 2 Samuel 7:18 or Psalm 110:4 or Proverbs 25:6 holds an important key to Genesis 22:1; indeed, *Genesis Rabbah* cites all of these, but not Genesis 22:3, to explicate Genesis 22:1. The midrashic interpreter will tend to look to the verse further away, thereby demonstrating the Bible's deep underlying unity.

The fact that Genesis 22:1 appears in a Torah scroll next to Genesis 22:2 and not right next to the verses from Psalms, Deuteronomy, Isaiah, Ecclesiastes, Micah, Samuel, Psalms, and Proverbs that *Genesis Rabbah* cites when explicating 22:1 is simply a result of the limitations of the technologies with which humans write. It is not possible to put Genesis 22:1 next to all the verses related to it when writing on a leather scroll or, for that matter, when printing a book. Here we arrive at a crucial aspect of the midrashic conception of the Bible. *For the rabbis, the Bible is not really a book at all.* It is not a scroll, and it is not a text (at least not in the way any other text known to humanity in the first millennium CE, and almost all the second millennium, was a text). *Rather, the Bible is a hypertext, a database with myriad internal connections spanning the whole canon.*[14] These connections link any one verse to many other verses, which were in turn linked to a large number of additional verses. Thus, a given verse had several literary contexts, each of which implied several additional contexts. The physical data-storage technologies available to humanity in the midrashic era (indeed, in most of the postmidrashic era up until the late twentieth century as well) allowed a verse to be physically contextualized next to only a few other verses. But in reality (that is, reality as the classical rabbis conceived it), any one biblical verse was part of a matrix of verses, each of which invoked additional matrices.[15] To be sure, one part (we might say, one row) of any verse's matrix was the context produced (or, rather, made obvious) by the written scroll on which scripture was imperfectly recorded; this row links, say, Genesis 22:1 to 22:2 and 22:3 and might be referred to as the *surface context* or *local context*. But that row, that surface context, was not necessarily the most important aspect of the verse's matrix. Thinking of scripture as if it were text in the way that Homer's poems or Justinian's laws are texts would severely limit the interpreter, because such thinking would point the interpreter toward surface context alone. The surface context would suggest various meanings which might be legitimate ones intended by the divine author; but those were unlikely to be the deepest or most interesting meanings, and for the classical rabbis scripture was above all interesting and deep.

Producing meaning from any utterance (whether a poem or a narrative or a note from one's spouse about what to pick up from the supermarket on the way home) is a matter of contextualizing the utterance properly. For the rabbis, the correct context of a biblical verse includes not only, and not even primarily, the local context (as it would for a medieval rabbinic interpreter or for a modern literary reader)—that is, the correct context is not the poem or narrative in which the verse appears. The context, rather, is the whole Bible; or, rather, the context includes individual verses from throughout scripture. The challenge, then, was to figure out which verses elsewhere in the Bible were related to the verse under consideration.

Characteristic 4. To the extent that a midrashic interpreter wanted to unpack some of the supercharged meaning that God loaded into a single biblical verse, he[16] needed to figure out which verses in other books relate directly to the verse under discussion—because while any verse in the Bible was *potentially* related, only some verses were in fact related. How, then, does the interpreter make the relevant connections? A given verse might contain a rare word, a hard phrase, some elements that do not seem to fit easily in their immediate context. Those textual oddities may appear in another verse elsewhere in scripture or may recall some other verse. The oddity suggests that the two verses are connected with each other—that is, that reading them side by side, or reading one in light of the other, might produce some insight or allow one to glean an additional piece of information that was initially not clear from either verse by itself. Of course, to understand the first verse in light of the second, it will often be necessary to relate the second verse to a third verse. In such a case, only when the third verse is added to the hypertextual matrix will the relevance of the second verse to the first become clear. Unfortunately for the reader of midrash, the text of a given midrash may simply assume that the reader knows that one has to understand the second verse in light of the third; the midrashic text may not explicitly mention the third verse at all. This can create the appearance of a non sequitur to the modern reader who does not realize that elsewhere in rabbinic literature another scholar has connected the second verse to the third.[17]

Concrete Examples

From among thousands of examples in midrashic literature that display these characteristics, space permits consideration of a few midrashim on a single passage. In Numbers 11:16, God directs Moses to choose seventy men from among the elders of Israel who will become prophets; the men accorded this honor were to station themselves alongside Moses at the Tent of Meeting. Numbers 11:26 informs us that two of these men, Eldad and Medad, did not go out to the Tent of Meeting, yet they became prophets nonetheless and broke out into prophesying inside the Israelite encampment, some distance from the Tent. In verses 27–29, a lad ran and informed Moses that they were prophesying, whereupon Moses's assistant Joshua said, "My lord Moses, restrain them!" Moses, however, approved of their prophesying and rebuked Joshua for being jealous on his behalf.

According to *Numbers Rabbah* §15.15 (15.19 in some editions), Eldad and Medad were rewarded for acting with humility. Because they decided to remain in the camp rather than accepting the honor of being publicly recognized as prophets, their prophetic status was greater than that of the other elders in five ways. In what follows, I examine the midrashic derivation of one of these ways. The midrash says of Eldad and Medad,

> For minimizing their own stature, they became greater than the elders [i.e., the other sixty-eight prophets] in five respects. The elders' prophecies contained predictions concerning only the next day, as the biblical text says, "Tell the people, 'You will become holy concerning the morrow'" [Numbers 11:18]. But these two issued prophecies concerning what would happen years later, as it states, "Two men remained in the camp" [Numbers 11.26]. What did they predict? There are those who say that they prophesied [concerning the end of days], predicting the fall of Gog and Magog. And there are those who say they prophesied concerning what would happen forty years later [at the end of the Children of Israel's time in the wilderness, specifically] that Moses would die, and that [his assistant] Joshua would lead them into the Land of Israel. This is clear, since Joshua said to Moses [Numbers 11.28]: "Joshua the son of Nun answered."

The midrash tells us that Eldad and Medad prophesied concerning the far future, predicting either the fall of Gog and Magog at the end of days or the death of Moses forty years after their own prophecy was issued. It is worthwhile to study the first possibility more closely. The evidence suggesting that Eldad and Medad spoke concerning Gog and Magog is not at all clear from the local context in Numbers 11. It becomes clear, however, when one examines Numbers 11:26 (which the midrash cites rather cryptically to support this reading) together with Ezekiel, chapter 38. That chapter contains the biblical account of the ascent and fall of Gog, a leader from the land of Magog. According to Ezekiel's prophecy, Gog will assemble a multinational force to attack Israel, only to fall in a defeat that will usher in the restoration of the nation Israel to its land at the eschaton. A crucial element that provides a link to Numbers 11:26 appears in Ezekiel 38:17, which reads (and I translate quite literally), "Thus says the Lord Yhwh: Are you the one concerning whom I spoke in ancient days through my servants the prophets of Israel, who prophesied during those days years that I would bring you against the Israelites?" The Hebrew of this verse is odd, since the word "years" does not fit into the syntax of the sentence. This is precisely the sort of textual oddity that attracts the rabbis' attention, suggesting to them that the text might be read another way that will reveal a connection to another verse elsewhere in the Bible. In this case, as in many others, the rabbis base their reading on the fact that Hebrew in their days was written without any vowels. Consequently, they suggest that the word "years" (Hebrew, *shanim*) should be read as "two" (*sh^enayim* —the same exact letters, but with different vowels). This yields the translation, "Are you the one concerning whom I spoke in ancient days through my servants the prophets of Israel, who prophesied during those days, two of them, that I would bring you against the Israelites?" In this rereading of Ezekiel 38:17, the prophet Ezekiel recalls a time long before his own era ("in ancient days") when two prophets together issued a prophecy concerning Gog and Magog. This implies the question, when in the Bible do we find two prophets prophesying in tandem? There is only one such place in all of Jewish scripture: the story of Eldad and Medad, in Numbers 11. Thus, the connection between Numbers 11:26 and Ezekiel 38:17 implied by the odd phrasing in the latter allows us to deduce an additional piece of narrative that is hidden in the former and becomes clear only when we use the interpretive key in the latter to unlock it. When Eldad and Medad prophesied, they predicted just what Ezekiel would one day predict: the rise and fall of Gog from the land of Magog.

In this example, we see the first, third, and fourth characteristics discussed earlier in play. (1) The biblical text, spoken or inspired by God, is supercharged with meaning. Therefore, when Ezekiel 38:17 reads "years," it also intends "two." (In this case, it is the unvocalized nature of the Hebrew text that allows the supercharging of meaning to occur.) (3) The Bible is a hypertext, in which verses in one book are linked to verses in another. When we read Numbers 11:26 in light of its distant twin, Ezekiel 38:17, the additional meaning of both verses becomes clear: the two prophets Ezekiel mentions were Eldad and Medad from the book of Numbers, and what they uttered in Numbers was the same prophecy found in Ezekiel. (4) A textual oddity (the word "years," which does not fit into the syntax of Ezekiel 38:17) stands out in one of these verses; when examined thoughtfully and with a mind toward connections with verses elsewhere in scripture, this word yields a meaning that links the verses together and releases some of the meaning supercharged into these verses.

It should be noted that our midrash is based entirely on the parallel between these two verses, yet nowhere does our midrash actually quote the verse from Ezekiel. Having mentioned Gog and Magog, the midrash assumes we know that they are discussed in Ezekiel 38, and it further assumes we will be able to identify which verse in that prophetic text poses a question ("What is the word 'years' doing here?"); finally, it assumes that we understand why the answer to that question provides insight into our text from Numbers. This midrash makes sense only to someone deeply familiar with the text of the Hebrew Bible (or to someone who pauses to look up the biblical source of the terms "Gog" and "Magog," who carefully reads the chapter from Ezekiel where they appear, who notices the syntactic problem in verse 17 there, and who thinks it through carefully). To someone who does not have this familiarity with scripture or who does not take the time to think through these texts and the issues they raise, the midrashic explanation must seem completely arbitrary.

What of the other explanation—that Eldad and Medad predicted the death of Moses and the ascent of Joshua to lead the people into the Promised Land? In this case, the role of hypertext (characteristic 3) is not crucial, but the supercharged nature of the text (characteristic 1) is. The midrash draws our attention to a few words within Numbers 11:28 itself: "And Joshua answered." The significant words, however, appear in the remainder of the verse, which the midrash does not quote, assuming that we know the rest (either by heart or because we take the trouble to look it up). The verse in full reads, "Joshua the son of Nun, who had served Moses since his youth, said, 'My lord, stop them!'" Why does this verse emphasize that Joshua had served Moses and had done so since his youth? After all, earlier biblical references to Joshua had already informed the reader of Joshua's role, so the mention of this information here must have special significance. And why does the text tell us that Joshua referred to Moses as "My lord" before asking that Moses put a stop to the prophesying? An answer to this question seemed clear to the rabbis, who differ from modern readers in viewing hierarchy as a given and the opportunity to serve an exalted master as an honor rather than a humiliation: Eldad and Medad must have said something that impugned Moses. Even more likely, given the verse's emphasis on the master-disciple relationship between Moses and Joshua, the two elders must have said something that cast doubt on that relationship or reversed its hierarchy. And whatever that prediction was, it must have been a true prediction, since Eldad and Medad were true prophets.[18] From these assumptions, it is a short, almost inevitable step to the reading that what angered Joshua was a prediction that his master would die and that he himself would inherit (or, from the disciple's point of view, usurp) the job of leading the nation into the Promised Land—an honor which rightly belonged, in the eyes of the disciple, to the master.

Our midrash in *Numbers Rabbah* §15.15 goes on to examine Numbers 11:27: "A lad ran to tell Moses and said, 'Eldad and Medad are prophesying in the camp!'" To this, the midrash adds, "Who was this? It was Gershom, Moses's son." That the midrash is unsatisfied with having an unidentified character reflects a frequent tendency of rabbinic exegesis: however innocuous some lack of specificity seems to modern eyes, for the rabbis, a divinely authored text cannot have any loose ends. Thus, this lad must have a specific identity (because a perfect scripture leaves nobody anonymous), and it is the interpreters' job to find it.[19] But how do the rabbis know the lad is Gershom? Here again, a text from elsewhere in the Bible provides the answer. In Judges 17–18, there is a story about various travels and tribulations of a particular Levite. Since a story as a whole has little interest to the rabbis, we can pass over the plot of this narrative and simply cite the verses that begin and end these chapters:

Judges 17:7: There was a lad from Bethlehem in Judah, from a family living in Judah, a Levite, and he dwelt there temporarily [$v^e hu\ gar$-$sham$].

Judges 18:30: The Danides set up the cultic statue for themselves. Jonathan, the son of Gershom, the son of Ma^{na}sseh, and his descendants were priests for the tribe of Dan until the time of the exile.

A scribal oddity in the second of the verses most likely attracted the attention of the midrashist. In the Hebrew text, the name "Manasseh" is written in a strange manner: the letter *nun* (equivalent to our *n*) is written in superscript. This suggests the possibility that we should read the name without the *nun*—and without the *nun*, this name would read "Moses." In other words, the Levite of this story in Judges may in fact have been a descendant of Moses (who was himself a Levite—that is, a member of the tribe descended from the patriarch Jacob's son Levi). The Levite was descended from Moses's son Gershom (a character mentioned in Exodus 2:22 and 18:3 and apparently alluded to in Judges 18:30); or perhaps the text in Judges does not intend literally to connect the Levite of this story with a Mosaic progenitor, but the text as it is traditionally written at the very least wants to remind us of Moses and his son Gershom. That hint is also evident, on second reading, in the very first verse of the narrative, Judges 17:1, which mentions that the Levite with whom the narrative is concerned lived in Bethlehem. More specifically, the text tells us that "he dwelt there." The Hebrew for "dwelt there," *gar sham*, sounds almost identical to "Gershom," the name of Moses's son; indeed, one could translate the phrase in question, "And he was Gershom." In short, the opening and closing verses of this story have a number of textual signals that attract the midrashic interpreter's attention: the odd spelling of Ma^{na}sseh/Moses and the play on the name of Moses's son Gershom. One additional feature needs to be noted: the Levite in question is referred to first of all, at the beginning of Judges 17:7, as "a lad"—in Hebrew, *na'ar*, the same word used of the seemingly anonymous lad in Numbers 11:27.

We have identified two separate problems in two different texts: the oddities in Judges require explanation, and so does the anonymity of the lad in Numbers. The vocabulary of the verses involved in these two problems shows that these texts are linked; both include the word *na'ar* (lad), and both relate to Moses. To the midrashic mind, these linkages (characteristic 4) demand that we read both texts closely (characteristic 1) and that we read each in light of the other (characteristic 3). It follows from the linkages that the two texts are hinting at one and the same lad—to wit, Moses's son Gershom, who, like Joshua, would be upset at the prediction made by Eldad and Medad. After all, the midrash has already established that their prophesy could be seen by Moses's disciples as an insult to Moses (though Moses himself did not see it that way). Gershom would have shared Joshua's desire to bring the matter to Moses's immediate attention, which explains why he did not merely "go" or "walk" but "ran" to the Tent of Meeting to tell Moses what was transpiring at the Israelite encampment.

We should also note the role of characteristic 2 in this midrash. The information in both texts is a matter of what is found in a few verses themselves. The larger narratives of Numbers 11 and Judges 17–18 play no role in the midrashic interpretation that the other three characteristics produced. If one reads the entirety of Numbers 11, it quickly becomes clear that the midrash does not attend to the narrative as a whole; many aspects of this short story are nowhere hinted at in *Numbers Rabbah* §15.15: the Israelites' complaints about their diet in the desert, Moses's anger at the nation's complaints, the quail, and the plague, to name a few. This midrash remains a midrash on a few verses from Numbers 11 and Judges 17–18 (just as the first explanation related to these few verses of Numbers 11 along with one verse from Ezekiel 38), not a holistic reading of the story that is Numbers 11.

As in the midrash that linked Numbers 11:26 with Ezekiel 38:17, the crucial biblical text with which Numbers 11 is linked is not quoted. In fact, in this case, it is not even alluded to. In the previous case, the words "Gog and Magog" at least suggested what biblical passage contains the crucial verse, but here the midrash does not even hint where the interpretive key lies. To a reader not deeply familiar with the text of the Hebrew Bible, the identification of the lad as Gershom must seem arbitrary if not utterly capricious. But to the reader who knows biblical texts very thoroughly and understands midrashic conceptions of how they function as hypertext, the identification seems not merely clever but inevitable, even natural. Since the Bible is an intensely complex unity (characteristic 3), whose verses (characteristic 2) must be read with great care so as to allow the emergence of the myriad meanings that God has introduced into the text (characteristic 1), the linkages between Numbers 11:27 and Judges 17:1 and 18:30 lead directly to the midrash's conclusion.

These few examples from a single midrash hardly begin to suggest the range of methods used by the classical rabbis to construct their interpretations, and in any event, surveying all those exegetical methods is not the concern of this chapter. I have not, furthermore, touched on the extent to which midrashim attempt to link extrabiblical traditions to biblical texts, though this is a crucial aspect of many midrashim.[20] What I hope to have made clear is how the rabbis regard the Bible's language as essentially, even ontologically, different from normal language. Because the Bible's language is divine, it functions radically differently from normal human language, and it demands to be read in ways that reflect this radical difference. Some later Jewish thinkers and interpreters accept this proposition, extending the notion of the radical ontological difference between scriptural and nonscriptural language even further.[21] Others reject it, insisting that scripture should be read as one would read any literary texts, while some accept this notion but minimize it or attend to other aspects of the nature of biblical language.[22] Modern Jewish thinkers and interpreters variously reject it, look back toward it wistfully, or attempt in one way or another to retrieve it.[23] But at no point does any Jewish thinker escape the midrashic conception of scriptural language.

NOTES

1. For information on the system of biblical passages chanted in regular synagogue worship, see chapter 2 by Elsie Stern in this volume.

2. I keep notes to an absolute minimum in what follows. Many introductions to midrashic reading and midrashic literature exist. Particularly useful brief introductions include Barry Holtz, "Midrash," in *Back to the Sources: Reading the Classic Jewish Texts*, ed. Barry Holtz (New York: Summit, 1984), 177–211; Burt Visotzky, "Midrash" and "Rabbinic Interpretation," in *The New Interpreter's Dictionary of the Bible* (Nashville: Abingdon, 2006–2009), 4:81–84, 718–720; and, at greater length, Hananel Mack, *The Aggadic Midrashic Literature* (Tel Aviv: MOD Books, 1989). On a more technical level, see Shmuel Safrai et al., eds., *The Literature of the Sages, Second Part: Midrash and Targum* . . . (Assen, Netherlands: Van Gorcum, 2006), especially the articles by Menahem Kahana and Marc Hirshman, 3–132; and Rimon Kasher, "The Interpretation of Scripture in Rabbinic Literature," in *Mikra: Text, Translation, Reading and Interpretation of the Hebrew Bible in Ancient Judaism and Early Christianity*, ed. M. J. Mulder (Assen, Netherlands: Van Gorcum, 1988), 547–94. For useful introductions to specific midrashic works and the secondary literature on them, see G. Stemberger and H. L. Strack, *Introduction to the Talmud and Midrash*, trans. M. Bockmuehl (Edinburgh: T&T Clark, 1991), 254–393; the essays by Kahane and Myron Lerner in Safrai, *Literature of the Sages, Second Part*, 68–104, 133–229; and the articles on these individual collections in *Encyclopaedia Judaica*, ed. Cecil Roth et al. (Jerusalem: Keter, 1971; 2d ed., Detroit: Macmillan Reference, 2007).

3. I use the term *classical rabbinic* to refer to the culture of the rabbis of the Talmudic era and the centuries immediately following, as opposed to referring to people with the title *rabbi* in the Middle Ages or modern era.

4. The *tannaitic* anthologies include works such as the *Mekhilta*, the *Sifra*, and the *Sifre*.

5. These post-tannaitic anthologies include several with the title *Rabbah* covering the Five Books of Moses (*Genesis Rabbah, Exodus Rabbah*, etc.) and the Five Scrolls (*Ruth Rabbah*, etc.), several with the title *Pesiqta*, the various *Tanḥuma* midrashim on the Pentateuch, to name only a few.

6. On these newer methods of interpretation, which entailed new ways of conceptualizing scripture, see the chapters by Meira Polliack and Robert Harris in this volume.

7. Studies of the interpretive method of the rabbis are legion. In what follows, I am deeply influenced by several scholars and their work: Isaac Heinemann, *Darkhei Ha-Aggadah* [in Hebrew] (Jerusalem: Magnes, 1970); Daniel Boyarin, *Intertextuality and the Reading of Midrash* (Bloomington: Indiana University Press, 1990); many publications by James Kugel, especially *In Potiphar's House* (San Francisco: Torch, 1990) and "Two Introductions to Midrash," in *Midrash and Literature*, ed. Geoffrey H. Hartman and Sanford Budick (New Haven: Yale University Press, 1986), 77–103 (originally in *Prooftexts* 3 [1983]: 131–55); and both the teaching and writing of Michael Fishbane, among whose essays those found in *The Garments of Torah: Essays in Biblical Hermeneutics* (Bloomington: Indiana University Press, 1989) and *The Exegetical Imagination: On Jewish Thought and Theology* (Cambridge: Harvard University Press, 1998) are especially relevant.

8. In identifying these four characteristics, I am influenced by James Kugel, who has famously identified four assumptions of ancient Jewish and Christian interpreters of scripture generally. The interpreters of whom Kugel speaks include, but are not limited to, the classical rabbis who produced the midrash. The four assumptions Kugel describes are:

(1) The Bible is a fundamentally cryptic document, which is in need of especially close and careful reading.

(2) The Bible is fundamentally *relevant*, so that it speaks to contemporary concerns.

(3) The Bible is perfect and perfectly harmonious; it contains no self-contradictions.

(4) Scripture is divinely sanctioned, of divine provenance, or divinely inspired.

These four assumptions are laid out in many of Kugel's works; see, e.g., *The Bible as It Was* (Cambridge: Belknap Press of Harvard University Press, 1997), 17–23, and *Traditions of the Bible: A Guide to the Bible as It Was at the Start of the Common Era* (Cambridge: Harvard University Press, 1998), 14–19. While the four characteristics I discuss are not the same as these four assumptions, Kugel's influence on my approach is clear.

9. Later Jewish mystics accurately summarized this characteristic of the midrashic view of scriptural language when they said, "There are seventy facets to the Torah." This saying appears often in medieval texts such as works by Nahmanides and the Zohar, as well as in late-medieval/early-modern works such as Isaiah Horowitz's *Sh^enei Luḥot Ha-Berit*. (Though often associated with the classical rabbis, this phrase appears only once in classical rabbinic literature, in *Numbers Rabbah* 13.15–16.)

10. Toward the end of the first millennium, scribes invented a system of dots

and dashes inserted into the old consonantal text of the Bible to represent vowels, but even today most Hebrew texts are written mostly with consonants and with only a few vowels; competent readers (nowadays, starting roughly in third grade) figure out the vowels from context.

11. On some implications of this tendency for Jewish conceptions of scripture, especially in ways that differentiate Jewish theological readings from the readings of modern Protestant canon critics such as Brevard Childs, see my comments in "The Scroll of Isaiah as Jewish Scripture, or, Why Jews Don't Read Books," in *Society of Biblical Literature 1996 Seminar Papers* (Atlanta: Scholars Press, 1996), 225–42.

12. The term appears only once in midrashic literature: *Tanḥuma* (Buber) *Vayera'* §46—but even there it refers not to a particular narrative unit but to what happened to Isaac.

13. Kugel, "Two Introductions to Midrash," 93.

14. In this regard, people of our times, who are familiar with computers, hypertexts, and databases, can understand the rabbinic conception of scripture much more readily than people only a few decades ago could.

15. While writing could not accommodate the matrix, it is important to note that memorization of a text (a nonphysical data-storage method) could do so, at least to some extent. On the importance of memorization and orality in midrash and its connection to midrash's verse-centeredness, see Kugel, "Two Introductions to Midrash," 94–95. On the importance of orality/aurality in conceptions of scripture in many religious traditions, see Wilfred Cantwell Smith, *What Is Scripture? A Comparative Approach* (Minneapolis: Fortress, 1993), index, 376, s.v. "Oral-aural," as well as William A. Graham, *Beyond the Written Word: Oral Aspects of Scripture in the History of Religion* (Cambridge: Cambridge University Press, 1987).

16. This is, historically speaking, the correct pronoun.

17. Similarly, whether as a result of scribal practice, printers' conventions, or the original midrashist's discourse, it is often the case that a rabbinic text cites only the first few words of a verse, even though the relevant part of the verse appears later, in the section not quoted. In the period in which midrashim were first produced and transmitted, our contemporary system of chapters and verses did not yet exist. Consequently, to refer to, say, Genesis 1:1 a scholar would say, "In the beginning God created"—even if the crucial section for the point he was making involved the words "the heavens and the earth" later in the verse. The point of the citation was merely to let the audience know what verse was under consideration, not to repeat the whole text. The rabbis seem to have assumed that their audience knew the Bible more or less by heart, so that complete citation was not necessary. To a modern reader who does not pause to look up the whole verse (and maybe, just to be safe, the verse after it as well), midrashim often appear to be full of random comments and non sequiturs.

18. The midrash presumes that prophecy necessarily involves prediction. This

assumption, typical of postbiblical Jewish texts, is at odds with the Bible's own view, in which predicting the future played a fairly small role in a prophet's job description.

19. This assumption on the rabbis' part, of course, tells us much about their conception of the God who authored the text and the world that God created. In the classical rabbis' worldview, all things have a proper place, and ambiguity or liminality must be resolved.

20. On the relationship of tradition to scripture as well as secondary attempts to link the former to the latter (or to assert that tradition rather than scripture has conceptual priority), see chapters 3 and 4 by Steven Fraade and Azzan Yadin-Israel in this volume.

21. See chapter 10 by Moshe Idel in this volume, on concepts of Torah in Jewish mysticism.

22. See, in this volume, chapter 6 by Meira Polliack on Karaite and Rabbanite interpreters among the Sephardim, chapter 7 by Robert Harris on the French Ashkenazic school of Rashi and his followers, and chapter 8 by James Diamond on Maimonides.

23. See the chapters in this volume by Jonathan Cohen, Job Jindo, Marc Brettler, and Shalom Carmy on several modern Jewish thinkers and interpreters.

Chapter 6

Concepts of Scripture among the Jews of the Medieval Islamic World

Meira Polliack

The medieval Islamic period brought about great intellectual growth and a flowering of literary creativity among the Jews. Arabic language, thought, and literature, as well as Islamic religion and politics, represented a significant challenge for the Jewish communities who came under Islamic rule and whose social and cultural structures had been forged in the classical rabbinic age. During this period, and especially throughout the 10th to 12th centuries, Judaism was consolidated, and many of its central institutions took shape. A principal religious rift also occurred during this period between traditional rabbinic Judaism (or Rabbanism) and Karaism—a new sectarian movement which sprang up in the late 9th century in the Jewish intellectual centers of Babylonia and Persia. Karaism is a scripturalist Jewish movement which rejects the authority of oral Jewish tradition as canonized in rabbinic literature and upholds the text of the Bible as the sole source for Jewish religious law and practice. Karaites follow laws that differ from those of talmudic tradition in their interpretation of the biblical text. The Hebrew names by which the Karaites designated themselves (*qara'im, ba'aley miqra, beney miqra*) highlight their upholding of *miqra*, which is the uniform term for Scripture used in classical and medieval Jewish sources. Karaite Judaism quickly became centered, as an expression of its scripturalist ethos, around the Land of Israel and especially Jerusalem, where a Karaite school of learning was established in the early 10th century and thrived for around two hundred years. After the 12th century, especially as the result of the Crusaders' conquest of Jerusalem and the dispersion of the Karaite community to Byzantium and Egypt, Karaite scripturalism became somewhat mollified, as the Karaites gradually accepted the need for an authorized interpretive tradition of the Bible. Karaite Judaism exists to this day, mainly in Israel.[1]

One of the main factors that fueled the Rabbanite-Karaite rift was the renewed prominence of "Written Torah," that is, the Bible, in the cultural consciousness of the Jews of the Islamic world as of the 10th century. The Bible appears to have been conceived more and more as a textual entity in tension with "Oral Torah," or received tradition. Unease emerged as to the reliability and validity of this oral tradition, which had gradually undergone canonization in the midrashic, mishnaic, and talmudic corpuses, gaining the status of a complementary and sanctified interpretive tradition throughout the classical and early medieval periods. Some scholars have explained this unease in light of the central role Islamic scripture, the Qur'ān, occupied in the literary hierarchy of medieval Arabic literature. The tension regarding oral tradition resulted in part from the Arabization of the Jews, which reached a peak in the 10th century. This transformation entailed the adoption of the Arabic language and culture (including new genres of literature and philosophical and scientific thought). It also forged a new concept of the literate Jew, including the scholarly intellectual, which differed from that of rabbinic Judaism in pre-Islamic times.

This new literacy centered on the Bible as a textual reference system and on the individual skills of the interpreter as one who interrogates this reference system. One of its first manifestations was the undermining of the established relationship between the "oral" and the "written" in Jewish religious literature. Yet the written did not supersede the oral completely. Even the Karaites, who redefined Judaism as based on written tradition, did not reject the content of oral tradition altogether and engaged in wide debates with ancient rabbinic and talmudic sources. Nonetheless, a new type of interdependence was created in which "oral discourse effectively begins to function within a universe of communications governed by texts," as astutely described, albeit in a different context (of medieval Christendom), by the historian Brian Stock.[2] Whether of Rabbanite or Karaite persuasion, the Jews of Islam grappled with the effects of this shared new consciousness, which enforced a different evaluation of oral tradition, including midrashic tradition, as one which should be cast into a logical relationship with the written Bible and filtered into fresh textual modes that gave it a form of literary legitimacy.

Logic (and what some scholars would define as rationalism), whether juridical, philosophical, theological, linguistic, or textual, was a dominant feature within this new literacy. A scholar's accomplishments in logic and in linguistic control of a text enabled him to gain individual status as a Bible interpreter and to be judged by his personal level of knowledge and achievement. This ideal of what it meant to be learned undermined and even overpowered longstanding social norms by which belonging to a certain school of rabbis or to a certain rabbinic family functioned as one's main ticket of entry into the intellectual Jewish elites. In this new atmosphere, Rabbanites and Karaites alike sought original ways for understanding the Bible that could reflect and give expression to their expanding intellectual horizons and new cultural identity. Sa'adiah Gaon (882–942), who came from the forlorn town of Fayyūm in Middle Egypt, is the quintessential example of this development within the Rabbanite sphere. It was his intellectual brilliance, wider personal acumen, and exceptional literary creativity, in both the Hebrew and Arabic languages, which attained for him the seat of the Gaon, the head of the Babylonian Yeshiva of Sura in 928, despite the fact that he was an outsider from an unknown family. The Karaite Jews, nonetheless, formed the intellectual spearhead in internalizing these developments, due to their scripturalist ideology. This enabled them to embrace the new literary culture with less qualms than the Rabbanite Jews did, especially when it entailed the rejection of Jewish oral tradition.

Karaite Judaism has been portrayed by historians as the Jewish variation on the theme of *sola scriptura*, analogously to movements such as Christian Protestantism and Islamic Shi'ism, which aspire to reinstate a revealed text (in Judaism, *miqra* [the Bible]; in Islam, the Qur'ān) as the sole or major basis for religious law. Such scripturalist movements tend to deny or considerably delimit the role of "oral law" or "received tradition" (in Judaism, *torah she-be-'al-pe*; in Islam, *sunna*) and also have in common a messianic flavor. In the case of Karaite Judaism, this messianism manifested itself in an ideology of return to the Land of Israel, as the locus of written lore, and a rejection of life in the Diaspora, as a rabbinic invention which undermines the Bible's binding authority and jeopardizes the well-being and salvation of the Jewish people.

The rise of literacy among Arabized Jews of the 10th century is of no less import in explaining the Karaite-Rabbanite rift. Karaism signaled the ascendancy of a new cultural order whose hallmark was individual literacy. The unease expressed by various Jewish movements, since antiquity, with the rabbinic institution of oral law and the authority invested in it had become accentuated within this new order. There was a new self-perception in the air as to what it meant to be a Jewish man of letters, which is reflected in documentary sources such as letters and book lists as well as in new genres that permeate medieval Judaeo-Arabic and Hebrew literature. While Karaites were the first to respond to and to ride the wave of this new literacy, ultimately these developments inspired new conceptions of the Bible among Rabbanites as well.³ The term "Judaeo-Arabic" serves herein in its wider sense, to designate the unique culture of the Jews of Islamic lands, and not only in its stricter linguistic sense as a description of the type of Middle Arabic which the Jews were accustomed to transcribe into Hebrew letters.

Common Denominators: The Role of Scripture and Its Relationship with Oral Tradition in Medieval Judaeo-Arabic Culture

Despite their differences, the Jewish commentators, Karaite and Rabbinate, who wrote works on the Bible in the Arabic language share several characteristics which justify grouping them under the designation "the Judaeo-Arabic school of biblical exegesis." The interpretive endeavor of the rabbinic Sages had previously been a collective one, expressed in midrashic anthologies and talmudic tractates whose editors and collators often remained anonymous. As of the 9th century, more and more Jews authored their own exegetical works on the Bible which bore their name as authors. Though this practice was known among Hellenistic Jewish writers, it became largely antithetical to rabbinic tradition at large, which tended to de-emphasize personal authorship. The Judaeo-Arabic exegetes inaugurated a lasting form of individual programmatic exegesis among the Jews in that they strove to comment on all of the biblical books equally and from an individual standpoint. They prefaced their works with introductions which openly described their approach and methodology in relation to those of contemporaries and predecessors. The individual book-form composition also accounted for the personal communication of the author and reader. The latter is often constructed as the internal addressee of the exegetical process. Strewn throughout these commentaries are also various statements in which the exegete reminds the reader of his reasoning, albeit in relation to past traditions and contemporary views. Some of these views are cited within the context of an oral culture of biblical learning as "what we heard," while others are cited in the context of written culture as "what we read." Structurally, this novel genre emulated Arabic (Islamic) models of nonfictional and exegetical writing, yet its content was idiosyncratic to the longstanding traditions of Jewish Bible interpretation. The Judaeo-Arabic Bible commentaries had a three-layered structure. First the commentator cited a Hebrew biblical verse; then he translated it into Judaeo-Arabic (essentially classical (middle) Arabic transcribed into Hebrew letters); then he commented on it in Judaeo-Arabic from syntactic, semantic, thematic, and stylistic perspectives. Sometimes the very same commentaries were also produced in Arabic script, especially by Karaite exegetes. In such cases, the Hebrew biblical verse could also be transcribed into Arabic characters. The commentary continued verse by verse as a functional device, enabling the analysis and interrogation of the biblical text within cohesive discourse and literary units.[4]

In order to grasp the novelty of this form of commentary in Judaism, one must look to classical rabbinic literature, which at first glance may also appear to comment on the Bible consecutively. The formal structure of midrashic compilations (or *midrashim*) tends to follow the biblical text verse by verse, often dissecting the verse into smaller fragments of phrases. But the content of these compilations is not inherently consecutive or cohesive. Rather, midrashic compilations bring together clusters of varied, diverse, and often opposing interpretive comments on each verse and its minute fragmentations. Further, they sometimes focus on some verses and then skip large sections before moving on to another group of verses. Though the classical midrashim may contain interrelated comments, they are essentially anthologies of collated interpretations attributed to various Sages, with no overall evident cohesiveness between their parts, except that they are arranged formally in a manner that follows the biblical text consecutively. Their editors remained anonymous, and as literary works, their creations seem to reflect the collective exegetical endeavor of a certain school of rabbinic thought. At some stage, these interpretations were committed to writing, but they appear to have originated from an oral setting of biblical study and interpretive discourse which took place in *batey midrash* (schools/houses of learning) or in synagogues during the pre-Islamic period. The midrashic method of commenting on the Bible reflects the Sages' conception of the Bible as an "omnisignificant" divine text imbued with unlimited meanings, unlike any text originated by a human being. The new medieval commentary form was suited to different ways of thinking about, writing about, and reading the Bible among the book-cultured Arabized Jews.[5]

Before rabbinic midrashim, there did exist individually authored works on the Bible in antiquity, especially those by Philo and Josephus, and certain works of Second Temple and Qumran literature bear the stamp of individual Jewish authorship based on the Bible (e.g., the Book of Jubilees). The question of whether and how these literatures may have reached medieval Jewish circles and if and how they may have served as models for their innovations is fascinating and still needs to be explored.[6] From what is currently known, however, the Judaeo-Arabic exegetes, Karaite and Rabbanite alike, cite profusely from midrashic literature and engage openly with Arabic thought and literature, whereas they appear to be mostly unaware of the ancient and Hellenistic Jewish literary models. They do not engage with such sources or cite them directly, although some indirect channels of contact may have existed or may yet be uncovered. Judaeo-Arabic exegesis reflects, therefore, a new era of thinking and writing on the Bible among Jews.

This type of exegesis was distinctive of Karaite Judaism from its very beginnings. It is found in the Hebrew commentaries of the 9th-century Karaite Daniel al-Qumīsī and develops fully in the Judaeo-Arabic works of the great commentators of the 10th to 11th centuries: Yaʿqūb al-Qirqisānī in Babylonia and Salmon ben Yeruḥam, Sahal ben Maṣliaḥ, Yūsuf ibn Nūḥ, Yefet ben ʿEli, Abū Faraj Harūn, Yeshuʿah ben Yehudah, and others in the Jerusalem community of "returnees" (*shavim*). The same type of exegesis was also employed by the Rabbanite Geonim of Babylonia (Iraq), beginning with Saʿadiah Gaon in the early 10th century, as well as in Muslim Spain and North Africa during the 11th and 12th centuries, by Moses ibn Gikatilla, Judah ibn Balʿam, Isaac al-Kinzi, and Tanḥum ha-Yerushalmi. Common denominators among these commentators include systematic structure, exegetical terminology, and the content of the exegesis, which draws from a shared treasure of Jewish exegesis, on the one hand, and from a common mentality of Arabic language and culture, on the other hand. Even when the Judaeo-Arabic commentators or their families left the orbit of Islamic civilization and adopted Hebrew in place of Arabic as the language of their exegetical works (as when the Karaite interpretive enterprise moved from Jerusalem to Byzantium or when Rabbanites such as Abraham Ibn Ezra and the Kimhi family moved from Muslim Spain to the lands of Christendom), these commentators continued to integrate into their Hebrew works the heritage of the Judaeo-Arabic tradition of Bible interpretation as they directed it toward a new audience.

This Judaeo-Arabic hermeneutic tradition applied logical and contextual tools to biblical exegesis. Rationalist thinking, of the kind that relied on logical argumentations within a juridical or philosophical context, became an essential accomplishment of the Jewish literate classes, who acquired it through their wide reading of Arabic scientific, philosophical, and theological works. By internalizing these disciplines to a degree unknown among rabbinic Jews in pre-Islamic times, they created a new hermeneutical consciousness in three basic respects relating to the language, literature, and history of the Bible.

First, Judaeo-Arabic exegetes generally conceived the language of biblical texts to be governed by conventions which rule all forms of human communication and which can be analyzed through the use of specific tools, mainly, those of grammar. Saʿadiah Gaon gives clear expression to this stance in the introduction to his *Translation and Commentary on Genesis*, in which he states, "The Torah was given in one of the languages." His approach recalls the dictum attributed to a mishnaic sage, Rabbi Ishmael: "The Torah speaks as human beings do." Though some medieval Rabbanite exegetes drew on this affinity to justify their linguistic approach, there is a difference between Rabbi Ishmael's hermeneutics and that of Saʿadiah and the Karaite exegetes.[7] These latter give voice to a scientific (secularizing) conception of biblical language, viewing it as a system of signs comparable to those of other languages and denying it an inherent mystical or mythological dimension. Accordingly, the divine origins of the Bible are not to be sought in the texture of its language, as in the conceptions of classical midrash (omnisignificance, indeterminacy of meaning, atomization, etc.) but in its ideas and content. The rabbinic Sages' conception of the divine essence of scriptural language distances it from the ways of human discourse. Judaeo-Arabic exegesis abandons this conception, though not always and often not in an openly declared fashion. The Bible could now be analyzed as a piece of literature, even if its content was still perceived as divinely originated or inspired.

Judaeo-Arabic grammarians and exegetes inherited a science of comparative linguistics from the Arabs and applied it to Hebrew scripture. The seeds of grammatical and lexical study of biblical Hebrew were planted in the great works of 10th- to 11th-century linguists, be they David ben Abraham al-Fasī, Yūsuf ibn Nūḥ, or Abū Faraj Harūn among the Karaites or Saʿadiah Gaon, Judah Ḥayyūj, and Jonah Ibn Janāḥ among the Rabbanites. This linguistic framework enabled the consecutive and contextual analysis of the biblical text to be largely based on the specialized understanding of its lexicon and grammar. The Karaites made this approach a fundamental aspect of their exegetical system, in terms of lexical, grammatical, and discourse analysis.⁸ This led, in turn, to particular Karaite innovations in the understanding of the Bible's genres, style, and poetics.

Second, Judaeo-Arabic exegesis reflects an appreciation of the Bible as literature. The term "contextual exegesis" has sometimes been applied in describing this approach, yet this term fails to distinguish it from midrashic exegesis. Both midrashic and Judaeo-Arabic exegesis were interested in context, but in very different ways. Judaeo-Arabic exegetes turn the immediate context of a particular verse (the verses that precede and follow it within a passage) into the main focus of interpretation, conscious of the double-binding relationship between the part and the whole. Midrashic exegesis was more apt to draw on the extended context and so interpreted a verse in light of a different passage within the same narrative or, more often, in light of a completely different narrative that contains an analogous theme. Judaeo-Arabic exegesis is generally much stricter when drawing on analogies within the wider context of a biblical passage. It mainly refers to the same narrative or book or, less frequently, to other biblical books, and even then the framework for comparison is restricted to the same genre or historical period and is governed primarily by linguistic and textual (rather than thematic and associative) criteria. Hence the term *literary exegesis* seems more suitable in characterizing the unprecedented understanding of the narrative, rhetoric, stylistic, and editorial devices of biblical literature as explored by the Judaeo-Arabic exegetes. The Karaite exegetes, in particular, believed these devices served the biblical composers (be they the authors, the editors, or both) to create a cohesive literary composition. Rabbanites in Muslim Spain (such as Moses ibn Gikatilla [first half of the 11th century] and Moses ibn Ezra [1055–1138]) later developed this innovative approach in new directions in their own Judaeo-Arabic exegetical and poetic works.⁹

Third, a growing historical consciousness concerning the social and material realities of biblical times and their differences from medieval times enabled the Judaeo-Arabic exegetes to distance themselves from the biblical text (and era) and to consider critically the midrashic tendency to blur the world of the exegete and the world of Scripture. This discomfort with midrash, expressed subtly in Rabbanite sources and more bluntly in Karaite ones, is another common feature of Judaeo-Arabic exegesis. Karaites were more apt than the Rabbanites to employ lengthy historical reasoning in their works on the Bible. In the Rabbanite sphere, contemplating the historical aspects of a biblical story or prophecy became a dominant mode among the commentators of the 14th and 15th centuries, such as Profayt

Duran (1350–1414) and Don Isaac Abravanel (1437–1508), who represent the Renaissance period in Jewish exegesis.

In this complex exegetical consciousness lies the contribution of medieval Judaeo-Arabic exegesis to the development of Jewish Bible interpretation as a whole. In the Karaites' call to return to Scripture and their rejection of talmudic literature and its interpretive methodology, they paved the way to the wider adoption of these features. The Karaites' ideological stance enabled them to embrace the fundamental transition that took place in medieval Jewish culture as the result of its encounter with Islam. They gave open and initial expression to the understanding of the Bible as a text, that is, as a product of written communication (even if it had an oral core transmitted from God to his prophets) and as part of a "universe of communications" in which texts "emerged as a reference system both for everyday activities and for giving shape to many larger vehicles of explanation."[10] These developments empowered individual writers as well as readers who acquired the tools of literature, composition, structure, and eloquence within a literate mentality.

The Relationship between Bible and Tradition: Legal Exegesis and Nonlegal Exegesis

Legal Exegesis

The degree of derivation of legal (*halakhic*) norms from the Bible was one of the key issues that divided Karaites and Rabbanites. There were conceptual as well as exegetical aspects to this dispute. While the Karaites, in an ongoing attempt to base Jewish legal practice on Scripture alone, maintained that the Bible had to be rescrutinized, the Rabbanites upheld the authenticity of classical rabbinic tradition by continuing to sanctify Oral Law as a foundational base, complementary to Written Law, in the derivation of Jewish halakhah.

The Karaites widened the basis for halakhic derivation from the Bible to include all of its twenty-four books. Halakhah could thus be derived directly not only from the books of the Pentateuch (as in rabbinic lore) but also from Prophecy and the Writings. The widening of the sanctified written basis from which law can be deduced was necessary given that there was no recourse to a sanctified oral tradition as a "complementary" legal source to written tradition. Another exegetical manifestation of the newly charted relationship between the Bible and tradition was the rejection of interpretive authority and authoritativeness. In other words, the revered place of a chain of tradition, as passed on from a renowned rabbi to his pupil in a particular circle or school, was replaced by the individual's freedom to interpret. This freedom was not without bounds. It relied on the new literate mentality as discussed earlier and on an acquired education in the rational and linguistic tools of biblical study. But once one mastered these tools, one was given the chance to use them irrespective of one's personal and familial background and regardless of status or scholarly class (though not regardless of the gender divide: women appear to have been barred from this newly emerging scholarly world, whether Rabbanite or Karaite).[11] In the case of the Karaites, the rejection of these socially authoritative structures was given higher legitimacy since it further endorsed their wider dispute with and undermining of rabbinic tradition. As a consequence, they did not only encourage, similarly to some Rabbanites, the individual's freedom to interpret but also endorsed exegetical inventiveness per se as well as interpretations which undermined or subverted what came to be perceived in rabbinic tradition as the "established" meaning of the biblical text.

Some Muslim thinkers of the time, especially among the Shi'ites, also focused on the unreliability of the transmission chain which traced certain Muslim oral traditions (*Ḥadīth*) back to the Prophet Muhammad. Early Karaite sources go further by comparison, unequivocally rejecting the actual institution and literary embodiment of Jewish Oral Law in the mishnaic and talmudic corpus. It was this (legal) aspect of rabbinic tradition which particularly troubled them. The Karaites did not accept that rabbinic Oral Law embodied any kind of live or authentic legal tradition which could hail back to Moses, and they did not even see in it remnants of such a tradition. Rather, it was a concept invented by the Rabbis in the Second Temple period to establish their own interpretive authority, over and above the authority of others, in determining the meaning of biblical law. This purported legal authority was more disturbing to the Karaites than the Rabbis' authority in determining the meaning of other genres in biblical literature, due to the practical binding dimension of religious law in Judaism. In the Karaites' view, this mistaken rabbinic tradition plunged the Jewish people into a state of sin, wherein they were performing wrongly and even transgressing the God-given commandments of the written Torah in order to follow the devices of men (*miṣwat anashim melumadah*, "a commandment learned by rote"; cf. Isaiah 29:13). This transgression explained the Jews' extended exile, loss of sovereignty, and humiliation among the nations.

The following excerpt from Yefet ben 'Eli's allegorical commentary on Zecheriah 5:5–8 exemplifies this viewpoint:[12]

> And in the end of the time of the exile those books which the people claim to have been [derived] from Moses will become obsolete, and no one will follow them. They will go back, instead, to the written Torah, as it is said (Deuteronomy 30:8): "And you shall again obey the voice of the Lord," . . . and no one will turn to the Mishnah nor to the Talmud for they will know they are "a commandment of men learned by rote" (Isaiah 29:13). . . . He said (vs. 8): *"This is the wicked one"*—and he named her a wicked woman in order to demonstrate that they are sinners before God, since they composed these [talmudic] books and compelled the nation to believe in them and to act according to them and condemned to death those who disagreed with them. They did not say: so we reason, and so it occurred to us, and do search yourselves O Israel as we have searched. Had they done so, they would have been saved from the condemnation of the Lord of the Universe. . . . And so all the Karaite scholars used this method and established what appeared to them as the truth and encouraged people to search (themselves), so much that a man is entitled to disagree with his father and the father will not say to him, "why have you disagreed with me?", and a student with his Rabbi. . . . And his saying (vs. 8) *"and he thrust her back into the container, and thrust down the leaden weight upon its mouth"*—means that they sealed the Mishnah and Talmud and did not leave a path for those who came after them to establish not even a single letter.

The Karaites' conception of the innate falsity of Oral Law as expressed in this passage is inextricable from their historical-philosophical attempt to explain what they saw as the regrettable political state of the Jewish people. The rejection of Oral Law as a mistaken interpretive tradition would enable the spiritual lifting of the perpetual state of sin in which the Jews had existed since Exile. It was perceived as a necessary step in rectifying their national predicament.

The time required, however, to reinterpret all of Scripture meant that the Karaites could not replace oral traditions at a satisfactory pace. With regard to the legal corpus of the Bible, this presented an existential problem which left them in limbo: not beholden to the accepted norms yet at the same time not fully committed to new ones. The Karaites' justification in their eyes, however, was that they had begun the process of revision that would break a millennium of interpretive deadlock. They understood this process as one of trial and error and demanded candidness in this respect, partly in counterreaction to what they perceived as rabbinic conceit in espousing the heavenly and flawless derivation of oral law. These concerns find poignant expression in the following section from the 10th-century Karaite Yefet ben 'Eli's introduction to his commentary on Deuteronomy:[13]

> From the Giver of Knowledge I ask that He steady us in the correct way, benevolently and with kindness, and that He open our eyes to his laws, ... forgive the errors and mistakes which may transpire, and that He absolve us from any admonition, for He knows our intention, for we do not intend to be at variance with Him, but we seek the truth. [He knows] that we are interpreting the words of the [Karaite] scholars, may God have mercy on them, and may He establish them, for they opened the eyes of the people of Exile who dwell in darkness, in which we are now, and taught them, and instructed them and directed them away from transgression, on which they were set, to the way of the truth and to the law of the Lord of the Universe.

Nonlegal Exegesis

Nonlegal exegesis of the Bible also divided Karaites and Rabbanites. Since exegetes of both orientations were less bound by a theological framework in their discussions of the biblical stories, it is in respect to the narrative portions of the Bible that their newly acquired Judaeo-Arabic culture seeps through their readings and that their innovative approaches and methods of interpretation become apparent. Biblical narrative (including historiography) provided an outlet for a more inventive reading of Scripture, whose themes and structures could be elaborated in ways akin to the art of fiction, whereas biblical texts charged with legal (and hence practical) as well as prophetic or poetic implications were more restrictive in the types of readings they sanctioned.

The Karaite exegetes of the 10th and 11th centuries, and especially the great 10th-century commentators Ya'qub al-Qirqisānī and Yefet ben 'Eli, exhibit a heightened consciousness of biblical narrative per se, when compared to Rabbanite commentators of the same era, such as Sa'adiah Gaon or Samuel ben Ḥofni. Focusing their intellectual acumen on the Bible as a self-referential text, Karaite exegetes disassociated their exegesis from preexisting sanctified midrashic, and especially homiletic, models, on the one hand, and continued a form of discourse with the interpretive content-matter of midrashic sources, on the other hand. Yet unlike their Rabbanite counterparts, they were free of the need to integrate classical rabbinic midrash into their conception of Scripture or to find a way of harmonizing this conception with midrash. For them, classical rabbinic midrash represented just one more "opinion" on the Bible, sometimes relevant in its linguistic and contextual reasoning, at other times irrelevant. The Karaite exegetes did not refrain from using exegetical explanations found in classical rabbinic literature when they found them relevant in illuminating the meaning of a verse or passage. Yefet ben 'Eli and other Karaite exegetes sometimes quote rabbinic works; more often, they present known talmudic views anonymously.

In the Rabbanite sphere, however, reckoning with classical midrash was an inevitable part of the new exegetical enterprise. Rabbanites could not openly relegate midrashic tradition to the margins. They could not accept such a cultural or spiritual position toward the classical works of the Sages, despite the new mentality which caused them to feel uneasy with it. Their reservations as to the decontextualizing (and in their definition illogical) tendencies of certain types of midrash had to be more subtly expressed, especially in the early pioneering stages, when the polemic with Karaite Judasim was at its highest intensity. In Rabbanite exegesis of this era, even within a nonlegal context, a process of intricate harmonization with midrashic sources is apparent, especially in Sa'adiah's works and those of his pupils.[14] In the 11th and 12th centuries, these tendencies somewhat slackened in Rabbanite exegesis as well: Judaeo-Arabic Rabbanite commentators who lived in Muslim Spain and North Africa, such as Moses Ibn Ezra and Tanḥum ha-Yerushalmi, became less engaged in harmonization with midrashic homilies. In Christian Europe, however, commentators who had cultural links with Judaeo-Arabic tradition (such as David Kimhi [1160–1235]) yet wrote in Hebrew made renewed efforts to integrate midrashic tradition into their exegetical scheme. As a cultural parallel, it is striking to note the similarity between the enterprises of Sa'adiah (882–942) and Rashi (1040–1105), the first in the Islamic sphere, the second in that of Christendom, in trying to integrate midrashic homilies into their quintessentially medieval hermeneutic, in which language and context as well as logical thought represent a new paradigm for reading Scripture. Whereas in Ashkenaz (Christian Europe) the approach that came to be known by the

Hebrew term *peshat*, focusing on the plain meaning of the text, was relatively short-lived (it flourished mainly within the school of Rashi's disciples in northern France of the 11th to 13th centuries), in the Islamic sphere—as well as in Christian northern Spain and southern France, which had historical connections with Islamic culture—there developed a longstanding tradition of nonhomiletic exegesis which lasted from the 9th to the 14th centuries and beyond. In Arabic, the term used to designate such a type of context-bound exegesis highlighted its relationship to the "surface/apparent" meaning of the text (*ṭhāhir*), but this term is not identical with Hebrew *peshat*, and its translation from Arabic into Hebrew as *peshat*, already in medieval times (by Judah Ibn Tibbon), caused confusion. The couching of this context-bound exegetical enterprise in the philosophical and scientific language and culture adopted from the Arabs, as well as its fueling, sharpening, and distilling within the Karaite-Rabbanite polemic, forged a much stronger orientation toward a linguistic-contextual-literary-historical orientation in biblical study among the Jews of the Islamic world. This tradition was eventually adapted from its original Judaeo-Arabic language into Hebrew and further transformed within Hebraic culture in the works of commentators such as Abraham Ibn Ezra, who was born in Muslim Spain and emigrated to Christian lands, David Kimhi, and Moses Nahmanides (1194–1274). In this manner, it eventually found its way into the Renaissance works of later Jewish commentators such as Profayt Duran and Don Isaac Abravanel, who developed independent literary treatises on specific biblical themes and narratives.[15]

The Karaite Impetus to the Linguistic, Literary, and Historical Aspects of Judaeo-Arabic Exegesis

Expertise in the Biblical Hebrew as a Prerequisite to Biblical Study

The Karaites considered the detailed study of biblical Hebrew as a prerequisite to the pursuit of the Bible's meaning. They developed the lexical and grammatical study of the Bible, often as a conscious substitute to its homiletic expansion in classical rabbinic and medieval Rabbanite tradition, subjugating all analysis of Scripture to its primary linguistic control. Karaite biblical study, at the height of its achievements throughout the 10th to 11th centuries, was conducted through the interrelated disciplines of grammar, translation (into Arabic), and exegesis.

The Karaite tradition of Hebrew grammar originated in centers of grammatical study in the East during the late 9th and early 10th centuries and was brought to the Land of Israel by Karaite scholars who migrated from the Persian regions, sometimes via Iraq. An important figure among these was Abū Ya'qūb Yūsuf ibn Nūḥ, who wrote a grammatical commentary on the Bible, known as the *Diqdūq*, during the second half of the 10th century. Ibn Nūḥ established in Jerusalem a Karaite "house of learning" or "learning compound" (*dār lil-'ilm*; *ḥaṣer*), in which other famous Karaite scholars were active. It is possible that the special fusion between the branches of grammar, translation, and exegesis typical of Karaite biblical study crystallized within the Jerusalem school, in an atmosphere of open intellectual debate in pursuit of the Bible's meaning.

Grammar and exegesis were intertwined in early Karaite thought much in the way that early Arabic grammar was closely associated with Qur'ānic exegesis prior to the work of Sībawayhi, the founder of Arabic grammar. In both traditions, grammar was primarily conceived as a tool in the clarification of the meaning of Scripture, and only later did it become an independent discipline. The Karaites' subordination of grammar to exegesis enabled them to perceive that form and meaning were inextricably connected. Thus, a leading principle in Ibn Nūḥ's Hebrew grammar is that "one category of linguistic form consistently has one type of meaning. In order to establish the precise meaning of the Biblical text, therefore, it was thought to be essential to analyse the form of words."[16] The Karaites' concern with linguistic form arose from their understanding that a direct link exists between form and meaning. This understanding is also reflected in their Arabic Bible translations, which were designed to represent, as much as possible, the original word order and syntax of the Hebrew text. In contrast, Sa'adiah Gaon's translation of the Torah became separated from his lengthier commentary on it at an early stage of its transmission. This was probably due to the functional differentiation which Sa'adiah himself initiated, wherein his interpretive translation was deemed a self-sufficient mode of addressing the biblical text. In the same vein, the Karaites' lengthier commentaries, which served as the third layer of their Bible compositions, were generally bound to the immediate literary context of the annotated passage.

The Bible as Literature

The leading Karaite exegete of the 10th century, Yefet ben 'Eli, was able to pursue the linkage between form and meaning a step further, by applying it to discourse analysis. Yefet developed the innovative Karaite approach to the Bible by concentrating on the narrative and literary techniques employed by its supposed authors and editors. He widely introduced into his commentaries a novel theoretical Arabic concept, that of the biblical *mudawwin* (composer-compiler), which is also found in the works of other Karaite exegetes of this period, though in a less developed form. His unshared vocation was to establish the canon of Karaite Bible translation and exegesis. Between 960 and 1000, Yefet devoted himself exclusively to the vast undertaking of producing a translation and commentary on all three divisions of the Bible, beginning with the Pentateuch and then going on to the Prophets and Writings. Yefet created a work of a summarizing nature, a "summa" of Karaite Bible exegesis up to his time. His recourse to exegetical opinions other than his own was not only essential to his canonizing task but also formed a live reflection of the egalitarian ethos of early Karaite biblical study, an ethos which is best captured in the dictum attributed to 'Anan ben David (reported by Yefet himself), "Search diligently in the Torah and do not rely on my opinion." While the primary focus of Yefet's commentaries is linguistic-contextual, he added to this tradition a distinctively literary layer of discussion, concerned with the discourse analysis of the wider thematic unit in the text under discussion and with the formation of the biblical text. In this context, he identified patterns of expression typical of biblical literature, as well as wider structural characteristics of certain biblical types and genres.

The exegetical concept of the *mudawwin* served Yefet as a composite literary term blending several functions into one overall concept, which signified the entity or entities responsible for the *form* or *texture* of Hebrew scripture. The theoretical nature of the term is further underlined by its uniform application in Yefet's discussion of various biblical genres (narrative, historiography, prophecy, law, and poetry) and in all three divisions of the Bible, wherein the *mudawwin* is mostly and deliberately left unidentified as a historical figure. The *mudawwin*'s predominant function is to control and carry out the narration process of the biblical text. At times, this aspect converges with his secondary role as the redactor-editor of the biblical text, responsible for its stringing together into a cohesive whole.[17]

Yefet discusses certain formal techniques and structures of biblical narrative (such as resumptive repetition, elision, dialogue ordering) which have a particular effect in the buildup of narrative meaning. He identifies these techniques as issuing from the hand of the *mudawwin*. It appears, therefore, that Yefet understood the work of the biblical *mudawwin* to be concerned with the exercise of control over the flow, positioning, and gapping of the data within the narrative span. In this, there is some parallel with modern literary theory, which distinguishes the "narrator" or "authorial-narrator" from the actual, biographical person of the "author" who composed the text and which considers the "narrator" as a literary device, a fictitious entity, a varying "point of view" as the teller of the story. Whereas modern literary criticism of the Bible considers various devices employed by the biblical narrator, such as gapping, to have been mastered by the biblical authors in order to create complex literary effects (for example, characterization, the buildup of tension, or the creation of irony), Yefet relates to these in exegetical terms, focusing on their interpretive significance in the understanding of the biblical story.

No parallel has been uncovered between the Karaite usage of the nominal form *mudawwin*—in any of the senses of author-composer, authorial narrator, or editor—and medieval Qurʾānic exegesis. Nevertheless, the Arabic term *tadwīn* and the root *dawwana* are quite rife in Ḥadīth literature, wherein they connote the process of the writing down of traditions relating to the Prophet Muhammad and their collation as books. These traditions were transmitted orally in the first centuries of Islam, and there was a fierce opposition to their commitment to writing which was only resolved in the 9th century.[18] The *mudawwin*'s comprehensive and groundbreaking application by Yefet to biblical literature appears therefore to be original to Karaite thought. It reflects a wider Karaite perception of the nature of the Bible as a literary work, whose core may have been transmitted orally in biblical times but was effectively turned into a written oeuvre, a book, during the time of the Prophets, at the latest, and certainly before the Second Temple (rabbinic) era.

The Bible as History

In the history of biblical interpretation, questions concerning the Bible's origins, historical background, and credibility have often been arrived at through the identification of literary cruxes. Critical study of the Bible as it emerged in the 18th and 19th centuries linked questions of literary genre and those of historical background. The medieval Karaite study of the Bible as literature raised similar questions. Naturally, these were not defined through a modern conception of "origins" or "sources" but focused on the nature of the world described in the biblical text. It was not only the literary contextualization of biblical study which led the Karaite exegetes to explore the connection between the biblical text and the "real" world of its time but also the attempt to remold this study within the mentality of a rationalist age affected by a significant rise of literacy (similar, in this respect, to the era of Enlightenment, which fostered modern critical study of the Bible). Already in early 10th-century Karaite works, we find a keen and unprecedented interest in questions such as: What kind of reality is the biblical text describing? Is it describing events that actually occurred in historical times? If so, in what ways, and what does it choose to leave out? Yefet and other Karaite exegetes of the Jerusalem school engaged in such questions especially in their commentaries on the prophetic books as well as in relation to texts with a pronounced historical setting (such as Genesis, Samuel, Ruth, and Esther). Not surprisingly, it is Yefet's older contemporary, the major Karaite philosopher and exegete Abū Yūsuf Yaʿqūb al-Qirqisānī, who provides these questions with a wider philosophical and theoretical basis. Qirqisānī, who was active in Iraq in the first half of the 10th century, is mainly known for his commentary on the legal portions of the Pentateuch, known as *Kitāb al-anwār wal-marāqib* (*The Book of Lights and Watchtowers*), a milestone in the development of Karaite halakhah, philosophy, and historiography. Qirqisānī also wrote programmatic commentaries on Job, Ecclesiastes, and Genesis. Mostly extant are portions from the Commentary on Genesis, which exist in a "short" or "abridged" version and in a "long" version. These appear to have formed part of his commentary on the nonlegal portions of the Pentateuch, known as *Kitāb al-riyāḍ wal-ḥadāʾiq* (*The Book of Parks and Gardens*). Qirqisānī's preamble to *Kitāb al-riyāḍ* discusses the validity of rational speculation on the Bible, after which are presented thirty-seven propositions about biblical interpretation.[19]

These propositions clarify Qirqisānī's opinion concerning the nature of the Hebrew language, the composition of the Bible, and other textual features. Several of Qirqisānī's hermeneutic rules grapple with the question of whether the Bible contains a "reliable" depiction of the reality of biblical times. Qirqisānī asks, for instance, whether the Bible, when describing non-Israelite nations, cites their words in the original language (thus suggesting that these nations spoke Hebrew) or translates their tongues into Hebrew. Furthermore, are there signs in the text as to whether their words were transmitted in the original? In the same introduction Qirqisānī contends that the Torah mentions place names according to how these were known in the time of Moses (whom Qirqisānī, unlike Yefet, openly and unequivocally identified as its composer [*mudawwin*]) and not in accordance with how they were known at the time in which the events are recounted as taking place (for instance, the time of Abraham). Qirqisānī, like Yefet, takes pains to distinguish between the words in the story which originate from the narrator-compiler and the words which originate (as real historical utterances) from the characters and which are merely reported or "told" by the narrator-compiler.[20]

In this and in other respects, Qirqisānī attempts to distinguish between the fictive world of the Bible as a book and the nonfictive historical world of the events recounted in it, which were transmitted orally over a certain period of time. These questions were not only the result of Qirqisānī's philosophical mind-set or Yefet's literary astuteness. They are also emblematic of the newly found literacy among the Jews of the medieval Islamic world. For, as noted by Stock, the rapprochement between the oral and the written typical of such an era plays "a decisive role in the organization of experience.... At a more abstract level, philosophers revived the opposition between what was really taking place when events were described in words and what was merely thought or said to be taking place."[21]

Concluding Remarks

The major contribution of the Judaeo-Arabic Karaite exegetes lies in the transition they brought about toward a new type of understanding which espoused the in-depth analysis of the Bible's language (grammar and lexicon) and carried it through into new dimensions of discourse analysis, literary structure, and narrative technique. These had been left largely unexplored by rabbinic exegesis. Historical sensibilities became an integral feature of their literary approach. Even though they were capable of applying varied interpretive modes to the biblical text, including midrashic-like allegorizing or actualizing (messianic) readings, the Karaites' rejection of the sanctity of Oral Law, and of midrashic tradition as a binding reading of Scripture, and their refocusing on the Bible as a self-contained text fostered a new path in Jewish Bible interpretation. This path echoed wider needs of a new era of literacy among the Jews of the medieval Islamic world, and gradually it also found expression in the works of the Rabbanite Judaeo-Arabic exegetes as well. The flowering of Karaite exegesis depended on the principle of individual freedom and acquired learning in the investigation of Scripture and the rejection of received authority. These are known hallmarks of a literate culture. The works of the Judaeo-Arabic Karaite exegetes, especially those by Yefet ben 'Eli, appear to have reached Spain. They were also kept alive through the Hebrew translation enterprise undertaken by the Karaite exegetes in Byzantium during the 12th century.[22]

From this period, however, the unique features of classical Judaeo-Arabic Karaite exegesis began to diminish within Karaism. The fervent anti-Karaite Rabbanite polemic took its toll, while the Crusaders' conquests dealt a blow to the Karaite center in Jerusalem, its scriptural-messianic ethos, and its emphasis on living in the Land of Israel. But there was also the inevitable dwindling of a revolutionary spirit in the face of the hardships and problems of reality. A situation in which, as Qirqisānī puts it in his *Kitāb al-Anwār*, "scarce two of them [the Karaites] are to be found who agree on anything" meant disarray in managing the Karaite communities and sustaining their religious life. Consequently, from the 12th century, the Karaites consolidated their own version of a sanctified tradition of biblical interpretation, albeit less binding (and less ancient) than that of rabbinic tradition.[23] Karaites still encouraged personal freedom of interpretation, but its ways became inhibited and charged with harmonization. The time of Karaite innovation in biblical study had effectively ended by the 12th century, but the unique Karaite contribution to the medieval Jewish conception of Scripture continued its innovative effect in the works of the great Spanish Jewish exegetes and well into those of the Renaissance.

NOTES

1. On Karaite history and literature, see further Fred Astren, *Karaite Judaism and Historical Understanding* (Columbia: University of South Carolina Press, 2004); Yoram Erder, "The Mourners of Zion: The Karaites in Jerusalem in the Tenth and Eleventh Centuries," in Meira Polliack, ed., *Karaite Judaism: A Guide to Its History and Literary Sources* (Leiden, Netherlands: Brill, 2003), 213–35; Moshe Gil, "The Origins of the Karaites," in Polliack, *Karaite Judaism*, 73–118; Meira Polliack, "Medieval Karaism," in Martin Goodman, ed., *The Oxford Handbook of Jewish Studies* (Oxford: Oxford University Press, 2002), 295–305.

2. Brian Stock, *The Implications of Literacy: Written Language and Models of Interpretation in the Eleventh and Twelfth Centuries* (Princeton: Princeton University Press, 1983), 3.

3. On the relationship between the rise of literacy and the formation of heretical and reformist religious groups, see ibid., 88–240.

4. See Daniel Frank, *Search Scripture Well: Karaite Exegetes and the Origins of the Jewish Bible Commentary in the Islamic East* (Leiden, Netherlands: Brill, 2004); Geoffrey Khan, ed., *Exegesis and Grammar in Medieval Karaite Texts* (Oxford:

Oxford University Press, 2001); Uriel Simon, *Four Approaches to the Book of Psalms: From Saadiah Gaon to Abraham ibn Ezra* (Albany: SUNY Press, 1991).

5. "Late" midrashic compilations dated in the eighth and ninth centuries, such as Pirqe de-Rabbi Eliezer, often retell the biblical story, thus reflecting a transition in the Jewish literary tradition from anthological rabbinic collections to coherent works by individual authors.

6. See Meira Polliack, "Wherein Lies the Pesher? Re-questioning the Connection between the Medieval Karaite and Qumranic Modes of Biblical Interpretation," *Jewish Studies, an Internet Journal* 4 (2005): 151–200; Eve Karkovski, "Many Days without the Truth: Loss and Recovery of Religious Knowledge in Early Karaite Exegesis," in Joel L. Kraemer and Michael G. Wechsler, eds., *Pesher Nahum: Texts and Studies in Jewish History and Literature from Antiquity through the Middle Ages, Presented to Norman Golb* (Chicago: University of Chicago Press, 2012).

7. See Mordechai Z. Cohen, "'The Best of Poetry': Literary Approaches to the Bible in the Spanish Peshat Tradition," *Torah U-Madda* 6 (1995–96): 15–57.

8. See Geoffrey Khan, *The Early Karaite Tradition of Hebrew Grammatical Thought: Including a Critical Edition, Translation and Analysis of the Diqduq of Abu Ya'qub Yusuf ibn Nuḥ on the Hagiographa* (Leiden, Netherlands: Brill, 2000).

9. See, for instance, Mordechai Z. Cohen, "The Aesthetic Exegesis of Moses Ibn Ezra," *Hebrew Bible/Old Testament: The History of Its Interpretation*, ed. M. Sæbø (Göttingen, Germany: Vandenhoeck & Ruprecht, 2000), I/2:282–301.

10. See Stock, *Implications of Literacy*, 3 (and further discussion on 4–57).

11. Nevertheless, it appears from various sources (exegetical, halakhical, and documentary) that Karaism did have an appeal to medieval (and especially to the literate) Jewish women by way of offering them an opportunity for positive involvement in their creed (an issue that deserves a separate study).

12. See Polliack, "Medieval Karaism," 312–15.

13. See ibid., 316–19.

14. See Haggai Ben Shammai, "The Tension between Literal Interpretation and Exegetical Freedom: Comparative Observations on Sa'adya's Method," in J. D. McAuliffe, B. D. Walfish, and J. W. Goering, eds., *With Reverence for the Written Word: Medieval Scriptural Exegesis in Judaism, Christianity, and Islam* (Oxford: Oxford University Press, 2003), 33–50.

15. See, in this context, Michael G. Wechsler, *Strangers in the Land: The Judaeo-Arabic Exegesis of Tanhum ha-Yerushalmi on the Books of Ruth and Esther* (Jerusalem: Hebrew University Magnes Press, 2009).

16. See Khan, *Early Karaite Tradition*, 12, 132–133.

17. See Meira Polliack, "Karaite Conception of the Biblical Narrator (*Mudawwin*)," in J. Neusner and A. J. Avery-Peck, eds., *Encyclopaedia of Midrash*, vol. 1 (Leiden, Netherlands: Brill, 2005), 350–74; Meira Polliack, "The 'Voice' of the Narrator and the 'Voice' of the Characters in the Bible Commentaries of Yefet ben 'Eli," in C. Cohen et al., eds., *Birkat Shalom: Studies in the Bible, Ancient Near Eastern*

Literature, and Postbiblical Judaism, Presented to Shalom M. Paul on the Occasion of His Seventieth Birthday, vol. 2 (Winona Lake, IN: Eisenbrauns, 2008), 891–916.

18. See Gregor Schoeler, *The Oral and the Written in Early Islam*, trans. U. Vagelpohl (London and New York: Routledge, 2006), 111–41.

19. See Hartwig Hirschfeld, *Qirqisani Studies* (London, 1918); Leon Nemoy, *A Karaite Anthology* (New Haven: Yale University Press, 1952), 60–68.

20. This kind of distinction is reminiscent of the modern differentiation between the functions of "seeing" and "telling" in narrative theory. See Hirschfeld, *Qirqisani Studies*, 52.

21. See Stock, *Implications of Literacy*, 4. See further exemplification of the interpretation of the Bible as history in Meira Polliack, "Historicizing Prophetic Literature: Yefet's Commentary on Hosea and Its Relationship to al-Qūmisī's *Pitron*," in J. L. Kraemer and Michael G. Wechsler, eds., *Pesher Nahum, Texts and Studies in Jewish History and Literature from Antiquity through the Middle Ages, Presented to Norman (Nahum) Golb* (Chicago: Oriental Institiute, Chicago University, 2011), 149–84.

22. See Daniel Lasker, "Karaism in Twelfth-Century Spain," *Journal of Jewish Thought and Philosophy* 1 (1992): 179–95.

23. See Astren, *Karaite Judaism and Historical Understanding*, 124–57.

Chapter 7

Concepts of Scripture in the School of Rashi

Robert A. Harris

In considering the definition of a "Jewish conception of Scripture," it is just so right on many levels to begin with Rashi's Torah commentary: Jewish children have begun their own studies with this work almost since the very generation in which he wrote it. Rashi, or Rabbi Solomon ben Isaac (1040–1105), lived in Troyes, in Champagne country in northern France. Though as a young man he studied in the great centers of rabbinic scholarship in Germany, Rashi's fame rests on the Bible and Talmud commentaries he wrote after his return to France. These commentaries provide a unique blend of ancient, traditional approaches to Torah (midrash, see later in this chapter) and a newer, literary method that came to be called *peshat* (contextual or "plain sense" understanding; again, see later). In the introduction to his very first comment of his Torah commentary, Rashi tackles (among other issues) the question of "What is Torah?":

> Said R. Isaac:[1] He ought to have begun the Torah [with the words,] *This month shall be for you* [*the beginning of the months*] (Exodus 12:2), for that passage contains the first commandment that Israel was commanded. And what is the reason that he began with [the narrative of] creation? On account of [the idea expressed in Psalms,] *The strength of His deeds he has declared to his people, to give to them the inheritance of the nations* (Psalm 111:6). For should the nations of the world say to Israel, "You are bandits, for you have conquered the lands of the seven [Canaanite] nations," [Israel] could say back to them, "The whole world belongs to the Holy One, Blessed be God. God created it, and gave it to those for whom it was fit in his eyes. According to His will did He give it to them, and according to His will did He take it from them and give it to us."

This opening comment addresses the very essence of Torah.[2] Contrary to the Christian charge that Jews slavishly and carnally adhered to "the Law" and missed the "true" allegorical meaning of Scripture (that bespoke Christianity),[3] Rashi avers that the Torah is Divine Instruction that includes far more than law alone. Rashi claims that the Torah deliberately encompasses as well the sacred, instructive narrative of Genesis and the beginning of Exodus.[4] Thus, for Rashi as for the rabbis of classical antiquity, "Torah" is not only law but also narrative, poetry, prophecy, indeed, even archival list; it is pointedly *not* Christian *nomos* (law) but rabbinic *oraita* (instruction), all-purposeful, Divine teaching and instruction.

To gain an understanding of the Jewish conception of Scripture among Rashi and the other rabbinic exegetes of the northern French school, one needs to turn to a quintessential statement of rabbinic thought to which these medieval scholars were themselves heir: the Mishna famously states, "Moses received Torah from Sinai."[5] Here one must make clear that what is *not* being stated is that "Moses received *the* Torah (that is, the Pentateuch) at (the revelation of God to Israel) at Sinai"; such a statement would surely not have required confirmation by the Mishna! Rather, the statement indicates the essential rabbinic claim about Torah, namely, that alongside the Written Torah (the Pentateuch and, for that matter, the entire Hebrew Bible, Tanakh), God also revealed the Oral Torah, that is, all of the teachings that are typically understood by the rubric "Rabbinic Judaism." For Rashi and the northern French rabbinic exegetes whom this chapter will treat as the "School of Rashi," this belief about the Divine nature of both the Written Torah and the Oral Torah is the sine qua non of their entire "theology of Scripture" (were they to have considered having one).[6] For these French rabbis, as for their ancient forebears and contemporaries, the concept "Torah" could not only mean the Hebrew Scriptures but rather encompassed all of the midrashic teachings of the ancient Sages, both legal and moral, as well as the conventions of Rabbinic Judaism conveyed by the term *halakhah*, the practice of Jewish law. In a sense, a medieval midrash, Exodus Rabba (47:1), envisions this "theology of Torah" most comprehensively: "At the moment when the Holy One was revealed at Sinai to give Torah to Israel, He said it to Moses according to its order: Scripture, Mishna, Talmud and Aggadah, as it is said: *God spoke all these words* (Exodus 20:1): even that which a student asks a rabbi was already said by the Holy One to Moses at that moment [of revelation at Sinai]."

In the foregoing discussion, I have employed the term *midrash*, and it is high time that we arrive at an understanding of this concept. The Hebrew root of this word is *derash*; in biblical Hebrew, this root generally means "to seek" or "to demand" or "to inquire" (typical usages can be found in Genesis 25:22, Deuteronomy 4:29, Isaiah 55:6). In later biblical Hebrew, the root came to be used specifically for an act of searching out meaning in the Torah book: "For Ezra had dedicated himself to study the Teaching of the LORD [literally "to search in the Torah of YHWH"] so as to observe it, and to teach laws and rules to Israel" (Ezra 7:10). This usage was particularly significant in rabbinic thought and became the bedrock of rabbinic method for finding significance in Torah: "midrash," as it was employed in any of the many ancient rabbinic texts, came to be understood as "that which is (rabbinically) sought in Scripture." Thus conceived, all of ancient rabbinic literature (Mishna, Tosefta, Talmud, and the many collections of midrashim), whether legal or nonlegal in nature, encompasses books of midrash.

A term that has gained currency in describing the classical rabbinic (i.e., "midrashic") point of view regarding Scripture is "omnisignificance," a term coined by James Kugel. Kugel defined this as

> the basic assumption underlying all of rabbinic exegesis that the slightest details of the biblical text have a meaning that is both comprehensible and significant. Nothing in the Bible . . . ought to be explained as the product of chance, or, for that matter, as an emphatic or rhetorical form, or anything similar, nor ought its reasons to be assigned to the realm of Divine unknowables. Every detail is put there to teach something new and important, and it is capable of being discovered by careful analysis.[7]

Kugel accurately describes midrashic discourse as including "a thoroughgoing lack of interest in any deducible principle of composition in the Bible, or in explaining peculiarities of expression stylistically."[8] As we shall see, it is precisely the development away from omnisignificant conception of Scripture and toward a contextual, essentially literary conception that is the subject of this chapter.

Omnisignificant, midrashic understanding of Scripture's essence changed dramatically in Europe during the so-called Renaissance of the 12th century (a period that encompasses much of the 11th and 13th centuries, as well).[9] I am referring to the development of *peshat*, either "plain sense" or "contextual" exegesis.[10] To be sure, this development found its roots in the changed patterns of interpretations that took place in the Karaite and (later) Rabbanite reactions to the rise of Islam and the concomitant cultural supremacy of the Koran and the Arabic language—which themselves eventually led to the biblical exegesis of Abraham Ibn Ezra.[11] These subjects are, alas, outside the bounds of this chapter. For our purposes, the rise of contextual exegesis in northern France ought to be seen against the background both of the 12th-century Renaissance (in Christian Europe) and, ultimately, of the world of Judeo-Islamic scholarship.[12] Briefly put, the scholars who championed this type of exegesis substituted the approach of those still committed to "omnisignificant exegesis" with other models rooted in such rabbinic expressions as *ain mikra yotzei midey peshuto* (Scripture does not escape the clutches of its context) or *dibra Torah kilshon bnai adam* (Torah has spoken according the language of humankind).[13] These latter sentiments, although also found in ancient rabbinic sources, were not much employed in generations immediately after the rabbinic period and were, in any case, never developed as overarching methodologies of interpretation.

Granted that medieval *peshat* or contextual exegesis is not midrashic, then, what exactly is it? After all, I have just claimed that it is "rooted in (ancient) rabbinic expressions," so how may we define it as the essentially new, non-midrashic type of reading it came to embody? We ought to admit one problem from the outset: the medieval exegetes who developed the concept of *peshat* never defined either their terminology or their methodology, and modern scholars have struggled to achieve consensus about just such a definition.[14] Perhaps the greatest advance in our understanding of medieval *peshat* exegesis was authored by the late Israeli scholar Sarah Kamin. In writing her magnum opus about the most influential of the medieval exegetes, Rashi, Kamin defined *peshat* in the following, concise formulation: *Peshat* is

> an explanation (of a biblical passage) according to its language; its syntactic structure; its (immediate) literary context; its literary type, within a dynamic interaction among all of these components. Put differently, an interpretation according to *peshat* is an interpretation that considers all of the linguistic foundations in its literary composition, and assigns to each of them an understanding within a complete reading.[15]

To be sure, we should keep in mind that this is a modern assessment, however insightful; again, none of the medieval exegetes ever seemed to feel the need to offer such a precise definition of either the term *peshat* or of the method that came to be associated with it. Moreover, we should remember as well that each of the exegetes worked within the framework of his own, unique method and that there was really no true consistency among their related-but-varied understandings of Torah according to *peshat*.

For northern French exegetes, the moment when the concept of "Torah" begins to shift from an exclusively omnisignificant understanding to one that enabled the development of contextual exegesis may be found in the much-celebrated methodological statement in Rashi's comment on Genesis 3:8: "I have come for no other purpose than [to explain] the plain sense of Scripture and for the Aggadah that settles a matter of Scripture and its sense as *a word spoken according to its character* (Proverbs 25:11)."[16] Rashi expands on this theme in the introduction to his Song of Songs commentary, part of which I produce here:

> *One thing has God spoken; two have we heard* (after Psalms 62:12). One scriptural verse yields many meanings, and the end of the matter is that no scriptural verse ever escapes the hold of its sense. And even though the prophets spoke their words in allegory [*dugma*], one must reconcile the allegory according to its characteristics and its order, just as the verses of Scripture are ordered one after the other. I have seen for this book [Song of Songs] many homiletical midrashim, for some of which the entire book is arranged in one midrash, whereas others are scattered in many books of midrash, on individual verses. But these are not reconciled according to the language of Scripture or the order of the verses. I have intended to capture the sense of the scriptural verses, to reconcile their explanations according to the order. And as for the midrashim—the rabbis have fixed them, each midrash in its place.[17]

Rashi's methodological comments provide a starting point from which we may consider Rashi's concept of "Torah." For while the ever-expanding midrashic universe of discourse (a some thousand-year process begun in the ancient world and continuing into the Middle Ages) continued to provide new homiletical and moral interpretations of Scripture in what we might imagine as a widening, *horizontal* concentric circle, Rashi's introduction of *peshuto*/"plain meaning" opened up new vistas of interpretation in a *vertical* direction. What I mean by the distinction between "horizontal" and "vertical" modes of interpretation is that as long as rabbinic exegetes continued to parse Scripture's meaning according to midrashic norms, the meaning of Scripture simply grew larger and more expansive—but rooted in the same type of (mostly homiletical) interpretation: while there are distinctions to be made between the hermeneutics of ancient midrashim and early medieval midrashim, these are merely distinctions of degree, and they are by and large quite similar. However, by "leaping"—vertically—out of the midrashic frame of mind (or by "thinking outside the midrashic box," if you prefer), the *peshat* exegetes forged a completely new universe of contextual, literary (and occasionally historical) discourse. Indeed, within a generation, Rashi's distinction paved the way for a fully contextual exegesis (*peshat*) practiced by R. Yosef Kara, Rashbam, R. Eliezer of Beaugency, and others.

Whereas the midrash-generating rabbis of the ancient and early medieval world envisioned Torah as an omnisignificant message encompassing God's will as revealed through both Written and Oral Torah, what might be said of contextual-*peshat* exegetes who imagined a "plain meaning" level of Scripture that embodied no necessary or inherent relationship to rabbinic tradition? Would their conception of Scripture be in essence a medieval precursor to modern historical-critical and/or literary biblical scholarship, or would it develop some degree of religious sensibility? If the latter, to what degree would it be in conversation with ancient rabbinic imagination, and to what degree would it forge its own unique contribution to the panoply of conceptions of Scripture that have manifested themselves since antiquity and continued into modern times? Let us survey some of the most prominent *peshat* commentators in an effort to answer these key questions.

One European *peshat* exegete was R. Yosef Kara (c. late 11th century), who actually hailed from Provence and moved north to Champagne country to study with Rashi. Becoming part of Rashi's immediate circle, Kara was one of the principal architects of the new *peshat* exegesis. As we shall see, he envisioned what has been termed by the contemporary Israeli biblical scholar Uriel Simon a "religious significance of the *peshat*."[18] Kara is well aware of the distinction between midrashic and *peshat* exegesis and suggests that a reader can find religious meaning also in the latter. Consider for a moment Kara's interpretation of 1 Samuel 1:17. Kara's long comment is ultimately contextual in nature; the following excerpt is essentially a brief aside that is likely rooted in an oral response to a student who had suggested a midrashic interpretation of the passage:

> Know well, that when Scripture was written, it was written completely, with every explanation and need taken care of, so that future generations would not stumble in it. In its place, it lacks nothing. Moreover, one does not need to bring proofs from another place, and certainly not midrash,

for the Torah was *given completely and written completely* (Psalm 19:8), and lacks nothing. Whereas the midrash of the Sages is for the purpose of *glorifying Torah and enhancing it* (Isaiah 42:21). But anyone who doesn't know the context of Scripture [the method of *peshat*], and prefers to incline toward a midrashic explanation, is similar to one who is drowning in a river, and the depths of the waters are sweeping him away, and who grabs hold of any old thing that comes into his hand to save himself. Whereas had he paid attention to the word of the Lord, he would have investigated the true explanation of the matter and its context and would have fulfilled that which is written: *If you seek it as you seek silver, and search for it as one searches out treasure, then you will understand reverence for the* LORD *and find knowledge of God* (Proverbs 2:4–5).

Note that the last part of Kara's comment is a sermon in the service of *peshat* exegesis: the pronominal antecedent in the verses from Proverbs ("If you seek *it* . . . and search for *it*") is a general reference to biblical "wisdom," whereas in Kara's explanation it becomes a referent of the *peshat* method that he has been advocating. However, the clear implication is that contextual exegesis can yield religious knowledge ("reverence for the Lord and . . . knowledge of God") that is outside the bounds of Oral Torah and rabbinic interpretation. However, what type of religious knowledge might this be? Unfortunately, Kara does not make this explicit. For the present, let us at least suggest a possibility: perhaps, behind the oblique religious message that Kara advances is the ancient rabbinic value placed on "the study of Torah for its own sake" (*talmud torah lishama*). This principle, which I will abbreviate as "selfless Torah study," is highly prized in rabbinic literature;[19] for now, let us adduce the treatment of the principle in the brief rabbinic treatise generally entitled *Qinyan Torah*:[20]

> Rabbi Meir said: Anyone who engages in Torah study for its own sake merits many things. Not only that but the entire world is worthwhile [having been created] for that one alone. Such a one is called "[God's] beloved friend; one who loves the Omnipresent, who loves [God's] creatures; one who gladdens the Omnipresent, who gladdens [God's] creatures; one whom [selfless Torah study] clothes with humility and reverence; one whom [selfless Torah study] enables to be righteous, pious, upright, and faithful; one whom [selfless Torah study] keeps far from sin and brings close to merit."[21] Humankind is benefited by this one's counsel, insight, understanding, and strength, as it is said: *Counsel is mine and insight, I*

am understanding, Mine is strength (Proverbs 8:14). [Selfless Torah study] grants to such a one rulership, governance, and wisdom in judgment; revealed to this one are the secrets of Torah, and he becomes like a fountain that increases in power, like a river whose flowing does not cease. Such a one is modest, patient, and forgiving of insult. [Selfless Torah study] magnifies and exalts such a one beyond all deeds.

As it is presented in this powerful homily, "study of Torah for its own sake" is pointedly *not* study that leads, say, to the rulings of Jewish law or to the practice of Jewish liturgy or to the development of any religiously authoritative Jewish theological observation. It rather is something that stands on its own. And highly prized though it might have been in the study of Talmud—where a non-authoritative rabbinic legal argument might occupy the attention of the talmudic redactor for great lengths—it had never been articulated as a principle by those who developed midrashim that expounded biblical verses. Rabbis had, on the contrary, generally composed midrashim to articulate legal, moral, or theological insights that were, among other things, meant to guide Jewish communities in the practice of Jewish law or to instruct them about moral behavior or the nature of the one true God. In these senses, midrash was assuredly not "study of Torah for its own sake." However, one can make a pretty good argument that *peshat*, on the contrary, was exactly that: *peshat* commentaries do not purport, for example, to instruct about Jewish behavior, to justify the often untoward actions of biblical heroes, or to develop any type of systematic theology. *Peshat* exegesis is solely concerned with the explication of scriptural literature (the Bible's contents) and composition (what we might call its poetics). Most of the prominent exponents of *peshat* methodology do not even address the theological underpinnings of their project, as Kara appears to do on occasion; perhaps the principle was a given, understood intuitively and by mutual, unspoken agreement, or perhaps no need for a principled argument was ever felt. All that we know for certain is that none of its northern French practitioners wrote any tractates to justify the application of *peshat* methodology to biblical texts.[22]

Kara returns to the theme of knowing God through contextual explication of Scripture in his comment on Isaiah 5:8–10.[23]

> Incline your ear and surrender yourself to Scripture! For each and every Scriptural text that the Rabbis have expounded—may their souls dwell in goodness!—inasmuch as they told a midrash about it, they themselves

[also] said about it: "No Scriptural passage ever escapes the hold of its context" (BT Shabbat 63a). For we have no greater principle than contextual exegesis.

Therefore do I say that you have no greater principle in [the study of] Scripture than contextual exegesis. Thus did Solomon, King of Israel, say: *Incline your ear . . . to the words of the sages, apply your heart to my wisdom* (Proverbs 22:17). The explanation [of this verse] is: even though it is a commandment for you to "hear the words of the Sages," apply your heart to knowing me—according to the body of the word, "to know them" [i.e., the Sages] Scripture does not say; rather to know me [i.e., God, through Scripture]. Thus far have I explained them [biblical passages] according the Bible's style and its context.

Again, what interests us here is Kara's valuation of Scripture's status as "Torah," that is, a source of religious teaching in ways that are independent of the traditional rabbinic posture. While Kara does not articulate precisely what he might mean by the distinction between knowing God through the intervention of rabbinic midrash versus knowing God "directly," as it were, through Scripture, his latent theology seems to adumbrate the *sola scriptura* (by Scripture alone) arguments advocated by early, "proto-Protestant" Christian reformers (Waldensians, Wycliffites, and others), to wit, that study of Scripture alone (independent of the theological and liturgical traditions of the Western Church) was sufficient to lead the good Christian life.[24] While ostensibly a similar sentiment animated early Karaite Judaism as well (particularly in the 9th to 11th centuries), no rabbinic authority ever came close to the same type of argument.

The dedication to wholly contextual, *peshat* exegesis, irrespective of the challenges it might offer to traditional, midrashically based rabbinic Judaism, held true for certain northern French exegetes—even when they addressed biblical legal texts, the rabbinic halakhic (legal) interpretation for which is far from contextual. R. Samuel ben Meir (Rashbam) was a grandson of Rashi and one of his most distinguished disciples, and in the midst of the 12th-century Renaissance, he became one of the most prominent exponents of the contextual (*peshat*) method of biblical exegesis. Rashbam famously adjures midrashic interpretation in his own Torah commentary while steadfastly professing his loyalty to rabbinic interpretations as the necessary concomitant to ongoing Jewish living; thus, he drew a distinction between "reading" a text and observing the norms that rabbinic Judaism would posit were inherent in the text. While he never wrote a treatise detailing ideological underpinning for maintaining his position, he did articulate his basic premise in his introduction to the legal section of the Torah (at Exodus 21:1):

> Let knowers of wisdom know and understand that I have not come to explain halakhot, even though these are the essence of Torah, as I have explained in my Genesis commentary [e.g., at Genesis 1:1; 37:2]. For it is from the [apparent] superfluities of Scriptural language that aggadot and halakhot are derived. Some of these can be found in the commentary of our Rabbi Solomon, my mother's father [i.e., Rashi], may the memory of the righteous be for a blessing. But I have come to explain the contextual meaning of Scripture. And I will explain the laws and halakhot according to realia [literally "the way of the world"]. And [I will do this] even though the halakhot are the essence, as the Rabbis taught: "halakha uproots Scripture" (BT Sota 16a, with emendation).

Rashbam's statement raises more questions, perhaps, than it does offer answers.[25] On the one hand, Rashbam establishes that the rabbinic understanding of biblical law (*halakhot*) is the most essential aspect of Torah. This should not surprise us: Rashbam was one of the most respected rabbis of his generation and composed a commentary on the Babylonian Talmud that more than established his reputation as one of the greatest rabbinic scholars of all time.[26] He was well known as a rabbinic pietist,[27] and despite some medieval criticism that may have been directed against his total commitment to *peshat* methodology, no one ever doubted his standing as a rabbinic authority. Thus, let there be no thought that Rashbam thought that people should observe biblical law or that Jews could somehow choose between it and rabbinic halakha. However, that being the case, what value or meaning does Rashbam see in this purely theoretical law?

However frustrated one might be from Rashbam's failing to address this question directly ought not prevent us from assaying an opinion about a possible answer. Recently, I have been writing about the ways in which the 12th-century exegetes found in the Bible the very literary and structural devices that, in a later age, came to define what "literature" is.[28] My thesis has been that Jewish and Christian biblical exegetes working primarily in northern France during the 12th-century Renaissance essentially "invent" the notion of literature through their contextual (*peshat* or *ad litteram*) reading of biblical composition and their attention to what we would call its literary qualities. A corollary of this same point is to consider that the

12th-century exegetes invent "the reader" as we have come to understand the term. Before their time, Jews and Christians who considered the biblical text did so primarily as "religious truth seekers" (again, the root *derash*); they were determined to find in Scripture support for or evidence of their own (Jewish or Christian) religious views and practices. Following the advent of contextual exegesis, "readers" could consider dimensions of the meaning of biblical texts without necessary regard for religious underpinnings—this was a paradigm shift whose proportions we have yet to fully comprehend.[29] Thus, in Rashbam's introduction to the legal corpus of the Pentateuch, he was essentially advocating a place for an independent, grammatically based, and literarily intuitive reading whose theoretical value, he believed, had been established by the ancient rabbinic authority in the axiomatic talmudic ruling oft cited by his grandfather Rashi and others of his teachers: "no Scriptural passage ever escapes the hold of its context." It is true that Rashbam says even less about the possible religious value of this level of meaning than did his elder colleague R. Yosef Kara. However, in what Rashbam believed to be the sanctioning of *peshat* endorsed by the talmudic sages, we might see yet another self-validating appraisal of the Bible's own context as independent, sacred meaning.

Rashbam's willingness to engage in contextual exegesis that is at variance with rabbinic interpretation of legal passages in the Torah is as steadfast and constant as he proclaims here programmatically: he will interpret biblical law as just that—biblical law, not rabbinic halakhah. Whereas Rashi would, on occasion, deviate from accepted rabbinic interpretation of biblical law,[30] Rashbam does this all through his commentary, as any perusal of his interpretations of, for example, the entire Deuteronomic legal corpus demonstrates. One famous case involves Exodus 13:9. Talmudic tradition understands this passage as requiring Jews during their morning prayers to don a set of leather boxes (known as *tefillin*) filled with miniature parchment scrolls of selected Torah passages. Rashbam, however, does not understand these verses as referring to a ritual practice at all. Rather, he maintains that they present a figuration of "mindfulness" on an intellectual or spiritual level. (It is important to recall that Rashbam nonetheless fully accepted the authority of the Talmudic requirement to practice the *tefillin* ritual daily; the authority of the religious law for him is guaranteed by the law's presence in the Oral Torah and does not depend on the talmudic rabbis' attempt to anchor it exegetically in Exodus 13.9.) Again, unlike R. Yosef Kara, Rashbam does not articulate any ideational or religious orientation to his contextual interpretations; apparently, he relies on his repeated claim that rabbinic interpretation is the "essence" (Hebrew, *iqqar*) and bedrock of the Torah. However, it is not as clear that the absence of some Kara-like homily in the service of *peshat* necessarily means that he would consider *peshat* exegesis to be of no value whatsoever beyond intellectual exercise. What it does mean, however, at the minimum, is that Rashbam maintains what I termed the "vertical" addition of *peshat* interpretations as part of the concept of "Torah" alongside that of the "essence" that he considers midrashic rabbinic interpretations to convey. It is important to remember that, in Rashbam's eyes, even though *peshat* interpretations are apparently ideologically inferior to the *iqqar*, "essential" level of rabbinic midrash, they are nonetheless a systemic part of what is now a fully two-tiered text. Thus, for Rashbam, Torah is *multivalent* in that (a) it conveys an essential, midrashic meaning that finds its roots in God's revelation of Oral Torah at Sinai (and as passed on by rabbinic tradition) alongside that of Written Torah; and (b) it conveys a contextual, *peshat* meaning—never losing it, ever (again, "Scripture never escapes the hold of its context")—that is rooted in the ability of individual, attentive intellects to bring this to light.

Thus, while the traditional rabbinic adage "*shivim panim la-Torah*"— "the Torah conveys an infinite number of possible interpretations"—still holds, now this no longer means only midrash but *peshat* interpretations as well. Moreover, Rashbam considers that one ought not to speak of "the" *peshat* but rather many *peshatot*, that is, contextual interpretations. He famously declares this to be so in his comment on Genesis 37:2:

> Lovers of reason should become enlightened and understand that, as our Rabbis tell us, no Scriptural verse ever loses its contextual [*peshat*] meaning. Although it is also true that the main aim of the Torah is to teach us aggadot, halakhot, and laws, which are derived by hint or by the use in Scriptural verses of superfluous words or by means of the thirty-two rules of Rabbi Eliezer ben Rabbi Yosi the Galilean or the thirteen rules of Rabbi Ishmael. In their piety the early scholars devoted all their time to the midrashic explanations, which contain, indeed, the main teachings of the Torah. But, as a result, they became unfamiliar with the deeper aspects of the text's contextual meaning. . . . Our Master, Rabbi Solomon, my mother's father [Rashi], who illumined the eyes of all those in exile, and who wrote commentaries on the Torah, Prophets, and the Writings, also set himself the task of elucidating the contextual meaning of Scripture. And I, Samuel, son of his son-in-law Meir, may the memory of the righteous be for a blessing, argued it out with him [Rashi, i.e., privately] and in his presence

[in the study hall]. He admitted to me that if he had the time, he would have written new commentaries in accordance with the fresh interpretations of the contextual meaning [*peshatot*] that are innovated day by day.

Now, it is of course possible or even likely that when Rashbam employs the plural term *peshatot* in this comment he is thinking of many contextual interpretations, each on a different verse, and in their totality, these represent the "interpretations . . . that are innovated day by day." At the same time, one gets a sense of the type of study-hall discourse as described by Rashbam here—with free-flowing exchanges, heated rhetoric, changing opinions—and one cannot ignore the possibility that what he has in mind is as much the many possible contextual interpretations of each verse —analogous to the multilevel midrashic interpretations provided through the ubiquitous midrashic convention *davar aher . . . davar aher*, "an additional interpretation . . . an additional interpretation." In that case, then, the concentric circle of *peshat* further widens to include even the always contemporary rhetorical debates as to what constitutes Torah and its now even more fluid interpretation ("the fresh interpretations of the contextual meaning—*peshatot*—that are innovated day by day").

Even the very authorship of Scripture comes under scrutiny in the *peshat* school. Whereas the rabbis of classical antiquity had addressed the subject of the authorship of the various biblical books and had decided on the resolution of the question, the rabbinic exegetes of 12th-century northern France felt no compunction about addressing the question anew—and providing whatever answers they found to meet the evidence. First, let us review the position of the Babylonian Talmud (Bava Batra 14b–15a):

> Who wrote them [i.e., the books of the Bible]? Moses wrote his book and the portion of Balaam and Job; Joshua wrote his book and eight verses in the Torah; Samuel wrote his book and Judges and Ruth; David wrote the Book of Psalms through the agency of eighteen elders. . . . Jeremiah wrote his book and the Book of Kings and Lamentations; [King] Hezekiah and his council wrote Isaiah, Proverbs, Song of Songs, and Koheleth; the Men of the Great Assembly[31] wrote Ezekiel and the Twelve ["Minor" Prophets], Daniel and the Book of Esther; Ezra wrote his book and the genealogies in Chronicles until his (own time).

We will not analyze this statement to any degree other than to contrast some of its conclusions with the contradictory commentary of several northern French rabbinic exegetes. Let us begin with a portion of R. Yosef Kara's comment on 1 Samuel 9:9. This biblical verse calls attention to the distance in time between its author and the events being narrated: "Earlier in Israel, when a man went to inquire of God, he would say, 'Let's go to the seer,' for what today we call a prophet used to be called a seer." Reading this verse, Kara thought it utterly impossible to deduce that Samuel could have written it:

> Thus you learn that when this book was written, people had already resumed calling a seer a "prophet," from which it follows that this book was not written during the days of Samuel. For when you review all of Scriptures, you do not find that a prophet was called a "seer" in any place except here, where [Saul] says: *where is the house of the seer?* (1 Samuel 9:18). Thus, you have learned that it was the generation of Samuel that is called *formerly in Israel* (1 Samuel 9:9), or the generation immediately afterward, and it is regarding that generation that Scripture says for the prophet of today [was formerly called a seer]. Our Rabbis, whose memory is a blessing, said that Samuel wrote his own book (BT Bava Batra 14b); May the One who gives light to the earth turn darkness into light and the crooked into the straight!³²

Kara's humorous "prayer" aside, a number of serious issues are at stake here: "Who wrote the Bible?" is indeed one of them. But perhaps no less significant is the challenge issued against the authority of the Sages of the Talmud, whose conclusions could be and were subjected to the rigors of *peshat* analysis. However, despite this comment's invective tone, nowhere in it does Kara call into question the sanctity of the biblical text or the God who oversees the conduct of the world. This is an important point: from the vantage of the literary analysis to which he subjected the text, Kara could consider the human authorship of Scripture—even a different human authorship than that sanctioned by the authority of the ancient rabbinic tradition—and still consider it "sacred Scripture."

In considering the question "Who wrote the Bible?" R. Eliezer of Beaugency was one of several northern French rabbinic exegetes who considered the role of the redactor in the composition of the biblical text. Not much biographical data is known about Eliezer, though he was most likely a disciple of Rashbam and was active in the mid-12th century.³³ A prominent example of his awareness of the redaction of biblical books is his commentary on Ezekiel 1:1–4. Observing that verses 2–3, cast as a third-person narration, interrupt the flow between the first-person narration that begins in verse 1 and continues with verse 4 and following, Eliezer comments,

> And I saw visions of God. . . . I looked, and lo, a stormy wind . . . : Ezekiel's words did not continue from the beginning, and even his name he did not make explicit, since the context of the book will make it clear below.[34] . . . And, relying on this, he allowed himself to abbreviate. . . . But the redactor who wrote all of his words together added to what [Ezekiel] had left unclear and abbreviated, in these two verses.

This comment attributes two biblical verses to a *sofer*, which I have translated as "redactor" since Eliezer claims that this person "wrote all of Ezekiel's words together." On the surface, this is less radical than it might otherwise seem; after all, the Babylonian Talmud had attributed the authorship of the book not to the prophet Ezekiel himself but rather to the "Men of the Great Assembly." However, just beneath the surface is the striking observation that God had not revealed God's own self to this "redactor" (nor to "those Men"); the "redactor" was not a prophet! At least, none of the medieval exegetes who refer to *sofrim, sadranim, kotevim, ba'alei ha-sefer*, and so on (some of the preferred medieval designations for "redactors")[35] ever refer to them as possessing prophetic status. The implication ought to be clear: R. Eliezer and other exegetes attributed portions of the biblical text to people with whom God did not "speak"—and none of these exegetes considered that the sanctity of the biblical text was in any way diminished by this consideration. Thus, to at least a certain degree and in certain particular circumstances, the northern French rabbinic exegetes included in their "conception of Torah" texts that were manifestly composed by human beings and not God.

Lest one think that observations such as these are possible with prophetic texts but not Torah itself, I conclude through consideration of one final text. This is part of Rashbam's comment on the opening verse of the Torah, Genesis 1:1. You may recall that I began this study with a citation of Rashi's comment on the Torah's first verse: *lo hayyah tzarikh le-hathil et ha-Torah*, which though it is usually translated as "the Torah only needed to have begun," I instead deliberately translated using a transitive verb (as had Rashi), "He ought to have begun the Torah." Rashi had thus considered the process of writing with an active verb and a singular subject (though it must be admitted that the subject of Rashi's imagination, being left unstated, could as easily refer to a Divine Author as it could to a human author, and—for Rashi—it probably in some sense did refer to God). The same is pointedly not true with regard to his grandson Rashbam's gloss, the implications of which I would like to closely examine. Rashbam writes as follows:

> The following is the true contextual meaning of the passage, which follows the Scriptural pattern of regularly anticipating and explaining some matter which, though unnecessary to the immediate context, serves the purpose of elucidating some matter to be mentioned further on, in another passage.... Moreover, this entire section, concerning the six days of creation—Moses wrote it for anticipatory purposes to make explicit to you (the reader) what God said when he gave the Torah (Exodus 20:8–11): *Remember the Sabbath day and keep it holy . . . for in six days did YHWH make heaven and earth and sea, and all that is in them, and he rested on the seventh day.* For this reason it is written (Gen. 1:31), *there was evening and there was morning, the sixth day*, a reference to that same sixth day, the end of the creation process, of which God spoke when he gave the Torah. That is why Moses related to Israel this entire chapter about creation—in order to inform them that what God said was true. In other words, Moses said, "Do you think that this world has forever existed in the way that you now see it, filled with all good things? That is not the case. Rather, *bereshit bara elohim*—that is, at the beginning of the creation of the heaven and the earth, when the uppermost heavens and the earth had already been created for some undetermined length of time—then, the earth which already existed, was unformed and void—that is, there was nothing in it."

I want to call your attention to Rashbam's observation of the literary device of prolepsis,[36] or literary anticipation (foreshadowing) at play here in the opening narrative of the Bible: "Moreover, this entire section, concerning the six days of creation—Moses wrote it for anticipatory purposes to make explicit to you . . ." More literally rendered, Rashbam writes that "Moses placed this section early" or "Moses moved this section forward." In other words, in contradistinction to the ancient midrash (rooted in Proverbs 8:22), alluded to by Rashi, that God created Torah "at the beginning of His way"—even before God had created the world—Rashbam considers Moses to be the author of the Torah: it is Moses who chooses to include the Creation narrative at the beginning of the Torah, so that the reader will not "be astonished" (*sheh-lo titmah*) when reading the Sinai narrative (specifically, Exodus 20:8–11) that makes passing reference to God's creation of the world. Brilliantly, Rashbam imagines even the circumstances that would lead Moses, as author/redactor of God's Written Torah, to decide to include the Creation narrative at the beginning of the Torah: Moses observes, as it were, the astonished Israelites at the foot of Mount Sinai who are hearing for the first time that the God who took them out of Egypt is the same God who created the world! This God, while communicating in oral, Divine speech to the entire nation on Mount Sinai, surprises the Israelites in the course of commanding them to remember the Sabbath, in commemoration of God's own rest following the work of creation. Moses, in consideration of the Israelites' surprise and in anticipation of that of the future reader, decides to include the Creation narrative we call Genesis 1. The point is that, for Rashbam, it is Moses who "authors" the written text of Torah, or at least "arranges" the structure of the Torah's contents—and one can be certain that Rashbam would feel that this does not detract from the sanctity of the Torah one iota. God communicates to Moses and to the nation—and Moses faithfully represents the Divine communication in written discourse. This is a far cry from the conception of Torah in the ancient rabbinic midrash invoked by Rashi—and even farther from the one, cited by Nahmanides, that imagines the "original Torah" as a mystical "black fire on white fire."[37] For Rashbam, Written Torah is a human document, written in historical circumstances, albeit faithfully composed in response to Divine communication and command.

This chapter is perforce an introductory statement; neither is it comprehensive in terms of the totality of northern French exegesis, nor does it engage in examination of the compelling polemic that exists between it and Judeo-Islamic exegesis as represented by the arc of interpretative history spanning from Saadia Gaon to Abraham Ibn Ezra. However, even the sources we have managed to review have given us an idea both of the radical departure from old forms that the movement from *derash* to *peshat* represented, as well as the range of ideas pertaining to the 12th-century northern French school's "conception of Scripture."

NOTES

1. This is not Rashi's own father. Rather, Rashi appears to be citing a version of the Tanhuma midrash to which he had access. All translations of biblical and rabbinic texts in this article are my own.

2. I have treated this comment with a different agenda in an earlier article:

Robert A. Harris, "Rashi's Introductions to His Biblical Commentaries," in *Shai Le-Sara Japhet: Studies in the Bible, Its Exegesis and Its Language*, ed. Moshe Bar-Asher et al. (Jerusalem: Bialik Institute, 2007).

3. I.e., the idea that the "Old Testament" pointed to the Christian messiah. See Anna Sapir Abulafia, "Jewish Carnality in Twelfth-Century Renaissance Thought," in *Christianity and Judaism*, ed. Diana Wood (Oxford, UK: Blackwell, 1992), 59–75.

4. See Rashi's second comment on Gen. 22:2: Jerusalem is called "Moriah" because "from there did Instruction go forth to Israel." See also Targum Ps.-Jonathan to Isaiah 2:3.

5. Mishna Avot 1:1.

6. See Steven Fraade's chapter 3 in this volume, on Oral Torah.

7. James L. Kugel, *The Idea of Biblical Poetry: Parallelism and Its History* (New Haven: Yale University Press, 1981), 103–4. See also Yaakov Elman, "The Rebirth of Omnisignificant Biblical Exegesis in the Nineteenth and Twentieth Centuries," *Jewish Studies, an Internet Journal* 2 (2003): 199n. 1, http://www.biu.ac.il/JS/JSIJ/2-2003/Elman.pdf.

8. Kugel, *Idea of Biblical Poetry*, 105.

9. The classic study is still that of Charles H. Haskins, *The Renaissance of the Twelfth Century* (Cambridge: Harvard University Press, 1927); see also Robert L. Benson and Giles Constable with Carole D. Lanham, eds., *Renaissance and Renewal in the Twelfth Century* (Toronto: University of Toronto Press, in association with the Medieval Academy of America, 1991), in particular, Nikolaus M. Häring's essay "Commentary and Hermeneutics," 173–200; Thomas J. Heffernan and Thomas E. Burman, *Scripture and Pluralism: Reading the Bible in the Religiously Plural Worlds of the Middle Ages and Renaissance* (Leiden, Netherlands: Brill, 2005), in particular, Frans van Liere's essay titled "Andrew of St. Victor, Jerome, and the Jews: Biblical Scholarship in the Twelfth-Century Renaissance," 59–75; Brian Stock, *The Implications of Literacy: Written Language and Models of Interpretation in the 11th and 12th Centuries* (Princeton: Princeton University Press, 1983).

10. Robert A. Harris, *Discerning Parallelism: A Study in Northern French Medieval Jewish Biblical Exegesis* (Providence, RI: Brown Judaic Studies, 2004), 15–34.

11. For the development of Karaite biblical exegesis against the backdrop of Muslim intellectual and literary expression, see Meira Polliack's chapter 6 in this volume and references there, as well as Daniel Frank, "Karaite Exegesis," in *Hebrew Bible/Old Testament: The History of Its Interpretation*, vol. 1, *From the Beginnings to the Middle Ages (until 1300)*, part 2, *The Middle Ages*, ed. Magne Saebo (Göttingen, Germany: Vandenhoeck & Ruprecht, 2000).

12. See Avraham Grossman, "The School of Literal Exegesis in Northern France," in Saebo, *Hebrew Bible/Old Testament*, vol. 1, part 2, esp. 327–31.

13. On the former statement, see Sarah Kamin, *Rashi's Exegetical Categorization in Respect to the Distinction between Peshat and Derash* (Jerusalem: Magnes,

1986) [in Hebrew], esp. the first two chapters; David Weiss Halivni, *Peshat and Derash: Plain and Applied Meaning in Rabbinic Exegesis* (New York: Oxford University Press, 1991). On the latter, see Abraham Joshua Heschel, *Theology of Ancient Judaism* (London: Soncino, 1965) [in Hebrew], now translated as *Heavenly Torah as Refracted through the Generations*, trans. and ed. Gordon Tucker (New York: Continuum, 2005).

14. For a variety of approaches and translations by scholars writing in English, see Raphael Loewe, "The 'Plain' Meaning of Scripture in Early Jewish Exegesis," in *Papers of the Institute of Jewish Studies London*, vol. 1, ed. J. G. Weiss (Jerusalem: Magnes, 1964); Sara Japhet, "The Tension between Rabbinic Legal Midrash and the 'Plain Meaning' (Peshat) of the Biblical Text—an Unresolved Problem? In the Wake of Rashbam's Commentary on the Pentateuch," in *Sefer Moshe: The Moshe Weinfeld Jubilee Volume*, ed. Chaim Cohen et al., 403–25 (Winona Lake, IN: Eisenbrauns, 2004).

15. This is my translation of Kamin, *Rashi's Exegetical Categorization*, 14. Kamin's contribution has been brilliantly analyzed in a recent Hebrew article by Mordechai Z. Cohen, "Reflections on the Conception of *Peshuto Shel Miqra* at the Beginning of the Twenty-First Century," in *"To Settle the Plain Meaning of the Verse": Studies in Biblical Exegesis*, ed. Sara Japhet and Eran Viezel, 5–58 (Jerusalem: Bialik Institute; Mandel Institute of Jewish Studies of Hebrew University, 2011).

16. The translation of Rashi's comment includes my own conjectural emendation of one letter in the standard editions.

17. Like the comment by Rashi discussed previously, I have treated this introduction at greater length in Harris, "Rashi's Introductions."

18. Uriel Simon, "The Religious Significance of the Peshat," *Tradition* 23:2 (1988): 41–63.

19. For a brief presentation of rabbinic sources, see Hayyim Nahman Bialik and Yehoshua Hana Rawnitzki, *The Book of Legends = Sefer Ha-Aggadah: Legends from the Talmud and Midrash*, trans. and ed. William G. Braude (New York: Schocken Books, 1992), 414.

20. In the traditional Jewish prayer book, this is generally printed as "Avot, Chapter 6." However, it is not actually part of that Mishnaic tractate but, as contemporary rabbinic scholarship has demonstrated, replicates material found in several post-talmudic, midrashic collections.

21. I.e., the one who "studies Torah for its own sake" is called all of these things.

22. In roughly contemporary Christian circles, for example, a figure such as Hugh of St. Victor composed two treatises on the role of literal exegesis within the structure of Christian religious life. One of these was his *De scripturis et scriptoribus sacris*, on the study of sacred Scripture, and the other was the *Didascalicon*, "on the study of reading." For a translation of these two important works, see now Franklin T. Harkins and Frans van Liere, *Interpretations of Scripture: Theory*, Victorine Texts in Translation 3 (Turnhout, Belgium: Brepols, 2012). For Victorine biblical

scholarship, see Gilbert Dahan, "Genres, Forms and Various Methods in Christian Exegesis of the Middle Ages," in Saebo, *Hebrew Bible/Old Testament*, vol. 1, part 2, 196–236; Rainer Berndt, "The School of St. Victor in Paris," in ibid., 467–95.

23. I have treated this text in Robert A. Harris, "Structure and Composition in Isaiah 1–12: A Twelfth-Century Northern French Rabbinic Perspective," in *"As Those Who Are Taught": The Interpretation of Isaiah from the LXX to the SBL*, ed. Claire Mathews McGinnis and Patricia K. Tull (Atlanta: Society of Biblical Literature, 2006).

24. See Ian Christopher Levy, "Holy Scripture and the Quest for Authority among Three Late Medieval Masters," *Journal of Ecclesiastical History* 61:1 (2010): 40–68.

25. These questions and others have recently been raised in Sara Japhet, "Tension."

26. Most of this commentary did not survive the Middle Ages; only his comments on parts of two treatises are extant.

27. Famously reported by the 13th-century halakhist R. Mordecai b. Hillel Ashkenazi; see Harris, *Discerning Parallelism*, 25, n. 30.

28. See my articles, "Twelfth-Century Biblical Exegetes and the Invention of Literature," *Commentaria* 2 (2009): 311–29, and "The Reception of Ezekiel among Twelfth-Century Northern French Rabbinic Exegetes," in *After Ezekiel: Essays on the Reception of a Difficult Prophet*, ed. Andrew Mein and Paul M. Joyce (New York: T&T Clark, 2011).

29. Among other ramifications, it ultimately led to the scholarly method of critical inquiry, a crucial component of the university culture that consequently developed throughout Europe.

30. See, e.g., Rashi's interpretation of Exodus 23:2.

31. The "Men of the Great Assembly" was a legendary group of 120 postbiblical Jewish sages who were thought to bridge the gap between the last prophets and the earliest rabbis.

32. See Eran Viezel, "The Formation of Some Biblical Books, According to Rashi," *Journal of Theological Studies* 61:1 (2010): 29–31 and the scholarly discussion cited there, 31, n. 29.

33. Again, see Harris, *Discerning Parallelism*, 28–30.

34. See Ezekiel 24:24: "Thus shall Ezekiel be to you a sign; according to all that he has done you shall do. When this comes, then you will know that I am the Lord GOD."

35. Respectively, these Hebrew terms may be translated literally as "scribes," "arrangers," "writers," and "masters of the book." All of these terms, and others, were employed by medieval exegetes to describe the actions of those anonymous writers and compilers who were responsible for the biblical books as these came to be passed on. The northern French exegetes were quite articulate in addressing the role of the redactor, and there are far more examples of this than we can consider

in this chapter; see my article "Awareness of Biblical Redaction among Rabbinic Exegetes of Northern France," *Shnaton: An Annual for Biblical and Ancient Near Eastern Studies* 13 (2000): 289–310 [in Hebrew]; also Richard C. Steiner, "A Jewish Theory of Biblical Redaction from Byzantium: Its Rabbinic Roots, Its Diffusion and Its Encounter with the Muslim Doctrine of Falsification," *Jewish Studies, an Internet Journal* 2 (2003): 123–67; Aharon Mondschein, "Additional Comments on Hasadran and Hamesader," *Leshonenu* 67:3–4 (2005): 331–46 [in Hebrew]; and again, Viezel, "Formation of Some Biblical Books."

36. Rashbam's discovery of this has been well documented by contemporary scholarship. For a summary and description, see Martin I. Lockshin, *Rabbi Samuel Ben Meir's Commentary on Genesis: An Annotated Translation* (Lewiston, NY: Edwin Mellen, 1989), appendix 1, 400–421; and Sarah Kamin, "Rashbam's Conception of the Creation in the Light of the Intellectual Currents of His Time," *Scripta Hierosolymitana* 31 (1986): 91–132.

37. See Tanhuma Bereshit 1, and Nahmanides's introduction to his Torah commentary.

Chapter 8

Concepts of Scripture in Maimonides

James A. Diamond

There is virtually no facet of present-day Judaism that does not bear the imprint of the formidable intellectual legacy of Moses ben Maimon (1138–1204), whether it be in Jewish law (*halakha*), rabbinics, theology, philosophy, or biblical interpretation. Even the mystical tradition's (*kabbala*) inventive re-readings of Scripture can be seen as a negative reaction to his overpowering rationalist approach. He was a first in many respects. No fundamental tenets of Judaism to which Jews must subscribe existed prior to his introduction of thirteen articles of faith, what have since been generally assented to as the Jewish creed. He pioneered the first code of Jewish law (*Mishneh Torah*), organizing and systematizing what had previously been a vast rabbinic morass that only the most skilled Talmudist could possibly navigate. After assimilating much of the philosophical/scientific tradition of his day, as transmitted through Islamic sources, he authored the single most important and influential reconciliation between the Torah, Judaism's foundational document, and reasoned demonstrated truths with which it apparently conflicted. That treatise, titled the *Guide of the Perplexed*, continues to vex, challenge, inspire, provoke, and stimulate any serious discussion or thought since, addressing apparent dichotomies between religious texts, faith, and science. All of this he accomplished while leading his Jewish community in old Cairo and practicing medicine, acquiring an outstanding reputation as a physician in no less than Saladin's court.

The intellectual enterprise of reconciling reason and faith, or what has been referred to as Athens and Jerusalem, was not unique to Maimonides, who had his counterparts in Christianity and Islam as well. The names he was known by alternatively to the three traditions—Maimonides, Rambam, Musa ibn Maymun—attest also to the influence he had on all them, thus affording him a seminal place in the history of religious thought in general. A lengthy and complex tradition of biblical interpretation within Judaism preceded Maimonides, but it was primarily applied to law, ethics, and narrative gaps and anomalies in the Hebrew Bible. Since that biblical text on its face challenges virtually everything Maimonides held to be demonstrably true of the world and God, developing a fresh approach to it, devising sophisticated reading strategies, and establishing a new dictionary of biblical terms that could accommodate the "truth" were the centerpieces of his undertaking. In this sense, he radically advanced the history of biblical interpretation. Whether one opposed or agreed with Maimonides, the Hebrew Bible could never be read in the same way again.[1]

In the quest for human perfection which, for Maimonides, consists of whatever is attainable of the knowledge of the divine, Scripture is the textual bridge between God, the objective zenith of all knowledge, and His knowing subjects. This textual bridge, however, is littered with anthropomorphic descriptions of God that threaten to lead these subjects astray. Maimonides's characterization of scriptural language is most aptly captured by his adoption of a rabbinic hermeneutical maxim, whose application is subject to earlier rabbinic controversy,[2] that "the Torah speaks in the language of human beings" (*dibrah torah kelashon bnei adam*). What this implies for him is that there is a stark dichotomy between the Torah's true, sublime, abstract, and universal ideas and the deceptively mundane, crude, and parochial means by which it communicates them. Maimonides transformed what for the rabbis had been an exegetically conservative approach that constrained rabbinic interpretive latitude[3] with respect to biblical language into one that nurtures interpretive expansiveness to liberate esoteric truth from its mundane articulation.

Paradoxically, Scripture's graphic portrayal of divine activity and being relate to human conceptions of perfection (language of human beings) while at the same time constructing an anthropomorphic edifice of unmitigated imperfection—"everything that the multitude consider a perfection is predicated of Him, even if it is only a perfection in relation to ourselves—for in relation to Him, may he be exalted, all things that we consider perfections are the very extreme of deficiency" (GP, I:26, p. 56).[4] To cite but one example, Scripture applies motion to God, since lack of it in a human context is considered a disability and to deny God this function would upset the notion of divine perfection as understood by those who are philosophically unseasoned. However, to take Scripture at its word on this or any other physical capacity is to corrupt the notion of an incorporeal unified Being that is the Maimonidean God. That Maimonidean deity allows for no commonality whatsoever with existence as human beings know and experience it. Therefore the Jew's encounter with his or her sacred foundational text is fraught with an irresolvable tension between, on the one hand, discarding the text and extracting the philosophically pure notion masked by it and, on the other, preserving its original Sinaitic form intact. After all, Maimonides endorses what he interprets to be a rabbinic dictum that bifurcates scriptural parables between an internal layer of incalculable value and an external that "is worth nothing" (GP, Intro., p. 11). At the same time, he also mandates a dogmatic belief in the authenticity of the Torah that remains forever unalterable. This he posits as a fundamental principle of Judaism, the denial of which is tantamount to resignation of a Jew's membership in the Jewish nation.[5]

Medieval theologians and philosophers conducted their investigations and discourse in the shadow of a world largely constructed by a now outdated physics and astronomy that remained regnant science since Aristotle, its founding father. The question then arises as to the continuing relevance of Maimonides's interpretive project in his *Guide of the Perplexed*. If all that project amounts to is providing the tools for excavating this antiquated Aristotelian science and ancient cosmology from beneath Scripture's anthropomorphic surface, of what value is it to the contemporary reader of Scripture? However, the two questions Maimonides took great pains to answer continue to vex modern Jewish readers of the Bible. The first is the hermeneutical inquiry into the precise nature of the biblical text and its peculiar language, and the second is the existential quandary of how to remain loyal to both intellect and tradition without resorting to an either/or choice of renouncing one in favor of the other.[6] The hermeneutical agenda he set for a Jewish approach to reading Scripture has withstood the mounting scientific revolutions since his time, remaining as urgent and demanding as it ever was.[7] What stimulated Maimonides's twelfth-century disciple R. Joseph, the private addressee of the *Guide*, whose longing to *find out acceptable words* (Eccles. 12:10, p. 4) drove their master-student relationship, is as stimulating to twenty-first-century students of the Bible. The original biblical *acceptable words* discovered by Solomon, the traditional author of Ecclesiastes, are the exposition of parables (*meshalim*) of the previous verse (12:9), which he subjected to close scrutiny (*'izzen ve-hiqer*) in order to teach the people knowledge (*limmed da'at et ha-am*). Joseph's own striving for *acceptable words* draws him into the camp of that rare breed of person whom Maimonides, in the introduction to his thirteen principles of faith, identifies (with this very citation) as mimicking a Solomonic methodology. Such persons distinguish themselves from their literalist compatriots by an appreciation for parables and riddles, the preferred literary genre of the biblical and rabbinic traditions. They acknowledge that "all men of wisdom speak of the ultimate in lofty matters only by way of riddle and parable [*hiddah u-mashal*]."[8]

Depending on the audience, scriptural language either simplifies or complicates. For those who are averse to the rigors of rational thinking, the moral, social, and political messages of scriptural language provide comfort, while for the philosophically inclined, reading the Bible becomes an intricate, angst-ridden process of deciphering and unraveling.

Though contemporary scholarship tends to alienate Maimonides the philosopher from Maimonides the halakhist (rabbinic law expert), he remains consistent on the centrality he assigns to the enterprise of reading Scripture for Jewish faith. The *Mishneh Torah*, his comprehensive legal code, opens peculiarly for a work that purports to be a purely legal abridgment encompassing all of Talmudic law. It commences with a book titled *Book of Knowledge*, whose first subsection, the *Laws Concerning the Basic Principles of the Torah*, opens by identifying the very first commandments to first firmly establish in one's mind the existence of God, and then the unity of that God. The greater part of this chapter is concerned with the subtle art of reading Scripture, presenting a virtual digest of all the problematic terms descriptive of God that are dealt with in the *Guide*'s lexicography of biblical terms. All of them, whether they indicate features of a divine physiognomy, emotions, or attributes, are metaphors (*kinuim*), parables (*mashal*), or figures of speech (*melitsah*). Once Maimonides delivers a highly abstruse definition of divine existence and unity, there is a seamless transition to its scriptural antecedents with the phrase "It is explicitly set forth [*mefurash*] in the Torah and the Prophets."[9] Two internal scriptural proofs are cited as substantiating God's incorporeality, a staple feature without which His unity is misconceived. Since the verse *God is in heaven above and on the earth below* (Deut. 4:39) locates God in two places at the same time, violating the spatial limitations of physical bodies, He must be incorporeal. Then again, any analogy with the material world is ruled out, *for you saw no figure* (Deut. 4:15) at Sinai, as well as a subsequent declaration to Isaiah in which God renders himself wholly incomparable: *To whom will you compare me and with whom will I be identified?* (40:25). Prophetic revelation links up with Sinaitic reportage to form a scriptural continuum reinforcing a philosophical bulwark of divine unity. The latter verse also acts as a pivotal scriptural underpinning for Maimonides's negative theology developed in the *Guide*, which postulates that God can only be known by what He is not (I:55, p. 128). The "explicitness" of these prooftexts is grounded in philosophical sophistication.

The two pillars of Jewish faith, the existence of a creator God and of His absolute and indivisible unity, are rooted in Scripture, but only once the text has evolved from the apparent nonsense of its anthropomorphic language into "explicit" profundity. The task of the Jewish reader is to make Scripture speak explicitly as asserted in the *Mishneh Torah* (*mefurash*). Reading Scripture for Maimonides is a liberating venture for both the text and its reader. It should allow meaning to escape the pragmatic constraints of *human language*, whose linguistic reach only extends to "dark and lowly physical bodies that dwell in houses of clay and whose foundations are in the dirt."[10] As Maimonides's citation of this last Jobian verse implies, reading Scripture also reminds the reader of his or her own inferior state vis-à-vis the grandeur of the universe, thereby tempering reading by an ethics of humility that curtails any self-assured mastery of the text. At the same time, the term "clay," or *homer*, the standard Hebrew term for matter as opposed to form in the medieval Jewish philosophical lexicon, conjures up that aspect of the lowly existence that the reader must overcome by the exercise of "form," the nobler dimension, if he or she aspires to cultivate his humanity and find common ground between himself and God. If a reading does not penetrate the external, if it does not discern the "apples of gold" from their "silver filigree" casing, then existence itself will be mired in the *homer* that renders it indistinguishable from animal or unreflective existence.

The *Mishneh Torah* concludes with its grand vision of a utopian Messianic era when uniform sociopolitical harmony and comfort are merely the historical setting for the single universal preoccupation "to know the Lord."[11] The beginning and end of the Code therefore link up in what commences as the normative pursuit of the knowledge of God and culminates in its ultimate attainment within an environment where that pursuit becomes the norm. But at the same time, it is bracketed by an engagement with Scripture that allows it to speak *acceptable words*. Critical to Maimonides's conception of the Messianic period is its location along a historical continuum where the laws of nature are fully operative. It is a progressive evolution, not a caesura in the temporal flow initiated at creation when the "world follows its customary course" (*olam keminhago noheg*). In preparation for its eventuation, all those metahistorical prophetic visions entailing a breach in the natural order (such as *the wolf shall dwell with the lamb* [Isa. 11:6]) must be read figuratively, a literary strategy that itself will be vindicated, for "in the days of King Messiah the full meaning of those metaphors [*meshalim*] and their allusions will become clear to all."[12] Knowledge of God, the noblest of intellectual pursuits, is intertwined with an appreciation for Scripture, which elevates Scripture along with its reader and helps actualize the Messianic period. The nature of God and the nature of Messiah are inextricably bound in the process of correctly deciphering biblical language. A properly conducted understanding of such language promotes a philosophically coherent notion of both God and the Messianic age. Conversely, a crude literalist approach to biblical God-talk leads to a corrupt notion of the Supreme Being which ipso facto derails the arrival of the Messiah. Prophetic fantasies of the future must be read in the same vein as prophetic anthropomorphisms, and so the *Mishneh Torah* brackets all of human history as a constant struggle with the biblical texts.

Maimonides's program of scriptural interpretation always looks back toward its pre-Sinaitic antecedents in the attempt to recapture them. In the Maimonidean perspective, human history from its inception did not evolve along a linear progression of knowledge and achievement but rather could be charted along a series of peaks and valleys determined by monotheism's fortunes. What began as a universal subscription to a pristine belief in and worship of one God deteriorated into a widespread idolatrous culture in which virtually no trace of the authentic One remained in the mind of humanity. Were it not for Abraham's sui generis retrieval of a philosophically pure monotheism, the world would have been irrevocably doomed to theological and intellectual impoverishment. According to Maimonides, Abraham discovered the existence and unity of God on his own, long before the revelation of Torah to Moses and Israel at Sinai and thus without the benefit of Scripture.[13] After a lengthy process of vigorous internal reflection from infancy to middle age, Abraham reasons his way toward those truths that later become "explicitly" enshrined in the Bible. Jewish posterity is then left with a textual legacy of his findings that perpetuates his teachings posthumously. However, those lost "books" authored by Abraham fail to stem the tide of idolatrous ideology, which is so seductive as to draw the Jews enslaved in ancient Egypt generations later tightly within its pagan orbit. Scripture, for Maimonides, does not antedate the world as in the midrashic and kabbalistic tradition[14] but arrives on the historical scene to address an urgent human predicament, a decline in the commitment to the theological and philosophical truths which Abraham reintroduced to humanity but which his written oeuvre could not sustain. Discursive treatises are exchanged for a blend of laws and narratives better suited to preserve those principles which Abraham's literary strategy failed to do.

Maimonides describes the new measures God took, via Moses at the time of Egyptian enslavement, to salvage Abraham's teachings. From these measures, we can determine what elements those Abrahamic books lacked so that it could not gain the timelessness Scripture did—"He crowned them with mitzvoth and showed them the way to worship Him and how to deal with idolatry and those who go astray after it."[15] Law, ritual, and sanctions for transgression are the hallmarks of the Torah, the revised edition, so to speak, of Abraham's publications, which not only responds to the crisis of the moment but also guarantees its survival because it has been psychologically, socially, and politically adapted to withstand the vicissitudes of human nature. The *Guide* apprises us of a fourth ingredient—the parable —which externally might convey practical or political wisdom while internally signaling "beliefs concerned with the truth as it is" (GP, Intro., p. 12).

The Torah, then, is neither the midrashic blueprint for the universe nor the kabbalistic mind or body of God but rather is a document that is thoroughly human in its concerns and language. In that spirit, all its prohibitive and prescriptive regulations are drafted to promote "the welfare of the soul and the welfare of the body," the former entailing individual intellectual perfection and the latter an ideal corporate political body (GP, III:27, p. 510). But its humanity rather than its divinity is ingrained even deeper when it buttresses these laws with incentives and sanctions that encourage obedience and deter disobedience. Though it is within God's capacity to populate the world with perfectly obedient human beings, "He has never willed to do it, nor shall He ever will it" (GP, III:32, p. 529). Such thoroughgoing moral and intellectual consistency would run contrary to human nature, and "God does not change at all the nature of human individuals by means of miracles" (ibid.). Thus, the entire legislative and narrative components of the Torah in their systematic appeal to the human sensibility are testaments to both God's self-imposed restraint from interfering with nature and humanity's enduring process of overcoming its own foibles along a path of becoming rather than simply stagnant being.

Scripture, in its entirety, is intended as a textual preservative for the "fundamental principle implanted by Abraham," of God's existence, unity, creation, governance, and exclusivity, whose existence precludes the possibility of any other God.[16] Both in the *Guide* and the *Mishneh Torah*, the denial of idolatry is tantamount to the fulfillment "of the entire Torah, all the prophets and everything they were commanded from Adam to the end of time," while the affirmation of idolatry is tantamount to the Torah's repudiation.[17] This extends to those segments of the Torah intended to inculcate a moral regimen in people and to construct a socially viable, politically cohesive community. Ethics and theology are inseparably interlocked, since the ideal morality is one that is a function of the supreme religious mandate to mimic God's governance, or what is referred to as *imitatio dei*. To qualify as such, human conduct must approximate those characteristics the Torah ascribes to God while at the same time being wary of a true conception of God that cannot sustain such characteristics in truth. All those acts normally described by such biblical terms as *merciful, compassionate,* or *gracious,* which, as a rule, are humanly motivated by emotions, "by no means proceed from Him, may He be exalted, on account of a notion superadded to His essence" (GP, I:54, p. 126). Thus, these attributes ascribed to God are subject to the caveat that they do not signify any inherent qualities of God but are rather attributes of action which are dispassionately distributed in nature. Any other conception of the deity is idolatrous. Consequently, any human conduct that aspires to *imitatio dei* based on mimicking divine acts that emanate from innate moral traits is also idolatrous. Even conduct must be filtered through the prism of knowledge of God, which will produce acts that assimilate themselves to the extent of being considered godlike.

The Torah, then, is a philosophical text in its totality. Correspondingly, the *Guide* is an exegetical work dedicated exclusively to providing the tools for reading out of the Torah its philosophical subtext.[18] At the same time, it mimics the Torah in its demand for reading keys that unlock the secrets encrypted in its text. True to this vision of Torah, the *Guide*'s express agenda is primarily "to explain the meanings of certain terms occurring in the books of prophecy" (GP, Intro., p. 5) and secondarily to offer "the explanation of very obscure parables occurring in the books of the prophets but not explicitly identified there as such" (ibid., p. 6). The *Guide* advises its reader at the very outset that any chapter that does not patently deal with biblical terms does so implicitly as ancillary to others which do, or by obliquely hinting to a term intentionally suppressed for the time being. Such chapters seemingly devoid of biblical reference might also "explain one of the parables" or "hint at the fact that a certain story is a parable" (ibid., p. 10). The *Guide* could have just as appropriately been titled "How to Read the Bible."[19]

Since the *Mishneh Torah* purports to deal exhaustively with *halakhah*, what remains in Scripture to contend with is the physics and metaphysics covertly expressed therein. In the wake of this Maimonidean revolution, a new rabbinic mandate emerges vis-à-vis the enterprise of scriptural exegesis: rabbinic interpreters should strive to ensure the endurance of Scripture's esoteric truths. Maimonides provides a parable of the palace, which measures proximity to God in terms of intellectual sophistication and metaphysical concerns.[20] The conventional rabbi whom Maimonides describes in this parable involves himself solely with *halakhah* while accepting "fundamental principles of religion" "on the basis of traditional authority" rather than independent speculation. Such a conventional rabbi ranks low on the scale, skirting around the palace while never actually entering its precincts (GP, III:51, p. 619). Those who perceive Torah as simply a repository of ritual and legal minutiae of divine worship diminish its stature. On the other hand, those who mine Torah for its metaphysics ennoble it, and so a new scriptural authority is born. The *Mishneh Torah* sets the stage for the transition to this new authority when, in a companion text to the palace parable, it values *halakhic* concern as "a small thing," popularly accessible and aimed at promoting social well-being and psychological stability in relation to the far more sublime pursuits of physics and metaphysics, or the subject matter of the Code's first four chapters.[21] Although these prefatory chapters are interspersed with biblical verses and strategies for reading Scripture philosophically, Maimonides's prioritized understanding of Scripture informs the entire legal project of the Code. Approaching Scripture as a legal text is merely a preliminary, pragmatic stage in the new curriculum. This curriculum intends for its students to graduate into a medium for abstract truths. Maimonides's engagement with the rabbinic legal tradition is informed by this very same posture, as he professes in his *Mishnah Commentary*, "My method consistently is I will elucidate something any place where there is an allusion to matters of faith, for it is more important for me to expound on a fundamental of the fundamental principles than any other matter I teach."[22]

The Torah itself affords a fleeting glimpse of what its ideal form would be had it the luxury of not having to cater to human exigencies. Due to the frailties of human nature, the Torah, in its present form, blends "primary intentions" with "secondary," where the former are aimed at "the apprehension of Him, may he be exalted, and the rejection of idolatry" (GP, III:32, p. 527), while the latter couch the former in norms that are anthropologically palatable. Prominently illustrative of those necessary yet inherently distractive and misleading measures is the sacrificial cult which occupies a substantial portion of the biblical text, a pagan form of worship co-opted by the Torah to subvert idolatry from within. However, there was a previous revelation at the waters of Marah that Maimonides designates as free of secondary intentions, citing the midrashic identification of the *statute and judgment* (Exod. 15: 25) prescribed there as the Sabbath (inculcating belief in creation of the world in time) and the civil laws (to promote social cohesion and political stability) (III:32, p. 531).[23] This elusive image of a pristine revelation composed of pure "first intentions" is orchestrated to loom over all future encounters with the biblical text's final draft. The Torah, the end product of Moses's legacy, is always in danger of being read and interpreted oblivious of the message of Marah, in a way that confuses means with ends. In fact, prophetic anger and censure of national conduct is commonly provoked by behavior that is "ignorant of the first intention and not distinguishing between it and the second intention" (ibid.). Jewish religious history can be charted by the caliber of biblical interpretation: properly focused reading induces progress, while misreading impels decline. Maimonides has not only reinvented the text; he has transformed prophetic rebukes originally aimed at perverse conduct (such as Samuel's rebuke of King Saul's sanctimoniously hypocritical religiosity *listening is preferable to sacrifice* [1 Sam. 15: 22]) into a hermeneutical guide for discriminating secondary from primary intentions so as not to pervert the text. Though *listening* (*shamoa*) can metaphorically signify acceptance or obedience, it can also express "the sense of science and knowledge" (GP, I:45, p. 96). Ritual recedes into the background when the Torah speaks and is submerged in the overwhelming mandate to read, interpret, and understand its language. When applied to God, biblical *listening* expresses thought exclusively. Consequently, a Jew listens to his or her sacred text to stimulate thought and speculation, and not merely to determine behavior. Reading Scripture is then transformed into a genuine act of *imitatio dei*. At the very core of what "Abraham our father taught his children" is the *way of God* in order to emulate it.[24] By correctly interpreting the actions and characteristics of God, who is the central character in Maimonides's Torah, one also retrieves the Abrahamic legacy and reinvigorates his intellectual/spiritual revolution.

When Maimonides halakhically mandates that one allocate one's time evenly among the Jewish intellectual disciplines of written Torah, oral Torah, and Talmud,[25] he reconfigures these disciplines from their traditional molds. Subsumed under Talmud is the art of reasoning (logic, deduction, drawing analogies) and, more important, the subject matter of the "garden" (*pardes*), or physics and metaphysics. Once one attains intellectual maturity, one must abandon this study regimen in favor of exclusive devotion to Talmud "in accordance with the expansiveness of his mind (heart) and psychological composure [*yishuv daat*]." When the latter state is at its optimum, there is no longer any need to focus on the *halakhic* interchange and debate that pervades all of the Talmud—what is traditionally understood by that corpus—and there should be unmitigated intellectual engagement with those most esoteric of sciences known as the *Accounts of the Creation and the Chariot*. What Maimonides classifies then as "written Torah" here is a beginner's superficial familiarity with the contents of all of Scripture, namely, its narratives and laws, while the ultimate Talmudic enterprise is a reversion back to Scripture to elevate those superficial contents. One accomplishes this by utilizing the *Guide* and the beginning of the *Mishneh Torah* as linguistic compendia to expose the profound truths buried within Scripture. Both the elementary and graduated study of Torah involve reading the same text, but the disparity in intellectual sophistication renders entirely different products.

Just as the *Mishneh Torah* is structurally enveloped by the paramount endeavor of biblical interpretation, so the entire text of the Pentateuch, according to Maimonides, is anchored in an essential relationship between God and the world. This anchor must inform every interpretive encounter with the Pentateuch. Every single facet of existence, as a consequence of God's wisdom, is purposeful, even though we often fail to detect that inherent teleological wisdom when examining its various isolated parts. Opening and closing with this message, the Torah is imbued with the telos of all existence, for "it is upon this opinion that the whole of the Torah of Moses our Master is founded; it opens with it: *And God saw everything that He had made and behold it was very good* (Gen. 1: 31); and it concludes with it: *The Rock [zur], His work is perfect, and so on* (Deut. 32: 4)" (GP, III:25, p. 506). Though notionally these bookend verses capture the perfection of God's creation in which nothing is extraneous, they also demarcate a trajectory spanning the length of the Pentateuchal text from what God knows toward knowledge to which man must aspire. The all-encompassing goodness of creation envisioned by God at the end of the primal creation is accessible to human beings as the outermost limits of their intellect, since this very divine perspective is revealed to Moses at the summit of intellectual achievement when God passed His *goodness* before him (Exod. 33: 19) (GP, I:54, p. 124). Moses grasps how all things that exist "are mutually connected so that he will know how He governs them in general and in detail" (ibid.). This notion qualifies his pronouncement *The Rock [zur], His work is perfect* as authoritative. Because the text is indelibly stamped with the intellectual biography of its author, it invites the reader to retrace Moses's steps through the text from creation to its denouement in Moses's paean to God as the *Rock*, or "the principle and efficient cause of all things other than himself" (GP, I:16, p. 42),

This bracketing of the Torah is crucial. It sharpens the contours of what Maimonides considers the only truly authentic Jewish interpretive stance vis-à-vis Scripture. When Moses is on the precipice of the very acme of human knowledge, God instructs him to *stand erect upon the rock* (Exod. 33: 21), whose meaning, filtered through the Maimonidean lexicon, shifts from locus of place to locus of thought: "Rely upon and be firm in considering God, may He be exalted, as the first principle" (GP, I:16, p. 42) The opening narrative of the Torah must be read as a philosophically rigorous presentation of God as a "first principle," while its finale demands a continuously reflective engagement with it. Everything in between provides the literary enablement of that reflection and sustains its caliber of philosophical sophistication. By stipulating this cerebral activity as "the entryway through which you shall come to Him" (ibid.), Maimonides redesigned both the spiritual quest and its destination. Religion is no longer a praxis-centered journey toward existential devotion to God by way of obedience to commandments and performance of ritual. The religious quest is a contemplative one, whose primary activity is essentially the exegesis of a text. The ultimate aim of that exegesis is to pry loose the universal truth buried deep beneath all the text's different literary genres, be they poetry, narrative prose, or even legislation. In a verse from Psalms, *The nearness of God is my good* (73:28), "cognitive apprehension is intended, not nearness in space" (GP, I:19, p. 44). But the depth of interpretive engagement with the scriptural text is not exhausted by simply substituting one signification for another. Every verse catalyzes an elaborate network of terms and meanings developed by Maimonides through which it must be processed to enhance its own meaning and to advance the quest for truth. In this case, it is not only "nearness" that demands a philosophically nuanced treatment, but so does the value judgment of *good*. The "cognitive apprehension" signified by *nearness* consists in assimilating the cognitive content of *good*, which attracts the meaning we have seen assigned to it when God's *goodness* passed before Moses. That Mosaic assimilation of the *good* of all creation is the ultimate goal of cognizing to which all must aspire. The extent of that cognitive effort determines one's distance from God in thought. Scripture, for the disciple of Maimonides, represents an interpretive vortex from which both reader and text emerge in the exercise of intellect, or that divine *image* which God and humanity share in common (GP, I:1, p. 21).

During Maimonides's discussion of the meaning of "holiness" (*qedushah*) in the *Guide*, he cites a rabbinic rubric exempting discussions of Torah from the regular halakhic prescriptions of purity that allows them to be conducted even in a state of impurity—"The words of the Torah are not subject to becoming unclean" (GP, III:47, p. 595).[26] This rabbinic reference serves to dispel any perception of Torah as somehow ontologically unique or possessing some kind of inherent metaphysical quality as endorsed by the mystical tradition. The Torah is important for its contents. Since abstract teachings have no ontic reality outside the mind, they cannot contract impurities. This rabbinic rubric is also crucial because it reflects many of the Maimonidean conceptions of Scripture discussed previously. Scripture is available for reading, deciphering, and understanding, not for incantations or to provide some kind of refuge in what might be perceived as its magical apotropaic aura simply by chanting it.[27] For Maimonides, "uncleanness" can have three senses: disobedience of commandments in thought or action; dirt; ritual impurities contracted through, for example, contact with dead bodies (GP, III:47, p. 595). Of these three, ritual impurity and dirt must be ruled out when their converse is applied to Scripture. The remaining sense of uncleanness that can be used to determine its antonym (holiness) for Scripture is "disobedience and transgression of commandments concerning action or opinion" (ibid.). When Maimonides's disciples perceive their Scripture as "holy," what they are describing is their own compliant response with its practical and theoretical teachings. Just as God's glory and presence inhere neither in the world nor in the Sanctuary but are a function of human apprehension and discussion of Him (GP, I:64, p. 157), so Scripture's holiness resides in the human action and thought it provokes.

Finally, we return to the maxim with which our discussion began—*the Torah speaks in the language of human beings*—to explore its ramifications for a Maimonidean conception of Scripture. It is inextricably bound with another rabbinic adage that Maimonides adopts to capture the literary license of the biblical authors—"Great is the power of the prophets for they liken a form to its creator."[28] What this conveys is both the audacity and confidence of the prophets when articulating their visions of God in popular images. The rabbinic phrase *great is the power* always expresses "their appreciation of the greatness of something said or done, but whose appearance is shocking" (GP, I:46, p. 103). What I take this to imply is that to do justice to the biblical prophets' creative prose and poetry, Scripture must evoke shock in its readers rather than the comfort we so often believe Scripture is intended to provide. Reader response must correspond to authorial license, and if Scripture placates rather than disturbs, then it has been misread. The *great power* the Rabbis ascribed to themselves precisely captures what Maimonides envisions the role Scripture is to play in Jewish life and what constitutes authenticity in scriptural encounter. Paradigmatic of the rabbinic boldness characterized as *great power* is a talmudic illustration cited by Maimonides of a rabbi who conducted a prescribed ritual in a manner that did not conform with its formal legal requisite. In this particular case, a religious ritual related to family law was performed by the Rabbi alone, in direct contravention of established halakhic norms which required its execution in the presence of more than one person. This image, in its literary structure, encapsulates the loneliness and iconoclasm destined to imbue any Jewish relationship to Scripture that matures in the shadow of Maimonides's intellectual legacy. The Jew's engagement with Scripture perforce often entails a break with the community and with tradition since it calls for a hermeneutical boldness which measures up to that invested by its authors in drafting its enigmatic and parabolic composition.

Maimonides, taking his cue from the Psalter's admonishment, *Silence is praise to thee* (Ps. 65:2) (GP, I:59, p. 139), maintains that the ideal medium for apprehending the ultimate truth of all Being is the nonverbal and the nontextual. Consequently, all reading of Scripture tends toward the act of translation into the language of silence. In order to arrive at that destination, one must adopt a restrained approach to the text and guard oneself from being drawn into the beauty of its prose and poetry and landing deeper into its language rather than transcending it. Moses covered his face during his inaugural encounter with God: *And Moses hid his face, for he was afraid to look upon God* (Exod. 3:6). For Maimonides, this act evinces Moses's humility, awe, and self-restraint. It also provides the paradigm for the method and goal of reading Scripture: "When doing this, he should not make categoric affirmations in favor of the first opinion that occurs to him and should not from the outset strain and impel his thoughts toward apprehension of the deity [here read "text" in place of "deity"]; he rather should feel awe and refrain and hold back until he gradually elevates himself" (GP, I:5, p. 29).

NOTES

1. For a recent study of subsequent prominent Jewish philosophers, one in the seventeenth century and one in the twentieth, who seriously engaged the Bible in light of Maimonides's interpretive legacy, see my "Maimonides, Spinoza, and Buber Read the Hebrew Bible: The Hermeneutical Keys of Divine 'Fire' and 'Spirit' (Ruach)," *Journal of Religion* 91, no. 3 (July 2011): 320–43.

2. For but one example see BT *Sanhedrin* 64b. Typically the two sides of the debate on whether the Torah speaks humanly are identified with the tannaitic schools of R. Akiva and R. Ishmael. For Maimonides's use of this expression, see Abraham Nuriel, "The Torah Speaks According to the Language of the Sons of Man" (Heb.), in M. Hallamish and A. Kasher, eds., *Religion and Language: General and Jewish Philosophical Essays* (Tel Aviv: Tel Aviv University Pub. Projects, 1981), 97–103.

3. See Jay Harris's discussion of this exegetical principle in chapter 2 of *How Do We Know This? Midrash and the Fragmentation of Modern Judaism* (Albany: SUNY Press, 1995)

4. All references to the *Guide of the Perplexed* are to S. Pines's translation (Chicago: University of Chicago Press, 1963), cited as GP throughout the body of the chapter.

5. See the eighth and ninth principles in his *Commentary to the Mishnah* (*Mishnah im Perush Rabbenu Mosheh ben Maimon*), 6 vols., trans. Joseph Kafih (Jerusalem: Mossad Ha-Rav Kook, 1965) (hereafter CM), Sanhedrin, Perek Heleq. See also *Mishneh Torah* (MT), *Laws of Megillah Reading*, 2:18, where the Pentateuch survives even the Messianic era. References to MT are to the Shabse Frankel edition, 12 vols. (Bnei Brak, Israel: Hotsaat Shabse Frankel, 1975–2001).

6. The perplexed person envisioned by the *Guide of the Perplexed* is confronted by a clash between Torah and science that appears to be resolvable only by a stark either/or choice of either "renounc[ing] the foundation of the Law" or "turning his back" on his intellect, bringing "loss to himself and harm to his religion" (GP, Intro., p. 6).

7. Howard Kreisel has also argued in favor of a Maimonidean relevance that survives an outdated metaphysics in the sense that his "holistic" enterprise of an integrated worldview which deems practical philosophy inseparable from theoretical philosophy continues to challenge modern students of philosophy. See "Imitatio Dei in Maimonides' Guide of the Perplexed," *AJS Review* 19, no. 2 (1994): 169–211, esp. 203–5.

8. See CM, introduction to the tenth chapter of m. *Sanhedrin*.

9. MT, *Laws Concerning the Basic Principles of the Torah*, 1:8.

10. Ibid., 1:12, alluding to Job 4:19.

11. MT, *Laws of Kings*, 12:5.

12. Ibid., 12:1.

13. MT, *Laws of Idolatry*, ch. 1.

14. For the rabbinic sources claiming that the Torah existed before God created the world, see Ephraim Urbach, *The Sages: Their Concepts and Beliefs*, 2 vols., trans. I. Abrahams (Jerusalem: Magnes, 1975), 180–82. For the ramifications of a "pre-existent Torah" during the course of the history of Jewish mysticism from the Middle Ages, see Gershom Scholem, *Major Trends in Jewish in Jewish Mysticism* (New York: Schocken Books, 1954), 13–14.

15. MT, *Laws of Idolatry*, 1:3.

16. Ibid.

17. MT, *Laws of Idolatry*, 2:4; GP, III:29, p. 517, based on *Sifre Devarim* 54. See also BT *Shavuot* 29a; BT *Horayot* 8a.

18. See Alfred Ivry, "Strategies of Interpretation in Maimonides' *Guide of the Perplexed*," *Jewish History* 6, nos. 1–2 (1992): 113–30. Ivry asserts, "In its stated purposes, then, the *Guide* is a work of biblical exegesis with a clearly stated hermeneutic" (118), as opposed to a philosophical composition in the traditional Western form.

19. Considering the recent flurry of books bearing the title "How to Read the Bible" (at least nine by my count: Frederick Grant, James Kugel, Marc Brettler, J. Paterson Smyth, Edgar Goodspeed, James Fischer, Richard Holloway, Steven McKenzie, Jack Rang), Maimonides, by rejecting this title, considerately spared us a further perplexity of simply accessing his book.

20. For a probative analysis of this parable, see Hannah Kasher, "The Parable of the King's Palace in the *Guide of the Perplexed* as a Directive to the Student" (Heb.), *AJS Review* 14 (1989): 1–19

21. MT, *Laws Concerning the Basic Principles of the Torah*, 4:13.

22. CM, *Berakhot*, 9:5.

23. BT *Shabbat* 87b.

24. MT, *Ethical Traits*, 1:7.

25. MT, *Torah Study*, 1:11–12. Many of the manuscripts substitute *gemara* for *talmud*.

26. Also cited in MT, *Laws of Reciting Shema*, 8:4. One can recite the words of the Torah after having experienced a seminal emission, which would normally quarantine the subject from fully participating in religious life.

27. For a book-length treatment of Maimonides's antagonism to mystical currents that were germinating within Judaism during his life and that were to become staples of the kabbalistic tradition, see Menachem Kellner's *Maimonides' Confrontation with Mysticism* (Portland, OR: Littman Library of Jewish Civilization, 2006).

28. GP, I:46, p. 103, citing *Bereshit Rabbah*.

Chapter 9

Concepts of Scripture in Nahmanides

Aaron W. Hughes

Introduction: Cultural and Intellectual Background

R. Moses ben Nahman (1194–1270), customarily referred to as Nahmanides or the Ramban, is one of the towering figures of premodern Judaism. Scholar, commentator, halakhist, communal leader, and spokesperson, his career represents the creative intersection of the three primary trends of medieval Judaism: rationalism, traditionalism, and mysticism. Like the great Maimonides, with whom he is frequently compared and often too neatly juxtaposed, he was a product of the rich Iberian-Jewish intellectual tradition.[1] However, whereas Maimonides is often regarded as the last great representative of the rationalist school associated with the so-called Golden Age of Muslim Spain, Nahmanides was born in a Christianized environment, whose Jewish community was influenced less by Arabic learning than it was by the Jewish cultures of northern Europe. Nahmanides, thus, is at the vanguard of the new direction taken by Jewish culture in Christian Spain.

In order to put Nahmanides's life and thought in sharper focus, it is necessary to situate him against the larger intellectual and social backdrop that characterized the diversity of Jewish communities in the thirteenth century. This was a time of exchange and interchange between numerous Jewish cultures in northern Spain and France. Exhibiting different intellectual customs and local knowledges, these cultures were neither necessarily compatible nor reconcilable with one another. The rationalism associated with al-Andalus, the mysticism of Provence, and the Tosafist tradition of northern France all implied different sets of traditions and concomitant understandings of Judaism and Jewish texts.

At the crossroads of these cultures stood the commanding figure of Nahmanides. The rich diversity of his work and his role in numerous communal and intercommunal conflicts attest to his ability to draw on and appeal to numerous constituencies. Perhaps more than any of his immediate contemporaries, Maimonides included, he was able to mediate the tensions associated with these diverse Jewish cultures and, in the process, absorb the best that each had to offer. This is certainly not to imply that Nahmanides is a synthetic or derivative thinker; on the contrary, his work exhibits an uncommon comprehensive and multilayered quality. He could, for example, quite easily employ philosophical rationalism, expound on the mystical currents associated with the kabbalah, and, at the same time, uphold the conservatism of the rabbinic schools associated with northern France.

Biographical Sketch

Rabbi Moses ben Nahman was born in 1195 to a prominent family of the city of Gerona in the kingdom of Aragon in northern Spain, and he seems to have died sometime in 1270 in the land of Israel. In between the bookends of his life, the Tosafists in northern France had just revolutionized the study of Talmud, the great Maimonides had died in Egypt, and the first recognizable group of Spanish kabbalists emerged in the city of Nahmanides's birth.[2] At his death, he was known as a scholar, physician, rabbinic sage, orator, and defender of the faith against the attacks of the Church at the Court of Aragon.[3] Indeed it was on account of this latter role that he was forced to flee Aragon for the land of Israel in 1267. It was there that he wrote his commentary on the Torah, the synthesis of his life's work.

Recognized at a fairly young age as a great intellect, he soon became a communal leader, administering to the Jewish communities of southern France and northern Spain. On account of this, he was drawn into the controversies surrounding both the figure of Maimonides and his rationalist teachings.[4] He defended, for example, antirationalists in Montpellier against a ban imposed on them by pro-Maimonideans in Provence; yet he also wrote to the Tosafists of northern France encouraging them to withdraw their ban against Maimonides's *Guide of the Perplexed* and *Sefer ha-Madda*, the latter being the first book of his revolutionary *Mishneh Torah*.[5] His ability to defend both sides in these disputes has led some scholars to conclude that Nahmanides, whether because of polemical pressure or the need for intercommunal peace, hid his true opposition to the

Iberian-Jewish rationalist tradition.[6] It is perhaps easier, however, to see this tension as mirroring the creative tension inherent to his own thought, which attempted to grapple with numerous, often contradictory, ideas and ideals. Within this context, rather than simply to see Nahmanides as a conservative "antirationalist," it is important to note that he actually endorsed the nonliteral interpretation of rabbinic *aggadot*, or legends, something that placed him in the same camp as the rationalists of whom he was often critical.

In addition to functioning as a mediator in the Maimonidean controversies, Nahmanides played an important role in an official disputation at the court of King James I in Barcelona during July 20–24, 1263. Called to serve as the Jewish representative, Nahmanides's role was to defend the faith against the charges of Pablo Christiani, a Jewish convert to Christianity who had assured the king that he could prove the truth of Christianity from the Talmud and other rabbinical writings. Nahmanides agreed to the disputation, according to his account of it, only if he were granted complete freedom of speech. The disputation turned on the following points: whether the Messiah had appeared or not; whether, according to Scripture, the Messiah is a divine or a human being; and whether the Jews or the Christians held the true faith. Whereas Christiani relied on a Christological reading of both the Bible and the Talmud, Nahmanides countered with a traditional Jewish reading of the biblical text and the claim that the homilies of the Talmud must be understood nonliterally.

Although both sides claimed victory, the Dominicans subsequently charged Nahmanides with blaspheming Christianity, and they encouraged James I of Aragon to banish him from the kingdom. Eventually he ended up in the land of Israel, where he is credited with helping to reestablish Jewish communal life in the aftermath of Crusader repression and where he completed his commentary on the Torah.

The Importance of Scripture According to Nahmanides

Nowhere is Nahmanides's ability to mediate between different positions more on display than in his commentary to the Torah, the primary focus of this chapter. Perhaps this mediatory role is best epitomized in the two previous commentary traditions—the traditionalism of the French Rashi and the rationalism of the Spanish Abraham Ibn Ezra[7]—that he both struggled with and sought to emend in his own commentary. Drawing on their work, singling them out as his predecessors, Nahmanides effectively created a triumvirate that, in the words of Isadore Twersky, "still casts its shadow over all Bible study."[8] This triumvirate, which came to form the core of the sixteenth-century "Rabbinic Bible," the *miqraot gedolot*, effectively set out the exegetical problems and issues for the subsequent history of Jewish biblical exegesis.

Nahmanides's commentary combines all the major streams of medieval Jewish intellectual life: rabbanism, philosophy, and mysticism. In terms of rabbinic thought, Nahmanides emphasized the importance of tradition, based as it was on the infallibility of the ancient sages known as the *tannaim* and the *amoraim*. Nahmanides's relationship to philosophy, however, is a more complicated matter. Although he is often held up as the antithesis of the rationalism of Maimonides, such a characterization overlooks the many places in his commentary where he smoothly integrates philosophy.

Nahmanides's commentary is best known for its use of elements drawn from the kabbalah, a newly emerging mystical tradition that was associated with esoteric circles in northern Spain but that claimed to go back to Sinai and beyond. This new/old wisdom emphasized the mystical dimensions of the biblical narrative and the role of its language, Hebrew, in the process of creation. Its letters were not simply words on a page but cosmic principles ontologically connected to the divine presence. Nahmanides was one of the first thinkers to combine these teachings with the genre of sustained biblical commentary. Although his commentary may lack the "mystical systematization" of classic works such as the Zohar, it nevertheless did much to introduce, legitimize, and disseminate kabbalistic teachings to a large audience. Perhaps more than anyone, Nahmanides played a crucial role in enhancing the kabbalah's respectability and broadening its appeal.

It seems that Nahmanides originally wrote his commentary to the Torah as a way to interest the Jews in Jerusalem and the land of Israel more generally in the Bible. In the aftermath of the persecutions of the Crusading armies, these communities needed comfort in the face of displacement and uncertainty. Unlike other commentators who stressed scripture's rational or *peshat* (literal) dimension, Nahmanides holds that it is a dynamic text that unfolds before the reader on multiple levels. In his view and the hermeneutic that emerges from it, neither a monolithic rationalist nor *peshat* reading does the Torah, in its textual or cosmic totality, justice. Since he conceives of the Torah as a mystical, philosophical, literal, historical, and anthropological document, it must be understood and subsequently interpreted as a multilayered text. Linking all these levels together is the notion that the Torah mirrors the very purpose and rhythms of the Jewish people, from the creation of the universe until its future messianic fulfillment.[9] In his comments to Moses's Song at the Sea, for instance, Nahmanides writes,

> Now this Song, which is for us eternally true and faithful, offers an explanation of all that will happen to us. It begins by mentioning the mercy [*hahesed*] that the Holy One, blessed be He, bestowed upon us when he chose us as his portion. It then mentions the favors that He did for us in the wilderness, and how He bequeathed to us the lands of great and mighty nations. . . . [The enemies of Israel] inflicted all these evils upon us out of their hatred for the Holy One, blessed be He: because they do not hate Israel for having made idols like theirs, but only because they do not perform deeds like they do. . . . There is not in this Song any conditions of repentance or worship [of God as a prerequisite for the coming redemption], but it is a testamentary document that the evils will come and that we will endure them, and that He, blessed be He, will do with us "in furious rebukes" [Ez. 5:15]—but He will not destroy our memory. Rather, He will return and get satisfaction[10] and will punish our enemies *with His sore and great and strong sword* [Is. 27:1], and *forgive our sins for His Name's sake* [Psalm 79:9].[11]

Reminiscent of the Torah as a whole, Moses's Song contains information about both the distant past and future redemption. Because the Torah functions, on one of its many levels, as a blueprint for the unfolding of Israel's history, this means that levels or meanings hidden to previous generations become apparent only to the gaze of later ones.[12] Revealing the connection between Israel and God, the Torah also reflects, according to Nahmanides, the history of God himself by providing the skilled reader with insights into the inner dynamics of the Godhead. For this reason, the Bible must be read, and read again, as a constant source of wisdom, both old and new, that is grounded in the interpretive frameworks of the great works of the Jewish past. And it is for this reason that Nahmanides holds that the Torah cannot be exhausted by one interpretive lens and instead must be read both with extreme care and with an inclusive hermeneutic. It is necessary to read scripture in order to uncover its multiple layers of meanings and to try and ascertain how these layers connect with one another.

Nahmanides's Conception of Scripture

> The egg of the ant is as small
> as the outermost sphere
> of my limited understanding
> And my knowledge is imprecise
> When compared to the hidden matters of the Torah
> That lie hidden in her house and
> Concealed in her room;
> For every precious thing, every wonder,
> Every profound secret, and all glorious wisdom
> Are stored up with her,
> Sealed up in her treasure
> By a hint, by a word
> In writing and in speaking.[13]

With these words, Nahmanides begins his rich and multitextured commentary to the Torah. Nahmanides's goal, as indeed it is the goal of every biblical commentator, is twofold: to understand the biblical text within the parameters of its linguistic and historical context and to tease out the text's latent meanings. He writes, "Moses our teacher wrote this book of Genesis together with the whole Torah from the mouth of the Holy One, blessed be He."[14] Following rabbinic tradition, he holds that there exists forty-nine gates of understanding that Moses transcribed into the Torah either "explicitly or by implication in words, in the numerical value of the letters or in the form of the letters, that is whether written normally or with some change in form such as bent or crooked letters or some other deviations."[15]

The Torah, in other words, is inexhaustible. A narrow interpretive framework, according to Nahmanides, risks fragmenting both the Torah and, concomitantly, Judaism. This risk seems to have been behind his involvement in the Maimonidean controversy, wherein the various bans and counterbans threatened the unity of Judaism:

> The Torah will become like Two Torahs, and all of Israel [will become] two opposing groups. One group will agree with your decision, but the other will ignore your ruling. . . . If you decree something that [pro-Maimonideans] are necessarily unable to accept, they will ignore the *herem* of your group [literally, *minyan*] and they will say to you "we believe this." . . . *It is unlawful to declare a ruling on all Israel unless the majority*

is able to agree with it [BT Avodah Zarah 36a]. Why do you "devour the inheritance of the Lord" [2 Sam. 20:19]?[16]

Nahmanides, most likely owing to a combination of personal belief and political necessity, here stresses the importance of diversity in interpretative opinions. A perspectival approach to Torah, in other words, risks overlooking its inexhaustible richness. This richness, in turn, is connected to its language of revelation, Hebrew, which is full of sacral power. Nahmanides refers to it as a "sacred language" because it is the language of creation and of God's communication to Israel:

> I hold that this is the same reason why our Rabbis call the language of the Torah "the sacred language" [*lashon ha-qodesh*] because the words of the Torah and the prophecies, and all words of holiness were all expressed in that language, it is thus the language in which the Holy One, blessed be He, spoke with his prophets, and with His congregation. . . . He is called by His sacred names: El, Elokim, Tzebaoth, Shaddai, Yah, and the Great Proper Name [i.e., the Tetragrammaton]. In [this language] He created His world, and called the names *shamayim* [heavens], *eretz* [earth], and all that is in them, His angels and all His hosts—*He called them all by name* [Is. 40:26]. The names of Michael and Gabriel are in this Sacred Language. In that language He called the names of *the holy ones that are in the earth* [Psalm 16:3]: Abraham, Isaac, Jacob, Solomon, and others.[17]

Nahmanides's conception of Hebrew as a sacred language (*lashon qodesh*) provides a startling contrast to Maimonides's purely conventional and functional conception of Hebrew. This critical distinction plays a central role, as we shall see later, in the disagreements between the two scholars.

Nahmanides's approach to the Torah in the preceding passage, and more generally, is predicated on what he perceives to be an intersection of *peshat* and *sod*, the plain and secretive meanings, respectively. It is this intersection that permits Nahmanides to put in counterpoint a universally accessible meaning with a more esoteric or mystical one meant for the select. The former arises from the consensus of previous interpretive sources (e.g., Talmud, midrash, later commentators such as Abraham Ibn Ezra and Rashi); whereas the latter emerges from reflection on the divine Name that can only be hinted at in a commentary.

This juxtaposition is one of the defining elements of Nahmanides's commentary. Whether because he was writing very early in the historical emergence of kabbalah (e.g., before the final redaction of the more systematic Zohar) or because he was acutely aware that the Torah was not just a mystical text, his conception of Torah is highly inclusive. Unlike that of many later kabbalists, Nahmanides maintains a delicate equilibrium between the Torah's literal, mystical, and other meanings. A good example of this may be found in his discussion of the term *devequt* (cleaving) in Deuteronomy 11:22 ("and to cleave unto Him"). Although later kabbalistic interpreters often interpreted this to mean a form of *unio mystica*, Nahmanides does not confine its semantic range solely to a mystical experiential mode. In the verse's most literal sense, he argues that the meaning

> of the verse is one of admonition against idolatry, meaning that one's thought should not move from God to other gods, that one should not think that there is any substance to idolatry but instead that it is all emptiness and worthless. In this regard this verse is similar to *and Him shall you serve, and unto Him shall you cleave* [Deut. 13:5], the intent being to warn that one is not to worship God with anything besides Him, but to worship God alone, with one's hearts and deed.[18]

According to Nahmanides, Deuteronomy's call to cleave to God, on its simplest level, means that one should not or must not worship other gods or otherwise engage in idolatrous practice. Following this, however, Nahmanides writes that *devequt* can also refer to the practice of being close to God at all times: "It is possible that [the term] 'cleaving' means that you should remember God and His love always, that your thoughts should never be separated from Him *when you walk by the way, and when you lie down, and when you rise* [Deut. 11:19], so that when you are speaking to others by mouth and tongue, your heart will not be with them, but instead directed toward God."[19] According to Nahmanides, here *devequt* is not simply a negative term, used to denote the avoidance of idolatrous beliefs and practices, but now receives a more positive valence: to keep God constantly in one's thoughts, even when engaged in more mundane activities. Following this, Nahmanides writes that for some people even this is not enough and that for "such men of excellence it is possible that even in their lifetime, their souls *shall be bound to the bundle of life* [1 Sam. 25:29], since their very being is a 'residence' for the Divine Glory, as the author of the Book of the Kuzari [Judah Halevi] alludes."[20] In Nahmanides's deft hermeneutics here, we witness how the term *devequt* receives both a simple and a technical interpretation. For all, it refers to the importance of worshiping God and not other deities; for the few, however, it refers to a particular mode of mystical practice.

Within this context, Nahmanides is certainly informed by the kabbalistic tradition that sees the Torah as an esoteric text that is composed of the names of God. He writes, as we have seen, that Moses wrote the Torah directly "from the mouth of the Holy One, blessed be He."[21] In addition to this, however, Nahmanides argues that Moses also received the secret combinations of letters that represent another, deeper, aspect of the Torah and, by extension, the universe. We possess, according to him,

> an authentic tradition [*kabbalah*] that shows the whole Torah is composed of the Names of the Holy One, blessed be He, and that the letters of the words separate themselves into Divine Names when divided in a different manner.... It is said that the Torah is written with letters of black upon a background of white fire, and this is the form we have mentioned, namely, that the writing was contiguous, without break of words, which made it possible for it to be read by way of Divine Names and also by way of our normal reading which makes explicit the Torah and the commandment. It was given to Moses our Teacher using the division of words that expresses the commandment, and orally it was transmitted to him in the rendition that consists of the Divine Names.[22]

This passage is significant for several reasons. First, Nahmanides indicates, in typical mystical fashion, that the Torah represents the cosmos and, like it, conceals within itself inner mysteries connected to the divine presence. The mystical light that the initiated is to uncover within the Torah is synonymous with the mysteries of creation, both of which are connected to understanding the potencies associated with the names of God. This is, of course, a very daring statement because, as many subsequent kabbalists have claimed, such a conception of Torah negates or devalues the literal level of scripture, making it less about meaning than mystical value.

Yet, as we have seen, Nahmanides's conception of scripture was not just mystical or kabbalistic. He was well aware, for example, that Torah was meant for all Israel, and this intersection of the kabbalistic and the non-kabbalistic is, in many ways, one of the unique features of his understanding of scripture. Nahmanides's conception of scripture, to reiterate, is that of an endless and eternal font of wisdom. It is not something that can be exhausted with one hermeneutic—for example, literal, rationalist, or even mystical. This is what other commentators had done, some to great effect, but none succeeded in reading, according to him, the Torah in all its splendor. This is why Nahmanides was engaged in a constant, and often highly critical, conversation with his predecessors such as Rashi and Abraham Ibn Ezra and even his contemporaries such as David Kimhi (1160–1235).[23]

In order to get both a further and better sense of Nahmanides's conception of scripture, it is necessary to examine his commentary in counterpoint with others'. How he differs from previous commentaries—especially, Maimonides, Abraham Ibn Ezra, and Rashi—will ideally permit for a clearer articulation of Nahmanides's conception of the Torah and, by extension, his uniqueness.

Wrestling with Maimonides

As witnessed in the previous chapter, Maimonides is perhaps the most important and influential Jew in the premodern period. His works, along with interpretations of them and reactions to them by subsequent thinkers, were responsible for the formation of many trajectories within medieval Jewish intellectual and religious cultures. Nahmanides, as we have seen, was on one level critical of Maimonidean allegory, something that he felt subverted the literal and traditional reading of the Torah. In the opening pages of his commentary, for example, Nahmanides takes aim at those who believe, in Aristotelian fashion, that the world is eternal. Instead he makes *creatio ex nihilo* into "a root of the faith" and says that "he who does not believe in this and thinks the world was eternal denies the essential principle of the religion and has no Torah at all."[24]

Belief in creation, for Nahmanides, is the foundation of Judaism, for creation is the event that established the relationships among God, the world, Hebrew, and the Jewish people. Interestingly, Nahmanides does not simply counter a belief in the eternality of the universe with a literal reading of Genesis but instead argues that creation is a "deep mystery not to be understood from the verses, and it cannot truly be known except through the tradition going back to Moses our teacher who received it through the mouth of the Almighty."[25] Although he does not explicitly mention Maimonides here, it is certainly telling that he begins his commentary with a sharp criticism of an approach to scripture that imports foreign ideas onto the biblical narrative. True understanding of scripture, as Nahmanides indicates here, comes from penetrating the simple level of the text with the help of an authentic tradition that derives from Mosaic revelation.

The different hermeneutics of Nahmanides and Maimonides may be witnessed in their respective interpretations of prophetic visions. In the following passage, for example, Nahmanides is critical of Maimonides's discussion of the appearance of angels to Abraham under the oaks of Mamre in Genesis 18:1. First he summarizes Maimonides's discussion of the events:

> [Maimonides argues] that scripture first says that the Eternal appeared to Abraham in the form of prophetic visions [*maraot ha-navuah*], and then explains in what manner this vision took place, namely, that he [Abraham] lifted up his eyes in the vision, and *three men stood by him* [Gen. 18:2] *and he said, if now I have found favor in your eyes* [Gen. 18:3]. This is the account of what he said in the prophetic vision to one of them, namely, their chief.[26]

Maimonides's interpretation of these events, according to Nahmanides's summary here, glosses over the details of the account. For Maimonides, the meeting with the three strangers, the meal that he and Sarah cook for them, and the subsequent conversation that leads to the announcement that the aged Sarah will give birth occurred only in Abraham's imagination. Nahmanides continues:

> Now if in the vision there appeared to Abraham only men partaking of food, how then does scripture say, *And the Eternal appeared to him*, as God did not appear to him in vision or in thought? . . . [According to Maimonides], Sarah did not knead cakes, nor did Abraham prepare a bullock, and also, Sarah did not laugh. It was all a vision! If so, this dream came *through a multitude of business* [Eccl. 5:2], like dreams of falsehood, for what is the purpose of showing him all this! Similarly did the author of the *Guide of the Perplexed* [i.e., Maimonides] say in the case of the verse, *And a man wrestled with him* [Gen. 32:25], that it was all a prophetic vision. But if this be the case, I do not know why Jacob limped on his thigh when he awoke! And why did Jacob say, *For I have seen an angel face to face, and my life is preserved* [Gen. 32:31]?[27]

Nahmanides's criticism of Maimonides here is based on the latter's desire to downplay—or, indeed, to negate—the literal level of the biblical narrative. If scripture says one thing, asks Nahmanides, why should Maimonides interpret it in such a manner that it means something different? If Genesis claims that Abraham cooked a bullock or that Sarah laughed, why should we assume that they did not or did so only in a dream, as the Maimonidean interpretation seems to imply? Opposed to the Maimonidean interpretation, Nahmanides contends that one cannot, indeed must not, interpret prophetic visions solely as the products of the prophet's imaginative faculty.

The issue in this debate does not simply revolve around whether Sarah laughed. At stake is how one reads the entire biblical narrative and, accordingly, the commandments that define Judaism. Read from the perspective of the later Maimonidean controversies, of which, as we have seen, Nahmanides was intimately involved, this one example reflects the larger issue of what gets to count (or not) as an acceptable interpretation of the biblical text.

Another example of the debate between Maimonides and Nahmanides may be found in their treatment of Onkelos's "occasional" deviation from the literal sense of the text. According to Maimonides, Onkelos (author of a second-century Aramaic translation of the Bible) literally translated the verse "I myself [i.e., God] will go down with you to Egypt and I myself will also bring you back" (Gen. 46:4), despite the fact that he tended to remove all traces of God's corporeality. Maimonides's reason for this, according to Nahmanides, is once again that the narrative is part of a dream sequence wherein "God called to Israel in a vision of night" (Gen. 46:2). Nahmanides disagrees and looks to explain the verse using traditional sources:

> The reason Onkelos here literally translated *I myself will go down with you to Egypt* [and did not paraphrase it as "My Glory will go down with you"] is that he wanted to allude to that which the rabbis have said: "When they were exiled to Egypt, the Divine Presence went with them, as it is said, *I myself will go down with you to Egypt.* When they were exiled to Elam, the Divine Presence went down with them, as it is said, *And I will set my throne in Elam.*"[28]

Rather than explain the verse, as Maimonides does, by appeals to vision, Nahmanides here argues that the rabbinic conflation of the divine presence and God is more appropriate. Staying with Nahmanides's quarrel with Maimonides over Onkelos's hermeneutic for just a little longer, Nahmanides then asks why Onkelos paraphrased the divine corporeality found in the narrative of Jacob's ladder ("I am with you"; Gen. 28:15), which also occurred in a vision of night. Linking his disagreement with Maimonides to kabbalistic interpretation, Nahmanides writes,

> Onkelos could not have literally translated "and behold I am with you" [and was forced to paraphrase it as "and My word will be in your help"], because it is written here *And, behold, the Eternal stood beside him.* The wise individual will understand. Since Onkelos found the meaning of this verse not to be in line with its plain meaning, he therefore spurned [a literal translation], and thus he said, "My word will be in your help," instead of saying, "My word will be with you," as he said in the case of Moses. And may God show us the wonders of his Torah.[29]

Nahmanides here refers to the fact that the word for God used in Genesis 28:15 is the Tetragrammaton, which, in kabbalistic parlance, refers to the divine attribute of mercy. Instead Onkelos decided, again according to Nahmanides, to translate it as "my word," which symbolized the divine attribute of judgment (*din*).

Despite the fact that Nahmanides was familiar with the type of rationalism that Maimonides employed, his disagreement with him was one of the major engines that powered his commentary. A complete rationalist approach to scripture, one wherein dreams are invoked to explain textual "infelicities," is so problematic to Nahmanides because it not only puts the literal level of the Torah at risk (something he occasionally does himself) but subverts traditional Jewish reading.

Between Rashi and Ibn Ezra

Nahmanides writes at the beginning of his *Commentary on the Torah*,

> I will place as an illumination before me
> The lights of the pure candelabrum,
> The commentaries of our Rabbi Shlomo [i.e., Rashi]
> *A crown of glory, and a diadem of beauty,*
> Adorned in his ways,
> In Scripture, Mishnah, and Gemara
> The right of the firstborn is his.
> Upon his words I will meditate

> And in their love I will grow
> And with them we will have
> Discussions, investigations, and examinations . . .
> And with Abraham the son of Ezra
> We shall have open rebuke and hidden love.[30]

Much of Nahmanides's commentary on the Torah derives its energy from differentiating his own understanding of the biblical narrative from that of his predecessors. A sustained example should suffice to demonstrate this. He faults both Rashi and Ibn Ezra for misunderstanding the grammar in the opening verse of Genesis. This, according to him, leads them to misunderstand the account of creation. Nahmanides writes,

> *In the beginning* [Heb.: *bereshith*]. Rashi wrote: "if you wish to explain [the word *bereshith*] in accordance with its plain meaning [i.e., the fact that it is in what grammarians call the construct state], it must be explained like this: at the beginning of the creation of the heaven and the earth, the earth was formless and void and there was darkness, then the Holy One, blessed be He, said, *Let there be light.*" If so, the whole text leads into the creation of light.
>
> Rabbi Abraham [Ibn Ezra] explained it similarly. However, he claimed that the letter *vav* in the word *va-ha'aretz* is not a connecting letter [that adds new information but rather is specifying something further about what has already been mentioned]. He points to many such instances in scripture. The meaning [for him] is that at the beginning of the creation of the heaven and dry land, there was no habitable place on earth; rather, it was unformed and void and covered with water, and God said *Let there be light*. According to [Abraham Ibn Ezra's] opinion, only light was created the first day.[31]

According to Nahmanides, both Rashi and Ibn Ezra in their desire to understand the simple meaning of the text actually misunderstand it. Instead, Nahmanides writes,

> Now listen to the correct and clear explanation of the verse in its simplicity. The Holy One, blessed be He, created all things from absolute nonexistence. . . . Everything that exists under the sun or above it was not made from nonexistence at the outset. Instead He brought forth from total and absolute nothing a very thin substance devoid of corporeality but having a

power of potency, fit to assume form and to proceed from potentiality into reality. This was the primary matter created by God; the Greeks call it *hyle* [matter] . . . and from this *hyle* He brought everything into existence and clothed the forms and put them in a finished condition.[32]

Although we witnessed Nahmanides's opposition to Maimonides in the previous section, Nahmanides here resorts to philosophical explanation to understand the verse against the more literal and *peshat*-oriented interpretations of Rashi and Ibn Ezra. Yet rather than connect this discussion to Greek-inspired philosophy, he makes the claim that this teaching derives not from foreign sources but from the *Sefer Yetsira*, a text popular among kabbalists and that tradition claimed was written by Abraham.[33]

Speaking more generally, Nahmanides is for the most part favorably disposed to Rashi's commentary. His relationship to Ibn Ezra, however, is even more complicated (recall his "open rebuke and hidden love" for the great Spanish commentator cited earlier). Nahmanides tends to agree with Ibn Ezra on the level of his grammatical analyses; however, he frequently faults him for his unwillingness to examine the deeper, spiritual claims of the biblical narrative. Concerning the special blessing that God gives the seventh, or Sabbath, day—"And God blessed the seventh day and He sanctified it" (Gen. 2:1)—Ibn Ezra claims, according to Nahmanides, "that on the seventh day there is a renewal of procreative strength in the body and in the soul, a great capacity in the functioning of the reasoning power." Nahmanides agrees, to an extent, but then goes on to mine the deeper significance of the verse in question:

> The truth is that the blessing on the Sabbath day is the fountain of blessings and is the foundation of the world. *And He sanctified it*, so that it [i.e., the Sabbath] draws its sanctity from the Sanctuary on high. If you understand my comment, you will grasp what the Rabbis said in [the midrashic collection] Bereshith Rabbah concerning the Sabbath: ["Why did He bless the Sabbath? It is] because it has no partner," and that which they further related [that God said to the Sabbath]: "The congregation of Israel will be your partner." And then you will comprehend that on the Sabbath there is an additional soul.[34]

Here, Nahmanides moves well beyond Ibn Ezra's conception of the verse in question to argue for the relationship, on both an existential and mystical level, between Israel and the Sabbath.

Conclusions

Nahmanides's conception of scripture is multifaceted. Drawing on the work of previous scholars such as Maimonides, Rashi, and Ibn Ezra, Nahmanides was nonetheless discontented with their readings of scripture. As such, he sought to emend, correct, and transform previous understandings of the Torah by employing a hermeneutic that sought, simultaneously, to uncover the literal, rationalist, and mystical levels of the text. Nahmanides's commentary to the Torah, indicative of his approach to scripture more generally, is predicated on a sustained and engaged conversation with earlier generations of commentators, on his deep sense of traditional Jewish reading, and on his innovative attempt to connect the truths of the kabbalah with the traditional genre of biblical commentary. These features have all contributed to make Nahmanides one of the most dynamic and influential readers of the Bible in Jewish history.

NOTES

1. See Diamond's chapter 8 on Maimonides in this volume.
2. Gershom Scholem, *Origins of the Kabbalah*, ed. R. J. Zwi Werblowsky, trans. Allan Arkush (Princeton: Princeton University Press, 1987), 365–475. Other important studies on the influence of kabbalah on Nahmanides include Elliot R. Wolfson, "'By Way of Truth': Aspects of Nahmanides' Kabbalistic Hermeneutic," *AJS Review* 14 (1989): 103–78; idem, "The Secret Garment in Nahmanides," *Da'at* 24 (1990): xxv–xlix; Moshe Idel, "We Have No Kabbalistic Tradition on This," in *Rabbi Moses Nahmanides (Ramban): Explorations in His Religious and Literary Virtuosity*, ed. Isadore Twersky (Cambridge: Harvard University Press, 1983), 51–74.
3. Biographies of Nahmanides include Solomon Schechter, "Nahmanides," *Jewish Quarterly Review* 5 (1893): 78–121; Charles B. Chavel, *Ramban: His Life and Teachings* (New York: Feldheim, 1960); Jacob Even-Hen, *Ha-Ramban* (Jerusalem: Ganzach Rishon LeTziyon, 1976); Nina Caputo, *Nahmanides in Medieval Catalonia: History, Community, and Messianism* (Notre Dame, IN: Notre Dame University Press, 2007), 1–18.
4. For general background, see David Jeremy Silver, *Maimonidean Criticism and the Maimonidean Controversy, 1180–1240* (Leiden, Netherlands: Brill, 1965); and, more recently, Hava Tirosh-Samuelson, *Happiness in Premodern Judaism: Virtue, Knowledge, and Well-Being* (Cincinnati: Hebrew Union College Press, 2003), 246–90.
5. Bernard Septimus, "'Open Rebuke and Concealed Love': Nahmanides and the Andalusia Tradition," in Twersky, *Rabbi Moses Nahmanides (Ramban)*, 14.

6. See, e.g., Yitzhak Baer, *A History of the Jews in Christian Spain*, 2 vols. (Philadelphia: Jewish Publication Society of America, 1966), 1:245–47.

7. On Rashi and Ibn Ezra, see chapters 6 and 7 in this volume, by Polliack and Harris.

8. Isadore Twersky, introduction to Twersky, *Rabbi Moses Nahmanides (Ramban)*, 4.

9. Caputo, *Nahmanides in Medieval Catalonia*, 54.

10. For this rendering, see Moshe Greenberg, *Ezekiel 1–20* (Garden City, NY: Doubleday, 1983), 115.

11. Ramban, commentary to Deuteronomy 32:40. The Hebrew text is found in *Perush ha-Ramban al ha-Torah*, 2 vols., ed. Haim Dov Chavel (Jerusalem: Mosad ha-Rav Kook, 1959), 2:490–91. English translations here and in what follows are my own. For the reader unfamiliar with Hebrew, an excellent English translation of the commentary may be found in *Commentary on the Torah*, 5 vols., trans. and annotated by Haim Dov (Charles Ber) Chavel (Brooklyn, NY: Shilo, 1999), 5:367–68. For the sake of convenience, in passages that follow, I put the page number from this English translation in parentheses.

12. See Moshe Halbertal, "The Minhag and the History of Halakhah in the Teaching of Nahmanides" (in Hebrew), *Zion* 67 (2002): 25–56. On the role of history more generally in Nahmanides's thought, see Haviva Pedaya, *Ha-Ramban: Hitalut—Zeman Mahzori ve-Tekst Kadosh* (Tel Aviv: Am Oved, 2003).

13. Ramban, introduction to *Perush ha-Ramban al ha-Torah*, 1:xv–xvi (1:3–4).

14. Ramban, introduction to the Book of Genesis, 1:1 (1:7).

15. Ramban, introduction to the Book of Genesis, 1:3 (1:10).

16. Haim Dov Chavel, *Kitvei Rabbenu Moshe ben Nahman* (Jerusalem: Mosad ha-Rav Kook, 1964), 1:341–42.

17. Ramban, commentary to Exodus 30:13, 1:492–93 (2:518–19).

18. Ramban, commentary to Deuteronomy 11:22, 2:395 (5:136).

19. Ibid.

20. Ibid.

21. Ramban, introduction to the Book of Genesis, 1:1 (1:7).

22. Ibid., 1:6–7 (1:13–14).

23. See, for example, his comments to Genesis 1:26 and 35:16.

24. Ramban, commentary to Genesis 1:1. On the concept of "articles of faith" in premodern Judaism, see Menachem Kellner, *Dogma in Medieval Jewish Thought: From Maimonides to Abravanel* (Oxford: Oxford University Press, 1986).

25. Ramban, commentary to Genesis 1:1

26. Ramban, commentary to Genesis 18:1, 1:103–4 (1:226–27).

27. Ibid., 1:104–5 (1:227).

28. Ramban, commentary to Genesis 46:1, 1:251–52 (1:552).

29. Ibid., 1:252 (1:552–53).

30. Ramban, introduction to *Perush ha-Ramban al ha-Torah*, 1:xv–xvi (1:5).

31. Ramban, commentary to Genesis 1:1, 1:13–15 (1:22).

32. Ibid.

33. On the role of this text in medieval Jewish thought, see Raphael Jospe, "Early Philosophical Commentaries in the *Sefer Yezirah*: Some Comments," *Revue des études juives* 149 (1990): 269–415.

34. Ramban, commentary to Genesis 2:3, 1:30–32 (1:60).

Chapter 10

Concepts of Scripture in Jewish Mysticism

Moshe Idel

The correlation between any Jewish theology and the conception of scripture that accompanies it is one of the most characteristic features of Jewish thought.[1] All theological systems in Judaism have produced their own conceptions of Torah. These varied conceptions of Torah provide a lens through which one can study the development of Jewish concepts of God.

Biblical and midrashic theologies, in both legal and narrative texts, reflect a God who gives law and who directs the processes of history. Maimonides's God is a much more abstract, philosophical deity, and his understanding of the Torah assumes the presence of philosophical concepts. The Jewish mystical movements concerned with what is known as kabbalah began to arise in Europe in the twelfth century, and in these movements a conception of God as *Ein Sof*—infinite, transcendent, yet related to the world through several manifestations known as *sefirot*—came to the fore. Together with this understanding of God, a view of the Torah as infinite, transcendent, yet connected with the world (or better, connecting to it) emerged as well. Similarly, earlier mystical theologies of *heikhalot* literature (that is, prekabbalistic Jewish mysticism of the Talmudic era) entailed their own conceptions of Torah related to magical powers. This chapter describes connections among these earlier and later conceptions of Torah in various types of Jewish mysticism.

Torah as God's Name and Body

One of the most prominent and influential concepts of Torah that occurs in Jewish mystical literatures is that the Torah contains or even consists of names of God that are otherwise not known and that these names have the power to affect God and/or to affect the material world. Thus, for some mystics, the revelation of Torah was a revelation not only of a set of laws and narratives but of God's names, which is to say, God's very essence; revelation yielded not only information and guidance but a key with which to come into relationship with God.

According to this way of thinking, the Torah has two levels: an overt or manifest level and a hidden or secret level. The overt level was revealed to Moses at Mount Sinai, and it contains the narratives, laws, and poems known to anyone who studies or even simply reads the Torah. (Most midrashic interpretations, which one can arrive at through close reading, belong to the Torah's overt level.) The hidden level, according to the *heikhalot* mystics of the Talmudic era, was revealed to a famous sage of the Mishna, Rabbi Yishmael,[2] and also to those *heikhalot* mystics who delved into the secrets of *Shi'ur Qomah*, the literature that discloses the measurements of the divine body. Some mystics also regarded this hidden level of Torah as having been revealed to Moses at Sinai. Thus, one early medieval magical text, *Sefer Shimmushei Torah* (a *heikhalot* text dating to the Talmudic era or shortly thereafter), avers that at the time of the revelation of Torah, Moses ascended to heaven and received from various angels there secrets of the divine names found in each section of the Torah. These secrets included specific magical or mystical uses to which these divine names could be put. While Moses made the overt level of the Torah (that is, the laws and narratives found in the Torah) known to all Israel, Moses transmitted the hidden level of the Torah only to his nephew Eleazar, who succeeded Moses's brother Aaron as high priest; Eleazar transmitted it to his son and successor Phinehas, and through a continuing process of transmission, this esoteric heavenly knowledge ultimately came to the mystics of the rabbinic era themselves.[3] According to both *Sefer Shimmushei Torah* itself and the text known as *Shi'ur Qomah*, it is possible to use the secrets the angels vouchsafed to Moses (or Rabbi Yishmael) to read the Torah in a manner differing from the more widespread methods.[4] This esoteric reading yields its practitioners the ability to perform magical acts.

Further, this notion of an alternate, esoteric reading of the Torah's words at times relates to another idea that appears in *heikhalot* literature. The *heikhalot* mystics, like the rabbis, believed that the Torah existed already before the creation of the world; after all, according to the rabbis (at the beginning of *Midrash Genesis Rabbah*),[5] God used the Torah as a blueprint for creating the world; thus, Torah is the instrument through which

God created the world. If this is so, then the question needed to be asked: what was this preexistent Torah written on? It could not, after all, be written on leather (like Torah scrolls used in synagogues), since the animals from whose skin leather is made had not yet been created; nor could it be written on any other matter, since matter did not yet exist. Midrashic texts that show affinities to the literature of the *heikhalot*[6] provide an answer: the Torah was written on God's own arm. More specifically, the arm of God consisted of white fire, and the Torah was written on it in black fire. (Incidentally, here we must recall that, contrary to what many people nowadays assume, neither biblical nor rabbinic texts believe that God is completely incorporeal; for the Bible and classical rabbinic literature, it is a given that God has a body, though this body may be made of a substance that differs from a normal human body.)[7] This link between the preexistent Torah and the limbs of God's body also shows up in the similar language used in *Shi'ur Qomah* and *heikhalot* texts to describe the extraordinary size of both the divine limbs and the preexistent Torah. In this conception, the Torah at its esoteric level, like God, has the form of a human being. For prekabbalistic Jewish mystics, the secrets of the Torah revealed to Moses or to Rabbi Yishmael enable a different way of reading its words, so that the adept reader can come to gaze on the limbs of God to which Torah gives access or, perhaps, to see the limb of God that the Torah in fact is. Intensive study of the Torah on this esoteric level allows one to see God, because at this level, the Torah is on the body of God.

This confluence of ideas becomes clearer in the writings of the earliest kabbalists. The term *kabbalah* refers to the hidden meanings of ritual practices and to the esoteric doctrines that emerged in the twelfth century in the Provence region of southern France, spreading from there to Spain, Italy, and other parts of the Jewish world; these doctrines assume many forms but are especially concerned with the doctrine of *sefirot* and with the impact of the rituals upon them. The *sefirot* are manifestations of God (or, alternatively, powers emanating from God) that enter into the created world; each of the ten *sefirot* embody or reflect a particular aspect of God, such as Wisdom, Justice, Mercy, or Royalty.

The writings of thirteenth-century kabbalists display a concept of Torah based on two fundamental principles, which were described by the modern scholar of kabbalah Gershom Scholem:[8] the Torah is conceived of as a name of God (or a series of divine names), and the Torah is conceived of as an organism. The conception of Torah as an organism grows out of earlier conceptions which emphasize that the Torah has the form or shape of a human being. This concept usually appears together with the notion of the Torah as a divine name, and in fact these are two aspects of a single conception of Torah that the earliest kabbalists inherited from their predecessors, the *heikhalot* mystics. (To be sure, the *heikhalot* texts that have survived to the present day do not explicitly portray the Torah in anthropomorphic form, but a description of this sort is likely to have been found alongside these texts' anthropomorphic depiction of God.) One example of the notion of Torah as divine name appears in a commentary on the Song of Songs by Ezra ben Solomon, a thirteenth-century kabbalist from Gerona (a Spanish center of kabbalah located close to Provence.) Ezra writes,

> All the Torah is spoken directly from the mouth of God, and it contains not a single superfluous letter or vowel, because all of it is a divine edifice hewn from the mouth of the Holy One, blessed be He. . . . If a person were to remove a single letter [from the Torah], it would be as if he destroyed a whole [divine] name and a whole world . . . for the commandments are the very body of purity and holiness.[9]

The connection between the Torah as divine name and as divine body comes through more clearly in these passages from the work of another thirteenth-century kabbalist from Gerona, Jacob ben Sheshet:

> Whence do we know that His name is His body? From the verse [Proverbs 10:7], "A wicked man's name will rot." Is it really the case that a name can rot? Rather, a body rots [and thus we learn that these two words are interchangeable, that the Hebrew word for "name" can also mean "body"]. This is the reason that it is forbidden to utter [God's] name in vain and for no purpose. . . . Oaths [which are made "By the name of God"] are taken by holding on to an object such as a Torah scroll, because the Torah is God's name. . . . We have learned that one who takes an oath by means of a Torah has taken an oath by God's name, and whoever takes up a Torah scroll is mentioning His name. . . .
>
> "Let us make humanity in our image" [Genesis 1:26]. Rashi explicated "in our image" as meaning "according to a mold made from us." One can say: there was no mold in God's presence [since the world had only just been created] other than the Torah—that is, the 613 commandments [found in the Torah]. Those [commandments] were the mold with which He created humanity.[10]

The identifications, "God's name = God's body" and "name = Torah," recall Ezra ben Solomon's words quoted earlier, suggesting that we can equate "body" (which may be parallel to the "divine edifice" in Ezra's statement) with Torah.

In all likelihood, what stands behind the teachings of these kabbalists is a notion drawn from the *Shi'ur Qomah* literature, that the Torah—on its esoteric level—is the full height of God's body. But one should note some differences between these notions as they appear, say, in a prekabbalistic work such as the *Sefer Shimmushei Torah* and in these thirteenth-century kabbalistic works. In the former, a relatively small number of esoteric names of God can be derived from specific verses throughout the whole Torah, if one has access to the secret knowledge revealed to Moses or Rabbi Yishmael. For the kabbalists (not only the two cited here but others as well—in particular, Nahmanides),[11] not only can specific verses serve as a source of divine names, but the Torah in its entirety can be transformed into a long series of divine names. Doing so requires correct knowledge of how to redivide its constituent letters into this series of names, without regard for how those letters form Hebrew words and sentences on the Torah's overt level. Further, for kabbalists, the Torah is full of names of God, while for the earlier *heikhalot* mystics, the Torah also contains names of various angels. (Many kabbalists, including Nahmanides, resemble the *heikhalot* mystics in maintaining that one can use knowledge of these divine names embedded in the Torah for magical purposes.)[12] An additional kabbalistic perspective that coexisted with the one just described also deserves mention: to wit, the notion that the Torah not only contains esoteric divine names but is itself one long divine name. These two notions (the Torah as containing divine names, and the Torah as a divine name), viewed together, return us to the idea that the Torah is the body of God: the individual divine names found throughout the Torah are individual limbs; when combined, these individual limbs/names form the whole body of God, which is to say, form the Torah's text, which is one long and mysterious appellation for God.

These kabbalistic conceptions of Torah were often linked with doctrines of the *sefirot*. In some early kabbalistic systems, the second-highest[13] *sefirah*, Ḥokhmah or Wisdom, stands for the primordial or heavenly Torah; the sixth-highest *sefirah*, *Tiferet* or Glory, stands for the Written Torah (that is, the Bible); and the lowest *sefirah*, *Malkhut* or Kingship, is associated to the Oral Torah.[14] From this point of view, the Torah (in its various definitions) was projected onto the divine realm. Kabbalistic symbolism of this sort facilitated a move from the earthly practice of studying Torah (on its overt level) to a practice through which the mystic formed contact with heavenly forms of the Torah (on its esoteric level). Thus, R. Moses ben Shem Tov de Leon, a late thirteenth-century kabbalist in Spain (an influential kabbalist who was closely associated with the authorship, redaction, and/or dissemination of the Zohar, which is often viewed as the central text of kabbalistic tradition), writes,

> God has bequeathed this holy Torah to Israel from above to bequeath to them the secret of His name, Blessed be He, and to [enable Israel to] cleave to Him [or to His name], so that all the worlds will be equal according to one secret and one outcome, and so that all are linked [to each other] and descend according to the secret of His Name, Blessed be He, in order to show that as this name [or He] is infinite and limitless, so is this Torah infinite and limitless. . . . Since the Torah is "longer than the earth and broader than the sea" [Job 11.9], we must be spiritually aware and know that the essence of this existence is infinite and limitless. And behold that the essence of His existence descends from the source of the supernal rank, from where all the essences expand. We should know that the source of the [supernal] rank is the secret of the Torah, since you already know that the supernal rank is the first and supernal point and is the secret of the Torah.[15]

De Leon employs here the biblical image of infinity in relation to the second *sefirah*, Ḥokhmah or Wisdom. For de Leon, not only does the infinity of the Torah reflect God's infinite wisdom, but intimation of part of this infinity provides a way for a kabbalist to cleave to Him, to assimilate to the divine. The Torah is seen in a highly instrumental way, as a path toward a unitive experience that avoids any specific reasoning that addresses its particular textuality. De Leon assumes that it is the presence of God as author that ensures the infinity of the text. At the two extremities of the *sefirot* chain that leads from the Infinite and Transcendent *Ein Sof* down toward the world, we find two forms of the Torah, and the study of the lower form of Torah (which includes both the Bible and rabbinic tradition) enables the mystic to reach the higher.

A related understanding of the Bible is found in the work of a kabbalist whose identity is not firmly established but who was a contemporary of R. Moses de Leon. The author of *The Book of [Divine] Unity* presents this detailed explanation of the manner in which someone may have a sense of direct contact with divinity through the biblical text:

> God gave us the entire Torah in perfect form, from [its opening words in Genesis 1:1,] "In the beginning," to [the last words of the Torah in Deuteronomy 34:12,] "in the eyes of all Israel." Behold, how all the letters of the Torah, by their shapes, are the shape of God, blessed be He: combined and separated letters, . . . curved ones and crooked ones, superfluous and elliptic ones, minute and large ones, and inverted ones, the calligraphy of the letters, the paragraphs that begin on a new line and those that begin after a blank space on the same line as the end of the previous paragraph . . . , all of them.[16] This is similar to, though incomparable with, something someone paints using [several] kinds of colors; likewise the Torah, beginning with the first passage until the last one, is the shape of God, the Great and Formidable, blessed be He, since if one letter be missing from a Torah scroll, or if one is superfluous, or if a paragraph that should begin after a blank space on the same line as the previous paragraph were [written] at the beginning of a new line, or if a paragraph that should begin on a new line were [written so that it began] after a blank space on the same line as the previous paragraph, then that scroll of Torah is unfit [and, according to rabbinic law, cannot be used for liturgical reading but must be repaired or buried in a cemetery], since it does not contain the shape of God, blessed be He, the Great and Formidable, because of the change caused by the shape. And you should understand this! And because it is incumbent on each and every Jew to say that the world was created for him,[17] God obliged each and every one of them to write a scroll of the Torah for himself, and the concealed secret is that he made God, blessed be He.[18]

According to this text, God is reflected in the scroll of the Torah because of the special rules in rabbinic law specifying how its words are spelled and its letters formed. Further, this presence can be copied. Jews are obliged to reproduce the scroll precisely because of this type of reflection of the divine within the text. For this author, the Torah is an icon, because the Torah reflects the divine form. Moreover, this author's iconic vision assumes the literal nature of the divine, given the fact that the forms of letters constitute the divine shape. This formal correspondence between the lower and higher, along with the anthropomorphic nature of the actual biblical text, changes the basic approach toward the Bible from one deeply concerned with the meaning of its words and sentences to an approach that is unconcerned with these verbal meanings. This latter approach attends to an aspect of the text that precedes and underlies the text's semantic meanings. What counts is not the specific meaning or meanings of the canonical text but its status as an icon, as a carrier of divine presence. It should be stressed, nonetheless, that the two approaches (the semantic approach to the overt Torah and the iconic approach to the esoteric Torah) are not mutually exclusive: the same person can study and use the Torah from both points of view.

This oscillation between the literal/semantic structures and the anthropomorphic/iconic ones occurs also in the work of a mysterious kabbalist known as R. Joseph of Hamadan. In his *Commentary on the Rationales of the Commandments*, Joseph draws detailed parallels between Torah on the one hand and anthropomorphic visions of the *sefirot* and God on the other:

> Why is it called Torah? It has paragraphs that must start on a new line [these are known as "open paragraphs"] and paragraphs that must start after a blank space on the same line as the preceding paragraph [these are known as "closed paragraphs"], referring to the image of a building and the form of man, who is like the supernal, holy, and pure form. And just as there are joints in man connected to each other, in the Torah there are closed paragraphs, as in the case of the structure of the paragraph beginning with the words, "When Pharaoh let out" [Exodus 13:17]. The secret of the song "Then Moses Sang" [Exodus 15:1] is the secret of the joints of the Holy One, blessed be He. And the song "Give ear, heavens" [Deuteronomy 32:1] is the secret of the ear of the Holy One, blessed be He, and the secret of "Then Israel Sang" [Numbers 21:17] is the secret of the divine circumcision.... The positive commandments correspond to the secret of the male, and the negative commandments correspond to the secret of the female and to the secret of the [lowest *sefirah*,] *Shekhinah* [Presence or Dwelling] and to the secret of *Malkhut* [Royalty—another name for *Shekhinah*]. This is the reason why the Torah is called Torah, because it refers to the likeness of the Holy One, blessed be He.[19]

R. Joseph of Hamadan presents an interesting interpretation of the word Torah. The Hebrew noun *Torah* is generally understood to suggest "instruction," but here the medieval kabbalist interprets it (quite legitimately, from a linguistic or etymological point of view) to mean "reference." In the more typical usage, Torah/instruction descends from the supernal realm to humanity below, but for this kabbalist, the word implies movement in the opposite direction. The lower entity, the Torah, reflects a higher one, and thus it paves the way to an understanding of the divine through comprehension of the structure of the text. This understanding is based on the identity of form between portions of the Torah and the limbs of the divine body (which, in turn, is conceived as sharing its shape with a human body). However, for R. Joseph, this symbolic function does not operate on the Torah's overt or narrative level by introducing a divine myth paralleled by and reflected in mundane events. Rather, what counts is the shape of the portion of the canonical text, not its content.

As in *The Book of [Divine] Unity*, Hamadan assumes that God and the Bible are identical or at least isomorphic—that is, they share a similar or identical structure. However, what is fascinating in the material just quoted from Hamadan's *Commentary on the Rationales of the Commandments* is not the avowal of this isomorphism but the attempt to correlate specific sections of the biblical text with specific limbs of the supernal Man (i.e., the divine body). The significance of this relationship is captured in this passage:

> Happy is the man who knows how to relate a limb to another [i.e., a human limb to a divine limb] and a form to another [form], which are found in the Holy and Pure Chain, blessed be His Name, because the Torah is His form, blessed be He. He commanded us to study Torah in order to know the likeness of the Supernal Form; as some kabbalists said, [quoting Deuteronomy 27:26,] "Cursed is whoever will not keep this Torah up." Can the Torah fall? This [verse should be taken as] a warning for the cantor to [lift the Torah scroll up and thus to] show the written form of the Torah scroll to the community for them to see the likeness of the Supernal Form. Moreover, the study of the Torah brings someone close to seeing supernal secrets and the Glory of the Holy One, blessed be He, for real.[20]

This passage discusses knowledge of the structural affinity between human limbs and forms and the divine ones. The cognitive movement is expressly upward. The form of the letters in the Torah is assumed to play the same role as in the human body; the latter is an icon enabling the contemplation of the supernal form. This explains the custom of showing the open scroll of the Torah to the members of the community after the reading of the weekly portion in synagogue. However, the formal correspondences between the lower and higher limbs should be understood in a broader sense. The expression "limb to limb" is reminiscent of another recurrent phrase in R. Joseph of Hamadan's work: "a limb that holds up," which means that the lower limb not only corresponds to but also supports the supernal one. He is arguing that performance of the commandments by a certain limb strengthens its parallel limb found on high, which is one of the *sefirot*. Thus, the contemplation of the higher from the vantage point of the lower is not the only, and perhaps not even the most important, type of relationship between certain shapes here below (the human body and the Torah) and the structure of the *sefirot* on high. The lower not only knows the higher but also contributes to making it (as seems to be the case in the passage quoted earlier from *The Book of [Divine] Unity*) or supports it (as is the case in R. Joseph of Hamadan's books). This influence is theurgical in nature (the term *theurgy* refers to a human activity intended to influence divinity, whether in God's own inner state or in God's relationship with humanity). This theurgical influence is only possible because of the affinities between three isomorphic structures: the Torah, the human body, and the ten *sefirot* which form the divine realm.

R. Joseph writes elsewhere in his *Commentary on the Rationales of the Commandments*,

> Woe to whoever believes that there is nothing more than the plain meaning of the Torah,[21] because the Torah, in its entirety, is the name of the Holy One blessed be He. The [Talmudic] sages of blessed memory already hinted at this [when they said] that whoever says the whole Torah is from heaven except for this letter is a heretic and has no portion whatsoever in the World to Come.[22] Because the Torah in its entirety is the name of the Holy One, blessed be He, it consists of inner [i.e., spiritual] things . . . such that no creature can comprehend the greatness of its rank other than God, blessed be He, the supreme and the wonderful One who created it. And the Torah of the Holy One, blessed be He, is within Him, and in Him there is the Torah, and this is the reason why kabbalists said that "He is in His name, and the Name is in Him." He is His Torah, and the Torah is made of the holy and pure chain, in [the image of the] supernal form, and it is the shadow of the Holy One, blessed be He.[23]

The profound affinity between God, name, and Torah is obvious in this passage. God forms the hidden layer of the Torah, and from this point of view, He is within the Torah. However, this anthropomorphic isomorphism has an additional and very important layer: the human and divine limbs are parallel not only because they possess a similar structure but also because of their dynamic affinities. Ritual activities, the rituals or the commandments performed by human limbs, are related theurgically to the divine limbs. In other words, the realization of this isomorphism, based on knowledge and contemplation of the higher by means of the lower structure, leads from one stage to another.

The relationship between contemplation of Torah on its esoteric level and theurgy was made explicit by R. Menahem Recanati, an Italian kabbalist of the late thirteenth and early fourteenth centuries. He wrote, "All the sciences altogether are hinted at in the Torah, because there is nothing that is outside of it [the Torah]. . . . Therefore the Holy One, blessed be He, is nothing that is outside the Torah, and the Torah is nothing that is outside Him, and this is the reason why the sages of the kabbalah said that the Holy One, blessed be He, is the Torah."[24] This is a crucial example of the mapping of the supernal realm onto types of human practices; God and Torah are identical, which means that God is called by the word *Torah*. A fascination with the profound affinities among God, Torah, and man is found in a classic of kabbalah, written by R. Meir ibn Gabbai, an influential sixteenth-century kabbalist. He envisioned the Torah as isomorphic to both God and man and acting as an intermediate entity:

> The Torah is, therefore, the wholeness of the grand and supernal Anthropos, and this is the reason why it comprises the 248 positive commandments and 365 negative commandments, which are tantamount to the number of the limbs and sinews of the lower and the supernal man. . . . And since the Torah has the shape of man, it is fitting to be given to man, and man is man by virtue of it, and in the end he will cleave to man.[25]

Thus, the Torah becomes an intermediary man, a link between humanity down here and the supernal Anthropos in heaven: "The intermediary which stirs the supernal image toward the lower one," or, according to another passage, "the Torah and the commandments are the intermediary which link the lower image to the supernal one, by the affinity they have with both."[26] These quotations are simply examples of kabbalistic treatments of the Torah as the image or icon of God. Others can be found in later kabbalistic sources. According to these sources, the parallel among God, Torah, and man—who all share the same structure—allows the kabbalist to ascend on high.

Instrumental and Talismanic Uses of Torah in Later Jewish Mysticism

The notions that the Torah is a name of God and thus in some senses an icon of divine presence has far-reaching consequences in later Jewish mysticism, especially in Hasidism in eastern Europe. The Hasidic movement arose in the eighteenth century in what is today Poland and the Ukraine, spreading to most of eastern Europe; with the destruction of European Jewry in the Holocaust, Hasidism is now centered in Israel and parts of the United States (especially in New York). Hasidic theory and practice raise crucial issues pertaining to the concept of scripture—that is, to the basic question of what scripture is and what it does. These include the question of how a Jew uses Torah to access God, how a Jew accesses Torah itself, the extent to which it is important for a person to understand the Torah used to access God, what we may refer to as phonic talismanics (the idea that the very sounds of Torah are carriers of a divine power which human beings can utilize to affect God or the world), and thus finally the question of the relationship between scripture and magic. In these Hasidic texts, we see a transcendence of meaning (both of the plain sense and the esoteric one) in favor of oral performance, which effects the restitution of the primacy of spoken language.[27] These sources insist that scripture, or the Written Torah, is in essence an oral phenomenon and that only in its oral state does it fully function in the manner ontologically unique to scripture.[28]

Let me start with a short survey of topics that are related to the practice of reading the Torah in early Hasidism. The founder of Hasidism, Israel Baal Shem Tov (c. 1698–1760), also known as "the Besht," has been reported by his grandson, R. Moshe Hayyim Ephrayyim of Sudylkov, as holding the following view:

> How is it possible to take the Holy One, may He be blessed, so that He will dwell upon man? It is by the means of the Torah, which is indeed the names of God, since He and His name are one unity, and when someone studies the Torah for the sake of God and in order to keep His commandments and abstains from what is prohibited, and he pronounces the letters of the Torah, which are the names of God. By these [activities] he genuinely takes God, and it is as if the Divine Presence dwells upon him as it is written [Exodus 20.21]: "in all places where I pronounce the name of God" (which is the holy Torah, which is in its entirety His names), then "I will come to you and I bless you."[29]

According to the Besht, then, by studying the Torah for the sake of the "name" (namely, of the Tetragrammaton), the mystico-magical scholar is conceived as if "he thereby takes the name, and he draws onto himself the dwelling of the Divine Holy Presence."[30]

One of the most important followers of the Besht was Rabbi Dov Baer, known as the Great Maggid of Miedzirec (1704–1772). He seems to have continued and elaborated his master's assessment:

> He [God] contracted Himself within the letters of the Torah, by means of which He has created the world.... The *Tzaddik* [the righteous man; also, the leader of a Hasidic group], who studies the Torah for its own sake, in [a state of] holiness, draws the Creator, blessed be He, downward within the letters of the Torah, just as in the moment of the creation.... By the pure utterances, related to the study of the Torah, he draws down God within the letters.[31]

Here the Hasidic master elaborates on the concept of *tzimtzum* (contraction), a core notion in the kabbalah of the sixteenth-century Rabbi Isaac Luria and his followers. According to Luria, to create the world, the infinite and boundless deity contracted Itself to make room for the world. Our Hasidic text relates this concept to the notion of Torah we have been examining: the divine transcendence that characterized the deity before the moment of creation contracts into, or limits itself within, the particular letters of the Torah, which serves as the paradigm for the subsequent creation of the world. As a cosmogonical paradigm, those letters are also a reification of the divine in His contracted aspect. We may call this reification "linguistic immanence": in the letters of the Torah, the infinite and transcendent becomes real and even concrete in this world.[32] The Torah as revealed to man, when studied by the mystic, serves as the tool for the re-creation of cosmogony: the act of studying evokes and reproduces the first constitutive moments of the world by invoking the divinity into the letters. However, as the quoted text explicitly states, it is not the written aspect of the letters but their utterance aloud, namely, the individual performance of each of the letters by the righteous, that effects this re-creation of the world's first moments. Thus, the study aloud of the Torah is a case of what we may call phonic talismanics: it is the sound of the Torah's letters that have power over creation and even in some sense over God. In other words, the sound of the Torah's letters can be used for magical purposes (they have power over creation) and for theurgic purposes (they have power over God).

This invocation of the divinity by a phonic talismanics should not be distinguished from a strong mystical purpose: the sounds of the Torah's letters also allow the *tzaddik* to cleave to the immanent God. The Great Maggid has already expressed this view in various ways, and only a very few of them will be discussed here. In a collection of his teachings entitled *Or Ha-Emet*, we find what seems to be one of the most magical of the Hasidic formulations of manipulating God by means of the sacred text, again in the context of the divine contraction:

> It is as if God has contracted Himself into the Torah. When someone calls a man by his name, he puts all his affairs aside and answers the person who called him, because he is compelled by his name.[33] Likewise, God has, as it were, contracted himself into the Torah, and the Torah is His name, and when someone reads/calls out[34] the Torah, then they draw God, blessed be He, downward toward us, because He and His name are one total unity with us.[35]

The hidden affinity between God, His Name, and the Torah is a fundamental assumption that informed many of the Hasidic views of talismanic magic. Though close affinities and sometimes even explicit identities between these three topics recur in many kabbalistic texts since the thirteenth century, in Hasidic literature, the talismanic implications of such a view were explicated in a rather extreme manner: these Hasidic texts assume that God can be compelled by His name to descend. Extreme as this magical assumption is, the mystical implication is also evident: the ones who call God's name will cling to the descending deity, thus attaining a mystical union.

Similar views can be found in writings of one of the Great Maggid's most important students: Rabbi Shneor Zalman of Liady, the founder of the Habad (or Lubavitch) school of Hasidism, which is one of the most intellectualistic trends in Hasidism in general. In the following passage, Shneor Zalman discusses a common Hebrew term for the Bible, *miqra*. Though this term is often translated into English as "scripture," this translation is misleading, since the term comes from the Hebrew root *qr'*, which means not "write, put down in script" but "call, read aloud." Consequently, Shneor Zalman claims that the Bible is called *miqra*

> because one calls [or reads] and [subsequently] draws down the revelation of the light of the Infinite, by means of letters, even if one does not

comprehend anything at all. . . . The drawing down is specifically by means of the letters, and this is the reason that despite the fact that he does not understand the meaning, he is able to draw [the revelation of the light of the Infinite] down, whereas in the case of the Oral Torah, clothed as it is within [the *sefirah* of] Ḥokhmah, he cannot draw it down unless he understands.[36] In the case of the Written Torah, however, he draws down even if he does not understand, as it [the drawing down] does not depend on understanding to such an extent [as is the case with the Oral Torah] because the source of the drawing down is higher than [the *sefirah* of] Ḥokhmah, etc. This means that it [the drawing down] is [done] by means of the letters, and this is why the Written Torah is called *Miqra*—because we call [*qore'*] and [then] draw [down] by means of the letters.[37]

As mentioned earlier, in Hebrew the verb *qore'*, translated here as "calls," stands also for "reading." Here the reading of the Torah is understood more as a recitation, actually as a calling of God, an invocation which is very powerful because it is done by means of letters, whose origin is higher than the realm of Ḥokhmah, the second *sefirah*. Moreover, according to another passage, this drawing down occurs by virtue of a special feature of the biblical text, which is conceived as constituting a continuum of divine names. A most interesting parallel of our passage by the same author argues again that "the whole Torah consists of the names of God, blessed be He, which are the aspects of the letters of the Torah, and this is the reason that it is called *miqra*, which is derived from the term *qeri'ah* [understood as "calling"], because he calls Him by His names, and because of this He makes Himself available."[38] In this context, the *hamshakhah*, the drawing down, is explicitly mentioned, inter alia defining the whole Torah as drawing down from Ḥokhmah.

The longer of the two passages by Shneor Zalman quoted above introduces a remarkable distinction between the different ways the two Torahs are understood to function. On the one hand, the Written Torah is conceived of as having been voiced as part of ritual in general, and as part of magic in particular, which is not conditioned by the understanding of the Torah's content. On the other hand, the Oral Torah is described as having to be understood, namely, as undergoing a process of epistemological assimilation that does not comprise the act of verbalization. Only when this epistemological assimilation takes place can the drawing down occur. Prima facie, this distinction involves a double contradiction: the Written becomes oral, and the Oral become written. However, these contradictions can be explained as part of the sociological background of Hasidism: the Hasidic master invests the ritual of reading the Torah with an efficacy that does not depend on the cognitive capacities of the performer. Such an approach allows strong mystical experiences, which are caused by the descent of the divine power into the voiced letters of the canonical text. On the other hand, the study of the Oral Torah (the study of which is more elitist, because Talmudic study occurs especially in academic settings and not among the masses of Jewry) is envisaged as having a magical effect only if it involves understanding. Thus, the Oral Torah remains the prerogative of the rabbinic elite, but now this elite is deprived of a special status as magicians, at least insofar as the activation of the canonical texts are involved: God is compelled to be present by the inner structure of the voiced Written Torah performed in public, even by an unlettered but pious Jew.[39]

Torah as Intermediary

We have seen that the Torah as God's name serves as an intermediary, allowing God to descend into the world. We can conclude this survey by noting some texts which propose movement that goes in the other direction: the Torah allows human beings to ascend to a heavenly realm.

Some kabbalists developed a theory reminiscent of the great chain of Being. Here the lower realms are the impression (Hebrew, *roshem*) of the higher ones, with God at the top. A related theory defines the Torah as the souls of the people of Israel and considers that the Torah consists of the divine names. This triune vision enables the passage of the soul, via the Torah and the divine names, to God.[40] The following passage is one major example of this view, taken from Rabbi Isaiah Horowitz's early seventeenth-century work *Shnei Luḥot Ha-Berit* (*Ha-Shelah*), a widely read classic of somewhat more popular kabbalah:

> The Holy One, Blessed be He, and the Torah and man are linked to each other. . . . As the sages of truth [the kabbalists] said, the Torah is the impression of the Divinity, and man is the impression of the Torah, since the revelation of His divinity is the secret of His holy names, and the Torah is, in its entirety, His names. . . . The Torah consists of the souls of Israel, both the revealed Torah . . . and the primordial, preserved Torah, which is the root of the souls of the chosen few. And man is the impression of the Torah. The vast majority, almost all of them, are the impression of this

revealed Torah, . . . and the rank of the soul of the chosen few is from the primordial Torah.[41]

Unlike the more formalistic approaches discussed earlier, such as that of Joseph of Hamadan (which presuppose some type of distance between the isomorphic elements), Horowitz assumes a much more organic linkage. There is something congenital in the three elements mentioned in the preceding passage in that the entity that causes the impression still lingers in the imprinted entity. This is why the study of the Torah involves perhaps less a movement beyond a fallen plight than an actualization of a divine aspect found in man. Following Horowitz (and others including Menahem Azariah of Fano and Meir ibn Gabbai), Rabbi Ze'ev Wolf of Zhitomir, a late eighteenth-century Hasidic author, presents a Platonic process of ascent to the supernal source, deemed possible by the means of the Torah:

> The Torah is the impression of the divinity, and the world is the impression of the Torah. . . . An enlightened person concentrates his heart, spirit and soul to divest everything in the world from materiality, and cause the embodiment of the spiritual form . . . by his comprehension of the embodiment of the divinity, which dwells there, within the letters of the Torah, which are embodied as well in the entirety of the world, which was created with the Torah, and they animate everything. And this is the power of the enlightened one that he can divest himself of the material form and be clothed in the spiritual form.[42]

Here the Torah serves as an intermediary between the creator and man. The letters of the Torah represent what I termed earlier the linguistic immanence of the divine within the created world. The Hasidic mystic can restrict his contemplation solely to letters of the Torah and attain the divine source. The divine immanence or its extension in the Torah and hence in the world is presented in a concrete, nonsymbolic manner, but here (as opposed to what we saw earlier in the texts by the Maggid of Miedzirec and his disciple Shneor Zalman of Liady) the Torah serves as a scale of ascent to the divine, rather than the divine's descent toward man. The descent of the divine via the letters of the Torah is an interesting kind of divine accommodation (though not a regular one which implies attuning the message to the intellectual or moral level of the recipient). By means of linguistic immanence, there is ontic accommodation involving the divine presence in the mundane sphere, not only its symbolic representation.

This is the gist of another interesting passage in early Hasidism, in which the unitive concern is combined with what I call the talismanic model. Rabbi Menahem Nahum of Chernobyl, a Hasidic master active in the second part of the eighteenth century, writes,

> Man must pronounce the letters while being in a state of cleaving to the "Primordial Speech" through which he can draw downward the "Primordial Speech"—which is an aspect of God—to Israel in a general way. Since this is the quintessence of the revelation of the Torah, which is an aspect of God and is in His Name, part of God is drawn and infused into the Children of Israel, by means of speech that emanates from the Primordial Speech.[43]

On the same page, R. Menahem Nahum writes that the ideal study of the Torah is "for its own sake." This is a common rabbinic idea, and in the original Hebrew, the idea of "its own" is conveyed by a pronominal suffix spelled with the letter *h*. Menahem Nahum therefore interprets this common rabbinic idea to mean that ideal Torah study is "for the sake of the letter *h* [whose numerical value in Hebrew is five and thus refers to study for the sake of] the five locations, which is Primordial Speech." He interprets Torah study as being for the sake of the five locations in the mouth where vocalizations are produced. Thus, Torah study is defined as primarily vocal and also ideally intended to be so.

These passages represent only a sampling of the varied ways that scripture is viewed in Jewish mystical texts. Additional types of Jewish mysticism (in particular the ecstatic kabbalah) could not be adduced here for reasons of space, and further nuances in the literatures surveyed could not be described. Several themes, nonetheless, emerge from the varieties of scriptural experience seen in our survey. For Jewish mystics, scripture contains several types of information, accessible at exoteric and esoteric levels. Moreover, scripture does not only serve as a source of information and guidance; it also contains the very presence of God, through the names of God from which it is built. Consequently, scripture is not only something to be understood but something to be used, a localization of the sacred.

NOTES

1. *Editor's Note*: This chapter is based on two pieces by Moshe Idel, which have been abridged and combined by Benjamin D. Sommer: "The Concept of Torah in

Heikhalot Literature and Its Metamorphoses in Kabbalah," *Mechqerei Yerushalayim Bemachshevet Yisrael* 1 (1981), 23–84 [in Hebrew]; and chapter 5 from a forthcoming book, *Powers of Language*. Material from the third chapter of Idel's book *Enchanted Chains: Techniques and Rituals in Jewish Mysticism* (Los Angeles: Cherub, 2005) has also been incorporated. Notes in this chapter are kept to a minimum; full documentation can be found in the works which this essay summarizes.

2. This is the same Rabbi Yishmael whom Azzan Yadin-Israel discusses in chapter 4, but the *heikhalot* mystics' view of Yishmael is vastly different from the memories of him that appear in the midrashic texts Yadin-Israel discusses.

3. The relevant passage from *Sefer Shimmushei Torah* appears in the edition of Adolph Jellinek, *Bet ha-Midrash* (Jerusalem: Wahrman, 1967 [1853–1877]), 1:58.

4. It is possible that the Talmud, in BT *Shabbat* 88b–89a, alludes to these secrets that Moses received in heaven. This passage states that upon ascending on high, Moses received, in addition to the Torah, certain "gifts." See further Idel, "Concept of Torah," 25–26, 33 n. 33a.

5. Genesis Rabbah Par. 1 sec. 2 and parallels. This motif became especially important in kabbalah. See, e.g., Zohar 1:134a–b and 3:35b. On the preexistence of the Torah in midrash, see also *Genesis Rabbah* Par. 8 sec. 2 and parallels.

6. See *Midrash 'Asert Ha-Dibbrot*, ed. Judah David Eisenstein (New York: Eisenstein, 1915), 450; *Tanchuma Vayyelekh* §2 (123a); see further references in Idel, "Concept of Torah," 43–44nn. 59–61.

7. On the thoroughly anthropomorphic conceptions of God in biblical and rabbinic literature, see Alon Goshen-Gottstein, "The Body as Image of God in Rabbinic Literature," *Harvard Theological Review* 87 (1994): 171–95; Yair Lorberbaum, *The Image of God: Halakhah and Aggadah* [in Hebrew] (Tel Aviv: Schocken Books, 2004), 12–104; Benjamin D. Sommer, *The Bodies of God and the World of Ancient Israel* (New York: Cambridge University Press, 2009), esp. 1–10, 38–79.

8. See Gershom Scholem, "The Meaning of the Torah in Jewish Mysticism," in *On the Kabbalah and Its Symbolism*, trans. Ralph Manheim (New York: Schocken Books, 1996), 32–86, esp. 37.

9. Text available in Idel, "Concept of Torah," 49–50 (also in C. D. Chavel, *Kitvei Rabbeinu Moshe ben Nachman* [Jerusalem: Mossad Ha-Rav Kook, 1963], 2:548).

10. The first quotation is from Jacob's work *Faith and Trust*, the second from his *Who Responds with Upright Utterances*. For the texts, see Idel, "Concepts of Torah," 50 (Hebrew text in Chavel, *Kitvei*, 2:418), 51–52.

11. See chapter 9 in this volume, on Nahmanides, by Aaron Hughes.

12. See Moshe Idel, "On Angels and Biblical Exegesis in Thirteenth-Century Ashkenaz," in *Scriptural Exegesis: The Shapes of Culture and the Religious Imagination; Essays in Honour of Michael Fishbane*, ed. D. A. Green and L. S. Lieber (Oxford: Oxford University Press, 2009), 211–44.

13. *Sefirot* were often organized in sets that can be viewed from top to bottom and left to right. The three highest ones (which are closer to the transcendent God

as Infinite or *Ein Sof*) are referred to as the first through third. The remaining ones are sometimes referred to as the lower seven, and these might be seen as more immanent or involved with this world.

14. On the crucial distinction in rabbinic Judaism between Written Torah (that is, the Hebrew Bible) and Oral Torah (that is, rabbinic tradition, including but not limited to the Mishna, the Talmuds, and the midrashim), see chapter 3 by Steven Fraade in this volume.

15. R. Moses ben Shem Tov de Leon, *Sefer Ha-Rimmon*, 326.

16. In this sentence, the author refers to various special ways that words and paragraphs are required to be written in a Torah scroll used for liturgical reading in synagogues.

17. Here the author refers to a tradition found in a rabbinic text, *Tanna de-Bei Eliyahu*, ch. 25.

18. For the text from the unpublished work, see Idel, "Concept of Torah," 62–64.

19. For the text from this unpublished work, see ibid., 64–65.

20. For the text from this unpublished work, see ibid., 65.

21. The Hebrew translated here as "plain meaning" is *peshat*; see further concerning this term in Robert Harris's chapter 7 in this volume.

22. For this teaching in rabbinic literature, see BT *Sanhedrin* 99a.

23. For this unpublished text, see Idel, "Concept of Torah," 66–67.

24. See Recanati's *Commentary on the Rationales for the Commandments*, ed. H. Liebermann (London: Mekhon Otzar Ha-hokhmah, 1962), fol. 2ab; I checked the version found in MS Paris, BN 825, fols. 1b–2a. This quotation was reproduced in R. Isaiah Horowitz's early seventeenth-century work *Shnei Luhot Ha-Berit* (*Ha-Shelah*).

25. For the text from ibn Gabbai's *Avodat Ha-qodesh*, see Idel, "Concept of Torah," 75.

26. These quotations are also from Gabbai's *Avodat Ha-qodesh*, 36d.

27. On this issue, see also Elliot Wolfson, "Beautiful Maiden without Eyes: Peshat and Sod in Zoharic Hermeneutics," in *The Midrashic Imagination*, ed. Michael Fishbane (Albany: SUNY Press, 1993), especially 190. On the distinction between reading for understanding and reading for ritual purposes, see Moshe Halbertal, *People of the Book: Canon, Meaning, and Authority* (Cambridge: Harvard University Press, 1997), 13–14.

28. The notion that Written Torah was originally Oral Torah and in essence always remains this way has roots in classical rabbinic literature; see the discussion in Benjamin Sommer, "Unity and Plurality in Jewish Canons: The Case of the Oral and Written Torahs," in *One Scripture or Many? Canon from Biblical, Theological and Philosophical Perspectives*, ed. C. Helmer and C. Landmesser (New York: Oxford University Press, 2004), 123–25; and David Kraemer, "The Formation of

Rabbinic Canon: Authority and Boundaries," *Journal of Biblical Literature* 110 (1991): 624–26.

29. Moshe Hayyim Ephrayyim of Sudylkov, *Degel Mahaneh Efrayyim*, 119–20.

30. Ibid.

31. R. Elimelekh of Lisansk, *No'am Elimelekh*, fol. 8a.

32. See Moshe Idel, *Hasidism: Between Ecstasy and Magic* (Albany: SUNY Press, 1995), 215–18.

33. The Hebrew phrase here (*she-hu asur bi-shemo*) means figuratively that God is imprisoned in or bound by His Name. The view that God is bound is reminiscent of Song of Songs 7:6, in which the king, understood in many Jewish texts as an allegory for God, is caught or bound (Hebrew: *asur*) in tresses. Compare, however, to Scholem's view that, in addition to light and sound, "even the names of God are merely symbolic representations of an ultimate reality which is unformed, amorphous" (*On the Kabbalah*, 8).

34. The Hebrew verb *qore'* means both "to read" and "to call." For the magical significance of this verb in the *Heikhalot* literature, see Peter Schaefer, *Hekhalot-Studien* (Tübingen, Germany: J. C. M. Mohr, 1988), 259. In our context, the role of the biblical phrase *qore' be-shem Yhwh* (see Psalm 99:10 and Joel 2:17) should be examined.

35. Dov Baer, *Or Ha-Emet*, fol. 14c.

36. Note that Shneor Zalman here differs from the widespread understanding of the *sefirot* described earlier, according to which the second *sefirah*, *Hokhmah*, stands for the primordial or heavenly Torah; the sixth, *Tiferet*, stands for the Written Torah; and the lowest, *Malkhut* (also known as *Shekhinah*), is associated to the Oral Torah. According to Shneor Zalman in this passage, however, *Hokhmah* is associated with Oral Torah, and the highest *sefirah*, *Keter*, is implicitly associated with Written Torah.

37. This author emphasizes that the source of the letters and of speech in general is higher than that of knowledge, because the knowledge stems from the second *sefirah*, *Hokhmah*, while the speech stems from the first *sefirah*, *Keter*. This stand is explicated in more details elsewhere in the same book; see *Liqqutei Torah* (Brooklyn, 1979), *Huqqat*, IV, fol. 59a. This is a very important passage, as it explicitly describes the source of speech as higher than that of knowledge, a stand I am not acquainted with elsewhere in kabbalah.

38. Shneor Zalman, *Derushim le-Rosh ha-Shanah*, V, fol. 59a.

39. A similar view is found in a teaching ascribed to a grandson of Rabbi Shneor Zalman of Liady, Rabbi Menahem Mendel Schneerson of Lubavitch (1789–1866; he should not be confused with his great-great-great-grandson [and also great-great-grand-son-in-law, twice over] of the same name [1902–1994], who also served as Rebbe or *Tzaddik* of the Lubavitch community); see Hayyim Liebersohn, *Tzeror Ha-Hayyim* (Bielgoria: Azriel Hayyim, 1913), fol. 30a. The hyposemantic

approach evident in the works of these Habad rebbes recalls the views of a famous kabbalist from the city of Safed in the Galilee, Rabbi Moshe Cordovero (1522–1570), who emphasized the importance of performance while marginalizing the role of understanding.

40. On the emergence of this triunity, see Abraham J. Heschel, "God, Torah, and Israel," in *Theology and Church in Times of Change: Essays in Honor of John C. Bennett*, ed. E. LeRoy and A. Hundry (Philadelphia: Westminster, 1970), 81, 89 n. 60.

41. Horowitz, *Ha-Shelah*, I, fol. 9a, 11a.

42. Ze'ev Wolf, *Or ha-Me'ir*, fol. 239b

43. Menahem Nahum, *Me'or Einayim*, 171.

Chapter 11

Concepts of Scripture in Martin Buber and Franz Rosenzweig

Jonathan Cohen

The thought of Martin Buber (1878–1965) and Franz Rosenzweig (1886–1929) continues to exert a profound influence not only on theologians and philosophers of religion, both Jewish and Christian, but on biblical scholars as well. Their work has been foundational for readers who want not so much to deny as to move beyond historical and philological approaches that obscure biblical literature's religious and humanistic vitality. Buber and Rosenzweig bring God back into the picture and thus represent a gesture of return to older modes of biblical interpretation. Still, their approach does not simply restore medieval or midrashic approaches to scripture. It rather shifts the locus of authority from the biblical text itself to a space between the reader and the text, a space wherein the voice of the divine can still be heard by contemporary readers.

The spiritual path of Buber and Rosenzweig moved from the universal, humanistic values of German culture and philosophy back toward the intimate sphere of Jewish tradition. While Buber was raised for a time in the home of his traditionally observant scholar-grandfather Solomon, and although there are scholars who attribute an important spiritual influence to Rosenzweig's observant great-uncle Adam, for both Buber and Rosenzweig, the milieu of German thought and culture was a "native language," and it was the Hebrew Bible and other Jewish canonical texts that they often experienced as an "other." This "other" had to be encountered, or reencountered, such that its message could once again "speak" to a fully developed, modern European sensibility. For this reason, Leo Strauss characterized Buber and Rosenzweig, together with Hermann Cohen, as central figures in what he called a "movement of return"[1] from the outside in. Tragically, the cultural community that was to be the chief beneficiary of the philosophical and interpretive projects of Buber and Rosenzweig was decimated by the Holocaust. Nonetheless, these two thinkers address the "very great difficulties"[2] experienced by modern Jews who strive to reappropriate the Bible and its tradition in the contemporary world.

Buber and Rosenzweig did not share an identical theology, and they differed widely on significant theological issues. Buber regarded the Jewish people as a "history-making"[3] nation and as a political entity. He was concerned with the theological significance of its historical way through time and with the theological meaning of its renewed ingathering in a specific place—the land of Israel. Although he was a maverick Zionist, one who called for accommodation with the native Arab population of Palestine and favored a binational state, he was a Zionist nonetheless. He believed that the restoration of the Jewish people to an independent, "whole" national life was crucial for the spiritual renewal of a people called upon to expose its "whole" life to the commanding voice of God. Although he saw Jesus as an icon of the "underground Jew" (as he did the Chasidim and Spinoza), he believed that much of Christianity had developed into an objectified religion characterized by creed, dogma, and catechism ("belief *that*" as opposed to the "belief *in*" he thought was more characteristic of Judaism).[4] Rosenzweig, although he occasionally expressed a certain sympathy for the Zionist project, remained, theologically, a non-Zionist. For him, the Jewish people should not be understood as a history-making nation but rather as an ahistorical ethno-religious community existing under the aspect of eternity. Its task was not to walk a "way" through historical time but to persist outside of time as a holy people whose perennial intimacy with God could be directly beheld in the repeated celebrations of the cyclical Jewish calendar. It was the legitimate and divinely ordained task of Christianity to walk the historical "way," gradually bringing the pagan nations closer to God through the mediation of Jesus and the Church.[5]

Perhaps the most famous disagreement between Buber and Rosenzweig concerns their differing approaches to the issue of Jewish law and its claim on the modern Jew.[6] Both Buber and Rosenzweig gave privileged place to the "command" of God heard directly by the individual, or the people, in the "presentness" of a particular situation. Such a command, perceived as coming down on one suddenly from the outside, often going against one's grain and running counter to what one would like to hear, engendering a sense that "I cannot do otherwise," is, in the moment, sensed as a genuine address from the Unconditional—brooking no conditions. For both Buber and Rosenzweig, it was of supreme importance that human beings make a constant effort to attune themselves to the possibility of revelatory moments such as these—to commands that "speak" in and through the unique circumstances of individual and collective life. Buber, however, felt that an ostensibly "religious" orientation that sanctifies a corpus of received and fixed law as the unchangeable word of God desensitizes the individual and the collective to God's direct command resonating in and through the very tissue of lived life. One becomes deaf to the "command of the hour" if one fills one's time and space observing a comprehensive, humanly constructed legal system, believing that in so doing one has followed God's timeless will. From a *religious* point of view, then, Buber could not see his way clear even to the selective appropriation of traditional Jewish law. Rosenzweig also distinguished between what he called "commandment" (direct address in the moment) and "law" (the regularization of observances undertaken by human beings in response to moments of revelatory encounter). He believed, however, that traditional practices had been, and could become again, *invitations* to encounter rather than *obstructions* to religious immediacy. For him, responsible love turns into marriage, a relationship that rekindles its intimacy constantly by way of recurring rituals and anniversaries.

Despite these important differences, Buber and Rosenzweig collaborated on a most ambitious project, a new translation of the Hebrew Bible into German, begun together in 1925 and continued by Buber after Rosenzweig's death until 1961. This translation was theologically and educationally inspired.[7] Buber and Rosenzweig did not seek to "Germanize" biblical Hebrew such that it would transmit a clear message to the masses who are supposedly in need of a predigested religious instruction. It rather sought to Hebraize the German rendition of the Bible so that the spoken quality of the commanding biblical address could be recovered by way of the literary stimuli inscribed in the original Hebrew. In their theologies of the Bible and in their theological hermeneutics and aesthetics of Bible reading and interpretation, the thought of Buber and Rosenzweig overlapped greatly.

What Kind of a Book Is the Bible?

In discussions of the character of the Hebrew Bible, scholars often set forth univocal theses that bespeak an either-or approach. The Bible is regarded as *either* divine *or* human; it is considered a work similar to *philosophy* or a work of *practical* instruction for the nonphilosophical majority, a species of *history* (claiming to be "empirical" and "veracious") or a species of *literature* (thereby "mythical" or "fictional"). Some claim that the Bible is a book that can be reduced to a set of *theological* tenets. Others describe it as a book that, despite its narrative, exhortatory, and prayerful components, actually centers on a *law*.[8] Buber and Rosenzweig did not believe that the Bible could be understood by reducing it to any of these categories. For them, the Bible is both like these other types of books and unlike them.

First of all, Buber and Rosenzweig did not regard the Bible as an esoteric book that is accessible only through discretely "religious" or "mystical" experience. True, the Hebrew Bible, for Buber and Rosenzweig, is both the record of and the witness to a series of genuine encounters between great religious spirits, the Israelite people, and their God—a veritable "dialogue between heaven and earth."[9] This record, however, has been mediated by finite human beings who see the world and events in a human way and who employ all the modes of expression proper to human beings. Since human beings narrate their individual and collective lives within the medium of time, the Bible can and should be seen as a kind of history—both like and unlike what moderns conventionally understand as history. The "secular" tools of historical investigation can and should be applied to the Bible, although they should not be regarded as exhaustive. Since human beings use language, as well as all the literary forms attendant on language, the Bible can also be seen as a kind of literature that points beyond itself without undoing itself as literature. It is therefore proper to employ the best "secular" literary tools at our disposal in order to disclose the form-content relations that are inscribed in the biblical text, for only by doing so will the "religious" message of the text be released.[10] Since human beings form worldviews in response to perennial existential questions, the Bible can also be regarded as a species of philosophy or theology. It is a unique species, however: narrative (describing the vicissitudes of a relationship) and not propositional (composed of a system of "objective" statements). Now the Bible certainly gives law pride of place, but it is a law that does not exist for the sake of obedience or regulation but rather for the purpose of constituting a community with a common "personality" and solidarity that can face its God as an integral whole.

How Is God Encountered, and How Is He Encountered in the Bible?

Before we go on to speak in more detail about the modes and forms used in characterizing the "texture" of the Bible, it is important that we ask, what are the modes and forms by way of which God makes His presence known or felt to human beings altogether, according to the religious testimony of Buber and Rosenzweig? For them, the "encounter," "meeting," or "dialogue" between God and human beings does not take place in some "extraterritorial" dimension of "mystical" religious experience. It takes place in normal individual and collective life. For example, we sense our very being and birth as a gift, and intuit that we have not given ourselves to ourselves, and so come to see ourselves as "created." Sometimes we sense that an insight has been placed within us or that a challenge has descended on us—an insight or challenge that we could not have generated ourselves and that even goes against our grain. As a part of this experience, we sense that we are "commanded" to do this and not otherwise—that doing otherwise would be unthinkable in the circumstances—and so experience "revelation." Sometimes, when we feel a hopeless anguish and sense that we have come to a dead end, a "hand" seems to reach down to lift us up. When we feel challenged to take that hand and not to revel in our despair, we intuit what "redemption" can mean.[11] For Buber and Rosenzweig, experiences such as these, on both the individual and the collective level, can represent genuine encounters with God and cannot always simply be reduced to "the unconscious" or "mass psychology." All reduction of the divine to the natural, of the divine to the human, of the human to the natural, and so on—represents a stunting of experience. For those who have not shut themselves off to the full range of human experience, for those who hold themselves open to all aspects of experience in a spirit of "absolute empiricism,"[12] encounter with the dimensions of creation, revelation, and redemption is eminently possible.

The theology of Buber and Rosenzweig, then, is a kind of dialogical religious personalism, testifying to a personal interaction between God and human individuals or groups, mediated by the events and "stories" of life—whether modest or grand. This mode of interaction is to be distinguished from the "philosophical mysticism" of classical metaphysics (wherein the human intellect strives to unite with the divine intellect) as well as from other forms of mystical experience (wherein human individuality and personality are overcome in favor of a striving for unity with the Godhead).[13]

For Buber and Rosenzweig, the wholeness, separateness, integrity, and authenticity of both the divine and human "persons" are part and parcel of the dialogical experience. In the theology of Buber and Rosenzweig, "monotheism," or the oneness and unity of God, does not function as a *descriptive-ontological* category, in contradistinction to polytheism or to intradeical multiplicity, but rather as a *prescriptive-existential* category: it derives from the norm that only two authentic, unified, and self-consistent beings can genuinely encounter and face each other.[14]

This God is the "father" and giver of all dialogical experience. Were it not for this God, then, in the words of Nachum Glatzer, we would live in a "neutral, blind, cold unconcerned universe."[15] Since God has "turned" to the world and to human beings, addressing them in an act of love and concern, the world has been "transformed into a place where man is addressed by the Thou and where he . . . may or may not give answer." God can be glimpsed behind all dialogical encounters between human beings —encounters based on the acceptance of others in their totality, on full mutuality of relationship, and on a resolve to refrain from even the most subtle forms of exploitation (i.e., not relating to others as mere objects of "interest" or sources of "enjoyment"). Such dialogical encounters may also take place between persons and objects or places in "nature," between persons and events, or between persons and texts. In all such encounters, the place, the situation, or the text "speak"; they address and challenge one to respond with one's "whole being." In truth, for Buber and Rosenzweig, a genuine response within the framework of an "I-Thou" experience such as this can only be made with one's whole self—never with one's thoughts, feelings, or actions alone.

Although it is sometimes difficult to conceive how "I-Thou" encounters could take place between a whole people and its God (since this would seem to mean that the people are responding "as one," thereby negating the inalienable uniqueness, authenticity, and integrity of the individuals composing that people), Buber and Rosenzweig assume that such "collective dialogues" can and do take place. At certain junctures in a people's history, it is "addressed" by events—and must respond as a people.

Although the God experienced by Buber and Rosenzweig is one and separate from the world and human beings, He is not abstract and removed from human experience. Neither, however, is He so available that he can be conjured up and manipulated for human purposes. He appears where and when He wishes, to whom He wishes, in accordance with His purposes, which are not always disclosed or readily intelligible. This living God is not a function of a human "anthropomorphizing" tendency. He Himself has chosen to meet human beings on their "ground" of space and time as a "speaking person."[16] It is not that we create God in our image—conceiving of Him as, say, a God of love on the model of our own love experience. Rather, as Rosenzweig says in his famous magnum opus, *The Star of Redemption*, "we love as God loves and because God loves."[17]

God's appearances, however, are always fleeting—and He can never be permanently identified with any thing, force, person, or creature in the world. He may take up "temporary residence" in certain objects, persons, situations, or places—but He is never the "God of" those objects, persons, situations, or places. One might call such manifestations "temporary incarnation," although it is not certain that Buber and Rosenzweig actually understand divine-human encounters quite this way. Often one senses that they experience God as "reflected" in things or "hidden behind" things—rather than residing, even temporarily, *in* things. God is never permanently incarnate in any particular place, thing, or person. Buber and Rosenzweig testify to having experienced encounters such as these personally. Their existentialist philosophy, wherein philosophers do not strive to be objective beholders of Being but rather accept themselves as finite, concrete subjects who are inextricably implicated in their philosophy, is properly called "experiencing philosophy." For Buber and Rosenzweig, the Bible and other texts, traditions, and practices were legitimated not by reason or by agreement with the principles of this or that philosophic system but by resonance with concrete, individual experience in its totality.

Buber and Rosenzweig did not merely *legitimate* the Bible from the standpoint of their own religious experience, however. They complemented their orientation to the Bible by regarding it also as a *source of legitimation* for personal experience. Ultimately, they could not remain content with individual experience as entirely self-legitimating. They sought sanction for their own dialogical experience in the sacred writings of their people and tradition and especially in the Bible. Eventually, they came to see the Bible as the quintessential and paradigmatic example of the dialogical orientation—a foundational text that both introduced the dialogical perspective into the history of the spirit and was the most effective in bringing about its proliferation.[18]

It should not surprise us, then, to find echoes of Buber's and Rosenzweig's experience of God in their interpretations of the Bible, as well as reverberations of what they might have regarded as a "biblical" God-orientation in accounts of their personal religious experience. Buber, for example, who, more than Rosenzweig, was concerned with the "historical nucleus" of the biblical saga, believed that the experience of the "fleetingness" of the manifestation of God—the disappearance of God from a particular place where He was seen or heard, His long absences, and His sudden, unexpected reappearances "elsewhere"—can be traced to the nomadic experience of ancient West Semitic tribes from whom the Israelites derived.[19] For them, God was the *melekh* of the tribe—the leader, adviser, and judge who "showed them the way"—in both the immediate and larger sense. Unlike the Be'alim and the Ashtarot of more settled tribes, the "God of the way" was never identified with a particular place, object, or region or with a particular "natural" process. He was not to be identified with the fertility of the earth or with a particular volcano-mountain, although His mysterious power and will might be tangibly felt *by way of* the bounty yielded by the soil or *by way of* the flames, smoke, and tremors coming from the mountain.

Rosenzweig, however, was also concerned that God not be identified permanently with any other being or "image." In a brilliant article called "On Anthropomorphisms," he compares a graphic portrait of the god Kronos, appearing in Homer, with an equally graphic description of the biblical God that can be found in a passage from the book of Samuel. The Homeric text he quotes, from the *Iliad*, reads as follows:

> Yes, and Kronos now nodded with gloomy brows.
> Yet the ambrosaic hair of the protector flowed around.
> The immortal head, shaking great Olympus.[20]

The details of the description of Kronos's head and head movements—the nodding with gloomy brows, the ambrosaic hair that flows around, the weight of the head that has the effect of shaking Mount Olympus—combine to form what can legitimately be called a *portrait*, wherein a series of attributes is presented with the kind of continuity that contributes to the formation of a picture or an image. In a passage quoted from 2 Samuel 22, however, we are presented with a description which, while no less vivid and concrete, reflects an entirely different experience of the ways of the living God:

> When I was afraid,
> I called to my God.

> From his court he heard my voice,
> My cry of despair was already in his ears.
>
> And the earth shook, trembled,
> The foundations of heaven quaked.
> Rocked for he was flaring up.
> The smoke from his nostrils rose up high.
> From his mouth fire licked out
> And glowing coals caught fire.
>
> He lowered the heavens, he descended.
> Bleak weather beneath his feet
> Riding on a cherub he flew on.
> Came shooting down on the wings of the storm.

In this passage, the various details of the description of God's characteristics are not linked to one another to form a portrait. Rather, each individual detail represents the beginning point of a line that runs either from God to the supplicating human being or from the human being to God. The human's call is met with a divine response—the image of the "ear" in which the cry of despair was "already" found communicates the immediacy of the divine response as experienced by the supplicator. God's response shakes heaven and earth—not as a function of God's *attribute* of, say, strength but as an expression of the intensity and totality of the manner in which the supplicant's sacrifice is answered. The details of the biblical description are all intended to evoke an *event* of meeting and interchange, rather than a portrait of the divine image.

The experience of God, then, as corroborated by the Bible—or, conversely, the biblical account of the experience of God, as corroborated by the experience of human beings—is the experience of a relating yet ephemeral God of challenge and response who appears when and where He wishes and to whom He wishes in accordance with His purposes—purposes that cannot be controlled or manipulated. Rosenzweig was particularly concerned to show that the biblical God has no fixed form. He has no permanent attributes, and the figures by way of which His presence is sensed cannot be assembled and fixed to form a stable image. Buber, who gave more theological weight to history and geography, was concerned to avoid a different kind of fixation of God, the kind that identifies God with particular places or natural processes—hence the God who moves through time (history) and space (geography) to accompany His chosen.

The Bible as a Locus for Encounter with God

If the encounter with God, for Buber and Rosenzweig, comes in and through the events of life, how can the Bible itself be understood as a medium of revelation? Why should God be encountered in the reading of a particular book, if He is in principle accessible to all through the vicissitudes of life itself? Buber and Rosenzweig believed that the Bible has proved to be the historical harbinger of the possibility of this kind of encounter in the thick of life. Further, they regarded the act of Bible reading itself, when undertaken properly, as an orienting event. For Buber and Rosenzweig, the Bible, by the very manner of its composition, directs us to the kind of dialogical reading that sensitizes us to the possibilities of dialogical encounter with God and human beings in life.[21]

The Bible also represents a most striking example of what Buber has called the "wondrous means of writing,"[22] wherein the living voice of God, carried through the events of meeting between God and Israel, and the enthusiasm of the human response to that voice have been preserved in a seemingly "frozen," written medium. The biblical narrative has been formed in such a way that, paradoxically, its written forms call forth its original "spokenness."

Sometimes this "spokenness" seems to be preserved immediately within the text. A certain passage *stands out* and *contrasts* with the literary artfulness of its surroundings. A well-considered narrative or a well-constructed poem is suddenly interrupted by a celebratory exclamation that, according to Buber, could only have been preserved from the midst of a living event —even though the biblical account may be covered over by layers of subsequent editing. One important example of this, for Buber, is the exclamation "Let YHWH be king for the ages, eternity" (Exodus 15:18)—a spontaneous expression of wonder and loyalty that erupts from the intricate Song of the Sea. This exclamation bespeaks what Buber calls a kind of "objective enthusiasm."[23] In borrowing this term from Jacob Grimm, Buber collapses the conventional distinction, so dear to professional historians, between "objectivity" and "subjectivity." This outpouring is certainly not a dry chronicle. Neither does it represent the ravings of an overenthusiastic "subjective" imagination (as Spinoza would likely have interpreted it). Rather, in the event, subject (the experiencing human being) meets subject (God, the ultimate saving Power revealed in the event). For Buber, it is not the ostensibly supernatural character of the "wonder on the sea"[24] that begot the enthusiasm expressed in the passage. Buber did not expect or desire that the modern reader inauthentically adopt a belief in the supernatural. Such a belief would alienate him or her from the categories of science and history, those prisms by way of which moderns make sense of experience, including the experience conveyed by ancient texts. It is, rather, the sudden and unexpected deliverance from the waters at the most crucial time that Buber saw as a miracle. The Israelite people, sensing themselves addressed by the event, respond with an effusion of allegiance to the One whom they perceive as having snatched them from the pursuer. God, the true king, not Pharaoh, will now be followed on the way. According to Buber and Rosenzweig, Bible readers who "hear" the "crying out" (*mikra*)[25] of the voice in the text in response to this event can relive the original sense of wonder that overwhelmed the people at the time and immediately relate it to events with a similar structure (sudden reversal in the face of danger) known in their own experience.

Another example of the kind of authentically and perfectly preserved spoken texts that Buber claims to have uncovered in the Bible can be found in the response of Gideon to the people in the book of Judges (8:22–23), when they ask him to "rule" over them. Gideon says there, "I will not rule (be king) over you and my son will not rule over you, God will rule over you!" The straightforwardness of this statement reflects a genuine impulse toward the personal and unmediated rule of God in ancient Israel—an aspiration to direct theocracy unencumbered by a deadening political or sacral system.[26] The one God of all calls for the consecration of all of life and the bringing of all forms of public and private conduct directly under God's responsibility and commandedness. For Buber, only response to this comprehensive call and command can redeem the contemporary world from its false division into discrete "sacred" and "profane" spheres. Religion and the fullness of life have become compartmentalized, such that people can dissemble that they have discharged their "religious" obligations through established ritual while the rest of life proceeds unaffected by responsibility in the presence of the Absolute. The living voice of direct divine "rule" over all of life, then, as echoed through the voice of Gideon in the biblical text, can and should be experienced as addressing the contemporary reader with the same immediacy as in ancient times.

Sometimes, however, the very "literariness" of the text, its textured and artful character, provides the stimulus for the recovery of its "spokenness." Rosenzweig, in his penetrating article "The Secret of Biblical Narrative Form," illustrates this phenomenon by way of reference to the creation story, the story of the building of the Tabernacle, and the famous conflict between Jacob and Esau for the blessing and the birthright.[27]

Before we look at some of these passages, let me provide some background on the connection between Rosenzweig's theological categories and his aesthetics of Bible interpretation. The Jacob and Esau story, for example, is told in what Rosenzweig would call an "epic" manner. Like all stories written in the epic mode, it is told as an "objective" occurrence that has happened in the past. Although many readers might be scandalized by elements in the plot (especially the mendacity of Rebecca and Jacob), no judgment is directly passed on the characters. The narrator does not take up a "subjective" posture toward events; neither is the reader directly called on to do so (as the reader most certainly is, say, in the story of the Flood or the story of the destruction of Sodom and Gomorrah). This aesthetic mode, the seemingly neutral articulation of a story, reflects the theological dimension of creation.[28] The natural world, with its lawful interconnections, appears before us as a *past given*, as an object, even though its artfulness also seems to point to a hidden, supervening intelligence and will. Just as one can aspire to behold the world as an interlocking, "objective" whole (in the manner of, say, classical philosophy or certain trends within modern science), so a work of art can be beheld with a view to articulating its oneness and wholeness—the manner in which all the parts are intelligibly interrelated—its "epic" aspect.

However, another mode of experiencing the world and also, microcosmically, works of art is available to us. According to Rosenzweig, this is the mode wherein a *particular* configuration of events that occurs to a *particular* individual at a specific time and space creates a *unique*, unrepeatable moment of meaning. One sees or hears something that speaks privately to one's idiosyncratic life story—and nothing is the same again. One senses that the course of one's life must change as a result of an event or an encounter with someone or something and that it would be untrue to the experience to continue with one's life as if nothing had happened. One is commanded to reorient oneself and conduct oneself otherwise. From a theological point of view, experiences such as this represent the dimension of revelation in Rosenzweig's thought.

Within the framework of Rosenzweig's aesthetics, moments like these are termed "lyric" or "anecdotal." A symphony, for example, can be beheld as a compositional unity and appreciated for the underlying plan that lies at the basis of its many vicissitudes. It often happens, however, that a *particular* juncture in the motion of the music "meets" us with a sudden, almost transforming power. Something in the *immediate* and specific configuration of sound strikes us and seems to shake us to our very being, releasing a new perspective and changing our self-understanding. In Rosenzweig's aesthetic terms, a "lyric" aspect of the music will have been "revealed" at that crucial moment.

As far as stories are concerned, Rosenzweig terms moments of meaning such as this "anecdotal."[29] In an "anecdotal" situation, a person vividly relates a story from his or her own immediate present directly to the immediate present of another human being who is listening. The story is not related as a considered, artistic composition but as the direct recounting of an event that has "just now" occurred, a story whose course and outcome directly affect the present of the listener. Such a story represents, for the listener, either the answer to a question (whether conscious or dormant) or a challenge that calls out for a response. Both Buber and Rosenzweig characterize this kind of storytelling as a dialogical opportunity par excellence.

The theological and aesthetic dimensions that have just been briefly introduced form the background for Buber and Rosenzweig's famous discussions of "leading words" in biblical narrative.[30] Biblical authors and redactors use "leading words" to unify and lend meaning to various story sequences, as well as legal passages. These leading words carry both the epic and anecdotal dimensions of biblical literature. One the one hand, the borders, character, and wholeness of a literary unit may be defined by repeated leading words that course through it. The repeated "doings" of God and "separations" of things in the first creation story give this famous narrative definite parameters, as well as a discrete texture. The first creation story presents us with a harmonious whole: the systematic, intelligible unfolding of the world as we know it. Both the world considered from this perspective and the story can be beheld as a unified, harmonious matrix, as an epic. When we come, however, much later on in the biblical narrative, to the story of the construction of the Tent of Meeting in the desert (Exodus 36–40), we find that words used to describe the sequence of God's "doings" in Genesis are used to describe human "doings" in Exodus. The word used to indicate that God has "concluded" His work is used to indicate that Moses has concluded, as supervisor, the work on the Tabernacle. This comes as a surprise, since the minute details of the construction of the Tabernacle seem so insignificant and mundane when compared to the grandeur of the creation story, and these key words have not occurred in this kind of sequence during the long interim between the two accounts. The reader is arrested by a sense of dissonance. What are these words doing here, and what could possibly connect these two disparate narratives? For Buber and Rosenzweig, what we have here is a deliberate puzzle that challenges the reader to respond. One can no longer continue harmoniously as before—one is stopped in one's tracks. Sometimes, at points like these, a "revelatory" moment will be released by the seeming disjuncture planted in the text.

The surprising repetition of the Genesis word pattern in the Tabernacle narrative generates a lyric illumination. With the creation of the world, God acts to build a home for human beings. With the building of the Tabernacle, God shows the pattern of the structure to Moses, but all of the "doing" must come from human hands.[31] Humankind must build a home for God within the home God built for humankind. The Tabernacle narrative, then, generates a command that we become partners with God in completing creation, that we take part in a reciprocal "home building." Once an illumination like this descends on one, one senses that one cannot authentically steer the course of one's life in the same way again.

If we turn again to the Jacob narrative, it will become apparent that the reader cannot help but be scandalized by the course of events, even if the narrator is silent. Jacob is to inherit the way of God from Abraham and Isaac, the way of righteousness and justice. In order to ensure that he receives both the blessing and the birthright from his father, Jacob, on the instigation of his mother, deceives his father by dressing like his brother in order to receive the blessing (*beracha*), and he exploits Esau's fatigue and hunger in order to gain the birthright (*bechora*). This is hardly consistent with God's way.

An irritant has again been planted in the text, which generates a question that gives the reader no rest. How could God (or the Bible) countenance the transmission of His way by devious, unjust means? What kind of a model is Jacob—who subsequently avoids looking his brother in the face by escaping to the land of Laban at the instigation of his mother? Does God realize His ends by encouraging injustice? The textual and moral dissonance reflected in this narrative seems to go unresolved.

The reader, then, is temporarily beset by what might be called a "planned discontent." Later on in the narrative, however, an important "leading word" will modify this discontent—although it will not (or at least should not) dispel it altogether. When Esau realizes that someone else has received the blessing meant for him, he cries out bitterly to Isaac and asks Isaac to bless him as well. Isaac, however, says (Genesis 27:36), "Your brother came with *deceit* [from the root *rmh*] and took away your blessing." The second-born has been awarded the blessing instead of the first-born, yet Isaac declares that the situation, terrible as it is, is irreversible. Jacob, however, later becomes not just the perpetrator of deceit but also its victim when, at Jacob's wedding party, Laban slips Jacob his first-born daughter, Leah, instead of the second-born, Rachel, whom Jacob had contracted to marry in recompense for the seven years he tended Laban's flocks. At that point, the narrative has Jacob exclaim (Genesis 29:25), "What is this that you have done to me! Was it not for Rachel that I served you? Why have you *deceived* me [from the root *rmh*]?" In Rosenzweig's words, "Just at the moment when Jacob must first acknowledge how scornfully his father-in-law and employer Laban is exploiting him in this strange land, the crucial word occurs again for the first time in a long while. . . . We become *suddenly* aware of the narrator's linkage of doing and suffering; and yet not once has the narrator stepped out of his role. The betrayed Isaac has unconsciously given the stimulus that his betrayer, now himself betrayed, unconsciously takes up."[32] The reader experiences a sudden illumination that constitutes a revelatory moment. The reader's question, generated when the key word was used for the first time, is addressed here, when the key word is played on for a second time. He or she has suddenly been awarded the insight that those who wrong others on the way to inheriting God's "way" will not escape redress. They must experience the same kind of suffering that they inflicted on the other, in order that they no longer close themselves off to their brother's cry (a similar insight is generated by the intricate plot of the Joseph story). Harmony, however, is not totally restored, and a sense of uneasiness persists at the act, "done under the authority of God,"[33] of the painful disenfranchisement of Esau—a seemingly unavoidable concomitant of the choice of Jacob and of any choice of brothers or peoples for a special destiny. God's coming to be known in the world would seem to involve both a revealed dimension (wherein a definite correlation between divine justice and humanly intelligible justice is vigorously proclaimed) and a "mysterious" dimension (wherein the course of events guided by God issues in consequences that "defy our understanding.")[34]

In biblical narrative, then, a revelatory, "lyric" moment—a dialogical response to a question—is planted within an "epic" story. The key word both arrests the plot and contributes to its continued unfolding. A "secret dialogue" is "extended"[35] through the narrative, without undoing its literary-aesthetic character. Revelation has been woven into creation; within the world of the text, the immediacy of the "lyric" moment or of the "anecdotal" exchange has been incorporated into the flow of the "epic."

How Should the Bible Be Read and Not Read?

Such moments of revelational-dialogical illumination, wherein questions are addressed or challenges are posed in the process of reading, can occur only if the reader of the Bible holds him- or herself open to the text in a certain way. Buber and Rosenzweig both felt that the contemporary reader should not approach the biblical text by way of a "hermeneutics of suspicion."[36] Such an orientation assumes that the biblical writers are consciously or unconsciously guileful about their motivations. For the suspicious reader, the self-presentation of the biblical text as the record of a divine-human encounter is not to be trusted, and the claims of the Bible in this regard are understood as deriving from something "deeper," like religious politics or mass psychology. Such a reader will consider it self-understood that an "enlightened" modern understands the text, its underlying motivations, and its overall project better than the text understands itself. On the one hand, such a reader may believe that he or she possesses an absolute explanatory scheme that can serve as an alternative to the one promulgated by the text (in the form of, say, Freudian psychoanalysis or Marxism). This alternative perspective would be considered capable of explaining all individual and social-cultural phenomena, in contradistinction to the false perspective with which the biblical text purports to account for these phenomena. On the other hand, the reader may deny the possibility of *any* universal, transhistorical, or transcultural perspective and interpret the diverse teachings that can be found in the Bible as a function of diverse historical or cultural contexts.

From the standpoint of Buber and Rosenzweig, such a reductionist orientation does not permit the text to speak in its own voice. True, Buber and Rosenzweig acknowledged the Bible's multiplicity of views and did not attempt to harmonize them. They did not reject the evidence adduced by biblical criticism that the Bible was written, edited, and compiled over a long period of time by numerous scribes and editors. Nonetheless, concerning what they saw as the most crucial point—whether the great spirits of Israel and the people of Israel as a whole had experienced a "dialogue between heaven and earth" and whether the imperative to take responsibility for all aspects of life in response to God's immediate command is always a live option—the biblical canon speaks with one voice and should be approached as such. The spirit of the final redactor—"R"—playfully referred to by Buber and Rosenzweig as "Rabbenu," our Rabbi or our teacher, "hovers" over the canon as a whole and speaks through it.[37]

The voice of the modern "enlightened" reader, then, does not have a monopolistic hold on what can legitimately be construed as the meaning of this or that biblical passage. The living voice of the text has an equal right to take part in a living event of meaning that must take place in the space *between* the reader and the text.

Neither should the biblical text be approached from within the framework of what might be called a "hermeneutics of progress" or "evolution."[38] This approach is somewhat different from the one just described. It does not necessarily regard the supposed truth of the Bible as the function and illustration of a "deeper" truth—more mundane though no less absolute and universal (psychoanalysis, Marxism, historicism). Following in the footsteps of modern Jewish thinkers such as Hermann Cohen and Erich Fromm, it regards the biblical tradition positively as the birthplace of modern humanism and as the source from which modern humanistic values can be traced. Scholars and educators who read the Bible in this spirit will often assign different sections of the Bible to different periods along an evolutionary scale running from "lower" to "higher" spiritual or psychological development. This hermeneutics of progress places the modern reader in a privileged position with regard to the ancient text. He or she, presiding over the discussion from the superior perspective of one who stands at the end of a long process of historical development, evaluates components of the text as to their relative "primitiveness" or "progressiveness." Such a hermeneutic approach prejudices the possibility of a genuine interpretive dialogue, since it allows no real parity between the voice of the text and the voice of the reader.

There is one more hermeneutic posture that would have to be ruled out if genuine dialogue between the reader and the text were to become possible. This orientation, instead of privileging the contemporary reader, privileges the biblical text as the repository of truth—or, in the more sophisticated versions of Leo Strauss and some of his students, as the repository of *possible* truth. From the standpoint of this orientation—alternatively termed a "hermeneutics of humility" or a "hermeneutics of reverence"—the contemporary reader is seen as flawed, not the ancient text.[39] According to Strauss, Allan Bloom, and others of this school, present-day readers are incorrigibly affected by the contemporary perspectives of historicism and cultural relativism. They live under the myth that no truth claim can ever be simply right or just. They see all claims as right only from a point of view that is determined by historical and cultural circumstances. This perspective effectively neutralizes and delegitimizes the truth question. Strauss and his followers see the abandonment of the search for the truth not as an advance but as a retreat from the activity that is most characteristically human. The Bible and other great texts, on the other hand, are preoccupied by the truth question and seek to respond to it by articulating what they regard as a true account of the human condition and the good life. Most contemporary readers, then, are constitutionally incapable of understanding the Bible on its own terms since that very question is out of bounds for them. According to this approach, the voice of the present-day reader must be muted, at least temporarily, in order that the Bible may speak with its own voice. Moderns must distance themselves from their modernity in order even to qualify as adequate readers.

A genuinely dialogical hermeneutic, such as the one promulgated by Buber and Rosenzweig, could not one-sidedly privilege either the reader or the text in the interpretive exchange. A dialogical exchange between human beings in general, and between a reader and a text in particular, implies a certain ethic of interpretation. Both voices—that of the reader and that of the text—must be given equal opportunity both to listen and to speak. Dialogue between the reader and the text must be holistic (each voice must be regarded as whole and integral—as greater than the sum of its parts), charitable, and reciprocal. Neither side should set about "using" the other side for its own purposes. The reader should not regard the text as a mere illustration of his or her own theories of human development. Neither should the reader regard him- or herself as merely a potential student or emissary of the magisterial truth of the text. Each party must bring his or her entire life situation or "horizon"—in all its concreteness and finitude—to the encounter, and both of these perspectives will figure in the "fusion of horizons" that will inform the interpretation.[40]

From the standpoint of a theology of dialogue, God can be heard and glimpsed in and through events, human deeds, and human speech and especially through that humanly spoken, written, and compiled "speech" known as the Bible—the text that brought, and continues to bring, the gospel of dialogicality to the world. Nonetheless, biblical voices, and the biblical voice as a whole, are historically and culturally situated, just as the contemporary reader is so situated. For this reason, dialogue, in the words of

Paul Ricoeur, must involve both "distanciation" and "appropriation."[41] Each party to the dialogue must make an honest attempt to regard the other *as* an "other," as someone who sees from a perspective deriving from a different biography or history. This consciousness of "otherness" works to prevent the imposition of one perspective onto another. Only after this stage of distanciation can there also be appropriation, the expansion of self-understanding and reorientation to life that results from the assimilation of aspects of the other's perspective into one's own.

Dialogue and Midrash—A Dialogue and a Synthesis

For some scholars, the characterization of the hermeneutic approach of Buber and Rosenzweig as merely "dialogical" has not seemed "Jewish" enough. While not disavowing the "dialogical" nature of their hermeneutics, such a scholar would refer to their mode of Bible interpretation as a species of modern "midrash." My own distinguished teacher, Eliezer Schweid, has used this appellation to characterize the project of Buber and Rosenzweig, noting that they did not relate to their dialogue with the Bible in the same way they related to other forms of dialogue.[42] They saw Bible as not just another dialogue partner—as if it were a matter of happenstance or pure choice that they should find each other and find meaning in their conversation. For them, the Bible was a "source" toward which they felt an a priori responsibility as inheritors of the Jewish tradition. They assumed that the Bible, as source, was endowed with the resources to address the special kind of alienation experienced by moderns such as themselves, the alienation caused by the predominance of the I-It relationship in modern life. Although these thinkers (particularly Buber, in Schweid's view) understood themselves as approaching the Bible in the spirit of pure dialogue, wherein both partners have an equal voice in determining if, when, and how a dialogue is to take place, it would be more appropriate to refer to their hermeneutic orientation as a species of modern midrash, wherein it is assumed in advance that the source has the potential to offer answers to the quandaries of the reader—if not immediately and totally, at least gradually and bit by bit. Michael Fishbane writes, in a similar spirit,

> The truth of midrash is not the truth of historical information or textual analysis. It is the truth of the *power* of scriptural words to draw a reader into an authentic relationship with the mystery of the world—a world

constituted by speech and . . . face-to-face relations. . . . To have taught us this, allusively, is Buber's enduring legacy. . . . The Bible is for Buber the rescued and ever-hearable speech of the living God. It is a Teaching which simply points out an *ongoing way*. This is also the teaching of midrash.[43]

Schweid and Fishbane are correct in modifying the description of the hermeneutics of Buber and Rosenzweig as dialogical by pointing out the midrashic dimension in their approach. In order to fully clarify the interaction between the dialogical moment and the midrashic moment in their biblical hermeneutics, however, it is first necessary to distinguish between dialogue and midrash as reading modes. Only then (as with all good dialogical relations!) can they be shown to interact.

As distinct from the mode of "pure" dialogue, the midrashic mode of reading does not assume an absolute parity and equality between the two partners. The source, the Bible, is assumed to be an infinite wellspring of meaning—one wherein the potential for far-ranging and infinitely applicable interpretations has been predeposited. The assumption of the midrashic interpreter is that he or she is not presenting, in his or her interpretation, any genuinely new content. He or she is rather activating a preexisting potential, a direction or possibility that was embedded in the text even before he or she set out to interpret it. The midrashic reader is, in the words of Gershom Scholem, merely "laying" this potential "open in the context of his own time."[44] True, the midrashic reader has an indispensable role vis-à-vis the text. Without the imaginative search of the midrashic reader for the text's address to the contemporary situation, the text would remain silent. This, however, does not put the reader on a par with the text. Neither does the message of the text for the modern reader subsist in the space in-between the two interlocutors. This meaning proceeds *from* the text and has merely been *activated* by the reader. Even if, from a strictly "historical" perspective, what the midrashic reader has derived from the text seems to have no precedent and seems totally original, it has, from a *metaphysical* perspective, already been "placed" in the text, such that (as the Talmud states in BT *Megillah* 19b and JT *Pe'ah* 13a/2.6) "whatever a bright student might offer as a *chiddush* [new interpretation] was given to Moses at Sinai."[45]

We can characterize the hermeneutic of Buber and Rosenzweig as a dialogue between dialogue and midrash. As in all successful dialogues, each party has undergone a transformation without losing his or her identity. In Buber and Rosenzweig's reading mode, normal dialogue has undergone an important change: one of the partners, the text, carrying within it the living speech of God, is also regarded as the founder and fountain of dialogicality in the world. It is the biblical text that called out the reality of dialogue to the world, bringing so many readers throughout the generations into its orbit. As such, the reader is not its equal.

However, while the midrashic mode has influenced the balance between the reader and the text for Buber and Rosenzweig, it has not undone its dialogical character. In fact, just as midrash has modified dialogue, dialogue has also modified midrash. The midrashic mode of reading assumes that the *chiddushim* [new interpretations] offered by qualified readers of subsequent generations are not fundamentally new. What they say represents an unfolding of the preexisting. Within Buber and Rosenzweig's hermeneutics, however, every dialogical encounter with the biblical text has (like all dialogues) a unique and unrepeatable character. The encounter has its own "face," as do the participants in it. Any new interpretation resulting from such an interaction between a modern reader and the text (even if the reader is not "qualified" from a traditional point of view) is a genuine *chiddush* that was never predeposited, even as a potential, anywhere. True, the Bible is the fount of dialogue and therefore should not be regarded as merely parallel to the interlocutors who have engaged with it over the generations. But its primacy consists in its uncanny ability to evoke and provoke dialogue. This value does not accrue to it by virtue of any *content* that it might, even potentially, contain.

According to Buber and Rosenzweig, the divine voice can only be heard in the context of an address, challenge, or question put to a listener or reader. It does not subsist "in" the text (as the symphony is not the score) but in the "space" between the text and the reader (in the event of the performance of reading). In this sense, the hermeneutics of Buber and Rosenzweig retains its identity as a dialogical hermeneutics. On the other hand, the source that has founded—and repeatedly proven itself capable of inviting—this kind of dialogical experience is the Bible. The dialogue between heaven and earth that has somehow been captured and preserved[46] in the biblical text has become a world-historical paradigm and inspiration for subsequent dialogue. This gives the biblical text a primacy and normativity of the kind assumed in the midrashic mode. This primacy, however, is only *formal* and not material. The *structure* of the relationship between the reader and the text has been modified, but the *content* of any new interpretation begotten by such a relationship must await the event of meeting itself.

NOTES

1. See Leo Strauss, *Philosophy and Law*, trans. Fred Baumann (Philadelphia: Jewish Publication Society, 1987), 8.

2. See Leo Strauss, *Jewish Philosophy and the Crisis of Modernity*, trans. Kenneth Hart Green (Albany: SUNY Press, 1997), 144.

3. The term "history-making" here is taken from Eliezer Berkovits, *God, Man and History* (Middle Village, NY: Jonathan David, 1959), 135, but it encapsulates Buber's thought concerning the Jewish people very nicely.

4. See Martin Buber, *On Judaism*, ed. Nahum Glatzer (New York: Schocken Books, 1967), 70; and Martin Buber, *Two Types of Faith* (New York: Harper & Row, 1961).

5. See Franz Rosenzweig's magnum opus, *The Star of Redemption*, trans. William Hallo (Boston: Beacon, 1971), 336–79.

6. For the famous exchange between Buber and Rosenzweig on the religious status of Jewish law, see Franz Rosenzweig, *On Jewish Learning*, ed. Nahum Glatzer (New York: Schocken Books, 1965), 81–85, 109–18.

7. See Everett Fox, "The Book in Its Contexts," in Martin Buber and Franz Rosenzweig, *Scripture and Translation*, ed. and trans. Everett Fox and Lawrence Rosenwald (Bloomington: Indiana University Press, 1994), xiii–xxvii. See also Steven Kepnes, *Text as Thou: Martin Buber's Dialogical Hermeneutics and Narrative Theology* (Bloomington: Indiana University Press, 1992) 41–60.

8. For a discussion of the supposed divinity or humanity of the biblical commandments, see Rosenzweig's essay "The Commandments: Divine or Human?," in *On Jewish Learning*, 119–24. For a discussion of the problem of the historicity of the Bible, see Martin Buber, *Moses: The Revelation and the Covenant* (Amherst, NY: Humanity Books, 1998), 13–19.

9. See the article by the same name, in Buber, *On Judaism*, 214–25.

10. For a profound discussion of the deciphering of human literary forms with a view to releasing theological insight, see Franz Rosenzweig, "The Secret of Biblical Narrative Form," in *Scripture and Translation*, 129–42. See also my article "Subterranean Didactics: Theology, Aesthetics and Pedagogy in the Thought of Franz Rosenzweig," *Religious Education* 94 (1999): 24–38.

11. For a description of the experiences of Creation, Revelation, and Redemption in everyday life, see Martin Buber, "People Today and the Jewish Bible," in *Scripture and Translation*, 13.

12. For Rosenzweig's notion of "absolute empiricism," see Franz Rosenzweig, *Franz Rosenzweig's "The New Thinking,"* ed. and trans. Alan Udoff and Barbara Galli (Syracuse: Syracuse University Press, 1999), 101.

13. See Julius Guttmann, *Philosophies of Judaism*, trans. David Silverman (New York: Schocken Books, 1973), 7–10.

14. See Martin Buber, "The Words on the Tablets," in *Moses*, 119–40.

15. This quotation and the quotation in the following sentence are from Nahum Glatzer, "Buber as an Interpreter of the Bible," in *The Philosophy of Martin Buber*, ed. Maurice Friedman and Paul Schilpp (La Salle, IL: Open Court, 1967), 375.

16. See Rosenzweig's essay "On Anthropomorphisms," in Franz Rosenzweig, *God, Man and the World: Lectures and Essays*, trans. and ed. Barbara Galli (Syracuse: Syracuse University Press, 1998), 135–45.

17. Rosenzweig, *Star of Redemption*, 199.

18. See Franz Rosenzweig, "The Secret of Biblical Narrative Form," in *Scripture and Translation*, 140.

19. See Martin Buber, *The Kingship of God*, trans. Richard Scheimann (London: Allen & Unwin, 1967), 94–120.

20. For the quotations from the *Iliad* and from Samuel, see Rosenzweig, "On Anthropomorphisms," 138–39.

21. See Michael Fishbane, *Garments of Torah* (Bloomington: Indiana University Press, 1989), 97.

22. See Buber, *Moses*, 139.

23. See ibid., 14.

24. See ibid., 75–77.

25. See Rosenzweig, "Scripture and Word," in *Scripture and Translation*, 42.

26. See Buber, *Kingship of God*, 59–65.

27. The following discussion is based on Rosenzweig, "Secret of Biblical Narrative Form," especially on 131–40.

28. On the parallel that Rosenzweig creates between Creation and Revelation as theological categories, and epic and lyric as aesthetic categories, see *Star of Redemption*, 188–95.

29. See Rosenzweig, *Scripture and Translation*, 131–34.

30. See, for example, Martin Buber, "Leitwort Style in Pentateuch Narrative," in *Scripture and Translation*, 114–28.

31. See Buber, "People Today and the Jewish Bible," especially 18–19.

32. Rosenzweig, "The Secret of Biblical Narrative Form," 136.

33. See Buber, "Leitwort Style in Pentateuch Narrative," 121.

34. Rosenzweig, "The Secret of Biblical Narrative Form," 137.

35. Ibid., 142.

36. For a penetrating discussion of the structure of the hermeneutics of suspicion, see Paul Ricoeur, *Freud and Philosophy: An Essay on Interpretation*, trans. Denis Savage (New Haven: Yale University Press, 1970), 32–36.

37. See Franz Rosenzweig, "The Unity of the Bible," in *Scripture and Translation*, 23.

38. For further elaboration of the distinctions between the hermeneutics of "suspicion," "progress," "humility," and "dialogue," see my article "Hermeneutic

Options for the Teaching of Canonical Texts: Freud, Fromm, Strauss and Buber Read the Bible," in *Courtyard: A Journal of Research and Thought in Jewish Education* (New York: Jewish Theological Seminary Press, 1999), 35–65.

39. See Leo Strauss, "What is Liberal Education?," in *Liberalism Ancient and Modern* (Ithaca: Cornell University Press, 1968), 7–8.

40. For the phrase "fusion of horizons," see Hans-Georg Gadamer, *Truth and Method* (New York: Continuum, 1994), 302–7.

41. See Paul Ricoeur, *Hermeneutics and the Human Sciences* (Cambridge: Cambridge University Press, 1981), 131–44, 182–93.

42. See Eliezer Schweid, "Martin Buber KePharshan Philosophi Shel HaMikra," *Mekhkarei Yerushalayim leMachshevet Yisrael* 2:4 (1983): 570–612.

43. Fishbane, *Garments of Truth*, 98.

44. For this quote, and for a systematic and penetrating description of the Sages' midrashic project, see Gershom Scholem, "Revelation and Tradition as Religious Categories in Judaism," in *The Messianic Idea in Judaism* (New York: Schocken Books, 1971), 282–303, especially 289.

45. Even the most sophisticated practitioners of "modern philosophical midrash," such as Levinas and Soloveitchik, read with these assumptions. See my article "The Educational Significance of Modern Philosophical Midrash," in *Educational Deliberations: Studies in Education Dedicated to Seymour Fox* (Jerusalem: Keter, 2005), 93–118.

46. For the Bible as "capturing" events of dialogue, see Kepnes, *Text as Thou*, 50.

Chapter 12

The Pentateuch as Scripture and the Challenge of Biblical Criticism
Responses among Modern Jewish Thinkers and Scholars

Baruch J. Schwartz

Introduction

The study of the Pentateuch among Jews in the two centuries following the appearance of modern Pentateuchal criticism had no choice but to cope with the fact that the systematic study of the Torah had become an academic enterprise carried out exclusively by Christian scholars and that its results were diametrically opposed to the tradition of Jewish learning.[1] Severe challenges to traditional Judaism emerged especially from what ultimately came to be known as the "Higher" Criticism of the Pentateuch. Higher Criticism, recognizing that the Torah contains the work of more than one author and that it achieved its current form by a process that took place over time, proceeds from the realization that the solution to the exegetical issues that make the canonical Torah so difficult to follow often lies in determining how the text was composed. Several theories regarding the origins of the Pentateuch and the process by which it evolved were proposed by the Higher Critics, each one equally at odds with the traditional Jewish view of the Torah. Best known of all these was a theory that crystallized toward the end of the nineteenth century and came to be known as the Documentary Hypothesis. According to this theory, four independent sources or, better, documents—each containing its own account of Israel's early history and its own version of the Mosaic laws—were combined to produce what we know as the Pentateuch or (according to many critics) to form a six-book work that extended from Genesis to Joshua. Source-critical scholars managed, with considerable success, to disentangle these documents (referred to by the abbreviations J, E, P, and D) from one another and to reconstruct their original forms. They then proceeded to assess each document's unique literary, theological, and legal features and to posit its probable origin, authorship, and historical background.

Just about every possible reaction to the challenges posed by Pentateuchal criticism has manifested itself among Jewish scholars who have attempted to respond to it, and this fact alone is enough to indicate from the outset that there is no definitive "Jewish" response to the critical study of the Pentateuch. We shall not attempt to trace the history of Jewish scholarship since the beginnings of Pentateuchal criticism but rather to examine some of its trends, with the aim of demonstrating that Jewish study of the Pentateuch since the onset of the critical approach has been remarkably diverse.

Jewish concern with the criticism of the Pentateuch may be divided into two main types: that which has arisen out of religious motives and that which has been primarily academic in character. The crucial difference between the two is that in the former category are Jews addressing the question of the role of the Pentateuch in the Jewish religion, while in the latter category are biblical scholars who happen to be Jews. In practice, however, it was only natural for the two types of concern to merge and for the distinction to become blurred, even in the writings of one scholar.

The Challenge of Pentateuchal Criticism

The traditional Jewish approach to the study of the Pentateuch, as it developed over the centuries from rabbinic times down to the present, stems from the belief that it was composed by God and verbally revealed to Moses; that its narratives are a factual record of (the world's and) Israel's origins and the establishment of its covenant with God and that they exist in order to teach and edify; that its laws are a comprehensive and fully harmonious body of commanded legislation, incumbent on the Jewish people forever; and that the body of rabbinic teaching designed to implement and supplement these narratives and laws is in fact their authoritative and correct interpretation, it too being, in some measure at least, of divine origin. Thus, the "Written Torah" is only a portion of the Torah: it is incomplete in itself and understandable only by recourse to that other body of revelation, the "Oral Torah."

In Judaism, the Pentateuch (and, to some extent, the whole of Scripture) came to be viewed as the eternal foundation on which all normative teaching—legal, ethical, ritual, philosophical—must ultimately be based, whether explicitly contained therein or not. The underlying assumption that enabled Judaism to consider the teachings of all generations to be the intended meaning of the Torah is that, being a transcript of divine speech, it is omnisignificant: all truth is contained in it, and each and every word, indeed every letter and every grammatical and stylistic peculiarity, bears independent and inexhaustible meaning. Though the precise manner and degree to which Jewish tradition has maximized or minimized the potentially limitless content of the Torah has varied over the centuries, it has always assumed a fundamental difference between the Torah, which it conceived as divine verbalization, and all other literature, which is simply the written record of human speech. The Torah, therefore, was studied in traditional Judaism both as a source text, with the aim of apprehending the precise connection between it and the extant rabbinic tradition, and as a living text, with the aim of deriving from it teachings of present significance. The Torah was not an object of research but rather a tool for edification. There existed no difference between the confessional and the historical; the historical significance of the Torah was confined to its narratives, the historicity of which was not questioned but was not held to be their sole, or even primary, significance.

As indicated earlier, Pentateuchal criticism (the groundwork for which was laid in the seventeenth century by philosophers such as Baruch Spinoza but which received its permanent form in the biblical scholarship of the late eighteenth and the nineteenth centuries) provides the strongest possible contrast to the traditional Jewish approach to the study of the Torah book. True, medieval Jewish commentators occasionally admitted that the Torah included post-Mosaic additions, that the physical characteristics and even occasional substantive details of its text had changed here and there over the millennia, and that the narrative was sometimes artistic and not strictly reportage. Still, critical thought concerning the Pentateuch proceeded from totally different premises. Its point of departure may explain the difference. Whereas Jewish learning was predicated on the notion of *divine* authorship, thus on the Torah's timelessness, critical thought began with the notion of *Mosaic* authorship, thereby encasing the Pentateuch in a defined historical context. Though the latter notion is adumbrated in rabbinic tradition, it found full expression in the writings of Philo and thereafter became prominent in Christian doctrine concerning the Old Testament.

The Torah, which for the Jews was the law of God, was for the Christians the law *of Moses*. Critical inquiry, which from its inception was a Christian enterprise, naturally began by questioning the latter, not the former.

Since, for Christian scholars, the human (though divinely inspired) origin of the Torah was a given, two essential postulates of critical thought arose quite naturally: first, that the historical meaning of the text is the only true one and, second, that the text—the Pentateuch taken on its own—is autonomous: it must be understood without any external body of tradition, since no interpretation is a priori authoritative. Though these two postulates are somewhat of a departure from the Christian tradition too, they are considerably more compatible with it than they are with the Jewish tradition. Christian thought was more inclined to view the age of Moses as definitive, since it in any case believed the Torah to be time-bound. Moreover, it had long rejected the authoritative nature of the Jews' "oral law." Jewish learning, on the other hand, attached little significance to the moment in history at which the Torah—said to have been composed by God six millennia before the creation of the world[2]—finally arrived on earth, and was quite traumatized by the idea that the body of rabbinic interpretation might be anything less than the revealed accompaniment to the divine text.

Viewed in this light, the substantive conclusions of classical Pentateuchal criticism can be appreciated in the fullness of the challenge they present to Jewish tradition. In essence, these conclusions number five:

(1) The Torah, and the religious teaching it represents—monotheism, a covenant with Israel, the concept of divine law, the laws themselves, and the narrative framework—are not "original"; the Torah is not a body of isolated and insulated, inner-Israelite, phenomena. Rather, it represents, both substantively and literarily, a stage in the evolution of ancient Semitic culture, of which the Israelites were a part. Its beliefs, narratives, and laws locate themselves along a cultural continuum, not in a cultural vacuum. This discovery removes the Torah from the exclusive realm of the divine and calls into question its timelessness; by demonstrating the Torah's counterparts and antecedents, it casts doubt on the necessity of assuming its revealed nature.

(2) The Torah is later than Moses. Not only does it contain passages that could not have been written in the time of Moses, the entire work—its structures, aims, themes, and every aspect of its style and content—bespeak a period following Israel's conquest of Canaan and the establishment of its national life there. This realization breaks the iron link connecting

the laws to the historical personality of Moses and indeed calls his very existence into question. The religious teaching reflected in the Pentateuch could no longer be viewed as the starting point of Israel's religion; indeed, for most biblical critics of the late nineteenth and twentieth centuries, the Torah reflects evolving expressions of the latest phase of Israelite religion, arriving on the scene after classical prophecy.

(3) It follows that the Torah reflects, and indeed exists in order to promulgate, the viewpoints of its period and its understanding of received tradition and is not an eyewitness account of events as they transpired. What is told is not necessarily historical fact but rather the literary creation of tradents and scribes, and what is commanded is not necessarily the a priori terms of a covenant made at Israel's birth but is rather the legislative norm of later generations, retrojectively attributed to earlier revelation.

(4) The Torah is not a unified literary work. Before the Torah attained its final form, there existed several "torahs" (in the classical form of the Documentary Hypothesis, the four documents known to scholars as J, E, P, and D), each complete in itself, each consisting of a narrative with a law code embedded in it, and each recounting events, and recording the laws, in its own unique way. These have been combined to create the canonical Torah. This realization had two distinct ramifications:

(a) The unity of the finished product notwithstanding, on the exegetical level the meaning of any passage was no longer to be determined in a way that forced it into harmony with the remainder of the Pentateuch. Only the original literary context—the document to which the passage belonged when it was composed—is decisive in determining its meaning. The Pentateuch could no longer be interpreted as if it were all of a piece; it was no longer the sum of its parts, since the parts did not supplement and integrate with each other.

(b) The crowning accomplishment of the critical approach, epitomized in the school of the late nineteenth-century German scholar Julius Wellhausen (1844–1918),[3] is the hypothesis that the four separate documents of which the Pentateuch appears to have been composed belong to separate periods of time and stand in a dialectical relationship with one another. The contrastive study of the documents reveals a developmental process. The literary study of the history of the Pentateuch is the evolutionary study of the history of Israel's religion.

(5) Hence, traditional Jewish learning, aimed at harmonizing the Torah into a unified whole, and at reading into the Torah the teachings of later generations as if they had been contained there all along, could no longer be accorded any methodological legitimacy. The modern critical method leads inescapably to the conclusion that the Torah and the "authoritative" rabbinic interpretation of the Torah are not identical. The Torah and Judaism are distinct phenomena.

Religious Responses to the Challenge

In the category of religious response are three groups: those who have been persuaded by modern criticism, coming to view it as grounds for religious reform and/or theological reconsideration; those who have attempted to discredit critical theory and thereby reinforce Jewish traditional learning, belief, and practice; and those who have attempted to arrive at some sort of accommodation between the findings of critical biblical scholarship and traditional Jewish belief and law.

The translations and commentaries of the German-Jewish philosopher Moses Mendelssohn (1729–1786) and his associates were the catalyst for the Jewish religious response. This is somewhat ironic, since Mendelssohn himself, though already aware of the work of the earliest critics, made no room for Pentateuchal criticism in his commentaries and generally demanded that legal texts be interpreted in accord with rabbinic law. He did, however, take several steps in the direction of legitimizing Bible criticism. He emphasized the aesthetic side of biblical literature, calling constant attention to its literary features and explaining them on stylistic grounds, thus cutting away much of the infrastructure on which rabbinic midrash was based, interpreting the text in ways departing from rabbinic tradition, and implicitly viewing the text of the Torah as human—subject to the rules, conventions, and styles of human literary creativity. On the philosophical front, he promulgated the doctrine that Judaism is not a faith but a legal system, theoretically enabling "orthopraxy" to accommodate heterodox views of revelation—including a critical view of the Pentateuch.

Jewish Reform

A scholarly acceptance of the method and findings of Pentateuchal criticism is evident as early as the writings of Leopold Zunz (1794–1886) and his younger contemporary Abraham Geiger (1810–1884). While Zunz and Geiger themselves were not overly interested in the Pentateuch, seeing its nationalism and particularism as running counter to the Reform agenda, their approval of scholarly inquiry into the Torah had an effect on the Reform movement itself. Early reformers in Germany were interested in peeling away from Jewish practice what they perceived as superfluous layers of rabbinic casuistry and over-stringency and in reducing the particularism they found incompatible with Emancipation. In this initial period, Reform leaders contented themselves with the goal of returning Judaism to its "pristine" biblical form. They maintained their commitment to biblical law, reaffirming its divine nature, asserting only that man-made layers of Judaism were subject to review and even repeal. But from the moment that Pentateuchal criticism insinuated itself into the Jewish intellectual and religious context, the nature of Reform underwent a major metamorphosis. The Torah, thus the Jewish religion per se, was a human creation; nothing, neither ordained nor written, was immutable. Ideas—democracy, equality, liberty, ethical behavior—took the place of revelation, and the Torah became the record of earlier attempts to express and actualize them. For instance, far-reaching measures (such as the displacement of the Sabbath to Sunday) that were unimaginable in the early days of Reform were a matter of course for later reformers. This was a direct result of the influence of Pentateuchal studies on the reformers: the realization that the law in its entirety had not been divinely dictated implied, for them, that it was not divinely mandated. Early reformers had accepted more-or-less traditional notions in the realm of theology; once their successors discovered the implications of Pentateuchal criticism, modified ideas of God became acceptable, and even the questioning of the very existence of the divine became legitimate. Though it cannot be denied that scientific skepticism concerning religion in general was the prime mover in all of these processes, in the Jewish world the single most influential factor serving to legitimize them was the critical study of the Pentateuch.

The trend toward radical religious reform, which therefore received its final push from the implications of Pentateuchal criticism, did not confine itself to official Reform movements in Europe and the United States. Eventually, some more traditional groups in both continents, ultimately including many Conservative rabbis and leaders in the United States, aligned themselves with this position: that the man-made, historically conditioned nature of the written Torah (to say nothing of the so-called Oral Law) entitled humans to accept or reject it as they saw fit, to "re-form"—create anew—the Jewish religion in each generation. The specific nature of reform has differed with time, place, and movement and has been characterized by greater or lesser loyalty and adherence to traditional Jewish law and practice, but this loyalty, even at its greatest, has been a matter of religious conservatism rather than a dogmatic commitment to revealed norms. The common denominator remains the same: the notion that Pentateuchal criticism has rendered the belief in Judaism as revealed religion obsolete.

Jewish Orthodoxy

Traditional rabbis remained aloof from the findings of, and the threat posed by, Pentateuchal criticism for some time. The yeshivah world of central and eastern Europe was unaffected in the main by secular learning, and the effect of modern biblical studies on the Torah commentaries produced by eighteenth-century rabbinic sages is confined to matters of grammar and lexicography. This tendency simply to ignore nontraditional learning has never ceased to prevail: even after the destruction of European Jewry in the Holocaust and the reconstruction of the traditional academies in America and especially in Israel in the late twentieth century, the emphasis on Talmud and disdain for secular knowledge, particularly in humanistic disciplines, led to an increased ignorance of critical study of the Bible and indeed to ignorance of the Bible itself.

Two interrelated factors in the eighteenth and nineteenth centuries brought occasional representatives of the rabbinic world into the critical discussion of the Pentateuch: the Jewish Enlightenment in western Europe and the threat posed by the reformers in these countries. Rabbinic orthodoxy thus entered the field of Bible criticism not out of any desire to further the study of the Pentateuch but rather as a reaction to a danger that it perceived as approaching from two directions: practical and intellectual.

Western European Orthodoxy's response is typified in the writings of S. R. Hirsch (1808–1888), who, like some of his eighteenth-century predecessors, was a vehement opponent of Reform. His polemical aim finds ample expression in his commentaries. He viewed the divine word as primary data not subject to inquiry and utterly rejected the idea that the ancient historical context in which the Torah came into existence could be of any importance in determining its meaning.

This disregard for history and this maximalist position with regard to the divine role in revelation ultimately became definitive of modern Orthodoxy, of which Hirsch is rightly seen as a founder. Hirsch's writings turned *traditional* Judaism into *Orthodox* Judaism by asserting that the belief in the divine origin of the Torah is the central tenet of the Jewish faith. Henceforth the lines were drawn: the "creed" of the Orthodox Jew consisted of the rejection of Pentateuchal criticism. A life committed to the classical mode of Jewish piety, it has been argued ever since Hirsch, is possible only if the Jew concedes that certain areas are closed to inquiry, that religious life is the result of a "leap of faith" in the divinity of the Torah—a faith that runs counter to reason. Though Hirsch advocated secular learning and modernity, he rejected any synthesis between them and the study of Torah. This obscurantism—the acceptance of the modern world and modern science in all areas other than Jewish learning—remained, more than almost any other single feature, normative in modern Orthodoxy throughout most of its existence.

Among Hirsch's more noteworthy successors was the commentary on the Pentateuch by British Chief Rabbi J. H. Hertz (1872–1946). Hertz was the apologist par excellence, explaining away or ignoring the discrepancies in the text and making highly selective use of the writings of non-Jewish scholars, generally when he found their positions sympathetic to the traditional view of the Bible. Though he was not a strict creationist and made some accommodation between the Bible and natural sciences, he was particularly fond of adducing the evidence of archeology to "corroborate" biblical narratives. Indeed, the tendentious argument that since archeological evidence occasionally provides partial verification of biblical history, the Bible is thus proven to be fully factual, and since the ever-unfolding evidence of ancient Near Eastern cultures provides a plausible background for the biblical accounts, the Bible should at least receive the benefit of the doubt, has made its way into scholarly circles as well. Hertz also launched into fierce diatribe against the Higher Critics and the Documentary Hypothesis. Hertz's Humash was the only commentary ever seen or read by hundreds of thousands of English-speaking Jews for much of the mid-twentieth century.

Attempts at Accommodation

Attempts to bridge the gap between traditional Jewish theology and the critical view of the Torah generally floundered on the apparent impossibility of maintaining Jewish law to be divine if the Torah is not the literal word of God and rabbinic law and teaching are often not the original sense of the Torah text. Mendelssohn's option—accepting Jewish practice on the strength of its legal status alone, or as a loyal bias in favor of tradition, and abdicating all doctrine in the theological sphere—remained the only modern solution. Occasional mention was made of, and partial solace found in, the medieval solution to the problem of post-Mosaic verses in the Torah, namely, that since in any case whatever is divinely authored is written down by prophets, it made no difference whether Moses or a later prophet actually recorded this or that verse.[4] Yet, although from the rational standpoint the findings of biblical criticism indeed seem compelling, it still appears to many that there is simply no way that traditional Judaism can accommodate them and remain intact.[5]

Only in very recent periods have some more serious attempts been made. The Israeli Orthodox philosopher Yeshayahu Leibowitz (1903–1994) argued that the commitment to Jewish belief and practice was independent of any theory with regard to the origin of the written Torah. Since the former depends entirely on the acceptance of the authority of the classical rabbinic Sages, the Torah text that they canonized is religiously relevant only as implemented by them. Earlier stages in Israel's religious development, evidenced in the Bible, are irrelevant and can be either studied or ignored without influencing traditional piety. Leibowitz's approach was part of his philosophy of Judaism, which posited that Jewish belief consists only of the conviction that the observance of commands as defined by the Sages is compliance with the will of God, irrespective of any belief regarding how that will became known to man.

Another attempt to admit Pentateuchal criticism without embracing Reform or denying revelation was made by David Halivni (1927–), a European-born scholar who spent most of his career in the United States.[6] He suggested that a written Torah was in fact dictated to Moses but that it—as is amply evident from biblical history and rabbinic tradition—was not accepted as binding by the Jews until the early Second Temple period, under Ezra. In the time intervening, postulated Halivni, the text had become flawed, so that the Torah that Ezra inherited, and that he and his successors (the early Sages) were to implement, was not identical to the one given to Moses. Thus, Halivni was able to take seriously not only the critical method of studying the Pentateuch but also its historical implications: that the biblical period and the literature it generated were dynamic, humanly conditioned, "time-bound" phenomena, not identical to the revealed word of God. The divine will is manifest rather in the Oral Torah, the beginnings of which in Ezra's time constituted a restoration of what God had originally commanded; thus, the Jew is required to comply with it and not with any literal meaning of the Written Torah. The latter is preserved for the purpose of midrash—determining, or artificially "deriving," from the sanctified document what was really commanded. Though Halivni's proposal was not without difficulties,[7] its appeal was that it allowed both the text of the Torah and the history of Israel's religion to be studied critically, without denying either the verbal revelation of a "Torah" to Moses or the divine mandate for preserving traditional law.[8]

Academic Responses to the Problem

In the second category of responses to Pentateuchal criticism are those offered by historical and literary scholars whose interest in the Bible is academic and for whom the critical approach to the Pentateuch is a method of scientific investigation to be employed or modified, and its findings are theories to be proven or disproved according to the weight of the evidence. The fact that Jewish religious teachers did not provide a single, persuasive solution to the theological issue made the number of biblical scholars to emerge from the ranks of Orthodoxy small, though not quite so small as may have been expected. Many traditional Jews entered biblical scholarship but simply steered away from Higher Criticism (that is, from studying the composition and dating of biblical books), preferring to concentrate on biblical language, textual criticism, literary art, the history of interpretation, or ancient Near Eastern studies; or they focused on biblical books other than the Pentateuch. It needs to be stressed, therefore, that Jewish scholars have been intimately involved with biblical studies in all of its facets, and what follows pertains only to the area of Pentateuchal criticism.

By the beginning of the nineteenth century, the Enlightenment had spread across Europe, and critical biblical scholarship had begun to develop its characteristic features. Jewish scholars, however, were late to enter the field. Only after Jewish interest in the Bible, which had been on the wane for several centuries, was stimulated and new opportunities for secular learning were opened up by western European countries to their Jewish residents, leading to a late eighteenth-century Jewish Enlightenment (*Haskalah*), did Jewish activity in the field begin to emerge.

Probably the first Jewish scholar to enter, rather than shy away from (or worse, simply dismiss), Pentateuchal studies was the German-born British rabbi M. M. Kalisch (1828–1885).[9] This remarkable scholar, trained in traditional Jewish learning, wholeheartedly embraced the critical approach to the Pentateuch and to the history of ancient Israel. His commentaries on Genesis and Exodus are philological-critical though not outstanding, but his encyclopedic commentary on Leviticus is by far the most thorough critical commentary written on a book of the Torah until quite recently. It makes extensive use of rabbinic and medieval commentators when these are found to be in accord with the demands of philological science, and it contains exhaustive, comparative study of ancient Near Eastern and classical sources that shed light on the Pentateuchal laws. Kalisch accepted the then-current view that the law, and the ritual law associated with the Documentary Hypothesis's P (Priestly) document in particular, belongs to a late, postexilic stage in Israel's development, but since he wrote before the appearance of Wellhausen's work, his reconstruction of Israelite religious history is unconstrained by the doctrinaire system imposed by Wellhausen's school. Unfortunately, the fact that he preceded Wellhausen caused his work, like that of most early and mid-nineteenth-century scholars, to be largely forgotten. It does not seem that Kalisch anywhere accounted for the anomalous acceptance of radical Pentateuchal criticism by a traditional Jew (Kalisch served as secretary to the British chief rabbi!); the intellectual honesty dictated by the climate of the age seems to have been his only standard.

Far more significant for the history of Jewish scholarship were the works of the German rabbi David Zvi Hoffmann (1843–1921), professor at, and ultimately head of, the Orthodox Rabbinical Seminary established by E. Hildesheimer in Berlin.[10] In some ways a spiritual disciple of S. R. Hirsch, Hoffmann differed from Hirsch in his affirmation of the applicability of philological tools to Jewish studies. He is rightly considered the first modern scholar to place the study of Talmud and rabbinic texts on sound philological footing, and many of the earliest critical editions of rabbinic texts, as well as the first strides in the higher criticism of Talmudic literature, were made by Hoffmann. He was, however, an arch-conservative in his approach to religion and Jewish practice, and though he did not feel that the historical study of the later stages of Jewish religious evolution posed a serious theological problem, he believed that the foundation on which rabbinic Judaism stood was the antiquity and divinity of the Pentateuch and the inseparability of the Written and Oral Torahs. Biblical studies were growing by leaps and bounds, and the accomplishments of the great linguists, historians, and commentators of late eighteenth-century Europe were too impressive to ignore, yet for Hoffmann, to embrace the now-dominant Wellhausenian model of the nature of the Pentateuchal literature was unthinkable.

Hoffmann's commentaries on Leviticus and Deuteronomy (a commentary on Genesis also appeared in Hebrew) work out his approach to the Pentateuch. As with rabbinic literature, he was strictly philological: the grammar and stylistic conventions of the Hebrew language were the prime tools of exegesis, and forced or fanciful interpretations were avoided. Yet, because he was a priori committed not only to the integrity of the Pentateuch and the incorruptibility of its text but also to a direct correspondence between the Pentateuch and Jewish law as it had crystallized in rabbinic times, the utilization of philological exegesis was not objective but rather directed at predetermined aims. As he states in the introduction to his commentary on Leviticus, the task of a commentator is generally tripartite: to determine what the text is saying (content), to explain how it is saying it (form), and to elucidate the relationship between the two. In the case of the Torah, however, the task is only twofold, since the content is already known. What the text means is what the rabbis have already determined it means; the task of the commentator is merely to show that this rabbinically determined meaning is in fact the sole, literarily and grammatically correct meaning and that the text as it stands is the best possible way of conveying it.

Hoffmann, like some of his earlier rabbinic counterparts, signals a departure from traditional Jewish learning. Medieval commentators would simply have admitted that the text seems to be saying one thing and the Talmudic sages interpreted it to mean something else—that is, *peshat* and *derash* are two separate categories. With the universal acceptance of philological norms, it became the order of the day to demonstrate that the rabbinic *derash* is in fact the *peshat*. Though the results of this approach were often forced or at least convoluted, Hoffmann proffered sound philological insights into the highly nuanced style of biblical writing. The fact that Hoffmann applied himself to the legal books of the Torah and not to its narrative portions is itself a major step forward, and his are still among the most precise and detailed commentaries on the legal texts ever written.

Hoffmann's expertise in rabbinic literature, and in particular in the fine points of *midrash halacha*, enabled him to include in his commentaries detailed, analytical surveys of the history and logic of rabbinic and medieval interpretation. These too endowed his commentaries with lasting value. They remain the clearest and most comprehensive tool for the student interested in how the Written Torah was understood by the talmudic Sages.

The second facet of Hoffmann's response to the critical study of the Pentateuch is also a direct outgrowth of his expertise in Jewish law. Hoffmann was for a long period the only Jewish scholar to contend systematically with the Wellhausenian approach to the history of Israel's religion. Hoffmann understood that the kernel of Pentateuchal criticism was not the sources themselves (which, by harmonizing the laws in nouveau-rabbinic fashion, he rejected) but the reconstruction of Israel's religious history that the chronological arrangement of the sources made possible. Hoffmann was the first modern Jewish commentator to accept the literary distinctiveness of the separate law codes in the Pentateuch. Though he believed the four codes to be the work of a single (divine) author, he recognized the distinctive style and content of each. In the case of the Deuteronomic Law and the Priestly Code, he attempted to account for the distinctive character of each code on the basis of its placement and role within the Pentateuchal narrative. He thus set out to reject what the critics saw as the substantive disharmony between the separate codes, and with it the assigning of separate chronological periods for each, without denying their actual existence.

In 1904 and 1916, he published the two parts of his *Die wichstigsten Instanzen gegen die Graf-Wellhausensche Hypothese*, in which he remonstrated, point by point, with the Wellhausenian reconstruction. This companion volume to his Leviticus commentary dealt almost entirely with what the critics referred to as P or the Priestly Code. There Hoffmann aimed at refuting the critical claim that the Priestly legislation was a late phase in Israel's evolution. Following the agenda established by Wellhausen, Hoffmann entered into detailed discussions of sacrifice, especially the paschal sacrifice, as prescribed by the Priestly Code, the stages in the law of profane slaughter, the festivals, and the laws concerning the priesthood. In his attempt to cut the knot the critics had tied between P and the exile, Hoffmann devoted several chapters to Ezekiel, arguing repeatedly that Ezekiel's prophecies drew on P (and indeed on D as well) and could in no wise be taken as earlier than the law. Here lies Hoffmann's most lasting contribution to Pentateuchal studies: the antiquity of the law, specifically of the Priestly law, stands on two pillars: its lack of connection with exilic or postexilic conditions and its antedating prophecy. Hoffmann argued persuasively for both of these.

Typical of Hoffmann's reasoning, it has to be admitted, was an implicit assumption that in order to uphold the traditional view of the origin and unity of the Pentateuch, it was enough simply to show some logical inconsistencies in the critical view and to call attention to occasional disagreement among the critics themselves. Hoffmann seems to have sincerely believed that exposing flaws in the critical method would suffice to delegitimize its findings and, by default, to reinstate tradition. It does not seem to have occurred to him that the critics could occasionally be wrong without tradition thereby being proven right.

The mention of a few Jewish scholars roughly contemporary with Hoffmann should suffice to show that his approach was not decisive or even characteristic and that throughout the period, Jewish scholars responded to Pentateuchal criticism in various ways. At one extreme, mention should be made of I. M. Wise (1819–1900) and Harold Wiener (1875–1929). The former, though a leader of American Reform, simply declared that the written Torah was divine, subject to only such inquiry as upholds its divine nature. The latter, a more traditional Jew devoted to Jewish rebirth in Palestine, also vigorously rejected Pentateuchal criticism but attempted, by scholarly means, to uphold the Mosaic authorship of the Torah. At the other extreme is the Polish-born American scholar Arnold B. Ehrlich (1846–1919), who, like Kalisch, diverged from the path of the conventional Documentary Hypothesis but engaged in his own brand of Higher Criticism, as well as extensive text-critical speculation, in his commentaries on the Torah and other biblical books. Ehrlich's work is characterized by a thorough acceptance of the critical method.

Though biblical scholarship continued to develop among Jews in America, it cannot be denied that the Jewish religious agenda exercised an influence on the directions it took, at least as long as it was mainly confined to the rabbinical seminaries. The great rabbinic scholar and religious leader Solomon Schechter, who vehemently opposed Higher Criticism (which he famously branded "Higher anti-Semitism"), refrained from appointing a critically oriented Bible scholar to the faculty of the Jewish Theological Seminary of America, of which he was the head, and his policy of keeping Pentateuchal criticism outside the pale of Jewish studies remained in force for decades, not only at the Seminary but in Jewish scholarship in general. The only real exception was the American-born Julian Morgenstern (1881–1976), who began to publish his source-critical and historical-critical studies of the Pentateuch in the early 1920s. He too was known for his idiosyncratic divergences from the accepted source theory; it would seem that among Jewish scholars, even those who accepted Higher Critical methodology could not shake their aversion to the theory associated with the name of Wellhausen.

Following the establishment of the Institute of Jewish Studies in Jerusalem in 1924, the Hebrew University of Jerusalem became a major center for biblical studies. Here, too, Pentateuchal criticism was initially avoided, and only with the passage of time did the growing community of biblical scholars in *Eretz-Yisrael* begin to take up this arm of the discipline. Not all of them were willing to do so with the same dispassionate objectivity they reserved for other areas of biblical studies. Noteworthy in this context is M. Z. Segal (1876–1968), professor of Bible at the Hebrew University from 1926.[11] Segal, born in Lithuania, received traditional rabbinic training as well as an English university education and began his career in biblical studies while serving in rabbinical positions in England. He applied the most rigorous critical methods in all areas of biblical studies, including the history of the Hebrew language and lexicography, biblical poetics, canonization, text criticism and biblical historiography, Apocrypha, and Dead Sea Scrolls. Yet when he came to the Pentateuch—and he did so regularly in his teaching, though he wrote on the topic only late in life (in his articles appearing from 1938 on; in his *Mevo HaMiqra* [1946]; and, in English form, in *The Pentateuch, Its Composition and Authorship* [1968])—he insisted not only on Mosaic authorship (with some minor exceptions) and literary unity but on the divinely inspired nature of the Written Torah. The Torah was sui generis for Segal; its origin was divine, and its literary nature had to be explained on the basis of that postulate alone.

Two scholars may be credited with having brought Pentateuchal studies to Jerusalem and thence to mainstream Jewish academia: the Italian-born rabbi Umberto (Moshe David) Cassuto (1883–1951) and the Ukrainian-born Yehezkel Kaufmann (1889–1963). Both, not surprisingly, were trained in European universities and had begun their scholarly activity in biblical studies before coming to Israel. Though Cassuto was the later to arrive (1939), his approach to the Pentateuch had already been articulated in an Italian article appearing some eleven years earlier ("Studi sulla Genesi," 1928) and presented in detail in his full-length work *La Questione della Genesi* (1934). Kaufmann had settled in *Eretz-Yisrael* in 1928 and published earlier contributions to biblical studies ("Probleme der israelitisch-jüdischen Religionsgeschichte") in 1931 and 1933, but his detailed work on the Pentateuch began to become available with the appearance of the first volume of his *Toledot HaEmunah Hayisre'elit* (*The History of Israelite Religion*) in 1937. The two scholars were independent of each other, owing first of all to their introverted personalities and dissimilarity of approach but also to the fact that Kaufmann was not invited to the faculty of the Hebrew University of Jerusalem until 1949, having spent the intervening years, his most productive ones, in Haifa.

It will be convenient to begin with Cassuto.[12] Cassuto was a trained and practicing rabbi and teacher of rabbinics, and in keeping with the enlightened tradition of the Italian rabbinate, he was well versed in scientific Judaic studies, as well as in the classics. His original field of research, however, was the history of Italian Jewry. Though he had published an important work on Deutero-Isaiah in 1911–13, it was only after he became professor of Hebrew at the universities of Florence (1925) and Rome (1935) that he began to concentrate on biblical studies. This new interest was reinforced by the discovery of the Ugaritic literature at the archeological excavation at Ras Shamra on the Syrian coast in 1929. Cassuto, an avid student of the Hebrew language and biblical stylistics, was fascinated by the potential contribution to interpretation that lay in the closely cognate literature of ancient Ugarit, and indeed, most of his original work in the Bible is in the class of comparative study of biblical and Canaanite vocabulary and style. In his groundbreaking *Sifrut Miqra'it ve-Sifrut Kena'anit* ("Biblical Literature and Canaanite Literature," published in 1942), he laid the foundations for the study of the literary affinities between the two cultures and in *The Israelite Epic* (1943) proposed the existence of a poetic tradition in Israel antedating the biblical prose narrative. The better portion of his biblical studies further develop this area of inquiry.

Cassuto's teaching and writing (he was chief editor of, and a major contributor to, the Hebrew *Enziqlopedia Miqra'it*) indicate, however, that the Torah literature was never far from his mind. In contrast to his unquestioning acceptance of the anonymous exilic prophet "Deutero-Isaiah," his approach to the Documentary Hypothesis may be characterized as skeptical in the extreme and ultimately quite hostile. As distinct from Hoffmann, he sought to refute the source theory by examining not the law but the narrative portions of the Pentateuch. Thus, he embarked on a painstaking study of Genesis, maintaining that the accepted criteria for separating the sources—style and usage, in particular, the use of the divine names Elohim and Yahweh—were not consistent and that the variation could be explained on other grounds and that the discrepancies in the narrative—such as contradictions, discontinuity, and repetition—were evidence not of separate narrative sources but rather of the wealth and variety of Israelite traditions, employed selectively and judiciously by the Torah literature in order to further its pure, monotheistic aims.

La Questione della Genesi arrives ultimately at the conclusion that the Torah in its entirety was composed in the early monarchic period, most probably during the reign of King David. Cassuto's primary justification for this determination seems to be that while he felt compelled to concede that only after national existence is established and secured does literary creativity begin, and therefore that the Torah literature could not predate the conquest and settlement, once the existence of separate sources is discredited and the connection with Canaanite literature established, nothing stands in the way of positing such an early date. Of course, having confined himself to Genesis, some of the finer points of the source division of which remain disputed even today, Cassuto placed himself from the outset in a position advantageous to his goal. More important, as his work was restricted to the narrative, whereas most of what was so persuasive in the Wellhausenian model of criticism stemmed from the relationship of the law codes, he failed to contend with much of the real substance of the Higher Critical approach. Ironically, the idea that the Torah book is essentially a narrative, in which the law codes have simply been inserted but whose main aim was to recount Israel's history, is a radical departure from Jewish exegetical tradition, which sees imparting the laws as the Torah's primary aim and the narrative as a framework for the legal codes. Here, Cassuto sided, perhaps unintentionally, with the critical assessment of the nature of the Torah literature.

As distinct from Segal, Cassuto seems to have been willing to sacrifice the traditional view of the Torah's origin, conceding that it was a human document, the gradual product of Israel's religious and literary spirit, dating from a period later than Moses, as long as he could argue that it was not so late as the critics supposed and that it was a unified whole. By granting in principle that sacred literature is created in the context of a historical setting, Cassuto thus actually embraced Higher Criticism fully; he merely rejected the specific theory, namely, the Documentary Hypothesis, that had come to dominate it.

Because Cassuto argues so vehemently for the unity of the Torah in its final form, claiming it to be the result of a single, early redactional process thoroughly consistent on the literary and theological levels, it would appear that his motivation was both apologetic and aesthetic. To his mind, the greatest threat posed by the Documentary Hypothesis was that of the atomization and eventual disintegration of the Torah book; moreover, his literary tastes simply refused to perceive criticism's real challenge to the Torah's internal cohesion, which had been assumed by two millennia of Jewish commentators and defended for so long on sophisticated exegetical grounds. Cassuto preferred to excuse the lack of literary harmony as characteristic of ancient literature, and it must be said that his case was not entirely without merit. Indeed, in the years since, the possibility that certain literary discrepancies are indeed stylistic features rather than evidence for sources has been given ever-increasing credence—though without Cassuto's blanket denial of the source theory.

The early years of biblical studies in Jerusalem, still characterized by a feeling that the primary task of the Jewish Bible scholar was to refute whatever Christian scholarship had to say about the origins of Israel, were sympathetic to Cassuto's approach. In the summer of 1940, he presented a series of lectures on the Documentary Hypothesis and the composition of the Pentateuch, later published in Hebrew and English. Here he summarized, in highly polemical and often ironic rhetoric, his arguments against the source theory as he had set them forth in his Italian work of six years earlier. Again he asserted that the whole of Higher Criticism rests on the existence of separate narrative sources; again he (mis)represented the Documentary Hypothesis as resting primarily on the use of the divine names; again he claimed that once doubt can be cast on this foundation, the entire structure collapses. Now, however, appreciating the spirit of the time and place, he all but omitted his own conclusions, couching them in vague and brief references and preferring instead to allow his listeners and readers to reach their own conclusions. His Italian work, meanwhile, in which his conclusions were spelled out, remained untranslated, unavailable to the scholarly community especially in the Jewish world. Thereafter Cassuto was widely believed to have succeeded not only in casting doubt on the Wellhausenian approach but to have proven the traditional doctrine of a Mosaic origin for the Torah. Undeservedly, Cassuto has since obtained a posthumous reputation in certain Jewish circles for having convincingly disproved Higher Criticism on purely scientific grounds—when in fact he did nothing of the sort.

Cassuto's method of dealing with the Torah narrative consisted mainly of emphasizing the overall structure and logic of the narrative, while explaining the occasional discrepancy as stylistic variety or the result of the amalgamation of oral tradition. He put this method to use in his commentaries on Genesis (chs. 1–12) and Exodus, in which, drawing on his comparative studies, he investigated affinities between Pentateuchal traditions and the epic, poetic, and mythological traditions of Canaan, carefully pointing out the similarities in order to stress the differences. Cassuto may be said to have reinstated one of the scholarly theories that preceded the Documentary Hypothesis, known as the Fragmentary Hypothesis, which was largely discarded in the late eighteenth century, while at the same time anticipating the redaction criticism popularized in the latter third of the twentieth century. Still it needs to be admitted that merely explaining the possible redactional logic of the final text does not rule out the preexistence of literary sources, nor does the possibility that oral tradition preexisted the sources themselves: many critics before and since have maintained the source theory while at the same time admitting the obvious—that the sources have a literary and oral prehistory.

The more significant drawback of Cassuto's approach to the Pentateuch is the refusal to consider seriously the connection between events in Israel's history and the development of its religion as reflected in its sacred literature—its law codes in particular. Though Cassuto mentions in passing that the harmonistic method he applies to the narratives is equally valid in the law codes, nowhere is this demonstrated, and it is doubtful that it could be. No attempt is made to address such central issues as the connection between the Josianic reform and the Deuteronomic law code or between the Priestly law and any period in Israel's history. Thus, Cassuto's work created the appearance of having contended with the Documentary Hypothesis, while in actual fact it simply redefined the agenda as confined to the weakest and least significant points and ignored the real historical focus of Higher Criticism.

Virtually all of the scholars whose work has been considered so far were in some measure influenced by Jewish religious sensitivity. While they lived and worked in the scholarly milieu, there remains something of a confessional element in their writings, and their objection to the critical study of the Pentateuch does not seem to have been motivated exclusively by scholarly considerations. This is only to be expected. Ultimately, full entry into Pentateuchal studies as defined by the scholarly approach is possible only for scholars who can thoroughly divorce themselves from the theological challenge. By the early part of the twentieth century, Jewish scholars of a new type began to appear on the scene. In the wake of Emancipation, Enlightenment, and secularism, religious belief and the traditional way of life had ceased to be the sole defining characteristics of Judaism. Judaism came now to be seen primarily as a peoplehood, the furtherance of whose national aims—its cultural rebirth as an ethnic group and ultimately its restored political sovereignty in its historical land—rather than the preservation of its religious integrity, occupied its most productive minds. Particularly in the growing community of Jews in *Eretz-Yisrael* but throughout much of the culturally nationalistic diasporic Jewish community, the study of the Jewish past, especially insofar as its ancient historical connection with its homeland and the antiquity, uniqueness, and spiritually advanced features of its culture were concerned, became the primary sphere of humanistic interest.

So it was that Yehezkel Kaufmann, who as a young scholar in eastern Europe and later in Germany and Switzerland had embraced the national-cultural revival that swept the educated Jewish world, ultimately settled in *Eretz-Yisrael*, there to devote his intense scholarly career to the earliest stages of Israel's national development. He pursued this study with the fullest possible acceptance of scholarly method. Kaufmann was not suspicious of science or critical inquiry, and he belonged to the new generation of Jewish literati—unencumbered by religious inhibitions, curious and innovative in the extreme, iconoclastic to a fault. Kaufmann rather rejected what he perceived as uncritical in the works of the critics: not critical inquiry per se but its misapplication, not objective, philological study but the highly speculative, preconceived, and at base negative view of Israel's ancient culture that informed much of the philological study of the Bible in the nineteenth century.[13]

Though Kaufmann made his major contributions to biblical scholarship, he was not only a Bible scholar. He was an independent thinker, an essayist on issues of Jewish national importance, and a historian par excellence. He aimed to write a comprehensive history of the Jews and of their religious civilization from ancient times down to the destruction of the Second Temple. *Toledot Ha-emunah* itself was begun with this express aim in mind and had been preceded (in 1929–30) by *Golah ve-Nekhar* (*Exile and Alienation*), in which Kaufmann imposed a systematic conceptual structure on Jewish history that was to inform all of his later works as well. He was ultimately prevented from carrying out his entire plan, preferring to concentrate on the earliest stages of biblical history. After completing three volumes of *Toledot*—arriving at the end of First Temple times—he turned to the study of the conquest of Canaan and remained occupied with this period, writing full-length commentaries on Joshua and Judges. *Toledot* came to a close with the appearance of the volume on the postexilic age (1957; Kaufmann died in 1963). But though the essence of the work was a strictly philological study of the biblical literature, the entire structure, as expressed in the name of the work, was religio-historical.

It bears emphasizing that Kaufmann was probably the first Jewish scholar to appreciate fully the import of Higher Criticism. Kaufmann alone recognized that the Wellhausenian structure was not simply a matter of how many authors participated in writing the Torah and how much substantive disharmony can be found in its pages. Kaufmann saw that the primary issues were historical, not strictly literary. Unlike Hoffmann and Cassuto, he comprehended, and accepted, the critical postulate that the biblical *literature* was the key to reconstructing biblical *history*. What he refused to accept was the manner in which the reconstruction was carried out. The broad scope of his vision enabled him to distinguish between what was persuasive and what remained open to question in the reigning critical theory.

On three central issues, all of which touch on the Pentateuch, Kaufmann differed from conventional critics. First and foremost, he rejected the notion that Israel's monotheism had evolved gradually from the paganism of the Semitic peoples. He was convinced that the faith of Israel was a radical and thorough rejection of the paganism that preceded it and that Israelite development began with the revolutionary new religious idea of one, sovereign, nonmagical, ethical, transcendent deity. Unique among biblicists both Jewish and Gentile, Kaufmann inquired into the essential nature of polytheistic paganism and concluded not only that biblical monotheism was a complete departure from it rather than a stage in its gradual metamorphosis but also that biblical literature is utterly unaware of the true nature of paganism, presenting it as mere "fetishism"—the worship of images of wood and stone—rather than the manipulative, efficacious magical cult of a pantheon of whimsical, cosmic deities embodying the universe and natural forces. By the time biblical literature began to develop, argued Kaufmann, Israel had no direct knowledge of the nature of polytheism. It follows that Israel's religion had been thoroughly pervaded by the exclusive monotheistic idea, that of a sole God managing events without concern for competing deities constantly undermining His labors, an omnipotent God uninfluenced by magical forces that could be manipulated to force or stay His hand, and most important, a moral God who could be counted on to act justly rather than arbitrarily or whimsically.

The importance of this line of inquiry in Kaufmann's writings of course goes far beyond its implications for Pentateuchal criticism.[14] Still, the latter is what concerns us here. If the monotheistic idea was fully formed from the outset of Israel's national life and indeed formed the kernel of Israel's culture from its inception, then one of the accepted grounds for viewing the Pentateuchal literature as a late stage in biblical tradition is undermined. The thorough monotheism of the Pentateuch, Kaufmann maintained, belongs to and reflects the earliest phase of Israel's religious creativity. Adopting this position, Kaufmann in a sense reinstated the traditional view of the growth of the biblical tradition: the Torah predated prophecy, indeed predated everything. This liberation from the tendentious critical view of the late, secondary nature of the Torah tradition enabled Kaufmann to place the Torah literature in the historical context to which it most naturally belonged: First Temple times, preexilic Israel. Yet Kaufmann was not motivated by any desire to restore respect for Jewish tradition per se but rather by a driving need to account logically and systematically for the nature of Israelite culture overall. In accord with his general philosophic view of the essence of national life, Kaufmann insisted that the organizing principle for all of Jewish history was its religious idea. Monotheism was in his view a *revolution* and not an evolution; the revolution came at the beginning; once it had occurred, all that followed evolved naturally. Thus, Kaufmann diverged from nineteenth-century thinkers by insisting on the autonomy of the genesis of spiritual phenomena, restricting Hegelian dialectic to the stages following the initial, innovative event. Kaufmann was not an apologist for the Jewish religion but a revisionist historian of the Jewish nation.

For Kaufmann, the internal, philological analysis of the Pentateuch was a given. He accepted the essentials of the four-source theory (though with occasional differences and preferring, along with Wellhausen and many others, to speak of JE as one amalgamated tradition) and endorsed the stylistic and terminological basis for the division. He had no quarrel with the identification of a unique priestly source, and he readily admitted both its distinctive nature and that of the Deuteronomic source, whose connection with the Josianic reform, as well as with the Deuteronomistic redaction of the historiography in Kings, he maintained. He argued firmly for the literary and legal independence of the law codes and their intrinsic connection with the narrative documents into which they have been embedded. He had no doubt that the sources of the Pentateuch represent stages in the evolution of the Israelite religion (once that process had been set in motion by the sudden appearance of the radically new monotheistic idea) or that the direction of development was from the "epic" sources (J and E) to the more thoroughly theologized/legalized ones (P and D). His acceptance of the essentials of the Documentary Hypothesis on the one hand and his philological expertise on the other enabled him to reevaluate the Wellhausenian scheme of Israel's history without rejecting the method itself. Kaufmann's singular and far-reaching contention was that the Priestly source—the identification and character of which was not in dispute—belonged to the preexilic period and was indeed earlier than the Deuteronomic source. Arguing with the Wellhausenian approach (as Hoffmann had before him, taking up in turn each of the chapters of the *Prolegomena*), Kaufmann set forth the preconceived and fallacious nature of the attempt to assign P to the exile. Israel's cult—its Temple and sacrificial system, its priesthood, its sabbaths and holy days, and its laws of purification and atonement—are an integral part of its national life and not an exilic "aftergrowth." Kaufmann demonstrated that the institutionalized worship of the God of Israel and the legal and literary tradition that its priestly custodians cultivated were integral, ancient, and pervasive elements in the national culture from earliest times. To show that the Priestly document actually precedes the Deuteronomic, Kaufmann had recourse to the interesting claim that P does not even mandate the centralization of sacrificial worship in a single Temple, that the Priestly legislation can be best understood as pertaining to the time period when local shrines were still legitimate, and that its Tabernacle narrative is not a reflection of the Jerusalem Temple specifically—and certainly not the postexilic Second Temple. The remarkable influence of D. Z. Hoffmann on Kaufmann's argumentation for a preexilic context for the Priestly Code is undeniable, despite the fact that the two scholars had quite different agendas.

The third pillar on which Kaufmann erected his newly constructed history of the Pentateuchal tradition is the outcome of the other two: the claim that the Torah literature precedes the prophetic. Here, too, it was not a matter simply of asserting which literary figures drew on which others but rather of providing a much-needed corrective for what Kaufmann saw as a crucial misunderstanding of the nature of biblical prophecy and its role in Israel's religious growth. The prophets did not invent monotheism; for Kaufmann they were its advocates and proponents, but their most important contribution was the new emphasis on the role of the ethical in determining Israel's national fate. The Torah literature had established the covenant relationship but had based it primarily on religious—essentially cultic—loyalty to YHWH; the prophets redefined the essential demand of Israel's God as being in the moral sphere. Thus, here, too, Kaufmann did not depart from conventional criticism in seeing classical prophecy as, in some sense, the high point of Israelite religion; yet he steadfastly maintained that the Torah literature was its starting point and progenitor. Here, too, the influence of D. Z. Hoffmann, especially as regards the relationship of P and Ezekiel, is recognizable.

Paradoxically, though Kaufmann was among the first Jewish scholars to dare to enter the field of Pentateuchal studies without inhibition or restriction, his work was for many years ignored in the main by biblical scholarship at large. There are at least three reasons for this: Kaufmann's oeuvre is part of a comprehensive attempt to deal with Jewish national existence; thus, it is directed most naturally at a Jewish readership. In this sense, Kaufmann's work is a function of time and place: the early twentieth-century Jewish cultural milieu. Second, and an outgrowth of the first, Kaufmann wrote virtually all his scholarly studies in Hebrew; translations were partial and appeared late and were confined to English until recently. Third, Kaufmann dared to question the very fundamental assumptions of (mainly German) biblical scholars without distancing himself from their methods. It would not be an exaggeration to claim that by attacking them on their own grounds, Kaufmann presented too formidable a challenge. Scholars found it simpler to ignore than to respond.

Not surprisingly, Kaufmann's influence has been felt primarily among his Jewish successors, who make up a considerably large portion of Jewish biblicists, living and deceased, in Israel and elsewhere. Constant reference to his work pervades all serious Pentateuchal scholarship produced by Jews, be it exegetical-philological or historical-phenomenological. Whether endorsed or challenged, he, not Wellhausen, is the starting point for academic Pentateuchal studies among Jewish biblical scholars. Jews are to be found among the leading figures in biblical studies today, and their highly disproportionate number among scholars dealing with the Torah literature is a direct result of Kaufmann's thorough and groundbreaking Pentateuchal studies. It can be said that Kaufmann signaled Jewish scholars' loss of inhibition and final surrender to scholarly method in studying the Pentateuch, while at the same time maintaining the traditional Jewish refusal to accept uncritically the consensus of Protestant scholarship. While Kaufmann may have been widely ignored in person, this legacy of his has been of abiding influence.

NOTES

1. Bibliographic references are kept to a minimum in this chapter. For a fuller bibliography, see the longer Italian version of this essay, "La critica del Pentateuco nell'ebraismo e negli studiosi ebrai moderni," in S. Sierra, ed., *La lettura ebraica delle Scritture*, 433–63 (Bologna: Dehoniane, 1995).

2. On this notion in midrashic and kabbalistic literature, see note 5 in chapter 10 by Moshe Idel in this volume.

3. See especially Wellhausen's *Prolegomena to the History of Ancient Israel*, originally published in German in 1878. An English translation by J. Sutherland

Black and Allan Menzies was published in Edinburgh by the publishers Adam and Charles Black in 1885; this edition has been frequently republished.

4. Joseph ben Eliezer Bonfils (Tov-Elem) remarks in his fourteenth-century remarks on the Genesis commentary of Abraham ibn Ezra (1089–1164), who alluded to the verses in the Torah that could not have been written by Moses, "Since we have to trust in the words of tradition and the prophets, what should I care whether it was Moses or another prophet who wrote it, since the words of all of them are true and inspired?" See Jon Levenson, *The Hebrew Bible, the Old Testament, and Historical Criticism: Jews and Christians in Biblical Studies* (Louisville, KY: Westminster/John Knox, 1993), 67.

5. Most recently, James L. Kugel, *How to Read the Bible: A Guide to Scripture Then and Now* (New York: Free Press, 2007).

6. David Weiss Halivni, *Peshat and Derash* (New York: Oxford University Press, 1991).

7. See Baruch J. Schwartz, "On *Peshat* and *Derash*, Bible Criticism and Theology," *Prooftexts* 14 (1994): 71–88.

8. Another approach is that of Rabbi M. Breuer, concerning which see chapter 15 by Shalom Carmy in this volume.

9. For his work, see M. M. Kalisch, *A Historical and Critical Commentary on the Old Testament* (London: Longmans, Exodus, 1855; Genesis, 1858; Leviticus, 1867–72); Kalisch, *Bible Studies* (London: Longmans, 1877).

10. Hoffmann's work on the Bible is not available in English. See D. Hoffmann, *Die wichstigsten Instanzen gegen die Graf-Wellhausensche Hypothese*, 2 vols. (Berlin: H. Itzkowski, 1904–1916); Hoffmann, *Das Buch Leviticus*, 2 vols. (Berlin: M. Poppelauer, 1906); Hoffmann, *Das Buch Deuteronomium*, 2 vols. (Berlin: M. Poppelauer, 1913–1922); Hoffmann, *Genesis*, ed. and trans. A. Westril (Bnei Brak, Israel: Nezach, 1971) [in Hebrew].

11. For examples of his work, see M. H. Segal, *Introduction to the Bible*, 8th ed. (Jerusalem: Kiryat Sefer, 1967) [in Hebrew]; Segal, *The Pentateuch: Its Composition and Authorship and Other Biblical Studies* (Jerusalem: Magnes, 1967).

12. For Cassuto's work in English, see *The Documentary Hypothesis and the Composition of the Pentateuch* (Jerusalem: Magnes, 1961), *A Commentary on the Book of Genesis* (Jerusalem: Magnes, 1961–64), *A Commentary on the Book of Exodus* (Jerusalem: Magnes, 1967), and *Biblical and Oriental Studies* (Jerusalem: Magnes, 1973).

13. Kaufmann's magnum opus in biblical studies is his *Toledot Ha-Emunah Ha-yisre'elit* [The History of the Religion of Israel from Antiquity until the End of Second Temple Times], 4 vols. (Tel Aviv: Dvir, 1937–56) [in Hebrew]. An abridged version of volumes 1–3 appeared in English as *The Religion of Israel*, trans. and abridged by Moshe Greenberg (Chicago: University of Chicago Press, 1960). The fourth volume appeared in full in English as *History of the Religion of Israel*, vol. 4, *From the Babylonian Captivity to the End of Prophecy*, trans. C. W. Efroymson

(New York: KTAV, 1977). A summary of his main views is also available in his essay "The Biblical Age," in Leo W. Schwarz, ed., *Great Ages and Ideas of the Jewish People* (New York: Random House, 1956), 3–92.

14. For a fuller discussion, see Job Jindo's chapter 13 in this volume.

Chapter 13

Concepts of Scripture in Yehezkel Kaufmann

Job Y. Jindo

The empirical conception of the Bible fostered during the Enlightenment advanced the notion that "the Bible is not the key to nature but a part of it; it must therefore be considered according to the same rules as hold for any kind of empirical knowledge."[1] The notion of the Bible as artifact entails a paradigm shift for those who regard it as Scripture—it challenges them to reconsider their own understanding of this foundational text, which gives structure to their very mode of existence.[2] This conception of the Bible, which purports to be free of traditional, theological presumptions, puts in question not only the Mosaic origin of the Torah but the very existence of the biblical God (if the Bible is a human creation, the God it portrays may also be a human creation, that is, a figment of the human imagination). No wonder, then, that engagement in biblical criticism by traditional Jews is, to this day, limited. In this respect, it is worthwhile considering the case of Yehezkel Kaufmann (1889–1963), often referred to as "the greatest and most influential Jewish biblical scholar of modern times,"[3] who authored a magisterial four-volume historical-sociological interpretation of Jewish history, *Golah ve-nekhar* (Exile and Alienation, 1928–32; henceforth *Golah*) and a monumental four-volume study of biblical religion and history, *Toledot ha'emunah hayisre'elit* (A History of the Israelite Faith, 1937–56; henceforth *Toledot*).[4]

Although raised in a traditional Jewish family, Kaufmann fully endorsed the empirical notion of the Bible.[5] He understood the Bible not literally as the living word of God but rather as a historical artifact produced in a particular setting of time and place. For him, the Bible was a text to be examined, at least in scholarship, by means of the general principles and analytical tools of empirical investigation. Kaufmann had no qualms about discussing the history of the formation and transmission of biblical literature.

Kaufmann was, however, an independent critical thinker, and he reconsidered practically all the major theses in modern biblical criticism. In particular, he objected to the then-regnant theory of the German Protestant biblicist Julius Wellhausen (1844–1918)—the notion of the Bible as a legacy of a minority phenomenon in ancient Israel, reflecting a gradual evolution of monotheism from polytheism, or a primitive natural religion, during the biblical period.[6] Instead, Kaufmann considered the Bible to be a collective product of ancient Israel, reflecting monotheism as a popular phenomenon from the beginning of the biblical period and as a religion fundamentally different from any other in antiquity.

Today, it is important for students of biblical studies to read Kaufmann's *Toledot* from two perspectives. First, it is a classic that has shaped contemporary Jewish biblical scholarship. Kaufmann's influence is manifest in the writings of distinguished Jewish biblicists of the succeeding generations such as Moshe Greenberg (1928–2010), Menahem Haran (1924–), Jacob Milgrom (1923–2010), Yochanan Muffs (1932–2009), Nahum Sarna (1923–2005), and Moshe Weinfeld (1925–2009).[7] Second, his work still has relevance for today's biblical and religious studies—especially for phenomenological analyses of biblical monotheism. Though at times repetitive and polemical, *Toledot* is distinguished by critical thinking, detailed textual analysis, and vast and multifaceted erudition. As such, it helps us to reflect on how to think about the Bible as a cultural artifact.

In 1929, Kaufmann, while still preparing the manuscript of *Toledot*, wrote, "It would seem that research into the Bible is considered at present as *trefah* [baneful for Jews] but, perhaps as a result of my work, biblical studies may generally come to be considered *kasher* [acceptable]."[8] This statement is equivocal in its use of the terms *trefah* and *kasher* (theological or cultural?) as well as the readership it refers to (religious Jews in particular or the broad Jewish readership, including the secular, in general?). Be that as it may, Kaufmann does not seem to have conceived of the empirical notion of the Bible as detrimental to Jewish identity. This chapter seeks to elucidate this conception of the Bible.

Formative Period: Kaufmann's Theoretical Framework

Kaufmann was born in 1889 in the province of Podolia, Ukraine, and died in 1963 in Jerusalem. His immigration to Palestine in 1928 roughly corresponds to the shift in his intellectual life—from the formative period of learning and researching to the vocational period of teaching and publishing. In the second period, he was a senior teacher of Hebrew subjects at a prestigious high school, the Reali Gymnasium in Haifa, from 1929 to 1949, and later, a professor of Bible at the Hebrew University of Jerusalem from 1949 to 1957. The first period is pertinent to the present topic, namely, his conception of the Bible.[9]

In the Russian Empire of the late nineteenth and early twentieth centuries, where Kaufmann was born and raised, the question of Jewish survival engrossed the minds of Jewish intellectuals. In the face of the onslaught of pogroms and repressive regulations for the Jews that threatened the existence of Russian Jewry, a Zionist movement was formed. Odessa, to which Kaufmann's family moved in 1907, was the center of a Jewish Enlightenment. A galaxy of the intellectual leaders of eastern European Jewry lived there, including a prominent Zionist thinker, Asher H. Ginsberg, better known by his pen name Ahad Ha'Am (1856–1927). In this circle, Judaism was conceived as a cultural entity and the Bible as a formative text of Jewish identity. For them, the Bible was a legacy of their ancestors—a product of what these thinkers referred to in Hebrew as *ruaḥ le'umi* or the collective spirit of ancient Israel.

In 1907, Kaufmann, who by then had acquired a solid foundation of traditional Jewish learning, started to attend the modern yeshivah of Chaim Tchernowitz (1871–1949) in Odessa and then, in 1910, the Academy for Jewish and Oriental Studies of Baron David Günzburg (1856–1910) in St. Petersburg.[10] The objective of these institutions was to integrate modern scientific scholarship with traditional study, thereby reinvigorating Jewish culture and learning in eastern European Jewry. In these institutions, Kaufmann developed an abiding interest in the riddle of Jewish survival, which, for his entire life, he sought to investigate according to the general principles of empirical analysis. For that reason, while Kaufmann espoused the notion of the Bible as a product of the *ruaḥ le'umi* of ancient Israel, he insisted on using the term *ruaḥ*, "spirit" or "mind," only in the empirical sense and not in a speculative Hegelian or romanticist sense, which was how the term was generally used among Jewish thinkers of this period.

The inquisitive rigor or what his then-classmate and lifelong friend Zalman Shazar (1889–1974), the third president of Israel, called the "zeal for truth" that characterizes Kaufmann's writings began to be manifest in this period.[11] In 1914, at the age of twenty-four, Kaufmann published his first major article, titled "The Judaism of Ahad Ha'Am," in which he refuted Ahad Ha'Am's seminal notion of Judaism as a product of the collective will to survival. Instead, Kaufmann argued that it was religion and not the presumed will that preserved the Jewish people as a distinct minority in exile. Kaufmann seemed to have little tolerance for what appeared to him as unfounded quasi-scholarship—including Ahad Ha'Am's. Throughout Kaufmann's work, there is a missionary sense of intellectual responsibility, from which he published empirical observations that even he knew his readership would not accept.[12]

Kaufmann in turn sought systematic training in modern secular education. In 1913, he entered Berne University in Switzerland to study philosophy, Semitic languages, and biblical studies. He completed his Ph.D. in philosophy (summa cum laude) in 1918, after which he went to Berlin, where he devoted himself to the study of history and sociology for about eight years until his immigration to Palestine. Around this time, Kaufmann also studied the writings of Willhelm Dilthey (1833–1911), a German philosopher of history and an intellectual historian who significantly influenced the development of hermeneutics, phenomenology, and the methodology of the social sciences.

Dilthey's influence—especially, his empirical analysis of a lived experience and worldview as reflected in cultural phenomena—in Kaufmann's work is apparent. In Diltheyan terms, Kaufmann conceived of the Bible as a cultural expression that manifests a lived experience of ancient Israel. He sought to explore how the monotheistic mind obtained a deeper insight into the structures and functioning of the world and life, as contrasted to the mind-sets of people in surrounding polytheistic cultures.

On the Historical Formation of the Bible— From Literature to Scripture

As an empiricist, Kaufmann has no trouble assuming that the Torah originally existed not as a fixed canonical "book" but as a kind of didactic "literature," the roots of which may reach back to the time of Moses. He understands the process of biblical canonization to be a gradual one, starting with King Josiah's religious reform and centralization of worship in 622–621 BCE (2 Kings 22–23)—a historical event inspired by a "book of the Torah" found in the Jerusalem temple, which modern biblical scholars agree was Deuteronomy or an earlier version of it. Accordingly, for Kaufmann, Deuteronomy is the first canonized book of the Torah that was accepted "as binding divine law,"[13] and the age of Josiah marks the "Archimedean point" in the history of the Pentateuchal literature—"the beginning of the emergence of the Torah *book* out of the Torah *literature*."[14]

Kaufmann maintains that the whole Torah was canonized as the people's "book of life" in the time of Ezra and Nehemiah in the fifth century BCE.[15] As the primary impetus behind this canonization, he sees the collective urge to restore the relationship to God. At that time, the Babylonian exile (ca. 586–538 BCE) was conceived as a result of Israel's failure to fulfill its sacred duties, and the only way for the people of Israel to end this period of "divine rage" and to restore their life in the promised land was to live solely according to the will of God. To do so, first they must know the divine will. Thus, the Torah was compiled by an authorized institution from independent sources hitherto circulating in different groups and consecrated as the "living word of God."[16] Next, the literature of the Prophets was collected and organized as supplementary to this canon, as was, in turn, the Writings a few centuries later. The Bible thus came to have its present shape as "Scripture" and the people of Israel as the "people of the Book."

Kaufmann insists that we recognize as real the presence of both stylistic and substantive discrepancies within and among biblical texts. He also points out a considerable number of unfulfilled prophecies in biblical literature.[17] The very presence of such "flaws" indicates for Kaufmann that contrary to the dominant scholarly view of an age of canonization, it was rather an "age of compilation, not of edition and revision, let alone of innovation,"[18] for had revisions occurred at this stage, such glaring flaws would have been corrected or edited out. To be sure, he admits, "there have been technical errors, and the order of chapters has been confused, owing to the fact that the book was compiled from several collections over a period of time. A few marginal remarks may also have entered the text."[19] But by and large, the later codifiers and compilers of biblical literature did not seek to "clean up" the text, whether stylistically or substantively, and this, he argues, is because each source had long been preserved and circulated in a given form.

Cultural Creativity and Empirical Investigation

Kaufmann thus conceives of the Bible as a historical artifact that must be studied like any other historical document. For him, biblical scholarship must abstain from any speculative metaphysics. He is thus an "empiricist" but, at the same time, not an empirical "materialist." In other words, he thinks that we cannot explain cultural creativity by material conditions alone and that we must take into account a category of *ruaḥ*, which, for him, is a primary and fundamental factor in cultural creativity, a factor equally as important as any other moment or element, be that material or social. By the term *ruaḥ*, he refers not to some Hegelian or romanticist concept but to an empirical category of historical experience, as does Dilthey. And to give an empirical grounding to this category, Kaufmann introduces a cultural phenomenon that he calls an "infinite variety of cultural creative forms"—in a turn of phrase reminiscent of Dilthey's "infinite variety of philosophical forms."[20]

Kaufmann questions two dominant approaches in modern historical studies, namely, dialectic idealism and empirical materialism.[21] The former approach, like Hegel or Wellhausen, seeks to explain the origin and history of a cultural phenomenon through a preconceived metaphysical paradigm, whereas the latter, like Marx or Durkheim, seeks to explain it through its physical and social settings and causalities. In Kaufmann's view, neither approach adequately accounts for the origin of the infinite variety of cultural forms as an empirical phenomenon, for such a phenomenon involves multiple, heterogeneous factors—material and nonmaterial, which in turn influence each other—along with contingent elements and therefore cannot be explained by general overarching principles.

Like Dilthey, Kaufmann asserts that as each individual has this creative potential or *ruaḥ*, so does each social group. Kaufmann insists this term be used only in an empirical sense as a collective potential of cultural creativity and not as an abstract metaphysical entity. For him, as for Dilthey, any cultural organic phenomenon with its own internal logic and principles, such as language or religion, involves this collective creative potential or *ruaḥ*.[22] Indeed, his overall thesis is that biblical religion, as a cultural system, is a product of the collective creative potential of ancient Israel—a system that involves a distinctive worldview that is categorically different from any polytheistic worldview.

Polytheism and Monotheism: Two Different Worldviews

Kaufmann points out that the Bible displays no cognizance of what he regards as fundamental to all polytheistic literature—namely, the notion of a primordial nature or causality that limits or conditions everything in the universe, including the divine sphere. He calls this category the "meta-divine."[23] It is "the womb of all being, contains the roots and patterns of all nature, and out of which the gods themselves have emerged."[24] That is, in the polytheistic system, deities contend not only with each other but also with a transcendent order, to which they themselves are subject. In biblical monotheism, what shapes the destinies of all beings in the universe is not preexistent causality but the absolute will of one supreme deity. Accordingly, for Kaufmann, the monotheistic statement "YHWH is one" signifies not only the numerical oneness but, more essentially, the absolute supremacy of the sovereign deity as one and only.[25] Kaufmann thus conceives the difference between polytheism and biblical monotheism not only as quantitative or arithmetic (i.e., one deity or many) but, more fundamentally, as qualitative and ontological (i.e., different conceptions of divinity altogether). The decisive difference involves *worldview* and *lived experience*.

According to Kaufmann, this fundamental difference between two religious systems gives rise to two different attitudes toward the world and life. Consider, for example, the apprehension of misfortunes, such as untimely death or natural calamities.[26] For the polytheistic mind, which perceives the world as an ordered entity operating independently of human existence, such enigmas or misfortunes could appear to be part of the process of a preexistent system, independent of human responsibility. That is, although there is a polytheistic notion of divine retribution for human injustice, not every enigma of life may be perceived in terms of sin, that is, morality. It then comes as no surprise when the polytheistic mind minimizes the purposeful and moral quality of such misfortunes.[27] On the other hand, for the monotheistic mind, which perceives the unfolding of the world as manifestations of the absolute will of a moral and just deity, misfortunes would not happen without cause. This mind could thus assume divine intent in calamities and identify their origin in the realm of morality. It then comes as no surprise when the monotheistic mind displays a tendency to maximize the providential and moral quality of the enigmas of life and attributes them to human responsibility.

Kaufmann also asserts that most advanced polytheistic systems display a tendency on the part of humans to be self-reliant. This tendency stems, in his view, from the implicit recognition that none of the gods is truly omnipotent and that they are frequently occupied with matters outside the human sphere, so that humans must, for the most part, fend for themselves and resort to other means to assume a measure of control over their own fortunes. This tendency is reflected, he argues, in the sophisticated systems of magic, divination, and cult, each of which, for the ancients, is a form of science processed and practiced according to causal reasoning and empirical observation. What lies behind these systems is the belief in the redeeming power of the intellect—that humans can thereby manipulate the supreme order on which both the gods and the world depend or, at least, can comprehend the workings of the universe for their own benefit. Consequently, the polytheistic mind develops a belief in the competence of human reason. In a monotheistic system, by contrast, any attempt to manipulate the world order is considered as a cardinal sin, for it signifies a challenge against the supreme deity who designs and establishes that very order. In this system, self-reliance is viewed as potentially detrimental, for it can overshadow—and thus diminish the reliance on—the supreme deity. In this respect, self-assurance is a sign of human arrogance, an act of self-deification. Kaufmann notes, "The [biblical] war against polytheistic idolatry was at the same time a war against the intellectual deification of reason, against the belief that intellectual knowledge could redeem humankind."[28] No wonder, then, if the monotheistic mind discredits the reliance on human reason (e.g., Jer. 9:22–23 [23–24 in many English tranlslations]; Ezek. 28; Prov. 3:5–7; 26:12) and insists, instead, on the undivided faith in the redeeming power of the absolute deity.

Accordingly, Kaufmann maintains that the polytheistic and monotheistic worldviews are categorically incompatible, requiring a mental breakthrough to move from one perception to the other, and this shift cannot be explained by a theory of gradual progression, such as Wellhausen's. Put differently, the conception of biblical monotheism is revolutionary, not evolutionary—it has no antecedents, as Kaufmann sees it, in human history.

Because biblical monotheism posits that there is only one creator and ruler of the universe, Kaufmann regards it as universalistic from the outset in terms of both self- and empirical understanding of ancient Israel. Biblical tradition portrays humankind as originally monotheistic—"that Adam, Cain, Abel, and the succeeding generations were worshippers of the one God"—and that idolatry was introduced only after the dispersal of humankind and the confusion of tongues, while the faith and worship of the one God was maintained by Abraham and his descendants.[29] This means, for

Kaufmann, that ancient Israelites themselves understood the religion of this deity, YHWH, to be universalistic from the outset—from the beginning of human history. On the other hand, he notes, empirical investigation cannot determine the historicity of this tradition prior to the Exodus, and he rather thinks of historical monotheism as founded during the time of Moses, as the Bible itself also attests indirectly. According to him, every level of biblical literature, even the earliest, is pervaded by the universalistic notion of the monotheistic deity. If so, the religion of ancient Israel that produced biblical literature was universalistic even before the formation of this literature. This means that the religion of ancient Israel, as a historical religion, was monotheistic from the outset—from the Mosaic age.

Kaufmann points out that biblical literature nowhere articulates, explicitly or systematically, the monotheistic worldview, which he deems to have permeated the entire cultural system of ancient Israel. This means, for him, that the monotheistic belief in YHWH was a cultural given in ancient Israel. In the Bible, furthermore, the idea of monotheism is expressed in symbols and popular forms, such as in the anthropomorphic depictions of the absolute deity. It is these observations that lead him to conceive of biblical religion and literature as a popular phenomenon, a product of the collective *ruaḥ* of ancient Israel—*ruaḥ*, of course, as always with Kaufmann, in the empirical sense—and not of some individual thinkers or limited circles of religious elites thereof.

At the same time, Kaufmann regards the Israelite, popular aspect of biblical monotheism as essentially arbitrary. Because biblical monotheism is fundamentally universalistic, it could have been conceived in any other place or age, and it is a matter of coincidence that ancient Israel intuited the idea of biblical monotheism. Only the medium—or the *ruaḥ*—through which biblical monotheism was intuited and objectified, but not its conceptual content, is Israelite and popular. Herein lies what Kaufmann reckons as the secret of Jewish survival: the accidental union of the Jewish people with the universalistic idea of biblical monotheism that transcends both land and peoplehood is what has enabled Jews to survive as a people in the Diaspora for centuries.[30]

Kaufmann, in stressing the notion that monotheism was deeply engrained in the collective consciousness and culture of ancient Israel, makes an argument that to this day appears to be too radical to be accepted in scholarship: that biblical authors did not understand true polytheism and instead regarded it as a fetishism—as a deification of material objects such as wood and stone. Because biblical authors' monotheistic perception of reality was fundamentally different from that of their neighboring societies, they were unable to understand the true experience of polytheism, as a "vital, fundamental, psychic experience";[31] that is, they were unable to conceive of and experience the world and life according to the notion of the metadivine. Thus, he concludes, "in the sphere of religious creativity," polytheism and monotheism "were two worlds, distinct and mutually incomprehensible."[32]

For Kaufmann, accordingly, startling resemblances that comparative scholars have identified between biblical and other ancient Near Eastern literature—such as in narrative, law, wisdom, prayer, ritual, and historiography—are only on the formal and not on the conceptual level. Biblical authors incorporated and appropriated the literary and cultural conventions they, or their culture, had inherited from their neighboring polytheistic cultures and transformed those conventions according to their own worldview, self-understanding, and value system. Indeed, to elucidate this transformation and delineate the history of biblical monotheism as reflected in biblical literature was one of Kaufmann's major objectives in his *Toledot*.

On the Inception of Monotheistic Insight—An Empirical Take

Like any major work, Kaufmann's study has compelled a host of questions and serious criticisms that include such fundamental ones as the following: What Kaufmann presents as a phenomenology of biblical monotheism may hold true, by and large, for the religion as portrayed in biblical literature, but is that the case also for the religion as actually practiced by ancient Israelites during the biblical period? The typological approach whereby Kaufmann discusses polytheism and monotheism accentuates the differences between the contrasted systems, but does he not thereby overshadow possible crossovers between the two? The results of his contrastive analysis between the polytheistic and the monotheistic systems are impressively clear-cut and edifying, but how thoroughly—and with what degree of sophistication and depth—did Kaufmann actually examine ancient Near Eastern literature? Or, put differently, did he not interpret the actual texts in a forced manner to meet his overall thesis of biblical religion? Kaufmann emphasizes the cognitive assumptions of biblical writings—especially, the idea of one supreme deity—but does he not thereby overlook the diversity of competing, oftentimes even conflicting, perceptions attested within biblical literature?[33] Is not the biblical notion of one supreme deity who transcends fate and nature—the notion that Kaufmann deems as unique to biblical monotheism—only a precondition for the idea of divine interpersonality with an enduring, external focus of interest—the idea that a deity can fully and continually engage in the interpersonal drama with humankind, which *is* perhaps the real uniqueness of biblical monotheism?[34]

Be that as it may, how does Kaufmann understand the *ontology* of biblical literature? Is the Bible (merely) a cultural artifact? Or is it still a text of divine origin? And how does he explain the inception of monotheistic insight, which he deems to permeate this literature? In fact, nowhere does Kaufmann discuss the issue of revelation. While the Talmudist Ephraim E. Urbach (1912–91) and other believing scholars criticize him for not engaging in such metaphysical issues, he insistently refuses to present any empirical explanation to the origin of monotheistic insight.[35]

Kaufmann asserts that the distinction between the "content" and "form" of cultural creativity must be maintained because the origin of such content, according to him, cannot be fully explained by empirical methods —only the form of a given content and the process of its transformation thereby can be described. For example, Homer's or Beethoven's artistic creativity—especially, the original insight that sparked in their *ruaḥ*, as well as the creative spontaneity of their *ruaḥ* involved in this process—cannot be explained from empirical observation alone.[36] Thus, Kaufmann notes, what empirical investigation can consider is only the history of a given cultural creativity after its inception.

In this respect, for Kaufmann, biblical monotheism is not different from any other original and creative work or thought by the human spirit or *ruaḥ*. It came into being—just like any other cultural product—in a particular setting of time and space. However, according to Kaufmann, we cannot empirically explain why this content, although universalistic in principle, was conceived nowhere in the world but in ancient Israel. For him, this discussion of "why" is outside the scope of empirical investigation. "In terms of form, we can say: the formation [of biblical monotheism], too, is nothing other than a novel and unique creation of the human spirit. However, in terms of content, this is not the case. Accordingly, we may have to presume a special intervention of providence. However, we have, at this point, exceeded the realm of empirical history and entered into the realm of faith."[37]

Kaufmann's statement on the "special intervention of providence" has no empirical value—for it is a statement of faith or speculation—as he himself acknowledges elsewhere.[38] Empirical reason cannot penetrate into what is behind the ultimate nexus of reality and, as such, cannot—indeed need not—seek to address such a metaphysical notion as divine existence or revelation.[39] For some readers, this critique of empirical reason, which de facto leaves room for postulating such a metaphysical notion, might strike them as resembling the monotheistic critique of human intellect described earlier. Note, however, that Kaufmann's critique stems not from a dogmatic but from an analytical premise: to overlook this epistemic limitation is to risk invalidating the value of the empirical research itself. And for the same reason, contends Kaufmann, the empirical analysis of biblical monotheism must stay clear both of excessive positivism, such as Wellhausen's, and of supernaturalism, such as Urbach's. For the former blurs the scope and limits of scientific investigation and thus presents speculative considerations as empirical, whereas the latter seeks to explain cultural phenomena through religious categories and thus mixes two different disciplinary horizons—empirical and theological—producing essentially idiosyncratic analyses. Paradoxically, it is through Kaufmann's intellectual integrity—and not, for example, a theological dogmatism—that we find his stance strikingly approximating the traditional position.[40]

Concluding Remarks

The foregoing observations should not form the impression that Kaufmann's project had no Zionist convictions. The very fact that he wrote his works in modern Hebrew—and not, for example, in German—indicates otherwise. It may be fair to say that, as a Zionist, Kaufmann sought to present his study of the Bible and Jewish history as an empirical ground in light of which his people would consider and determine their collective fate. In this respect, his *Toledot* may even be seen as a project of cultural recovery, perceiving the Bible, as did other cultural Zionists of his period, as a formative text of modern Jewish culture. The Bible was a starting point for shaping the identity of modern Jewry and, more specifically, was a possible identitarian bedrock for his people who were then returning to their homeland from all parts of the world after two millennia. If so, his lifework as a Zionist project was to contribute to this revival and to the making of modern Israel through his empirical investigation of the Bible and Jewish history.

Kaufmann's lifework, at the same time, was a project of cultural integration. It sought to internalize an empirical study of the Bible into Jewish intellectual life—a discipline generally avoided by his contemporary Jews for its potential detriment to Jewish identity. Demonstrating the validity of this internalization was not a cause but a natural consequence of Kaufmann's work.[41] For him, the empirical notion of the Bible as cultural artifact—which categorically relativizes the religious conception of the Bible as Scripture—is neither detrimental to nor incongruent with traditional Jewish learning, including the idea of revelation. What gives the Bible its ultimate value as the living text of the Jewish people is not its traditional scriptural conception but rather the perception of reality and life as reflected in the text. Concomitantly, it seems that the traditional notion of "the (entire) Torah from Moses," for Kaufmann, was empirically not untenable either. In his view, every Pentateuchal law and every biblical passage postulates the original insight of biblical monotheism, which, as he saw it, ultimately goes back to the Mosaic age. In this respect, the entire Torah—and in fact the Bible as a whole—is of Mosaic origin.[42]

Like any scholarly notion or thesis, Kaufmann's conception of the Bible must always be corrected or revised in light of new theories, methods, and findings. Nonetheless, his conception encapsulates a sincere response to the challenge of modernity, that is, to address, if not resolve, the seemingly irreconcilable tension between two independent sources of truth and knowledge—that is, between faith and reason—and as such, merits a significant place in Jewish intellectual history, in the ongoing process of integrating outside cultural influences.

NOTES

This chapter is intended for educated lay readers. A longer (original) version, which includes a fuller treatment of Dilthey's impact on Kaufmann, appeared in the *Journal of Jewish Thought and Philosophy* 19 (2011): 95–129. I thank David Bergman, Harald Halbhuber, David Perechocky, and Leslie Rubin for reading and commenting on earlier drafts of this essay. I dedicate this (as well as the original) essay to Yocheved Hershlag Muffs, who has always extended her love and joy to me and my family, and to the memory of Yochanan Muffs, my mentor, who introduced me to the profundity of Kaufmann's work.

1. Ernst Cassirer, *The Philosophy of the Enlightenment*, trans. Fritz C. A. Koelln and James P. Pettegrove (Princeton: Princeton University Press, 1951), 186. In this quotation, Cassirer refers to Spinoza's notion of the Bible.

2. On the responses and struggles of modern Jewry—especially in Germany and in Palestine—against biblical criticism, see Yaacov Shavit and Mordechai Eran,

The Hebrew Bible Reborn: From Holy Scripture to the Book of Books: A History of Biblical Culture and the Battles over the Bible in Modern Judaism, trans. Chaya Naor (Berlin: Walter de Gruyter, 2007).

3. Benjamin Sommer, *The Bodies of God and the World of Ancient Israel* (New York: Cambridge University Press, 2009), 2. See also Chaim Potok, "The Mourners of Yehezkel Kaufmann," *Conservative Judaism* 18, no. 2 (1964): 1; Moshe Greenberg, "Kaufmann on the Bible: An Appreciation," in *Studies in the Bible and Jewish Thought* (Philadelphia: Jewish Publication Society, 1995), 175; Jon Levenson, *The Hebrew Bible, the Old Testament, and Historical Criticism: Jews and Christians in Biblical Studies* (Louisville, KY: Westminster/John Knox, 1993), 44.

4. Only part of either work is available in English: *Golah*, vol. 1, chs. 7–9, translated by C. W. Efroymson as *Christianity and Judaism: Two Covenants* (Jerusalem: Magnes, 1988); the first three volumes of *Toledot*, abridged and translated by Moshe Greenberg as *The Religion of Israel: From Its Beginning to the Babylonian Exile* (Chicago: University of Chicago Press, 1960); the fourth volume of *Toledot*, translated by C. W. Efroymson as *History of the Religion of Israel*, vol. 4, *From the Babylonian Captivity to the End of Prophecy* (New York: Ktav, 1977).

5. Kaufmann's lifestyle and scholarship led his contemporaries to regard him as a secular Jew. However, Kaufmann seems to have been profoundly religious in his own way; see Zalman Shazar, "Yehezkel Kaufmann of Blessed Memory" (in Hebrew), *Ha-Do'ar* 43, no. 4 (1963): 59–61, esp. 61.

6. Julius Wellhausen, *Prolegomena to the History of Israel*, trans. J. Sutherland Black and Allan Menzies (Edinburgh: Adam & Charles Black, 1885). For Kaufmann's objection to Wellhausen's seminal thesis, as well as his position on the dating of the so-called priestly source, see Baruch Schwartz's chapter 12 in this volume. See also Moshe Weinfeld, "Pentateuch," *Encyclopaedia Judaica*, 1st ed., 13:231–62, esp. 239–42. Kaufmann notes time and again in his *Toledot* that modern biblical scholarship in general and Wellhausen's work in particular are replete with Protestant preconceptions, so much so that he refers to it as "Protestant biblical scholarship." On this, see Moshe Weinfeld, *The Place of the Law in the Religion of Ancient Israel* (Leiden, Netherlands: Brill, 2004), 3–74; Levenson, *The Hebrew Bible*.

7. As Sommer notes, one can consider much of the great, modern Jewish biblical scholarship—i.e., the works that are consciously Jewish—as a dialogue with Kaufmann; see Benjamin Sommer, "Dialogical Biblical Theology: A Jewish Approach to Reading Scripture Theologically," in *Biblical Theology: Introducing the Conversation*, ed. Leo Perdue (Nashville, TN: Abingdon, 2009), 1–53, 265–85, esp. 266–67n. 11. On the reception of Kaufmann by American Jewry (especially in the Conservative movement), see Ismar Schorsch, "Coming to Terms with Biblical Criticism," *Conservative Judaism* 57, no. 3 (2005): 3–22.

8. Kaufmann's letter to his former teacher Joseph Klausner (1874–1958), as quoted in Emanuel Green, "Universalism and Nationalism as Reflected in the Writings of Yehezkel Kaufmann with Special Emphasis on the Biblical Period" (Ph.D.

diss., New York University 1968), 14. The letter is preserved in the Joseph Klausner archive in the National Library of Israel (ARC. 4° 1086/444). I thank Rachel Misrati of the Department of Archives for providing me with a copy of this letter.

9. For Kaufmann's biography, see, e.g., Green, "Universalism and Nationalism," ch. 1; Thomas Krapf, *Yehezkel Kaufmann: Ein Lebens- und Erkenntnisweg zur Theologie der Hebräischen Bibel* (Berlin: Institute Kirche und Judentum, 1990); Avinoam Barshai, introduction to *Selected Writings on Jewish Nationality and Zionism*, by Yehezkel Kaufmann, ed. Avinoam Barshai (in Hebrew) (Jerusalem: World Zionist Organization, 1995), 13–117.

10. These institutions attracted distinguished instructors and aspiring students of the Jewish intelligentsia in Russia. The instructors in Tchernowitz's yeshivah included Hayyim Nahman Bialik (1873–1934) and Joseph Klausner (1874–1958); the instructors in Günzburg's academy included Shimon Dubnow (1860–1941) and Judah Katzenelson (pseudonym: Buki ben Yogli; 1846–1917). Students at Tchernowitz's institution included Joshua Gutmann (1890–1963; scholar of Jewish Hellenism), Zvi Woyslawski (1889–1957; Hebrew writer and literary critic), and Jacob Hellmann (1880–1950; labor Zionist leader and editor); at Günzburg's academy, students included Zalman Shazar (1889–1974; the third president of Israel), Solomon Zeitlin (1892–1976; Jewish historian), and Joseph Trumpeldor (1880–1920; an iconic figure of the founding spirit of modern Israel). On these institutions, see Green, "Universalism and Nationalism," 1–5, 17–26; Barshai, introduction to *Selected Writings*, 60–96; Zalman Shazar, "Baron David Günzberg [sic] and His Academy," *The Seventy-Fifth Anniversary Volume of the Jewish Quarterly Review*, ed. Abraham Neuman and Solomon Zeitlin (Philadelphia: Jewish Quarterly Review, 1967), 1–17.

11. Shazar, "Yehezkel Kaufmann of Blessed Memory," 59, 61.

12. Kaufmann's following statement in *Golah* aptly captures his uncompromising sense of intellectual responsibility: "I know that there are in what I write words which will be most difficult for our contemporaries to accept, but what shall I do? Other than what I have stated, I cannot say" (*Golah*, xiii; translated by Efroymson in Kaufmann, *Christianity and Judaism*, x).

13. Kaufmann, *Religion of Israel*, 208.

14. Ibid., 209; italics added. The phrase "Archimedean point" is from Moshe Weinfeld, *Deuteronomy 1–11* (New York: Doubleday, 1991), 16.

15. Kaufmann, *Toledot*, 4:409; idem, *History of the Religion of Israel*, vol. 4, 485–94.

16. Kaufmann, *History of the Religion of Israel*, vol. 4, 404–6.

17. Kaufmann, e.g., lists a series of prophecies in Jeremiah that never came true; see Kaufmann, *Religion of Israel*, 413–14.

18. Ibid., 210.

19. Ibid., 413–14. The comment specifically refers to the book of Jeremiah;

however, Kaufmann generally understands that the same kind of scribal errors can be found in other biblical texts as well.

20. Kaufmann, *Toledot*, 1:xxi–xxii. For Dilthey's "infinite variety of philosophical forms," see Wilhelm Dilthey, *Dilthey's Philosophy of Existence: Introduction to Weltanschauungslehre*, ed. William Kluback and Martin Weinbaum (London: Vision, 1957); Hans Peter Rickman, *Dilthey: Selected Writings* (Cambridge: Cambridge University Press, 1976), 133–54.

21. Here, too, Kaufmann seems to take his cue from Dilthey's work; see, e.g., Dilthey, *Selected Works*, vol. 1, *Introduction to the Human Sciences*, ed. Rudolf Makkreel and Frithjof Rodi (Princeton: Princeton University Press, 1989), 136–69.

22. Rickman, *Dilthey: Selected Writings*, 93.

23. See Kaufmann, *Religion of Israel*, 21–59, esp. 23n. 1, where this term is defined. Cf. also Mark Smith's critique of Kaufmann in his *The Origins of Biblical Monotheism: Israel's Polytheistic Background and the Ugaritic Texts* (New York: Oxford University Press, 2001), 12, 201n. 70. For a response to Smith's critique from a Kaufmannian perspective, see Sommer, *Bodies of God*, 274n. 125.

24. Yehezkel Kaufmann, "The Biblical Age," in *The Great Ages and Ideas of the Jewish People*, ed. Leo Schwartz (New York: Random House, 1956), 10.

25. See Kaufmann, "Religion of Israel" (in Hebrew), in *Encyclopedia Miqra'it*, 4:729–30; cf. Maimonides, the first chapter (esp. sec. 7) of "Basic Principles of the Torah," in *The Mishneh Torah*. This oneness, for Kaufmann, is indeed not numerical. Elsewhere he notes that biblical monotheism can assume the existence of other divine beings besides YHWH: "There is room in monotheism for the worship of lower divine beings—with the understanding that they belong to the suite of the One" (Kaufmann, *Religion of Israel*, 137).

26. Cf. what Dilthey calls the "enigmas of life." See David Naugle, *Worldview: The History of a Concept* (Grand Rapids, MI: Eerdmans, 2002), 82–98, esp. 86–88.

27. Here, it is not claimed that polytheistic deities have no interest in morality. Kaufmann himself states that polytheistic deities were also conceived as ruling according to the principles of justice and righteousness; see *Toledot*, 1:224–25.

28. Kaufmann, "Biblical Age," 92; the quotation is slightly modified according to the Hebrew original in *Mi-kivshonah shel ha-yetsirah ha-mikra'it* (Tel Aviv: Devir, 1966), 138.

29. Kaufmann, "Biblical Age," 14; idem, *Religion of Israel*, 221–23.

30. Kaufmann understands that religion alone can no longer serve this role in modern times, especially in the face of the secularism that dominates Jewish culture. For the preservation of Jewish identity, he thus holds, a territorial solution is henceforth inevitable.

31. Kaufmann, "The Bible and Mythological Polytheism," *Journal of Biblical Literature* 70 (1951): 195.

32. Ibid.

33. For a polyphonic analysis of biblical religion and literature from a Kaufmannian perspective, see Israel Knohl, *Divine Symphony: The Bible's Many Voices* (Philadelphia: Jewish Publication Society, 2003).

34. As Yochanan Muffs puts it, "only a being in control of nature (including [God's] own nature) can act with the freedom needed to involve Himself in the world of humankind"; Yochanan Muffs, *Love and Joy: Law, Language and Religion in Ancient Israel* (New York: Jewish Theological Seminary, 1992), 6. See also idem, *The Personhood of God: Biblical Theology, Human Faith and the Divine Image* (Woodstock, VT: Jewish Lights, 2005), esp. 55–60; Moshe Halbertal and Avishai Margalit, *Idolatry*, trans. Naomi Goldblum (Cambridge: Harvard University Press, 1992), 68–73.

35. See E. Urbach, "Neue Wege der Bibelwissenschaft," *Monatsschrift für Geschichte und Wissenschaft des Judentums* (1938): 1–22, esp. 3–4.

36. Kaufmann, *Golah*, 1:22; idem, *Toledot*, 1:xxiii–iv and esp. 2:41, where he notes, "It is impossible to 'explain' this spark of striking and original creativity. The birth of every novel and original idea happens with an unusual spark, and therefore, any attempt to explain it is inconsequential-imaginative."

37. Kaufmann, *Toledot*, 1:xxxix.

38. Kaufmann, "Biblical Age," 14; idem, *Mi-kivshonah*, 59.

39. Cf. Kaufmann, *Golah*, 1:22.

40. Kaufmann's epistemic stance is reminiscent of a Kantian stance, which is also espoused by Dilthey; see, e.g., Dilthey, *Selected Works*, vol. 1, esp. 8, 20–21, 248–49, 489–90. For this and for other reasons, Kaufmann is generally regarded as Kantian. Note, however, that this stance is already anticipated by Maimonides, whose work Kaufmann was certainly well versed in; see *The Guide for the Perplexed*, from part 1, ch. 71, to part 2, ch. 31, esp., pt. 2, ch. 22, where Maimonides refers to Aristotle's metaphysics as well as the axiom of the eternity of the universe as no more than a mere "speculation." A caution is thus in order: Kaufmann may not be so Kantian as he is generally assumed.

41. Consider Kaufmann's remarks in his letter to Klausner quoted earlier. As Kaufmann nowhere advocated the validity of the integration of biblical criticism into Jewish intellectual life in his *Toledot*, the demonstration of this validity, for him, was not an agendum but a natural consequence of the publication of *Toledot*.

42. Cf. Jacob Milgrom's argument according to which the general principles and rules of the Ten Commandments that may go back to Moses are what underlie the (composite) Torah canon in general and its laws in particular; Milgrom, "Can Critical Scholarship Believe in the Mosaic Origin of the Torah?," in *Leviticus: A Book of Ritual and Ethics* (Minneapolis: Fortress, 2004), 1–6.

Chapter 14

||||||||||||||||||||||||||||||||||||||||

Concepts of Scripture in Moshe Greenberg

Marc Zvi Brettler

Introduction

Moshe Greenberg was born on July 10, 1928, in Philadelphia to Rabbi Simon and Betty (Davis) Greenberg.[1] His parents were observant Jews who spoke Hebrew to their children, and he received private tutoring in Jewish texts in the early mornings, before attending public school. His father was the rabbi of a prominent Conservative synagogue, served as vice chancellor of the Jewish Theological Seminary, and was active in some progressive social causes. Greenberg studied as an undergraduate and completed his Ph.D. at the University of Pennsylvania. Greenberg's dissertation, completed in 1954 and published one year later, was on the Ḫab/piru, an ancient Near Eastern group connected by some scholars to the Hebrews. It was an Assyriological dissertation, which dealt with the possible etymological significance of this term in relation to the ancient Hebrews in only six pages. In 1954, the same year he completed his Ph.D., Greenberg received rabbinic ordination at the Jewish Theological Seminary.

Greenberg's adviser at the University of Pennsylvania was Ephraim Avigdor Speiser,[2] a master linguist, known for his work in Hebrew, Akkadian, and Hurrian languages and texts. Speiser believed that the Hebrew Bible was "the capstone" product of ancient Near Eastern civilization, a notion expressed in his Anchor Bible *Genesis* commentary in 1964.[3] These ideas are reflected in Greenberg's writings. Greenberg likewise followed his teacher in "integrat[ing] philological details into larger conceptual wholes" and in an interest in the "enduring impact" of the ideas of antiquity. A picture of Speiser hangs in Greenberg's Jerusalem study.[4] Adjacent to that photo is a picture of Yehezkel Kaufmann, the towering

Jewish intellectual who is discussed elsewhere in this volume.[5] Greenberg discovered Kaufmann's works in his father's library, and his first scholarly article was based on Kaufmann; he soon thereafter translated an article by Kaufmann for the *Journal of Biblical Literature*. The two corresponded for several years, and later Greenberg translated abridgements of Kaufmann's works in several forms. The two met only once, during Greenberg's 1954 trip to Israel; Kaufmann had died before Greenberg settled in Israel to teach at the Hebrew University in 1970.

Greenberg venerated Kaufmann. This is reflected in Greenberg's huge effort to make Kaufmann's insights accessible to the world of biblical scholarship, in the manner in which Greenberg addressed Kaufmann in his letters, and in comments Greenberg made after Kaufmann's death, in which he calls Kaufmann "the foremost Jewish Biblicist of our time and a profound interpreter of Jewish history."[6] Greenberg also modeled himself after Kaufmann; what Greenberg says about Kaufmann is true of Greenberg himself: that "all of his life's work is suffused with a devotion to his people" and that Kaufmann, in contrast to many in his generation, did not engage in pure empirical research but left "room for the answer of faith to the phenomenon of the Bible." Greenberg, like his mentor, "elevated the discussion of biblical thought above ecclesiastical dogma and partisanship into the realm of the eternally significant ideas." Finally, Greenberg appreciated Kaufmann's role as a Jewish nationalist who emphasized the crucial nature of Jewish religion as defining Jewish ethnicity. Although Speiser was Greenberg's main formal academic teacher, Kaufmann was the more influential figure.[7]

Greenberg breaks the mold noted by Moshe Goshen-Gottstein, who in discussing the participation of Jews in biblical theology observed, "The issue of biblical authority has never been a question which bothered Jews."[8] Jewish biblical scholarship has come of age, and although there are now many contemporary Jewish Bible scholars who approach the Bible from a historical-critical perspective, Moshe Greenberg is the one whose identity as a Jew most suffuses his work. He has written a wide range of self-reflective essays, touching on so many aspects of Jewish biblical interpretation.

Greenberg often writes from the double perspective of a university biblical scholar and a practicing Jew. He is unafraid to speak of God—not only "the God of Old"[9] but a contemporary deity. He has been personally (and not only academically) influenced by classical Jewish biblical interpreters, in whom he sees "a model of reverence toward the source of religion that does not entail blindness to the complexity of that source." He commends a Christian scholar (George Ernest Wright) for combining "historical inquiry and religious concern."[10] Although there are other Jewish biblical scholars aside from Greenberg who are interested in theology, no other scholars of that generation may be called theologians or, at the very least, theologically sensitive exegetes.[11]

Greenberg's Scripture

Greenberg does not merely interpret the Bible; he interprets Scripture and in his writing frequently uses the more theological term "Scripture,"[12] in addition to "Hebrew Bible." Greenberg's Scripture has the following seven main characteristics: (1) it is a Hebrew Bible, very close to the accepted Hebrew Masoretic text (MT); (2) it has a prehistory, but that prehistory is never as important as the text in its final form; (3) it contains fundamental values, many of which endure; (4) some of its contents are more important than others; (5) it has an authoritative status within Judaism; (6) it is aesthetically beautiful; and (7) Jewish interpreters are a significant resource for understanding it.

Many of these principles are shared with other Jewish biblical scholars, though few share them all, and none articulates them as clearly and consistently as Greenberg. In Greenberg's writings, they combine in a particular way that forms a Jewish theology of Scripture and are similar to what Brevard Childs sees as his goal in *Introduction to the Old Testament as Scripture*: "to take seriously the significance of the canon as a crucial element in understanding the Hebrew scriptures, and yet to understand the canon in its true historical and theological dimension."[13]

Greenberg's Biblical Text: The Importance of the Masoretic Text

The first task that most scholars of the Hebrew Bible engage in is textual criticism, typically understood as determining the correct or (more) original text that the scholar intends to expound.[14] Whereas many volumes of the *Anchor Bible* series contain extensive textual notes relating to potential errors or variants in the Masoretic text (MT), Greenberg's Ezekiel commentary omits such notes because he is very reliant on the MT, the standard Hebrew text that crystallized after the destruction of the Second Temple in 70 CE.[15]

Greenberg's strong preference for the MT is seen already in his *Understanding Exodus* (1969), where he assures his readers that this choice is not "dogmatic" but is because the MT is "the best witness" and because this was the main text studied for generations.[16] Greenberg justifies his position in a lecture he gave in 1978 in Göttingen, Germany, the capital of biblical textual criticism: (1) in the case of Ezekiel or other prophets, we can no longer recover the *ipsissima verba*, "the original words of the prophet"; (2) even if we have a more modest goal, of interpreting the text at the period of canonization, we must remember that "the notion of 'the hypothetical textual form' (in the singular) that existed at the time of canonization posits an identity between canonization and text stabilization that is flatly contradicted by all the evidence we have"; and (3) any reconstructed text is hypothetical, and the job of the exegete "is to interpret text in hand." Greenberg notes that textual criticism of the Bible should be different from textual criticism as generally practiced in the humanities since the biblical scholar must also consider the role of "faith communities" in producing the text.[17]

Greenberg shares this feature of what may be called textual conservatism—that his Scripture is MT, no more, no less—with many of the other Jewish figures explored in this volume. For most of them, retention of the MT is a religious value judgment,[18] while Greenberg has articulated alternative reasons for retaining MT when expositing biblical texts, allowing what has been called the *textus receptus* (received text) of the Jewish community to remain its *textus receptus*. Greenberg's position is not, however, fundamentalistic—he does, on occasion, suggest emendations or follow other versions than MT. His belief derives instead from what it means to study a biblical text as a text. However, when he is engaged in studying history of religion, and he believes that the MT does not reflect the early text, he follows an earlier reconstructed text, preserved in non-MT witnesses.

Yet in all cases, he is studying the Hebrew text of the Bible. Translations, he believes, have their place in terms of understanding certain problems of the Hebrew, but the Hebrew text is of paramount importance. His tremendous care for understanding the nuances of each Hebrew word and grammatical form is evident throughout his writing and explains his decision to publish his grammar of biblical Hebrew so early in his career, in 1965—to allow students an opportunity to encounter the Hebrew text in an unmediated fashion.[19]

Greenberg's Biblical Text: Final Form versus Prehistory

Much of biblical scholarship is concerned with recovering the prehistory of biblical texts—in understanding what sources have been combined to form the current text, how texts have grown through additions over time, how various "schools" have adapted and added to earlier documents. Greenberg has some interest in the first of these issues, especially in source criticism of the Torah, but polemicizes against these other efforts to understand a work's prehistory. His position has gained some traction in the scholarly world, in part because of the development of the literary study of the Bible, but it is not the majority position.

Greenberg is highly critical of scholars who rearrange prophetic units based on their personal aesthetic of what sounds best. As early as 1958, he attacked the important German scholar Georg Fohrer for offering a "desperate solution" to the structure of Ezekiel and not considering the problem of making the redactor of the book into a person who "violently destroyed" "an originally continuous and eminently sensible arrangement."[20]

The main place where Greenberg shows some interest in what is sometimes called excavative methods[21] is in *Understanding Exodus*, in which he shows in a masterful fashion the composite nature of Exodus 1–11. His main goal, however, is to understand "the present form of a given text." Although the text is composite, composed of sources, he is primarily interested in "the inner coherence of the book's elements," which he believes was created by what I call a strong redactor, who did not merely use a set of simple principles and scissors and paste but "created a structure whose design is his own." This was a very innovative position in the late 1960s, when the redactor was often seen as a hack. Instead, Greenberg's redactor, although he "did not venture to iron out inconsistencies," engaged in "skillful fusion," exhibited "art," and produced a work that "enrich[ed]" his earlier sources. Studying this final product is decisive since it "has had a continuing, profound effect on its readers for thousands of years." This shows clear connections to the canonical approach, especially as practiced by Brevard Childs.[22]

Greenberg's redactor created a new book by combining sources, and the meaning of the final product is more important than that of its constituent elements. In the case of Ezekiel, Greenberg does not believe that it is possible to find an original book that was supplemented by a school of Ezekiel, the predominant scholarly position when he was writing. Instead, in 1980, Greenberg created the term "Holistic Interpretation" to refer to his method of explicating Ezekiel,[23] and he used that method throughout his two volumes on Ezekiel and in several essays.

This method is the result of Greenberg's frustration at the way that most scholars analyze texts: "As presently practiced, this method [the historical-critical method] lacks empirically established criteria and therefore yields results too divergent to inspire confidence"; "its standards are drawn from too narrow a range of literature and lack the support of extensive descriptions of biblical literature in its own terms"; and the modern scholarly axiom "that the primary creation was free of tension and ambiguity" is wrong. Scholars enforce their suppositions on the text, rather than "attempt[ing] to adjust one's mind, through activating an appreciating-integrating critical faculty, to the signals that emanate from the received Hebrew text taken as a whole."[24]

For these reasons, he proposes,

> As an alternative . . . we propose a holistic interpretation, "emphasizing the organic or functional relation between parts and wholes" (Webster). As the religious person approaches the text open to God's call, so must the interpreter come "all ears" to hear what the text is saying. He must subjugate his habits of thought and expression to the words before him and become actively passive—full of initiatives to heighten his receptivity. For an axiom, he has the working hypothesis that the text as he has it has been designed to convey a message, a meaning.[25]

Greenberg shows the folly of various criteria that scholars propose for discerning what is secondary from the original. He also asserts that the complete MT is the important text of and for the community: "The holistic interpreter is prepared to risk failure in order to establish the claim of his cultural heritage on its heirs." But Greenberg generally does believe that by "listening to it [the text] patiently and humbly," the manner in which it coheres eventually becomes apparent.[26]

In this area, Greenberg is close to those modern Jewish biblical interpreters who also show less interest in the prehistory of the biblical text and concentrate on the texts' final form. Given that the search for a book's prehistory developed only as part of modern biblical scholarship, it is not surprising that here as well Greenberg agrees with his medieval predecessors. Greenberg, however, states that his is not a religious perspective: "This is no *a priori* stance, but my critical assessment of the evidence—of the biblical text as part of ancient Near Eastern literature on the one hand, and of the preconceptions of some modern critics on the other."²⁷

Similarly, in treating the book of Job, he resists discussing the theology of different layers of the text because he believes they cannot be discerned with sufficient certainty. Even in cases where a redactional hand is obvious in places in Ezekiel, Greenberg does not believe that the effort to discern layers is worth it, and he believes that, as in Exodus, redaction reflects "an intelligent choice" and yields a final text that can and should be interpreted. On the other hand, reconstructed texts are always more or less hypothetical in nature, and most of the criteria that scholars use for creating such texts are highly subjective. In addition, study of ancient Near Eastern documents and the Temple Scroll (one of the Dead Sea Scrolls) suggests that a single ancient author may have composed a text that seems uneven or composite to us. This evidence bolsters his approach of "explain[ing] the biblical books as we have them—as integrated, independent wholes."²⁸

The Bible's Existential Values

For Greenberg, the Bible is not an arcane ancient text; it contains "existential values" that should be of broad interest to the "cultural community" (as well as "the faith community"). This perspective is especially obvious in his early articles, before he moved to Israel in 1970, after which his explicit focus often narrowed to the Israeli Jewish community, though implicitly he often retains a broader audience. For example, Greenberg spoke recently on "the Bible as a means of reflecting ultimate concerns."²⁹

Already in 1959, Greenberg praises certain "humanitarian values" of the Bible. More recently, in outlining the goals of the *Mikra Le Yisra'el* commentary series, a modern Hebrew series that he coedited, Greenberg laments that most Israeli Bible scholars avoid "inquiry into the significance of the texts that they study," with the result that "that Bible is perceived as irrelevant." Instead, the commentator needs to explain the Bible's "worldview, and its meaning and significance." These comments mirror the praise that Greenberg offered for Kaufmann in the first volume of *Anchor Bible: Ezekiel*: "Yehezkel Kaufmann embodied a passionate commitment to grand ideas."³⁰

Many of Greenberg's works published after he immigrated to Israel still reflect a broad implicit audience. His 1970 essay "Rabbinic Reflections on

Defying Illegal Orders: Amasa, Abner, and Joab" was first offered at a gathering marking the Vietnam Moratorium in New York. In an essay from a 1980 meeting of Peace Now, the Israeli organization set up in 1978 to urge the Israeli government to remain engaged in the peace negotiations, he notes that when he was in the States, he was forced to think about civil rights and Vietnam issues. Greenberg, however, decided to devote more time and energy to such social issues within Judaism and Israel, and it is to that audience that most of his writing in the past thirty years is explicitly addressed. This is especially so in his essay "Biblical Grounding of Human Value," which he published four times in three languages; there he notes to an inclusive audience, "Of all the treasures of Judaism, there is scarcely one that deserves more publicity in our time than this emphasis on the value of a single human life." Thus, he believes that his goal as a Jewish biblical interpreter involves "systematic search for its 'truth,' in the universal-human sense as well as the particularistically Jewish." In fact, it is often unclear whether Greenberg, in offering particular value judgments in his Hebrew essays, is speaking only to a Jewish-Israeli audience or to a general audience. Such is the case, for example, when he addressed students at Ben-Gurion University in 1991 and talked about biblical studies and the students' quest for "self-understanding" and the importance of addressing "the inner-life of students," observations that are equally valid for university students outside of Israel.[31]

Greenberg quotes from a large number of sources of wisdom—Jewish and non-Jewish, ancient, medieval, and modern. The Bible is not his *only* source for existential values. It is an important source, and following both Speiser and Kaufmann, it is superior to its ancient Near Eastern sources. This may be seen in the laws of the Bible, especially those concerning capital punishment; in biblical prayer, which according to Greenberg "is the blissful experience of God that motivates praise, not the anxiety of need [found in ancient Near Eastern prayers]"; and in various short prophetic statements about justice.[32] For Greenberg, like his mentors, Israelite society is the pinnacle of the ancient Near East.[33]

A Hierarchy of Values

This claim that we must find these "existential values" is problematic: Given that the Bible is not a single text but is an anthology written by various authors over a millennium and contains a wide variety of values, to which "existential values" should we offer priority? Which of the various biblical texts and beliefs is most important? Greenberg offers three suggestions: (1) there are certain "postulates" that are expressed in the Bible and stand behind other biblical texts; (2) several biblical epitomes offer suggestions of what is most central; and (3) rabbinic texts may offer a guide to evaluating conflicting biblical texts that deal with important values.

The notion that there are certain postulates that stand behind aspects of the Bible is audacious: after all, as Greenberg clearly acknowledges, the Bible is a composite book, representing the work of many people in different places over a long time period. Yet he insists in his 1960 essay "Some Postulates of Biblical Criminal Law," his most reprinted essay, that such postulates or "underlying principles" do exist. He claims that the "uniqueness and supremacy of human life" is such a postulate and, further, sees his isolation of such postulates as a Jewish activity. He views Genesis 9:5—"But for your own life-blood I will require a reckoning: I will require it of every beast; of man, too, will I require a reckoning for human life, of every man for that of his fellow man!" (NJPS translation)—as the central expression of this postulate. By definition, a postulate may not be disputed, so such postulates are helpful guidelines for determining which variant biblical view is authoritative.[34]

Greenberg also believes that the key biblical beliefs are found in several texts which he labels "epitomes." These include the Decalogue and several texts collected in the Babylonian Talmud in *Makkot* 24a, including Psalm 15, Isaiah 33:15, Micah 6:8, Isaiah 56:1, Amos 5:4, and Habakkuk 2:4. In discussing the alleged obligation to conquer the (entire) land of Israel, he claims that such oft-repeated epitomes trump a smaller number of biblical texts that discuss land conquest. Such epitomes emphasize the interpersonal, prophetic idea of justice rather than national liberation and include the ideal of proper treatment of the non-Jew in your midst. Though these epitomes recognize God, they highlight the interpersonal. Greenberg discusses this idea in disproportionate detail while commenting on Ezekiel 18, which he also believes contains a list of such epitomes; he concludes that section by observing, "the predominance of sociomoral injunctions stems from the distinctively prophetic appreciation of them as the essence of God's requirement of Israel."[35]

Greenberg believes that when there are a variety of biblical positions on a particular issue, the rabbis may offer important insight into which is normative. Toward the conclusion of his essay on Israel and humanity, he notes, "Our sages left us a criterion to distinguish between what is more and what is less important, what is time-bound and what is eternal." The sages, for example, determine which of the various attitudes toward the "other" should be normative and negate, in essence, Deuteronomy's depiction of the ban or proscription (Hebrew: *ḥerem*) which insists that every person from the nations of Canaan be killed. He states this principle concerning the validity of rabbinic interpretation most clearly in a Hebrew essay on teaching Bible in school: "The rabbis are the ones who clarified, from among never-ending possibilities that had developed, which aspects of the biblical world-view would become Judaism."[36]

The Bible Has a Central Status within Judaism

For Greenberg, the Bible is "the books," the etymological meaning of the word *Bible*. He recognizes the importance of postbiblical works that are independent of the Bible, but the Bible's role is tantamount as the Jewish "foundation document": it is the "basic document that both edifies the community and enables it to retain its identity through continuity with the past," "the source and resource for Jewish culture." He wants his Israeli audience to "respect the Bible as a national treasure and as the foundation document of the people—a component of its identity." In talking to a novice teacher, he similarly emphasizes that "the Bible is the source of Jewish identity" and is the "beginning point of thought and of self-perception." In outlining "An Agenda for an Ideal Jewish Education," he lists first "*Love of learning Torah (i.e., the fundamental books and their offshoots)*" and comments on "Judaism's near deification of the Torah" and the crucial Jewish concept of "(the study of) Torah for its own sake" (*torah lishmah*),[37] which "brings one into contact with something inherently valuable—the literary record of the encounter of Jews with a realm that transcends the visible, the earthly." He is critical of a narrow application of the historical-critical method, its "disinterested objectivity," which leads to the neglect of the Bible by emphasizing that it is not merely ancient but antiquated.[38]

This central nature of the Bible for the Jewish community is already evident in Greenberg's earliest scholarly publication written in modern Hebrew, in a volume honoring Israel's prime minister David Ben-Gurion. There, he speaks of Ezekiel "determin[ing] the practice [Hebrew: *halakhah*] for generations of exile." Greenberg uses the word *halakhah*, the rabbinic term for normative legal practice (typically based on biblical precedent), suggesting that for Greenberg the entire Hebrew Bible may be normative.[39]

For Greenberg, the Bible is both necessary and, through its later interpretations, (almost) sufficient for Jewish life. He observes in relation to the Conservative movement in the State of Israel, "The function of the Jewish state in Judaism is to promote the realization of Torah in life and society. . . . The scope of Torah is total. Its ideal is to permeate life and society and shape all to the service and the greater glorification of God (*kiddush hashem*)."[40] It cannot, however, be a sufficient source for society in a simplistic manner. It is a complex and contradictory text, and it contains some repugnant ideas. He is concerned that Israeli students might be influenced to apply Joshua's attitude toward the Canaanites to the current Arab population. That is why the issue of his essay "How Should We Expound the Torah Now?" is so important for him—given the many contradictory voices in the text, and the variety of ways each text has been interpreted, what is authoritative? Only a person who believes in the centrality of the Bible would be concerned with this issue and would speak so forcefully and often about the problem of biblical texts that appear to be morally problematic.[41]

The Bible's Aesthetic Beauty

For Greenberg, the Bible is not only central but aesthetically beautiful. Here too he follows in the footsteps of several biblical scholars, many of them Jewish, who emphasize the beauty of the Bible.[42] He speaks of modern scholars finding in the Bible "design that bespeaks subtle intelligence." In his commentaries and essays, he frequently points out aspects of that design. For example, in *Understanding Exodus*, he notes word plays, an author's "exquisite touch," and the redactor's "rich weave." He admires the literary economy of the Garden of Eden story. These are among the elements he notes in his *Ezekiel* commentary: "a gem of literary adaptation and combination," alliteration and rhyme, a "rich blend of motifs," Ezekiel's "poetic range," "verbal artifices," meaningful assonance, "coherence of the whole [chapter], structurally and thematically," "art and design," "high-style" alliterative chiasm, "artful design," "skillful employment [of words]," "intricate, integrative construction," and "foreshadowing."[43]

There is a clear polemic in these observations—among the prophets, Ezekiel's diction is often considered poor and certainly not comparable to the soaring poetry of (First or Second) Isaiah. For example, the great early twentieth-century British scholar S. R. Driver says of Ezekiel, "He has imagination, but not poetical talent."[44] Greenberg disagrees—he criticizes others' "prosaic pedantry" in their suggested reworkings of Ezekiel's poetry and claims, "One cannot but admire the imaginative power of the prophet, in truth a master of figures." I cannot recall instances when Greenberg criticizes biblical rhetoric or emphasizes infelicities. For Greenberg, message and form are connected—and the message of the Bible and the manner in which it is conveyed are both, to use the words of Genesis 1:31, "very good."[45]

The Significance of Jewish Biblical Interpretation

Traditional Jewish biblical interpretation (Hebrew: *parshanut*) is of paramount importance to Greenberg and served in a variety of ways as his model. In contrast, *parshanut* plays a minor role in historical-critical biblical scholarship, in part because most scholars cannot read the difficult, unvocalized postbiblical Hebrew in which the medievals wrote, which is full of unmarked rabbinic references, but also in part because most scholars have been socialized to believe that precritical biblical interpretation (both Jewish and Christian) is unimportant. Greenberg argues forcefully and frequently that this perception is wrong and that engaging *parshanut* is important, for different reasons, both for the historical-critical scholar and for the scholar interested in the place of the Bible in Jewish identity.

Greenberg has a broad definition of *parshanut*, including not only classical rabbinic sources such as the Talmud and the midrashim and the medieval Franco-German and Spanish commentators but also Jewish figures such as Josephus and obscure commentators not found in the standard rabbinic Bible. He has written on the important grandfather-grandson pair Rashi (1040–1105) and Rashbam (ca. 1085–ca. 1174). He is highly critical of Bible scholars who neglect such medieval scholarship and often introduces studies on the historical-critical meaning of a unit with a survey of its history of interpretation, which he shows often sheds light on its meaning. *Parshanut* is significant enough to Greenberg that in the midst of writing his Ezekiel commentary, he took time out to edit and write for the first volume of the Biblical Encyclopedia Library: *Jewish Biblical Exegesis: An Introduction*.[46] There he claims that biblical interpretation is the pinnacle of Jewish expression and that these interpreters kept the Bible alive as "as the source and resource for Jewish culture"—a goal that Greenberg clearly shares.[47]

In the introduction, "Purpose and Method," to *Understanding Exodus*, Greenberg notes that the medievals are important for the philology of the text—what words and phrases mean; as he clarifies here and elsewhere, this is because of their encyclopedic knowledge of the Hebrew text. They are also useful for understanding "sentences and paragraphs" since they are less "atomistic" than moderns—they are what Greenberg later called "holistic." In his commentaries and essays, he adduces hundreds of cases where the medieval commentaries, ignored by so many, are helpful for critical scholarship, and he even observes in reference to his Ezekiel commentary that the modern scholars often take a step backward when compared to their medieval counterparts. Greenberg is partly responsible for the additional interest among mainstream biblical scholars in premodern interpreters.[48]

He offers additional arguments for the importance of *parshanut* for the Jewish and/or Israeli community who views the Bible as Scripture. As noted earlier, for Greenberg, the Bible is *the* Jewish foundation document —but it has only maintained that function through constant interpretation and reinterpretation, which modern scholars must be aware of and continue. He is very insistent that those who are teaching Bible in Israeli schools must be familiar with *parshanut* and, for different reasons, suggests it even needs to be included in the Israeli university Bible curriculum: both because it is part of the student's heritage and because the history of interpretation is a significant subdiscipline of the humanities. Indeed, as a historian of religion, Greenberg is very interested in "continuities and transformations," and the two-millennia-long history of Jewish interpretation of the same core text offers important insights in this area.[49]

Moshe Greenberg's Theology of Scripture: A Coherent Vision

The seven features of Greenberg's theology of Scripture noted earlier fit together. His Scripture is the Jewish Bible, which has been studied throughout Jewish tradition: the Masoretic Text, in Hebrew, without much concern for its prehistory (points 1 and 2). As medieval Jewish exegetes show (point 7), we may not change the text, but it is open to a wide variety of interpretations, which help keep it relevant for the Jewish and general communities (5, 3). In determining these values, we must use criteria to decide which passages from this composite text are most important; this includes denying the centrality of certain passages (4). Finally, the Bible is not only of great consequence for the values it teaches; it is also an aesthetically beautiful text (7), thereby enticing its readers to appreciate its values.

Greenberg's model for how the Hebrew Bible should be read in a Jewish and critical context has influenced both Jewish and non-Jewish scholars: it is powerful and often compelling. It is not, however, the only model that Jewishly engaged biblical scholars practice—it has not garnered widespread assent.[50] Following the example of Greenberg, I offer the following observations concerning his model "in the language of humility and contingency."[51]

One difficulty is the method's overreliance on the notion of "coherence," a frequent term in Greenberg's oeuvre, which he sees as the opposite of the atomistic readings of many modern biblical scholars. He adduces two reasons for preferring coherence. One is that coherence is "justified by the enormous power it [the Bible] has exercised on the history of culture," in other words, that the Bible has typically been read over time as a coherent work. Not all scholars feel the same weight of this cultural practice, and even Greenberg, as a historical-critical scholar, in other ways rejects some of the predominant ways that the Bible has been read over the past two millennia—so why must he, for tradition's sake, retain coherence? Greenberg's second argument is that the more anyone reads a text carefully, the more signs of coherence emerge. To my mind, this is problematic: others have shown that coherence may be in the eye of the beholder, rather than the author, and that people inevitably create coherence out of the most bizarre and diffuse texts (and situations).[52] Certainly, due to our nature as humans, who by nature make coherence out of messes, we *can* read any text as coherent—but *should* we? Furthermore, given that we know that ancient texts were composed over time and often incorporate preexisting texts and traditions, why should we bias our minds so strongly toward interpreting only the final form of the text?[53]

Greenberg criticizes others for finding in the Bible "a reinforcement of one's own predilections"; in insisting so strongly on a holistic Bible of all passages, is he truly meeting "the text on its own terms" or finding what he wants to see there? This dispute concerning whether redaction creates coherence is found in other disciplines as well. Recently, Noam Zohar has suggested that the redactors of rabbinic literature were strong redactors who attempted to create meaning through their editing activities,[54] while Steven D. Fraade has suggested that some material is well redacted and other is less so. Fraade's warning is apposite for Greenberg as well: "For the more we read and reread this kind of [rabbinic] text and it becomes lodged in *our* minds, the better its pieces seem to fit together, the more its language seems to echo, and the more its messages seem to coalesce."[55]

Related to this problem of creating coherence out of a composite text is the manner in which Greenberg determines, in cases where he acknowledges the multiplicity of biblical views on a single topic, which view is most important, where he determines how "the Bible, as it were, 'corrects itself.'" In a variety of places, he offers some hints of criteria he uses, most especially the position taken (by the majority of scholars? by those whom he favors?) in postbiblical Judaism. But is this the only possible or valid criterion? Might we instead look at a different majority opinion—perhaps that expressed in the majority of biblical books or (and this may be different) in the largest number of biblical passages or in the latest (most final) or earliest (most pristine) passage? Perhaps we may consider the opinion expressed most forcefully, however we might measure that? Or the opinion expressed in the most authoritative source (however we might measure that—is every passage in the Torah more authoritative than every passage in, e.g., Job?)? As my many question marks suggest, any of the alternative criteria that I am suggesting are open-ended and problematic—as are Greenberg's criteria.[56]

For example, it would be possible to dispute, I believe, that "the testimonies" Greenberg offers concerning Judaism's view of the other, in his essay "Mankind, Israel, and the Nations in the Hebraic Heritage," suggest a general positive Jewish attitude toward the other. Certainly, many biblical and postbiblical texts respect the non-Israelite or non-Jew—but should we see this as the main biblical and Jewish view? Similarly, he states that one of the four main biblical points concerning "the relation between the nation and its land in the Bible" is that the "purpose of residing in land is to be a holy people"—I see that as *a* central point in some sources but do not believe that it is predominant enough to be in a list of the "top four." Given that Greenberg believes that the Bible is multivocal and is central for both the Jewish and the general community, I wish that he had articulated more convincingly how these communities might determine which of the various conflicting biblical voices to honor.[57]

Despite these misgivings, I find Greenberg's model compelling—I feel the strong pull of its logic and clarity trying to sway me. Greenberg is no mere biblical scholar who happens to be Jewish but also a clear-minded and clear-voiced preacher—like Ezekiel, he is "a master of figures"—arguing very strongly for an attractive image of the Bible as Scripture within

Judaism. As I have shown, this vision is influenced by his upbringing and his mentors. But there is one more inspiration: Greenberg identifies strongly with the prophet Ezekiel, who had a "lofty conception of a prophet's responsibility in an age of ruin."[58]

NOTES

1. This essay was written while Professor Moshe Greenberg, who died on May 15, 2010, was still alive. He taught me much over the past three decades, through his writings, his classes, and many conversations. I studied with him in 1978–79, when I was a graduate student at Hebrew University. Over the past few years, we have studied together and talked on a wide variety of subjects, including this essay. I would like to thank him for his comments on a draft of this essay and for sharing with me his correspondence with Yehezkel Kaufmann. I would also like to thank the Shalom Hartman Institute, and especially its codirectors David and Donniel Hartman, for providing a convivial atmosphere for writing this essay. The following individuals offered helpful comments: Adele Berlin, Sidney Brettler, Mordechai Cogan, Tova Hartman, Alick Isaacs, Israel Knohl, Jacob Milgrom, Dena Ordan, Lenin Prado,Tina Sherman, Benjamin Sommer, Jeffrey Tigay, and Noam Zohar. The collections of Greenberg's essays are *On the Bible and Judaism*, ed. Avrahm Shapira (Tel Aviv: Am Oved, 1984; in Hebrew); *Ha-Segulah veha-Koach* (Tel Aviv: Kibbutz Hameuhad, 1986; in Hebrew) (a literal translation of this title is "Particularity and Power"; in a conversation on May 16, 2009, Greenberg suggested rendering it "The Pearl and the Power"); *Studies in the Bible and Jewish Thought* (Philadelphia: Jewish Publication Society, 1995). For a bibliography, complete through 1997, see Mordechai Cogan, Barry L. Eichler, and Jeffrey H. Tigay, eds., *Tehillah le-Moshe: Biblical and Judaic Studies in Honor of Moshe Greenberg* (Winona Lake, IN: Eisenbrauns, 1997), xxiii–xxxviii. All translations from modern Hebrew in this essay are my own.

2. On Speiser, see Moshe Greenberg, "Speiser, Ephraim Avigdor," in *Dictionary of Biblical Interpretation*, 2 vols., ed. John H. Hayes (Nashville, TN: Abingdon, 1999), 2:496–97, with additional bibliography there; and Abraham Winitzer, "Toward Assessing Twentieth-Century Ancient Near Eastern Scholarship: The Case of E. A. Speiser," in *Gazing on the Deep: Ancient Near Eastern and Other Studies in Honor of Tzvi Abusch*, ed. Jeffrey Stackert, Barbara N. Porter, and David P. Wright, 379–410 (Bethesda, MD: CDL, 2010).

3. E. A. Speiser, *The Anchor Bible: Genesis* (Garden City, NY: Doubleday, 1964), esp. xlix–l. Note, also, for example, his insistence on page 46 that the biblical flood story is superior to its Mesopotamian antecedents since only in the Bible was the flood "morally motivated."

4. Greenberg, "Speiser, Ephraim Avigdor," 497.

5. See chapter 13 in this volume by Job Jindo.
6. Greenberg, "Kaufmann," in *Studies in the Bible and Jewish Thought*, 175.
7. Ibid., 175, 184, 187–88.
8. Moshe Goshen-Gottstein, "Scriptural Authority: Biblical Authority in Judaism," *ABD* 5 (1992): 1017. For a discussion on Jews and biblical theology, see Jon Levenson, "Why Jews Are Not Interested in Biblical Theology," chap 2. in *The Hebrew Bible, the Old Testament, and Historical Criticism* (Louisville, KY: Westminster/John Knox, 1993), 33–61; there is also some relevant material on this topic in my essays "Biblical History and Jewish Biblical Theology," *JR* 77 (1997): 563–83; and "Biblical Authority: A Jewish Pluralistic View," in *Engaging Biblical Authority: Perspectives on the Bible as Scripture*, ed. William P. Brown (Louisville, KY: Westminster/John Knox, 2007), 1–9, 141–43.
9. I have borrowed this term from James L. Kugel, *The God of Old: Inside the Lost World of the Bible* (New York: Free Press, 2003).
10. Greenberg, "Prophecy," in *Studies in the Bible and Jewish Thought*, 416; Greenberg, "On Sharing the Scriptures," in *Magnalia Dei: The Mighty Acts of God: Essays on the Bible and Archaeology in Memory of G. Ernest Wright*, ed. Frank Moore Cross, Werner E. Lemke, and Patrick D. Miller (Garden City, NY: Doubleday, 1976), 455.
11. See Moshe Greenberg, "A Faith-ful Critical Interpretation of the Bible," in *Judaism and Modernity: The Religious Philosophy of David Hartman*, ed. Jonathan W. Malino (Burlington, VT: Aldershot, 2004), 210: "In dedicating this essay to David, I acknowledge my debt to him who persists in calling me provocatively a 'theologian' when I am no more than an exegete, though keenly aware of the ideal marriage of exegesis and theology, so rare in Judaism." Of a younger generation, the recent book of Michael Fishbane, *Sacred Attunement: A Jewish Theology* (Chicago: University of Chicago Press, 2008), is especially noteworthy, as is the more recent Benjamin D. Sommer, *The Bodies of God and the World of Ancient Israel* (Cambridge: Cambridge University Press, 2009), esp. 124–32.
12. See the comments of James Barr on Brevard Childs, in *The Concept of Biblical Theology: An Old Testament Perspective* (Minneapolis: Augsburg Fortress, 1999), 49: "[Scripture] is a distinctively religious usage that evokes holiness, authority, the Word of God." See also James Barr, *Holy Scripture: Canon, Authority, Criticism* (Oxford, UK: Clarendon, 1983), 1, where he glosses Scripture as a "written guide for religion."
13. Brevard Childs, *Introduction to the Old Testament as Scripture* (Philadelphia: Fortress, 1979), 71. Greenberg the canonical critic is especially evident in *Understanding Exodus* (New York: Behrman, 1969) and *The Anchor Bible: Ezekiel*, vols. 1–2, and in his volume of Hebrew collected essays, *On the Bible and Judaism* (in Hebrew).
14. On textual criticism, see Odil Hannes Steck, *Old Testament Exegesis: A Guide to the Methodology*, 2nd ed., trans. James D. Nogalski (Atlanta: Scholars,

1998), 40–46; and Emanuel Tov, *Textual Criticism of the Hebrew Bible*, 2nd rev. ed. (Minneapolis: Fortress, 2001).

15. See Tov, *Textual Criticism*, 187.

16. Greenberg, *Understanding Exodus*, 4.

17. Ibid.; Greenberg, "Ancient Versions," in *Studies in the Bible and Jewish Thought*, 218, 220–21; Greenberg, review of *Critique textuelle de L'Ancien Testament*, by Dominique Barthélemy, *JQR* 78 (1987): 140.

18. See the eighth principle of Maimonides, in Isadore Twersky, *A Maimonides Reader* (New York: Behrman, 1972), 420–21.

19. Greenberg, *Introduction to Hebrew* (Englewood Cliffs, NJ: Prentice-Hall, 1965).

20. Greenberg, "On Ezekiel's Dumbness," *JBL* 77 (1958): 102.

21. The (pejorative) use of this term was popularized by the literary scholar Robert Alter.

22. Greenberg, *Understanding Exodus*, 1, 61, 66, 107, 121, 192; Greenberg, "The Thematic Unity of Exodus iii–xi," in *Papers of the Fourth World Congress of Jewish Studies* (Jerusalem: World Union of Jewish Studies, 1967), 154. For discussion and literature, see Mark G. Brett, *Biblical Criticism in Crisis? The Impact of the Canonical Approach on Old Testament Studies* (Cambridge: Cambridge University Press, 1991); and Paul R. Noble, *The Canonical Approach: A Critical Reconstruction of the Hermeneutics of Brevard S. Childs*, Biblical Interpretation 16 (Leiden, Netherlands: Brill, 1995). Oddly, Noble never mentions Greenberg, and Brett mentions him only once.

23. Greenberg, "The Vision of Jerusalem in Ezekiel 8–11: A Holistic Interpretation," in *The Divine Helmsman: Studies in God's Control of Human Events Presented to Lou H. Silberman*, ed. James L. Crenshaw and Samuel Sandmel (New York: Ktav, 1980), 141.

24. Ibid., 145, 147; Greenberg, *Anchor Bible: Ezekiel*, 1:218; Greenberg, "MSRT HBRYT, 'The Obligation of the Covenant,' in Ezekiel 20:37," in *The Word of the Lord Shall Go Forth: Essays in Honor of David Noel Freedman in Celebration of His Sixtieth Birthday*, ed. C. L. Meyers and M. O'Connor (Winona Lake, IN: Eisenbrauns, 1983), 44.

25. Greenberg, "Vision of Jerusalem in Ezekiel 8–11," 145–46.

26. Ibid., 149; Greenberg, *Anchor Bible: Ezekiel*, 1:21.

27. Greenberg, "What Are Valid Criteria for Determining Inauthentic Matter in Ezekiel?," in *Ezekiel and His Book*, ed. J. Lust, BETL 74 (Leuven: Leuven University Press, 1986), 135.

28. Greenberg, "Ezekiel 16: A Panorama of Passions," in *Love and Death in the Ancient Near East: Essays in Honor of Marvin H. Pope*, ed. John H. Marks and Robert M. Good (Guilford, CT: Four Quarters, 1987), 143; Greenberg, "A Faith-ful Critical Interpretation of the Bible," 211.

29. Greenberg, "Faith-ful Critical Interpretation," 211; Greenberg, introduction to *Studies in the Bible and Jewish Thought*, xv.

30. Greenberg, "Asylum," in *Studies in the Bible and Jewish Thought*, 43; Greenberg, "To Whom and for What Should a Bible Commentator Be Responsible?," in *Studies in the Bible and Jewish Thought*, 236, 238; Greenberg, *Anchor Bible: Ezekiel*, 1:ix.

31. Greenberg, "The Biblical Grounding of Human Value," in *The Samuel Friedland Lectures, 1960–1966* (New York: Jewish Theological Seminary, 1967), 50; Greenberg, "Prologue: Can Modern Critical Bible Scholarship Have a Jewish Character?," in *Studies in the Bible and Jewish Thought*, 7; Greenberg, "Supplement: Moshe Greenberg," in *Visions of Jewish Education*, ed. Seymour Fox, Israel Scheffler, and Daniel Marom (Cambridge: Cambridge University Press, 2003), 146–47.

32. See later in this chapter.

33. Greenberg, "On the Refinement of the Conception of Prayer in Hebrew Scriptures," in *Studies in the Bible and Jewish Thought*, 89.

34. Greenberg, "Some Postulates of Biblical Criminal Law," in *Studies in the Bible and Jewish Thought*, 30, 32.

35. Greenberg, *Anchor Bible: Ezekiel*, 1:347.

36. Greenberg, *Ha-Segula veha-Koach*, 65; Greenberg, "An Approach to the Teaching of Bible in School," in *On the Bible and Judaism*, 297 (in Hebrew).

37. From his writing and from personal conversations, it is clear that Greenberg's conception of *torah lishmah* includes not only study, but application. In other words, it reflects the classical rabbinic notion, rather than that of Hayyim of Volozhin. (On this distinction, see Norman Lamm, *Torah Lishmah: Torah for Torah's Sake in the Works of Rabbi Hayyim of Volozhin and His Contemporaries* [Hoboken, NJ: Ktav, 1989]).

38. Greenberg, "Commentator," 235, 241–42; Greenberg, "Exegesis," in *Studies in the Bible and Jewish Thought*, 367; Greenberg, *Jewish Bible Exegesis: An Introduction*, Biblical Encyclopaedia Library (Jerusalem: Mosad Bialik, 1983; in Hebrew), 138; Greenberg, "Some Thoughts Concerning the Responsibilities of the Bible Teacher and His Preparation," in *On the Bible and Judaism*, 281–82 (in Hebrew); Greenberg, "We Are as Those Who Dream: An Agenda for an Ideal Jewish Education," in *Visions of Jewish Education*, 124; Greenberg, "Prologue," 6.

39. Greenberg, "Ezekiel 20 and the Spiritual Exile," in *Oz le-David* (Jerusalem: Kiryat Sepher, 1964), 433 (in Hebrew).

40. Greenberg, "The Task of Masorti Judaism," in *Deepening the Commitment: Zionism and the Conservative Movement*, ed. J. S. Ruskay and D. Szonyi, 137–45 (New York: The Jewish Theological Seminary, 1990), 139.

41. Greenberg, "The Attitude toward State Power in the Torah and the Prophets," in *Hasegulah*, 49 (in Hebrew).

42. These include M. Weiss, Sh. Talmon, M. Sternberg, S. Bar-Efrat, R. Alter, A.

Berlin, and others. (In conversation, Greenberg has emphasized his kinship with the literary approach of his Hebrew University colleague Meir Weiss, who was interested in the text rather than its prehistory.)

43. Greenberg, "Exegesis," 367; Greenberg, *Understanding Exodus*, 87, 170; Greenberg, *Anchor Bible: Ezekiel*, 1:113, 139, 163, 221, 338, 396, 444, 502, 514, 589, 644.

44. S. R. Driver, *An Introduction to the Literature of the Old Testament* (New York: Scribner, 1950), 296.

45. Greenberg, *Anchor Bible: Ezekiel*, 2:498, 571.

46. Greenberg, *Jewish Bible Exegesis*.

47. Ibid., 138.

48. Greenberg, *Understanding Exodus*, 405.

49. Greenberg, introduction to *Studies in the Bible and Jewish Thought*, xv.

50. See the older survey of modern Jewish interpretation in Baruch A. Levine, Jacob Neusner, and Ernest S. Frerichs, eds., *Judaic Perspectives on Ancient Israel* (Philadelphia: Fortress, 1987).

51. Greenberg, "Response to Roland de Vaux's 'Method in the Study of Early Hebrew History,'" in *The Bible in Modern Scholarship*, ed. J. Philip Hyatt (Nashville, TN: Abingdon, 1965), 43.

52. Marc Zvi Brettler, "The 'Coherence' of Ancient Texts," in *Gazing on the Deep*, 411–19.

53. Greenberg, "Commentator," 241.

54. Noam Zohar, *Secrets of the Rabbinic Workshop: Redaction as a Key to Meaning* (Jerusalem: Magnes, 2007; in Hebrew).

55. Greenberg, "Faith-ful Critical Interpretation," 212; Steven D. Fraade, "Sifre Deuteronomy 26 (ad Deut. 3:23): How Conscious the Composition?," *HUCA* 54 (1983): 245–301; the quotation is from 293.

56. Greenberg, "Faith-ful Critical Interpretation," 213.

57. Greenberg, "Mankind, Israel, and the Nations in the Hebraic Heritage," in *Studies in the Bible and Jewish Thought*, 370; Greenberg, "The Relation between the Nation and Its Land in the Bible," in *On the Bible and Judaism*, 110 (in Hebrew).

58. Greenberg, *Anchor Bible: Ezekiel*, 2:57; Greenberg, "The Designs and Themes of Ezekiel's Program of Restoration," *Interpretation* 38 (1984): 188.

Chapter 15

Concepts of Scripture in Mordechai Breuer

Shalom Carmy

To most outsiders who have heard of Rabbi Mordechai Breuer's "theory of aspects" (*torat ha-beḥinot*), Breuer is a dark figure who has devised for his rigorously Orthodox confreres a counterapproach to biblical criticism so potent that they now thrive on the data that should be poisoning their faith, like bacilli that have evolved resistance to antibiotics. Alternatively, he is seen as one who has constructed a halfway house where academically mobile refugees from Orthodoxy can measure themselves for the trappings of biblical criticism on their way up to some form of orthopraxy. Both are correct.

Like many Orthodox Israeli educators and thinkers of his generation, Breuer was born in Germany (1921), studied in Israeli yeshivot, had no formal academic training, and spent the first twenty years of his career as a high school teacher of Talmud and other religious subjects. Beginning in the late 1960s, he taught at a variety of postsecondary yeshivot and seminaries. Most of his early publications dealt with the history of the Masoretic text of the Bible, which has served as the accepted text of the Bible among Jews for over a millennium. A multivolume biblical commentary in Hebrew that is widely used among Orthodox and non-Orthodox Israelis (the *Daat Mikra* Bible produced by Mosad haRav Kook in Jerusalem from the 1970s on) was done under Breuer's aegis and includes his notes. This aspect of his work was widely accepted and played a major role in his award of the Israel Prize (the highest prize awarded annually by the State of Israel) in 1999.

Meanwhile, Breuer launched a series of programmatic papers, beginning in the late 1950s, that sketched a new Orthodox response to biblical criticism. Despite initial incomprehension, he persisted in refining his "theory of aspects" (*torat ha-beḥinot*), eventually writing several books of applied studies. On the one hand, Breuer maintains that all the literary phenomena adduced by the critics to show that the Pentateuch is the product of multiple authors are compatible with divine authorship. On the other hand, he insists that unitary authorship by a human being is impossible. In each instance when the critics posit multiple authors, Breuer too discerns different voices. One task of the religious student is to grasp each of these voices in isolation, unearthing the theology, narrative vision, or legal positions implicit in each one. Finally, one also investigates the ways in which the Torah as a whole integrates and mediates these voices. No human author, in his opinion, could have orchestrated this multiplicity of voices. Thus, either the critics are right, in which case we have a jumble of conflicting writers spliced together, or there is a divine Author expressing a complex message by employing different voices.[1]

This, in a nutshell, is Breuer's thesis. To appreciate his theological contribution, it may be instructive to step back from Breuer's confrontation with academic Bible scholarship and to identify the elements in his intellectual makeup that stand behind his orientation. Breuer's views can be seen as the crossroads of four different strands of Jewish thought.

First, Breuer was the great-grandson of R. Samson Raphael Hirsch (1808–88), founder of the Frankfurt school of neo-Orthodoxy, and the nephew of Isaac Breuer (1883–1946), the most creative exponent of that position in the first half of the 20th century. The elder Breuer produced his theology with a portrait of Kant on his study wall and a version of Kant's *Critique of Pure Reason* in his heart. Pure scientific reason yields an understanding of the world as a closed causal system but can say nothing about its possible transcendent origin. Thus, it cannot legitimately affirm or deny the metaphysical doctrine of creation. Mordechai Breuer adopted an analogous thesis for the Bible. Modern biblical criticism is absolutely reliable and "scientific" within its logical limitations: it can determine authoritatively that if the Torah (for it is the Pentateuch that is Breuer's primary focus of attention) is a humanly authored book, it *must* have been composed in exactly the way the critics have hypothesized. But whether the Torah is a humanly authored book is beyond the determination of science. If it is a divinely authored book, then the apparent evidence of multiple authors is to be explained differently; Breuer, we shall see, proposes his theory of aspects as the explanation.

As noted, the theory of aspects, as promulgated by Breuer, maintains not only that the complexities and stylistic multiplicity found in the Torah can be traced to divine authorship but also that they cannot be ascribed to one human author working alone. Such complexity in a human author may be unusual, but to me it is not implausible, and surely it is not impossible, as Breuer would have it. One may therefore learn a great deal from Breuer, and identify with other elements in his intellectual and theological framework, without subscribing to this strand in his background.

In fact, most Orthodox writers indebted to Breuer, including myself, do not adopt his quasi-Kantian outlook. Like Breuer, they are intrigued by some of the literary questions raised by the critics. However, the evidence for multiple authorship, or for the relative dating of texts, is not the unified and assured result of a systematic science, which must be embraced or rejected as a whole, but a collection of insights, interpretations, and speculations, sometimes more plausible, sometimes less so. We understand the considerations that lead scholars to ascribe Genesis 1 and Genesis 2 to different authors. We believe that the data leading to these considerations are worthy of being incorporated into any cogent interpretation of Genesis. Yet few, if any, would endorse Breuer's sweeping assertion that assuming the human authorship of the Torah entails, beyond the shadow of a doubt, that the human author of chapter 2 lived earlier than the author of chapter 1.

Breuer himself, early in his career, acknowledged the Kantian impact on his outlook but played it down afterward. In later years, he was more likely to explain his unwillingness to challenge the conclusions of the academy, within their circumscribed orbit, on pragmatic grounds, as a householder would acquiesce to the competence of an electrician within his narrow professional sphere. The unqualified affirmations of the Documentary Hypothesis in Breuer's programmatic essays can be ascribed, first, to a fixation on the consensus prevalent at the time he first devoted careful study to Julius Wellhausen (the deeply influential German Protestant biblical critic who lived from 1844 to 1918 and in whose work the Documentary Hypothesis reached its apogee) and scholars associated with him and, second, to a reluctance to reexamine it in detail. Nonetheless, the "two domains" approach to the general question of science and religious truth associated with his uncle remains in the background.

Second, Breuer's early programmatic essays are explicitly grounded in kabbalah, which devotes enormous attention to different *sefirot* within God, that is to say, different aspects in which He is experienced and the dialectic between them. Breuer claimed that the need to assimilate biblical criticism prior to combating it was first suggested to him by his colleague R. Yehuda Amital, whose own worldview is rooted in the mystical teaching of R. Abraham Isaac Kook, the Chief Rabbi of Palestine in the 1920s and '30s, whose mystical thought has been enormously influential on modern Orthodoxy. The early essays explicitly cite R. Kook, especially his view that heresy is overcome not through immediate rejection but via a dialectical confrontation in which the "palace of Torah" is rebuilt so as to take over what is valid in the heretical ideas.

Rabbinic tradition, not just mysticism, had much to say about different aspects of God. The Rabbis notably speak of His attribute of judgment (*middat ha-din*) and His attribute of mercy (*middat ha-rahamim*). Indeed, in discussing the names of God in Genesis, the Midrash states that God "intended" to create the world with the former, represented by the name *Elokim*, but saw that the world could not survive and joined it with the Tetragrammaton, representing mercy. From one perspective, judgment and mercy are contradictory and thus mutually exclusive. For Rabbinic consciousness, such contradictions are not only allowable; if religious reality is to be communicated in words, they are necessary. For Breuer, this kind of duality became a paradigm of the multiple voices expressed in the Torah. In Genesis 1 and Genesis 2–3, the different aspects of God are juxtaposed. In the flood story, the different strands are intertwined. The multiplicity of voices is not confined to different names of God. Other apparent redundancies are also grist for the exegetical mill. Where, for example, in Genesis 11–12, Abraham seems to leave for Canaan twice, the repetition is due to the dual motivation of his journey: one motive is natural, so to speak, beginning with Terah's interrupted migration; the other is driven by God's command. As we shall see, dual or triple themes, some of them in mutual tension, predominate in the legal sections of the Torah as well.

The third factor played little or no role in Breuer's intellectual formation but arguably facilitated the reception of his work from the 1970s on. One of the most widespread trends in both modern Orthodoxy and ultra-Orthodoxy in the 20th century is the so-called analytic school of Talmud study, often identified with the thought of the 19th-century Lithuanian Talmudic scholar R. Hayyim Soloveitchik (1853–1918) and his descendants (known, from the location of his yeshivah, as the Brisker [Brest-Litovsk] system of Talmudic study). One of the key terms of this school is "two *dinim*" (two laws). The Brisker scholar examines a set of Talmudic or medieval legal texts, excavating apparent tensions and conflicts therein. The solution to these difficulties is the discovery that what seems to be one principle is actually a bundle of ideas, as when the word *kavvana* means "purpose" in connection with the work prohibited on the Sabbath and "intention" in most other contexts, such as prayer, or that what seems to be one law, upon analysis, displays different features that must be accurately and sharply distinguished. The goal of this work is not primarily resolving apparent contradictions between texts but rather uncovering the complex conceptual structure underlying the legal system. This Talmudic methodology predisposes its practitioner to find conceptual multiplicity and distinctiveness where the uninitiated would perceive a vague and uneasy congeries of details beleaguered by problems and inconcinnities calling for local patchwork resolution.

The premier exponent of the Brisker method of study (or "Brisker Torah") in the United States was R. Hayyim's grandson, R. Joseph Dov Soloveitchik (1903–93). It may not be accidental that his philosophical and theological work is characterized by the phenomenology of different religious and cognitive types, usually juxtaposed rather than harmonized. In effect, this imposed the Brisker "two *dinim*" on living human experience. One of R. Soloveitchik's most influential essays, *Lonely Man of Faith*,[2] opens with an analysis of Genesis 1 and 2, contrasting the images of humanity in the two accounts of creation and using the biblical text as scaffolding for a theological anthropology revolving around two different aspects of human experience. R. Soloveitchik's interest is primarily philosophical and secondarily literary. R. Breuer, by contrast, is preoccupied with the literary issues. Yet the points of overlap are unmistakable.

In 1971, R. Aharon Lichtenstein, R. Soloveitchik's son-in-law and leading disciple, joined R. Amital as head of one of Israel's premier modern Orthodox institutions, Yeshivat Har-Etzion, thus transforming it into the major home of Brisker learning in the Religious Zionist community. For the next three decades, the Herzog Institute affiliated with this yeshivah was the most important arena of Breuer's teaching and influence. It is possible that students who found his early references to mystical doctrine obscure and confusing were better able to appropriate Breuer's ideas when grasped as a parallel to the powerful approach to Talmud that had conquered the classic world of Lithuanian-style yeshivot.

Last but not least, there is the long history of the *peshat/derash* distinction in Jewish biblical exegesis. From Rashi, Rashbam, and Ibn Ezra[3] down to the great eastern European traditional commentators of the 18th, 19th, and 20th centuries, such as the Gaon of Vilna, R. Naftali Zvi Berlin of Volozhin, R. Meir Simha of Dvinsk, it is affirmed that rabbinic legal exegesis (*derash*) is normative and, at the same time, that determining the "plain meaning" (*peshat*) is a legitimate pursuit, even when the two diverge.

Despite the adherence of the classical medieval authors to this principle, they never explicitly justified their dual allegiance. The explanations offered by moderns have generally followed ideological preferences. Theological liberals usually credit the medievals as having anticipated some of their own modern critical positions and dismiss their predecessors' protestations of fealty to tradition as lip service. Orthodox scholars committed to their own constructive project of Bible study, despite their awareness of the meager historical record, annex their medieval predecessors' achievement to their own practice.[4]

Let us illustrate with a well-known example cited by Breuer. The laws of Jewish servitude (*eved ivri*) are expounded in three separate portions of the Torah: Exodus 21:2–6, Leviticus 25:39–55, and Deuteronomy 15:12–18. The legislation of Exodus and Deuteronomy includes the eventuality that the slave refuses to go free when his term of servitude is up, prescribing that his master bore his ear through with an awl and subjugate him in perpetuity (*l'olam*). According to Leviticus, however, all slavery is terminated by the Jubilee year. In the Talmud (*Kiddushin* 21b), the Rabbis explain that the word *l'olam*, in this connection, means "for an extended term," not "forever." Even the recalcitrant slave eventually is given his freedom. *L'olam* in Exodus and Deuteronomy thus does not conflict with Leviticus's Jubilee-based universal manumission. Thus, the three texts, regarding this detail and others, can be amalgamated to form a consistent halakhic code.

The 12th-century French Talmudist and exegete Rashbam (R. Samuel ben Meir) insisted that the *peshat* meaning of *l'olam* is "forever." If he is right—and champions of the internal consistency of the Written Torah and the absolutely authoritative interpretations of the Oral Torah[5] maintain that the word *l'olam* means exactly what the Rabbis say it means—then we have two authoritative but contradictory interpretations of the word. The rabbinic explication of *l'olam*, according to Rashbam, is *derash*. It cannot be treated as the plain meaning of the verses in Exodus and Deuteronomy.

Following Rashbam, Breuer holds that Leviticus cannot be harmonized, at a *peshat* level, with Exodus and Deuteronomy. Each legal section articulates a different aspect of the Torah's teaching on Jewish servitude. The major theme of Leviticus 25 is that the children of Israel can never become genuine slaves: "they are My slaves, whom I took out of the land of Egypt" (Leviticus 25:55). In Deuteronomy, by contrast, the master is reminded, "You were a slave in the land of Egypt and God redeemed you" (15:15). This principle is elaborated throughout Deuteronomy's legislation: for example, in the law that obligates the master to provide the departing slave with "severance pay" (*ha'anaka*) or in the very fact that the master is consistently addressed in the second person. In Leviticus, freedom is the inalienable destiny of the slave—for it is the slave who left Egypt—whose servitude cannot extend into the Jubilee year: the master is alternatively referred to in the second or third person—in fact, Leviticus does not ignore the situation in which the master is a Gentile. In Deuteronomy, it is the master who reenacts God's act of redemption and who is therefore obligated to free his slave after the term of service. From the perspective of Exodus and Deuteronomy, stressing the master's responsibilities, the slave can forfeit manumission by declining to go free; these texts are oblivious to the slave's right to freedom. In that case, his bondage is renewed *l'olam*, in the literal sense, forever. Leviticus, however, is concerned not with the limits of the master's obligation but with the unconditional doctrine of freedom that knows no difference between master and slave and does not tolerate the possibility that the slave will relinquish his freedom and prolong his servitude.

Now if we were to isolate the sections in Exodus and Deuteronomy, oblivious to the aspect revealed in Leviticus, we would interpret *l'olam* according to Rashbam's plain meaning, and if this were all the Torah had to say on the topic, we would conclude that the Hebrew slave who declined freedom is subject to interminable servitude. Conversely, were the Torah's teaching exhausted by the Leviticus passage, we would leave out the aspects embodied in the other texts. *Peshat* does not harmonize but hardens and juxtaposes the multiple voices in the Torah. *Peshat* alone would yield a fragmented, inconsistent code of law. The work of *derash* is to reinterpret the verses that are, at the level of *peshat*, understood independently of one another and to fuse them in a grand synthesis. The word *l'olam* carries its plain, unforced, Rashbamian meaning in the isolated context, when the Torah speaks in one voice; when the Torah becomes polyphonic, *l'olam* must be reinterpreted in conformity with the whole, mobilizing a secondary, perhaps figurative sense of the phrase, one that would otherwise seem awkward and exceptional.[6]

This example takes us into the heart of R. Breuer's approach. We can look at this entire discussion as a response to source criticism: where its practitioners discern several conflicting sources, combined haphazardly by a series of redactors and eventually harmonized through rabbinic creativity, Breuer perceives the polyphonic voice of the *Ribbono shel Olam*, the Master of the universe, heard by the human auditor in its multifarious glory, formulated as a unified legal code through the agency of the Oral Law. From this perspective, the question Breuer is answering is how what appear to be conflicting passages, allocated to several different sections of the Torah, can add up to one message. But we can also take his work as a response to a different question: Why is there a duality of *peshat* and *derash*? Why are there multiple and sometimes divergent levels within traditional Jewish exegesis? This latter question was immanent in the tradition: sooner or later it was bound to arise and command the attention of traditional commentators independently of modern academic study.

The term *omnisignificance* has become popular in recent years to characterize a basic presupposition of traditional Jewish exegesis. For our purposes, this means that no feature of the biblical text, however minor it appears to be, is beneath the consideration of the commentator. Some votaries of *peshat* are inclined to identify this orientation with *midrash* (think of Ibn Ezra): within their *peshat* universe, certain details of orthography, elegant variation (i.e., parallelism), redundancy, deviation from predictable vocabulary or word order, even the arrangement of material, do not deserve the *pashtan*'s attention. Others (think of the 19th-century eastern European rabbinic exegete Meir Leibush Weiser, better known as Malbim) insist that true fealty to *peshat* forbids the reader to pass over these phenomena.

The very existence of *peshat* as a category of interpretation in tension with rabbinic tradition asserts the will to omnisignificance or at least multiplicity of significance. If, for example, the word *l'olam* is normatively interpreted as "for an extended period of time [until the Jubilee]," then the fact that the Torah chose a word that could plausibly mean "forever" is irrelevant unless one assumes that identifying the normative interpretation does not exhaust the reader's work. Increasing self-consciousness about this point has contributed to the triumph of the "omnisignificant orientation" among sophisticated traditional students of the Torah (including some scholars affiliated with Orthodoxy and other students interested in Tanakh who are not members of any academic community/institution). The same conservative tendency would encourage the traditional exegete to give credence to several different *peshat* options found among their predecessors, on the grounds that the Torah may permit multiple interpretations (in the Talmudic phrase "these and those are the words of the living God")[7] or, more prosaically, that the Torah chose language open to multiple interpretations, ambiguous language, because more than one interpretation is valid. Assuming that some of the contentions associated with biblical criticism highlight significant features of the biblical text, hitherto ignored or treated sporadically in the classical Jewish literature, traditionalists of this stripe would welcome the opportunity to develop new insights within the framework of their belief in *Torah mi-Sinai* (Torah given at Sinai). These insights would fully belong among the "seventy faces of Torah" regarded as legitimate and praiseworthy by the Talmudic rabbis (Midrash *Numbers Rabba* 13.15). From Breuer's point of view, the palace of Torah is all the more majestic because it incorporates responses to the challenges of the past two centuries.

Yet not every disagreement should generate dialectic; not every uncertainty is an ambiguity; not every textual divergence confronts us with a legitimate variant. Sometimes no more than one party to a disagreement in interpretation can be right; some uncertainties need to be eliminated if at all possible, rather than cherished as a source of profundity; a scribe may err with no extenuating literary or theological apologia. Paradoxically, the momentum driving the Orthodox cultivation of omnisignificance, once it embraces noncanonical sources and methods, may end up unwittingly "sanctifying" some of these profane resources mainly because they are there.

Thus, one may agree with Breuer's outlook and yet wonder whether he goes too far in annexing every speculation generated by the academic ingenuity and industry on exhibit in the literature he studied. Let us examine one example where Breuer's program intersects with early rabbinic and nonrabbinic exegesis. Consider a famous crux found in Leviticus 23. After giving laws concerning the Passover holiday in verses 5–8, verses 9–11 of this chapter direct the Israelites to offer a sheaf of barley on "the day after the Sabbath" (*mohorat ha-shabbat*; Leviticus 23:11). The same phrase occurs again in verse 15, which directs the Israelites to count seven weeks starting on "the day after the Sabbath." At the end of those seven weeks, another festival occurs, which is associated with the offering of the first fruit (*bikkurim*), that is, the holiday of Shavuot (that festival is described in verses 16–21). The crux involves the precise meaning of the phrase *mohorat ha-shabbat* in verses 11 and 15. According to rabbinic tradition, the phrase refers to the morrow of the first day of the festival of *matsot* (Passover), that is the sixteenth of the month of Nisan. Thus, the word *shabbat* here does not mean the Sabbath; rather, it refers to the first day of the Passover festival. On the day after the beginning of the Passover festival, farmers must offer a sheaf of wheat known as the *omer* at the Temple; counting seven weeks from the *omer* yields the date of the second festival, Shavuot. According to rabbinic tradition, the Sadducees (another ancient Jewish group who opposed the predecessors of the Rabbis) rejected this interpretation. In their opinion, *mohorat ha-shabbat* means the day after the Sabbath, the seventh day of the week (specifically, the first Sabbath after the first day of Passover). The *omer* is then brought on the Sunday following the fifteenth of Nisan, and Shavuot is celebrated seven weeks later, always on Sunday.

At the level of *peshat*, the dispute is clearly defined. Does the word *shabbat*, in this passage, have its ordinary meaning of the weekly Sabbath (the Sadducean position), or can it mean any day on which work is forbidden, in this instance the festival of Passover, which is the rabbinic tradition? The Talmud (*Menahot* 65b) records arguments attempting to establish the rabbinic view; such debates continued through the Middle Ages, with the Karaites replacing the Sadducees as adversaries, and continue to occupy modern commentators.[8]

If one adopts the rabbinic view as authoritative for the community's religious observance, is the deviant view nonetheless a plausible alternative that could be accepted as *peshat*, just as Rashbam considered his reading of *l'olam* as *peshat*? If so, then the Sadducee position, like that of the Bible critics with whom Breuer is engaged, presents legitimate philology. Were it not for authoritative tradition, it might well be accepted, and on local philological grounds, it might well be superior, on Breuer's view, to the interpretation that is in fact accepted. Presumably this view ought to be taken seriously not simply because it was asserted by a deviant group but because it is independently plausible or even persuasive. In fact, Breuer does adopt the Sadducee view as *peshat*, arguing that if the Torah meant by *mohorat ha-shabbat* the day after Passover, then the Torah could have said it more unambiguously.

In the Second Temple period, there was a third reconstruction of the date of Shavuot. The book of Jubilees schedules all holidays for the time of the full moon. Hence, Shavuot, for Jubilees, occurs on the fifteenth of Sivan, not the fifth, sixth, or seventh of the month of Sivan, as would be the case if one were counting seven weeks from the first day of Passover or the Sunday following those dates, according to the Sadducees. Offhand, this view has no philological basis in the text of Leviticus; it only makes sense on the premise of the Jubilees calendar. So the second question is whether even the Jubilees option may or should play a role in *peshat* interpretation?

Breuer's theory of Shavuot is one of his most complicated efforts. He attempts to integrate the many sections in the Torah dealing with the holiday and to do justice to the different appellations the holiday receives. In addition, he gives credence to the rabbinic commemoration of Shavuot as the day of the giving of the Torah, despite the fact that this identification is not explicit in either the narrative about Sinai (Exodus 19–20 and Deuteronomy 5) or in the legal portions devoted to the festivals, though Exodus hints at a date early in the third month (known in postbiblical Hebrew as Sivan). Consequently, Breuer arrives at three different themes connected with Shavuot, each of which, taken entirely on its own terms, would mandate a different date for the celebration. As noted, Breuer takes the Sadducee date seriously on the evidence of the biblical text. He also must posit that, since biblical holidays usually coincide with the full moon, the Jubilees dating is also a legitimate option, despite the total absence of this date in the Torah.

In a footnote, Breuer states, astonishingly, that he discovered the Jubilees text only after he had already deduced the full-moon dating independently.[9] It is conceivable that a creative thinker juggling the massive legacy of the Jewish biblical and rabbinic scholarship and the literature of source criticism could misplace the evidence of Jubilees. However that might be, one might consider the possibility that the regimen of seeking significance in all phenomena connected to biblical study may lead one to appeal to data that would otherwise be dismissed as flatly irrelevant. Theology and literary sensitivity promote a technique that takes on a life of its own. Thus, the theologically and literarily motivated impulse to omnisignificance may lead to theologically curious procedures and conclusions that Breuer himself finds it necessary to disavow.

Breuer's programmatic essays focus on the Higher Criticism, and his major volumes parallel its themes. His expertise on the Masoretic tradition also manifested itself in a similar approach to questioning of Lower Criticism. Here, too, Breuer teases out differences of interpretation from textual traditions and even from traditions of cantillation (*ta'amei ha-mikra*—the notations in the Masoretic text that serve both as a guide to a verse's syntax and as musical notation for chanting biblical texts in synagogue services). Here, too, one may raise questions about the proper limits of omnisignificance.

The book jacket of Breuer's collection of essays, *Pirkei Moadot*, describes it as a commentary of the Torah and the festivals from the biblical text and the words of the Rabbis. R. Breuer hardly, if ever, mentions the critics in the body of his oeuvre, except when he explains his method, when he discusses little else. Often he branches out far beyond the standard pale of Jewish biblical exegesis, as he explores the implications of his ideas for sundry halakhic subjects. Contrary to common opinion, the substance of his work is less to join combat with academic literary Bible study than to make his own distinctive contribution to traditional Bible study with the aid of the modern literary methods.

NOTES

1. Breuer's work in this area is found in the two volumes of *Pirkei Moadot* (Jerusalem: Horeb, 1989), dealing primarily with legal portions of the Torah and with the narratives outside of Genesis; the two-volume *Pirkei Bereshit* (Alon Shevut: Tevunot, 1998) on Genesis; and posthumously, *Pirkei Mikraot* (Alon Shevut: Tevunot, 2009), several chapters in which refine previously published essays. After the completion of this chapter, there appeared *Pirkei Yeshaayahu*, a commentary on Isaiah 1–6 (Alon Shevut: Tevunot, 2010), edited and with an introduction by Yosef Ofer and with a preface by Yohanan Breuer. This is a verse-by-verse commentary written in the 1960s, before Breuer's major works on the Torah: its primary methodological value lies in Breuer's comments on matters of Lower Criticism. Yosef Ofer, ed., *Shittat haBehinot shel haRav Mordechai Breuer: Kovetz Maamarim u-Teguvot* (Alon Shevut: Tevunot, 2005), contains Breuer's early programmatic essays and later uncollected remarks, together with a number of critical papers on his work. The two-volume festschrift *Sefer haYovel laRav Mordechai Breuer* (edited by Moshe Bar-Asher; Jerusalem: Aqademon, 1992) includes Breuer's bibliography to that date. For English statements by and about Breuer, see the following in S. Carmy, ed., *Modern Scholarship in the Study of Torah: Contributions and Limitations* (Hoboken, NJ: Jason Aronson, 1996): M. Breuer, "The Study of Bible and the Primacy of the Fear of Heaven: Compatibility or Contradiction?" (159–80); S. Carmy, "Introducing Rabbi Breuer" (147–58); and S. Z. Leiman, "Response to Rabbi Breuer" (181–88).

2. Joseph Soloveitchik, *The Lonely Man of Faith* (New York: Doubleday, 1992), originally published as a lengthy essay in 1965 in the journal *Tradition*.

3. Concerning these commentators, see chapters 6 and 7 by Meira Polliack and Robert Harris in this volume.

4. For an academic author aware that the historical question about the intent of the medieval *pashtanim* remains troubling, see Sarah Japhet, "The Tension Between Rabbinic Legal Midrash and the 'Plain Meaning' (Peshat) of the Biblical Text: An Unresolved Problem?" in C. Cohen et al., eds., *Sefer Moshe: The Moshe Weinfeld Memorial Volume* (Winona Lake, IN: Eisenbrauns, 2004. A more recent discussion of the subject is Moshe Arend, "On the concept of *peshuto shel mikra*," in *Ha-Mikra b-Rei Mefarshav: Sarah Kamin Memorial Volume* (Jerusalem: Magnes, 1994), 237–61. Arend himself grew up against the background of Orthodox debate about these issues in Israel at the time that Breuer was formulating his views; his essay thus conveys something of the atmosphere of those formative debates.

5. On the rabbinic notions of Written and Oral Torah, see chapter 3 by Steven Fraade in this volume.

6. See *Pirkei Moadot* I, 16–22, for discussion of the three passages. For the sake of brevity, I have left out Breuer's views on the distinctions between the Exodus and Deuteronomy versions. The persuasiveness of Breuer's account gains force from the accumulation of details and thus may not be evident from our isolated discussion of *l'olam*. For a complementary essay comparing both narrative and legal slavery passages in the Torah on the assumption that the Torah proceeds in a unified and consecutive manner, see my "'We Were Slaves to Pharaoh in Egypt': Literary-Theological Notes on Slavery and Empathy," *Hebraic Political Studies* 4:4 (Fall 2009): 367–80.

7. See BT *Eruvin* 13b and, for an analysis of this concept in Orthodox thought, Michael Rosensweig, "*Elu va-Elu Divre Elokim Hayyim*: Halakhic Pluralism and Theories of Controversy," *Tradition* 26:3 (Spring 1992): 4–23; also in *Rabbinic Authority and Personal Autonomy*, ed. Moshe Sokol (Northvale, NJ: J. Aronson, 1992).

8. See, for example, R. David Zvi Hoffmann's commentary to Leviticus, vol. 2, 113–52 (Hebrew translation by Z. Harshefer and A. Lieberman; Jerusalem: Mosad Ha-Rav Kook, 1954). For further discussion relating to Breuer's views on this verse, see his nephew, David Henshke, "The Morrow of the Sabbath—a New Outlook," *Megadim* 14 (1991): 9–26; Yoel Bin-Nun, "Reactions," *Megadim* 15 (1992): 99–101; and Henshke's response, "Two Contradictory Verses," *Megadim* 16 (1993): 116–18; and Bin-Nun's reaction, in ibid., 118; as well as Henshke, "From Whence the Counting of the *Omer* from the Torah?," in Bar-Asher, *Sefer haYovel laRav Mordechai Breuer*, 417–48.

9. *Pirkei Moadot* II, 352n. 2. For Breuer's final discussion of these verses, see *Pirkei Mikraot*, 207–22. The footnote about Jubilees is repeated verbatim at 208n. 7.

Chapter 16

Scripture and Modern Israeli Literature

Yael S. Feldman

The fascinating autobiography of Max Brod offers a witty insight into the role of the Hebrew Bible in the cultural life of the *Yishuv*, the prestate Jewish community in Palestine. Culled from his long experience (1939–68) as the dramaturge of Habima—Israel's national theater—Brod's humorous quip critiques the overabundance of unsolicited *biblical* dramatic scripts sent to him in the 1940s: "After rejecting five plays named 'Moses,' ten 'King Ahabs,' and a dozen 'Ezras,' I felt like hanging on my door a note explaining that it is preferable to read the Bible in the original rather than getting excited over its staged versions."[1]

Brod's recollection illustrates not only the popularity of the Bible in the literary production of the prestate *Yishuv* but also the tension he perceived between the "original," the biblical text itself, and its rewritten versions, whether on stage or on the page. This tension was not new, however: it has in fact accompanied the more than century-long bond between the Bible and modern Hebrew literature, as it had done throughout Jewish history in different fashions. Nevertheless, the Bible had a particularly important role in molding the modern, presumably secular, Jewish national identity, which emerged in eastern Europe in the 19th century and began to flourish in the Land of Israel in the early 20th century. A literary repository of ancient Israel, the biblical corpus now functioned as a nation-building text, precisely like other ethnic myths that had been recovered and disseminated under the banner of European romanticism and nationalism. As such, it affected all aspects of the Hebrew national renaissance, impacting its language and letters, psychology and ideology, aesthetics and ethics.

Recently, however, contemporary critics have contested modern national identities on the grounds that they are cultural "constructs," "products," or "inventions," even "imagined communities." Israeli identity has not escaped this critique. Indeed, one might well apply this assessment to the history of what was recently called Israel's "Biblemania." This mania gained momentum, according to Anita Shapira, *after* the establishment of the State of Israel, when Prime Minister David Ben Gurion "elevated the Bible to the chief intellectual focus of the young state."[2]

I would suggest, however, that this "elevation" was not a new invention. One can readily argue that the Bible has enjoyed this elevated status throughout Jewish intellectual history, despite the competition from later postbiblical sources. In the Jewish tradition as a whole, Robert Alter has observed, the Hebrew Bible had been "doubly" canonized—as a religious, that is, doctrinal, theological, or ethical model, as well as a literary (and linguistic) model.[3] The first aspect follows the "thoroughly unambiguous definition" of the canon as a list of books accepted as "genuine and inspired."[4] The second aspect derives from the literary dimension of the Bible, namely, its "brilliant literary artistry," its "imaginative imagery," or its "luminous poetic achievements."[5] Moreover, Alter avers, the Hebrew Bible is the great *enabler* of expression; it is "the great compendium of cultural references for its Hebrew readers, who are presumed to have a word-by-word familiarity with it: images, motifs, narrative situations are there to be called up by a writer with a flick of a phrase."[6]

In light of this historical continuity, the attempt to co-opt the Bible in the service of nascent Jewish nationalism is not surprising, nor can it be considered as mere "construction." On the contrary, it may illustrate the approach suggested by Anthony D. Smith and his cohorts.[7] For Smith, national identity represents a community's response to its down-to-earth emotional needs to connect with its ethnic myths, symbols, and memories.[8] The Hebrew Bible has apparently answered these needs throughout most of Jewish history, even if in different fashions.

Indeed, the people of Israel, in their bimillennial attempt to connect with their doubly canonized Bible, seem to have utilized, just like other communities, all three measures Smith attributes to such national efforts—reiteration, continuity, and appropriation. A new measure entered this process, moreover, in the modern era: secularization. Although of long standing, this element has only recently come to the forefront of academic discussion. One can even detect some bewilderment in contemporary scholars' attempts to pin down and define the nature of this recent leg of the process. Alter, for one, suggests that while for the medieval poets the two canonical aspects dwelled peacefully together, modern Hebrew writers have elevated the literary/linguistic canonization over the religious canonization, in an attempt to harvest the Bible's literary riches while combating its doctrine. Ruth Kartun-Blum, by contrast, labeled the result of the "modern dialogue between Hebrew literature and the Bible" as *Profane Scriptures*,[9] while Nehama Aschkenasy reversed the perspective, giving the process, like Alter, a more positive twist: a recent volume on the topic she edited is titled "Recreating the Canon."[10] David Jacobson on the other hand had named the retelling of *all* traditional Jewish narratives by 20th-century Hebrew writers as *Modern Midrash*,[11] whereas the late Gershon Shaked limited this label to the modern rewriting of the Bible per se: "Modern Hebrew literature, by giving a secular (and sometimes subversive) interpretation of the Bible, becomes a *modern midrash*."[12]

Significantly, Shaked's definition points to a major characteristic of the phenomenon—the simultaneous continuity and discontinuity ("subversion") in the retelling of any ancient myth or symbol. Not unlike the rabbis of old, contemporary Jewish authors, Israelis not excluded, are engaged in "making sense" of received scripture, in adjusting it to their own reality, hence the term *midrash*; unlike the rabbis, however, many of them have been doing this under the aegis of secularism, hence the qualifying adjective *modern*.

As I have recently argued, however, this definition lacks a crucial aspect of the modern phase of the spectrum under scrutiny here: in many cases, the presence of the Bible in modern Hebrew literature (and probably in other literatures—Jewish or not—as well) is mediated through the *premodern rewritings* of the Bible, from Rabbinic and Christian "midrash," through kabbalah and medieval liturgy, to medieval and premodern quasi historical "Chronicles." From this perspective, modern literature not only wrestles with scripture; it often reads and rewrites it through an altercation with and subversion of the midrashic retellings of previous generations, far and near.[13] That this characteristic is not well recognized is a testimony not only to the towering authority of the Bible throughout the generations but also to the workings of Zionist ideology that has for the longest time *privileged* the Bible as *the* canonic text, naturally at the expense of *post*biblical literary expressions.

While this preference has been attenuated in recent years, its impact still abounds. A major example is a recent comprehensive Hebrew anthology, *I Will Play You Forever*, subtitled *The Bible in Modern Hebrew Poetry*, which was edited by the Israeli poet, educator, and literary critic Malka Shaked.[14]

In the first volume of this eminently valuable work, Shaked collects over five hundred annotated poems, spanning from the Hebrew Enlightenment of the 19th century through contemporary Israeli poetry. In the work's no less substantial interpretative second volume, Shaked documents, categorizes, and sheds light on the complex relationship between the Bible and its people in modern times. This complex relationship—a palpable movement from attitudes of adoration and fascination to altercation and subversion—surfaces mainly upon reading volume 2. In this discursive tome, the author analyses a select number of poems from each section of the anthology (volume 1). Since the poems are presented mostly in chronological order, the discussion lends itself to a developmental interpretation. Yet it is not the *history* of modern imaginative rewriting of the Bible that is the organizing principle of the anthology itself. Rather, volume 1 principally follows the order of the biblical narrative, from Genesis through Writings (*Ketuvim*), and in each section the poems are arranged thematically rather than chronologically. As such, this anthology, although limited to poetry, may offer a useful bird's-eye view of the distribution of biblical themes and personalities in Hebrew literature of the past two centuries. The internal organization of volume 2, however, whose sections interestingly sport a different set of headings, adds a valuable insight not only into the modalities and twists of this corpus but also into the biases inherent in the contemporary interpreting community of this corpus.

The Genesis section of volume 2 is teasingly titled *Bereshit Aḥeret*—literally, "A Different Beginning" but also "A Different (Book of) Genesis," since the Hebrew word *bereshit* is also the Hebrew title for the first book of the Bible. This title transparently invokes the subversive potential of this modern dialogue. The different beginning is followed by the anticipated sibling rivalry (Abel and Cain), Noah and the Flood, and so on. The title of the section devoted to the patriarchs again hints at the contemporary interpretation that has colored the rereading of Genesis in recent years: "Fathers and Sons." As we shall see, the patriarchal narrative of Genesis has recently become Hebrew culture's treasure house for archetypal tropes for intergenerational conflict in the style of Freud and modern psychoanalysis. Even more predictably, a focal point of the discussion of the patriarchs is "the aqedah" (the Binding of Isaac)—a cue for another "bias" of Israeli Hebrew literature to be picked up later in this chapter. The list continues with sections devoted to "Leaders" (mostly Moses and the Judges), Kings, Prophets, and on to themes from Writings, with the Psalms occupying center stage.

Although my brief account cannot do justice to Shaked's comprehensive mapping of biblical themes in Hebrew poetry, it does offer two edifying insights into the problematic nature of our topic:

1. A quick glance at the poems devoted to the patriarchs and other "leaders" shows that *Isaac*, traditionally considered the least heroic of all biblical figures, *"stars" in more poems than do* Father Abraham or Moses—the father of all prophets—or famed King David or a popular hero like Samson. If this orientation is characteristic (and it is), then we must ask what is the meaning—theological but also psychological—of the twist taken by the modern Hebrew imagination on the veteran distinction between the so-called Father religion and the Son religion.

2. One cannot help but notice that the order of presentation of both volumes is governed by the principal male actors of the biblical narrative. *So where have all the women gone?* Amazingly, they are all grouped together under the rubric "Women" (*Nashim*) that *follows* the final "male" section. Here we find, again arranged by the biblical order, Eve, the Matriarchs, the women of Judges, David's wives, the heroines of the Scrolls (Ruth, Naomi, Esther), and so on and so forth. But how are we to understand this one exception to the rule, the internal order that governs the anthology? Are women given here "a section of their own" (some 100 pages out of 460 in volume 1 and 107 out of 617 in volume 2), or are they simply relegated to the women's gallery (*ezrat hanashim*), to their traditionally excluded location in Jewish culture and the synagogue, as author Amalia Kahana-Carmon bitterly complained some three decades ago?[15]

In what follows, I use the questions raised by the latest effort to map the presence of the Bible in Hebrew poetry as a starting point for my brief sketch of the history of the appropriation of one biblical motif in modern Hebrew literature, the *aqedah*. Following my recent study on the role of Isaac's near sacrifice and other biblical sacrificial tropes in the Hebrew national narrative of the past century, I focus here on psychological and gender problems involved in that appropriation. These problems emanate, I suggest, partly from the "gender trouble" inherent in the patriarchal narratives and partly from our own inability to part with both traditionally and contemporarily received gender stereotyping.

The persistence in the Israeli mind of the biblical narrative of the so-called sacrifice of Isaac is a fact well known to Israelis but less so to outsiders. Indeed, non-Hebrew speakers and readers often find it hard to believe that despite the presence of the epithet "Israel" in the names of both the land and the state, Israel's literary imaginary has been dominated not by its eponymous forefather, Jacob-Israel, who, as Genesis tells us, "*wrestled with God and with men and prevailed*," but rather by the less heroic, somewhat passive figure of Isaac. The fact is, however, that more than any biblical narrative, the story of Isaac's near sacrifice in Genesis 22 has become a focal trope in Zionist thought and Hebrew letters. As any Israeli "knows," the Binding is *the* metaphor for national sacrifice, and hence Isaac naturally stands for Israel's fallen warriors. A deeper look reveals that the aqedah has come to signify broadly diverse, sometimes contradictory *psycho-political* attitudes that range from stoic heroism and ideological martyrdom to passive victimhood, or its obverse: fanatic (often aggressive) resistance to such martyric heroism.

Moreover, whereas in the early days of the Zionist revolution, the Exodus from Egypt and the journey in the wilderness may have been serious contenders (in fact, in the early 1900s, H. N. Bialik, the Hebrew National Laureate poet, authored two poems on the journey in the wilderness: "The Dead of the Desert" and "The Later Dead of the Desert"), these themes clearly lost the race in the wake of World War II and the struggle for independence. Since the 1940s, the aqedah has become a key figure in Hebrew literature. Paradoxically, it gained its prominence due to its double semantic potential: Janus-like, it can represent both the *slaughter* of the Holocaust and the national *warrior's* heroic death in the old-new homeland.

Before I approach the psycho-political problems hinted by this dialectical semantics, a likely historical misperception must be corrected: while the appropriation of both the aqedah and Isaac to describe *mot qedoshim*, Jewish martyrdom, goes all the way back to medieval times (see the "Isaacs" populating Hebrew liturgy and so-called Chronicles composed in the Rhineland following the Crusades),[16] its military appropriation was the invention of the early 20th century. The product of the pioneers of both the second and third waves of Jewish immigration to Palestine in the early 20th century (1904–24), this rewritten aqedah slowly came to stand for the sacrifices and loss of life demanded by the pioneering project in the Land of Israel. Having escaped the bloodbath of eastern Europe, these young immigrants were determined now to exchange the role of the victim (*qorban*) for the role of self-sacrifice (also *qorban* in Hebrew!), *choosing* to give up their life on the altar of the motherland.

Nevertheless, the literary products of these immigrants attest that they did not necessarily identify with the *biblical* Isaac, and this for more reasons than one. Let us begin with what I call the patriarchal "gender trouble." A quick comparative glance at ancient sacrificial narratives will tell us that the story of Genesis 22 is unique when it comes to the *sex* of the sacrificial victim. A chasm seems to open between the biblical tradition —and perhaps ancient Near Eastern traditions at large—and the Greek tradition. While Jephthah's daughter is *unique* in the biblical corpus as a female virgin sacrifice, the notorious sacrifice of Iphigenia is *emblematic* of human sacrifice in Greek myth and ritual. Of course, Isaac is unique too in the Bible as a *named* (potential) male victim, but the *generalized* references to *forbidden child sacrifice* in the Prophets are all gendered as male. This gendered choice has had long-term implications for Jewish psychology and Zionist ideology—a topic I discuss at length in my study *Glory and Agony*. Here I wish only to point out that the biblical Isaac does not partake in the function usually preserved for male characters within the orbit of Greek culture, the notorious aggressive struggle with their father or son. Among its other transformations of pagan myth, the biblical aqedah has "substituted" male for female,[17] without, however, changing the power-relations structure of the narrative. Isaac fulfills the role of a female, as the troublesome story of Jephthah's daughter should undoubtedly remind us. In the scenario of Genesis 22, so diametrically opposed to the oedipal plot, in any of its versions, no conflict is acted out. Any potential aggression is repressed, and by both parties.

The spirit of the aqedah, then, even throughout its permutations, is not amenable to *mainstream* Freudian interpretations (and not only because of the absence of the maternal link in the famous triad!). The importance of this disjunction could not be exaggerated, especially once we recall that modern Jewish nationalism emerged from the same European climate that had engendered psychoanalysis. Zionism therefore bears the stamp of Freudianism, the oedipal conflict in particular, in both conscious and unconscious ways. As an ideology that valorized masculine activism and preached resistance rather than submission to any use of force, it was doomed to clash with the patriarchal psychology of nonconfrontation at the core of its own preferred Jewish canonic text, the Hebrew Bible. This lack of fit between Freudian psychology and biblical psychology was, I suggest, the first complication for the young Zionist pioneers' enthusiastic embracing of the patriarchal narratives in general and especially the aqedah as a symbol of national sacrifice. In view of the turn taken by Israeli authors (and politicians), one may rightly ask, I believe, how did Israelis manage to turn around a scene traditionally read as a trope of *obedience* (à la "feminine" resignation of Greek virgins) and to rewrite it as a trope of *violence* and *trauma*, now identified with the *oedipal conflict*? Moreover, how could the very same story give rise to two opposite readings that have been virtually ripping Israel apart for some time: in the first, Genesis 22 is a story of a *willing* self-immolation, in which father and son harmoniously "walked together"; in the second, it is a story about an act of violence against an innocent victim, one whose experience is *not* that of *fear and trembling* but rather of *trauma and pain*?

A full answer to this question is too long to be rehearsed here. Suffice it just to outline the high points of the story. I trace the invention of the Binding as a modern military sacrifice to Berl Katznelson, who in 1919 coined the paradoxical expression "*osher aqedah*" (the bliss/glory of self-binding) to describe the zeal and excitement felt by the first volunteers to the Jewish Legion in the British Army in World War I.[18] The next step was taken up by the next generation of pioneer-poets (that is, poets who came in the third wave of modern Jewish immigration into Palestine, from 1919 to 1923). Yet those young pioneering "Isaacs" were mostly fatherless—some literally orphaned, others miles away from the parents they left behind in Europe. This condition left a clear mark on their literary output. Often there was no "Abraham" in their literary reworking of the scene, nor was there an angel to stop the act. Yitzhak Lamdan (1899–1954), for example, eloquently delineates the difference between the biblical aqedah and his own. Waking from drunken stupor and noticing a picture of "*Aqedat Yitzhaq*" on his table, the poetic persona of a poem titled "*Aqud*" (Bound) desperately inquires,

> What do you intimate, an empty, open-mouthed bottle:
> "That there is rescue . . . as echoed in this picture"—?
> But this is not me, a different Isaac was there.
> Different was the binder, and different the binding.[19]

The nature of this difference need not preoccupy us for too long, for it is stated boldly:

> I *did* know where I was being led to
> nor was it God who commanded my going for a test.
> I myself so loved the journey
> that I didn't even inquire about the lamb.[20]

Lamdan identified, then, not with the biblical aqedah but rather with the Jewish *post*biblical portrayals of his namesake. Volunteering for his own immolation, his Isaac is ready for the possibility that the biblical "rescue" is not applicable in the here and now. We should not be surprised, then, that the midrashic intertext soon fully materializes: in the poem "On the Altar," for example, a martyric postbiblical gesture is replicated in the self-sacrifice of contemporary Isaacs:

> Here we are all bound, bringing the wood with our own hands
> Without inquiring whether our offering [*qorban olah*] is accepted!
> . . . .
> Let us then silently stretch our neck on the altar.[21]

Similar aqedah dialectics later animated the ironic representation of the Second Aliya pioneers (those who came to Palestine before World War I) in the work of S. Y. Agnon, Israel's Nobel Laureate. One source of the ironic treatment of Yitzhak Kumer, the hard-to-pin-down protagonist of Agnon's monumental 1946 novel *Only Yesterday*, may have been the gaping distance between the two opposing senses (and two dichotomous "economies") of the aqedah that claimed the author's attention at the time: the heroic willing self-sacrifice (*qorban*) of the pioneers of his youth in the "Land of Isaac," as I call it, and the tragic victims (*qorbanot*) of the Holocaust, the victimization of European Jewry that was taking place when he was completing this novel.[22] It should be noted, however, that this dialectics is in evidence already in his 1939 novel *A Guest for the Night*, often mistakenly read as a "Holocaust" novel. Here the issue comes up in a dispute between the pious Rabbi Shlomo and his heretical son Daniel Bach: the latter is willing to accept the martyrdom practiced by Jews throughout history (*qiddush hashem*) but not his own generation's victimization during World War I and its aftermath, described by him as "daily, even hourly binding [*aqedot*] on seven altars."[23]

Agnon's "Isaacs," both exilic and "in the land," were soon followed, however, by a different brand of literary willing Isaacs. Populating Israeli literature of the 1940s and 1950s, these new Isaacs naturally represented the sacrifices made by the young in the War of Independence. By then, however, the contemporary writers qua Isaacs were not orphaned anymore. Their "Abrahams" were right there, available to be typecast in the unsavory role of the one commanding the sacrifice. Beginning with Yigal Mossinsohn's emblematic 1949 play *In the Negev Plains*, Isaac was still a willing self-immolator, but not his own agent: he volunteers to *go along with* his father's plans, ready for the slaughter if needed (a contemporary version not only of Genesis 22's repeated phrase "and they both went together" but also of the medieval martyrdom shared by parents and progeny in the Hebrew Crusade Chronicles). However, center stage was given—paradoxically perhaps—back to the father. It is the contemporary Abraham who is now imagined not only as the source of the command but also as the one who either "volunteers" to take the blame or is blamed by the son.

This self-blame or blame can be quite tempered, as in Mossinsohn's play ("We're a cruel generation that kills our young sons! The old go on living —and the young are sent to their death") or in Haim Gouri's iconic poem ("But that hour / He bequeathed to his progeny. / They are born / With the knife [*ma'akhelet*] in their heart").[24] It can also be ferocious, as in Moshe Shamir's or S. Yizhar's unprecedented and unforgettable lines. Whereas the former puts his harsh indictment in the mouth of a bereaving father —"Nothing may interest me anymore or arouse my feelings save for the sphere of the *aqedah*; I brought a helpless infant into this world only to murder him, either with my own hands or through (God's) agent [*biyedei shaliah*],"[25] the latter puts them in the mouth of the "son," one of the eloquent fighters of his 1958 War of Independence mock epic *Days of Ziklag*: "I hate our Father Abraham for going to bind Isaac. What right does he have over Isaac. Let him bind himself."[26]

Clearly, Yizhar's protagonist found "Father Abraham" guilty for ostensibly choosing to sacrifice the other—especially the next generation—over sacrificing himself. It was this indignant moral judgment, sounded shortly after the Sinai Campaign (1956), that soon captured the imagination of the younger generation. In the 1960s, that peer group, later to be dubbed "the Isaac Generation," offered a new fictional spin on the old story. In their narratives, not only had the aqedah completely morphed from "binding" to "blood sacrifice," it also moved from the realm of traditional biblical/Jewish psychology to that of its neighboring culture, classical Greek drama. In contrast to the harmonious going together imagined in Genesis as well as throughout premodern Jewish history and even in some of the cultural products of the 1940s and 1950s, the aqedah now began to be reinterpreted as the Hebraic equivalent of the oedipal scene, and especially as a Freudian oedipal scene. Although this oedipalization of the aqedah was first introduced in Hebrew drama in the early 1940s,[27] the violent potentiality of this turn came to the fore only in the 1960s.

A. B. Yehoshua and Amos Oz are today the most familiar representatives of that group of budding writers of the 1960s, and their penchant for Freudianism is well known by now. Much attention has been lavished in particular on Yehoshua's special blending of the aqedah with the oedipal conflict, which peaked in his 1990 masterful novel *Mr. Mani*.[28] Rather than repeating here my analysis of his lifelong oedipalization of the aqedah,[29] I will briefly demonstrate the new turn of the 1960s by two less-known prose narratives of the time. In *The Battle*, a 1966 first novel by the kibbutz native Yariv Ben-Aharon, the reader is invited to enter, through long interior monologues (cf. Yizhar), the "mad ideas" of the young protagonist, Moshe. These ideas turn Moshe's feelings of filial inadequacy into manifest wishes for *violence and patricide*. Yet through historical contextualization—the son's first baptism by fire in the Sinai Campaign—the novel turns this psychological complex into a psycho-political argument that falls back on the familiar trope we are following here: "Isn't the way of the world that a son buries his father? . . . Don't then the fathers *bind and sacrifice their sons on the altar of war* as if they attempt to escape their own sentence? Shouldn't the father die for his own ideas? Is it my duty to bury him before he buries me? Namely, before his ideas are materialized?"

Needless to say, Moshe does not murder his father.[30] Possibly following Gideon, Oz's young kibbutz protagonist from his popular story "The Way of the Wind,"[31] he ultimately directs his aggression against himself. Was the kibbutz environment too oppressive, rendering its young authors unable to imagine any way out for Oedipus/Isaac except through suicide/self-immolation? Is this why Yehoshua was alone in managing to orchestrate, in *Three Days and a Child* and beyond, a last-minute rescue for his novelistic sons?[32] And is this why he was the one to openly lead a "vendetta" against the aqedah, illustrating in his masterful 1990 novel *Mr. Mani* how one should paradoxically "undo the aqedah by *acting it out*"? Was this the reason for his insistence that we must try to extinguish the mesmerizing magic of this story, because one can never be sure that "the knife will continue hovering in midair and not strike home instead"?[33]

A different weaving together of Freudian and biblical motifs took place in Amos Oz's tale "Wild Man," also published in 1966. Since I have analyzed this story extensively elsewhere,[34] I only use it here as a transition to my second focus in this chapter: the representation of women and their participation in the aqedah debate. Indeed, this little-remembered story is unique on several counts. It offers a glimpse into an unfamiliar chapter of ecumenical, intercultural, cross-millennial transmission of cultural tropes, exposing the universal implications of the Jewish-Israeli story unraveled here. No less important, it is remarkable for grafting the Bible's *female* sacrificial "heroine," Jephthah's anonymous daughter, over the conventional male trope, the aqedah. This blending shakes up a bit the androcentric nature of the modern retelling of biblical human sacrifice as it has unfolded so far, even if this was not Oz's original intention. It thus helps me introduce the following crucial question: how did the dialectics exposed in the brief history outlined here—both the typically "effeminate" characterization of the biblical aqedah and its oedipalization and hence masculinization by Israeli literature since the late 1960s—affect Israeli women writers?

Given the centrality of the biblical sacrificial trope in the emotional and psychic economy of Israelis at large, its male-specific gender naturally raised a question for women: how are they to enter a millennia-old conversation between son, father, and their paternal godhead in heaven? This problematic has been often expressed in the literature through the question "Where was Sarah?" This challenge is usually directed at both the biblical narrative that excluded the figure of wife and mother from its religious/national *urtext*, and the contemporary scene, where women, in Israel as elsewhere, were slow to enter open public debates over "national sacrifice" and hence were hesitant in engaging its major biblical trope.

We may say, then, that there was a certain structural mirroring between Hebrew culture up to the 1980s and the ancient scriptural tradition that had famously excluded Sarah from its religious sacrificial *urtext*. Sarah was not alone in this exclusion. More often than not, ancient sacrifice, especially *blood* sacrifice, was *not* the business of women in any religious cult, near and far. It is clear, then, that ancient Judaism shared with its neighbors its preference for *male sacrificers*. So the question is, how did Sarah's modern descendants fare in a contemporary world that inherited such a male-centered tradition of sacrifice and martyrdom?

If my reconstructed history is accurate, although women's interventions in the general debate over national sacrifice were few and far between, they were often ahead of their time, sensing the shifting underground and trying to offer their remedies. Some women *throughout the 20th century* did intervene—and often spearheaded a new approach to both contemporary and biblical issues. Among them we can count, to name just a few, the poet Rachel, who in the 1920s protested the application of the appellation *qorbanot* (victims?) to her generation, the Second Aliya, and in her poetry avoided at all costs the terms *aqedah* or *qorban*; theater critic Margot Klausner, who was the first to pan the oedipalization of the aqedah by the 1948 generation, arguing that there is no agreement between the Jewish and European-Freudian psychological systems; essayist/author Shulamith Hareven, who in the 1970s coined the term "The Isaac Generation" in her attempt to talk that very peer group out of their "aqedah fixation"; and artist Shoshana Heimann, who in 1975 pioneered a different, one could say "maternal," mode of aqedah painting, in which the angel was feminized rather than excluded.[35]

Since the 1980s, however, the Israeli picture has considerably changed: women's voices, previously few and far between, have been slowly entering the national conversation over sacrifice and its biblical tropes. Unsurprisingly, their interventions take many shapes. While many undertake the maternal role placed on them by nature and tradition, as either mourning or protesting mothers, others imagine stepping in the place of Abraham, only to critique and challenge him. Few cross the gender lines so that they can stand "in the place" of Isaac. Still fewer challenge in principle the necessity for a cross-cultural *urtext* that apparently has established filicide (n.b.: not ritual sacrifice) as the cornerstone of all monotheistic traditions (Freudianism not excluded) or the need for self-sacrifice, by either male or female protagonists.[36]

It is this *range* of female voices that is of interest here. Two contemporary variations on the aqedah may illustrate how broad the range of women's positions on this issue can be. These variations made their way into two very different works of fiction by two quite diverse female authors of the 1990s: the young author Orly Castel-Bloom (1960–), then Israel's new literary bête noire, and the seasoned author Shulamith Hareven (1930–2003), then at the height of her career as a writer and cultural commentator.

As if answering the 1980s' poetic chorus of mourning mothers, in *Dolly City*,[37] a bold postmodernist dystopia, Castel-Bloom used a *mother* to deconstruct the aqedah alongside other foundational Zionist utopias. In her rewriting, however, the major Jewish/Israeli paradigm is entrusted to the hands of a mother who is no less a "compulsive normative ritualist" and no less a "manic" performer of her share of the ancient rite than were earlier *paternal* enactors of sacrifice in the work of *male* writers—such as novelists A. B. Yehoshua and Amos Oz and scholar Shlomo Shoham.[38] Moreover, in contrast to feminist expectations, the maternal as fashioned by Castel-Bloom does not offer any mending of the deficient paternity exemplified by both old and modern rewritings of the aqedah and other filicidal narratives. On the contrary, in the Kafkaesque parody produced by Castel-Bloom, it is precisely due to excessive and obsessive maternal care that a male infant ends up on the operation table, cut to small pieces in a monstrous effort to guarantee his well-being. Not to worry: the infant does survive, but only after the author has made her gruesome point. What the point is exactly is debatable, but at least one reading may be that maternal instincts do *not* exempt their possessors from aggressive handling of their progeny or excuse them of responsibility for risking the next generation's life.

By contrast, in Hareven's biblical novella *After Childhood*,[39] an aqedah, a son sacrifice *nearly* enacted by a father (just as in Genesis 22), is presented as one of the Western sources of *male* violence. And whereas Castel-Bloom made up a *futuristic* fantasy, Hareven invented a different *ancient past*. In this Israelite past, she tested the validity of son sacrifice in the "morning after" the great adventures, the journey in the wilderness and the conquest of the land. It is within this tough quasi-historical reality that Hareven made up—for the first time in her career as a writer—a matriarch, Moran, who deliberately *refuses to partake in male pursuit of power*, be it earthly or divine. Thus, while her husband, the victim of the aborted aqedah of this story, is constantly on the lookout for military might, Moran refuses to join him on such adventures. When he invites her to partake in the conquest of a deserted but "well-protected" fort, she boldly states: "If her master wished, he could visit her at home. She had four small children. The trip was too much for her."[40] The demarcation lines seem to be quite tightly drawn here. Motherhood and male escapades do not mix. The male protagonist predictably meets his death in the deceptively well-protected fort, whereas the mother continues in her quest, preserving the life of sons and vines.

What are we to make of these presumably contradictory representations of the crucible of maternity and violence, of the role of contemporary "Mothers Sarah" in the sacrifice of sons to the Molochs of past or future "states of exception"?[41] What light do these small samples shed on the popular attribution to women qua mothers of a "different (moral) voice" (Carol Gilligan) and "maternal thinking" (Sarah Ruddick)? Or on Julia Kristeva's diametrically opposite conjecture that women have a special proclivity to political and religious extremism precisely because of "maternal masochism"? Moreover, would *any* essentialist generalization about women's *and men's* attitudes toward their national sacrifice, and through it to the great existential questions of peace and war, violence and pacifism, and other hoary binaries, pass the test of the historical and literary record?

My answer is negative, as can be surmised. To further illustrate my point, I conclude with three brief examples from the Israeli corpus. The first is Shin Shifra's terse poem "Isaac," hardly remembered today. Published in her 1962 book *Woman's Verse*, its bold critique conflates Cain, Abraham, and a contemporary Sarah, thus anticipating by some three decades Castel-Bloom's excessive Dolly, as well as a host of other challenges penned by male authors since the late 1960s:

> No ram was caught in the thicket
> for me.
> I bound
> and slaughtered.
> God had no respect unto me—
> He laughed.[42]

My second example is Michal Govrin's 1995 novel *The Name*.[43] In this intriguing novel, the author's first, it is a *daughter*, rather than a mother, who challenges the traditionally cherished trope of religious and national sacrifice/victim. She does this through a long odyssey in which she barely overcomes her obsession with the family secret, the memory of the Shoah, only to be allured by a no-less-obsessive, erotically charged orthodox ritual of self-sacrifice. Govrin leads her protagonist, however, toward the ability of saying *no*, of refusing the sanctified giving up of life expected of her, both as a Jew and as a woman.

Finally, I close with a fictional mother, recently imagined by a *male* author, David Grossman. In his haunting novel *To the End of the Land*,[44] it is the mother who both brings her son to the altar, so to speak (the army assembly point before a military campaign), and runs away to the end of the land in protest and in refusal to fulfill the Israeli maternal role of waiting and mourning. She not only rejects biblical tropes of sacrifice in general, mocking "parents and brothers and girlfriends, even grandparents, bringing their loved ones to the seasonal operation, she thinks, a final sale, a young lad in every car, *first-fruit offering* [*bikkurim*], a *spring carnival* climaxing in human sacrifice" (98), she also scorns herself, as a contemporary Sarah, for *participating* in the aqedah proper: "And how about you, she tells herself off, look at yourself, how politely and orderly you are bringing here your *almost-only son*, the one you love terribly, and *Ishmael* drives you in his taxicab" (ibid.; emphases added). Moreover, in my reading, her refusal is targeted at the Christological Marian proposition as well. By fleeing from the (ostensibly good) tidings (*boraḥat mibesora*, as in the Hebrew title), she plays an anti-Mary role, rejecting the annunciation of the future sacrificial lamb. I guess it is not by accident that the author suggests, behind her back, that she has *unknowingly* marked her son as an offering by naming him *Ofer* (Hebrew for "Bambi" but also a homonym for the verb "to offer") (331).

In summation, I believe that the publication date of Grossman's novel (2008) obviates, or at least complicates, the laments sounded recently by scholars over the erosion of the status of the Bible in Hebrew culture and literature. True, the Bible came under severe scrutiny in the aftermath of the 1967 and 1973 wars that engendered a new Israeli geopolitical map of extreme internal polarization. Divided along ideological, political, religious, and territorial lines, contemporary Israel is also split over its cultural and biblical heritage. While right-wing religious nationalists see themselves as the rightful contemporary heirs of divine authority embodied in the "sacred" canon, left-wing "liberals" of both religious and secular convictions contest their opponents' claim for exclusively holding the "correct" interpretation of the Bible and reject the latter's view of the Bible as an absolute moral authority.

The erosion in the Bible's status has manifested itself in the wars fought in the Israeli education system (e.g., how much Bible should be taught to grammar- and high-school students?),[45] as well as in the academic study of biblical archeology. However, the furor and public attention lavished on these "wars" in Israel (as these lines are being written, a four-page article on the latest biblical dig appears in the holiday magazine of the daily newspaper *Ha'aretz*) raise doubts about this alleged erosion.[46] Apparently, despite nominal appearances, the Hebrew Bible still carries weight, and its moral authority still counts, even for secular Israelis. Otherwise, why all the sound and the fury?

NOTES

1. Max Brod, *Ḥayei Meriva*, trans. from the 1960 German ed. by Y. Sal'ee (Jerusalem: Hasifriya hatzionit, 1967), 282.

2. Anita Shapira, "The Bible and Israeli Identity," in "Recreating the Canon: The Biblical Presence in Modern Hebrew Literature and Culture," guest ed. Nehama Aschkenasy, special issue, *AJS Review* 28, no. 1 (2004): 23.

3. Robert Alter, *Canon and Creativity: Modern Writing and the Authority of Scripture* (New Haven: Yale University Press, 2000), 21.

4. Ibid., 21.

5. Ibid., 32, 35, 39.

6. Ibid., 48–49.

7. Anthony D. Smith, *The Ethnic Origins of Nations* (Oxford, UK: Blackwell, 1986).

8. Anthony D. Smith, *Ha'umah bahistoria* [The Nation in History], trans. Aya Broyer (Jerusalem: Historical Society of Israel, 2003), 84.

9. Ruth Kartun-Blum, *Profane Scriptures: Reflections on the Dialogue with the Bible in Modern Hebrew Poetry* (Cincinnati: Hebrew Union College Press, 1999).

10. "Recreating the Canon," ed. Aschkenasy, special issue, *AJS Review* 28:1 (2004).

11. David Jacobson, *Modern Midrash: The Retelling of Traditional Jewish Narratives by Twentieth-Century Hebrew Writers* (Albany: SUNY Press, 1986).

12. Gershon Shaked, "Modern Midrash: The Biblical Canon and Modern Hebrew Literature," in "Recreating the Canon," ed. Aschkenasy, special issue, *AJS Review* 28:1 (2004): 61.

13. For more on these issues, see the introduction to my recent book, *Glory and Agony: Isaac's Sacrifice and National Narrative* (Stanford: Stanford University Press, 2010).

14. Malka Shaked, *I Will Play You Forever: The Bible in Modern Hebrew Poetry*, 2 vols. (Tel Aviv: Yediot Aharonot, 2005). Another example is the popularity of Meir Shalev's humorous contemporary spin-offs on the Bible: *Tanakh Akhshav* [The Bible Now] (Tel Aviv: Schocken Books, 1985), erroneously touted as "the *first* secular midrash" on the Hebrew Bible, and his recent *Bereshit: Beginnings in the Bible* (in Heb.) (Tel Aviv: Am Oved, 2008).

15. See my *No Room of Their Own: Gender and Nation in Israeli Women's Fiction* (New York: Columbia University Press, 1999) and "'A People That Dwells Alone?' Toward Subversion of the Fathers' Tongue in Israeli Women's Fiction," in "Recreating the Canon," ed. Aschkenasy, special issue, *AJS Review* 28:1 (2004): 83–103.

16. Shalom Spiegel, *The Last Trial: On the Legends and Lore of the Command to Abraham to Offer Isaac as a Sacrifice: The Akedah*, trans. Judah Goldin (New York: Behrman House, 1967).

17. Paradigmatically, no diachronic order is necessarily intended here.

18. For full details and a tracing of the Russian Orthodox roots of this expression, see Feldman, *Glory and Agony*, chap. 1.

19. Y. Lamdan, "*Aqud*" (Bound), in *In the Triple Harness* (Berlin: Shtibel, 1930), 30–31. All translations from the Hebrew are mine, unless otherwise stated.

20. Ibid.; emphasis added.

21. "*Al hamizbe'aḥ*" (On the Altar), in ibid, 30–31. Cf. Lamdan's "*nafshil eifo dumam tzavar al hamizbe'ah*" to the Aramaic *Targum* (translation) of Gen. 22. In modern Hebrew poetry, these self-immolating gestures had become emblematic of Jewish martyrdom: cf. Bialik's famous lines, "to go joyfully to their death, / *to stretch out their necks* / to every honed knife, / to every raised axe," in his 1898 poem "If You Wish to Know," in *H. N. Bialik: Shirim 1890–1898*, ed. Dan Miron (Tel Aviv: Dvir, 1983), 405.

22. S. Y. Agnon, *Tmol shilshom* (1946), translated by Barbara Harshav as *Only Yesterday* (Princeton: Princeton University Press, 2000).

23. S. Y. Agnon, *Oreaḥ nata lalun* (1939; repr., Tel Aviv: Schocken Books, 1975). Agnon's later works abound with rather traditional uses of the aqedah, e.g., *Ha'esh veha'etzim* (Tel Aviv: Schocken Books, 1971) and *Hadom vekisse* [Footrest and (Royal) Seat], in *Lifnim min haḥoma* [Inside the City Walls] (Tel Aviv: Schocken Books, 1976).

24. H. Gouri, "*Yerusha*," in *Shoshanat haruḥot* [The Rosette Compass] (Tel Aviv: Hakibbutz Hameuchad, 1960), 28; idem, "Inheritance," in *Words in My Lovesick Blood*, trans. and ed. Stanley F. Chyet (Detroit: Wayne State University Press, 1996), 27.

25. M. Shamir, "A Prelude to a Story," *Massa* (Sept. 7, 1953).

26. S. Yizhar, *Yemei Ziklag* (1958; repr., Tel Aviv: Am Oved, 1970), 2:804.

27. A. Ashman, *Ha'adamah hazot* (Tel Aviv: Bimot Hovevim Association of the Histadrut Center for Culture and Education, n.d.).

28. A. B. Yehoshua, *Mr. Mani*, trans. Hillel Halkin (New York: Doubleday, 1992).

29. See my essay "Between Genesis and Sophocles: Biblical Psychopolitics in A. B. Yehoshua's *Mr. Mani*," in *History and Literature: New Readings of Jewish Texts*, ed. William Cutter and David Jacobson (Providence, RI: Brown University Press, 2002), 451–64; on the trajectory of Yehoshua's flirting with both Oedipus and Isaac, see Feldman, *Glory and Agony*, 21–26, 176–80, 240–42, 284–300, 307–8.

30. Yariv Ben-Aharon, *Haqrav* [The Battle] (Tel Aviv: Am Oved, 1966), 179–80, my emphasis. It was to take Ben-Aharon a quarter of a century to have the protagonist of his next novel actually make good on his wishes in his novel *Peleg* (Tel Aviv: Ophir, 1993).

31. Amos Oz, "The Way of the Wind," in *Where the Jackals Howl*, trans. Nicholas de Lange (New York: HBJ, 1981).

32. A. B. Yehoshua, *Three Days and a Child*, trans. Miriam Arad (New York: Doubleday, 1970), 53–129; see Feldman, *Glory and Agony*, 178–80, 312.

33. Yehoshua, "Postscript: Undoing the Aqedah by Acting It Out," in *Bakivun hanegdi* [In the Counter Direction: Essays on *Mr. Mani*], ed. Nitza Ben-Dov (Tel Aviv: Hakibbutz Hameuchad, 1995), 394–98 [in Heb.]; cf. his "From Myth to History," in "Recreating the Canon," ed. Aschkenasy, special issue, *AJS Review* 28:1 (2004): 210. See Feldman, *Glory and Agony*, 21–25, 291, 297.

34. See my "On the Cusp of Christianity: Virgin Sacrifice in Pseudo-Philo and Amos Oz," *JQR* 97 (2007): 379–415; Feldman, *Glory and Agony*, chap. 4.

35. For detailed analyses, see Feldman, *Glory and Agony*, chaps. 1, 3, 5.

36. Ibid., chap. 6.

37. O. Castel-Bloom, *Dolly City*, trans. Dalya Bilu (London: Loki, 1997).

38. See Yehoshua's *Mr. Mani*; Oz's "Upon This Evil Earth" (an expanded version of "Wild Man") in *Where the Jackals Howl*, trans. Nicholas de Lange (New York: HBJ, 1981), 168–217; and psychologist Shlomo Shoham's essay "The Isaac

Syndrome," *American Imago* 33 (1976): 329–49; see also Feldman, *Glory and Agony*, 264–69.

39. Shulamith Hareven, *After Childhood*, trans. Hillel Halkin (San Francisco: Mercury House, 1996).

40. Ibid., 57–58, 178.

41. Allusions are to three male authors of very different colors: Martin Buber, Shlomo Shoham, and Giorgio Agamben.

42. Shin Shifra, "Isaac," in *Shir Isha* [Woman's Verse] (Tel Aviv: Mahbarot Lesifrut, 1962). In my translation, I use a King James locution to highlight the allusion to the biblical source.

43. Michal Govrin, *The Name*, trans. Barbara Harshav (New York: Riverhead Books, 1998).

44. David Grossman, *Isha boraḥat mibesora* (Jerusalem: Hakibbutz Hameuchad, 2008), translated by Jessica Cohen as *To the End of the Land* (New York: Knopf, 2010). Further quotations from this book are my translation of the original Hebrew edition and are cited in the text.

45. See, most recently, Yairah Amit, *The Rise and Fall of the Biblical Empire in the Israeli Educational System* (Even Yehudah, Israel: Rekhes, 2011).

46. Add to this scholarly publications on the topic not mentioned earlier, e.g., Nitza Ben-Dov, *Unhappy/Unapproved Loves: Erotic Frustration, Art and Death in the Fiction of S. Y. Agnon* (Tel Aviv: Am Oved, 1997); David Fishelov, *Machlefot Shimshon (Samson's Locks): The Transformations of Biblical Samson* (Tel Aviv: Haifa University Press and Zmora Bitan, 2000); Vered Shemtov, "The Bible in Contemporary Israeli Literature: Text and Place in Zeruya Shalev's *Husband and Wife* and Michal Govrin's *Snapshots*," *Hebrew Studies* 47 (2006): 363–84.

Chapter 17

Scripture and Israeli Secular Culture

Yair Zakovitch

"In the beginning was the word," was the book—the Hebrew Bible, which provides the foundation of our being. On that foundation Jews built, layer upon layer, the cultural house of the people of Israel: translations of the Bible, the apocrypha and pseudepigrapha, Jewish-Hellenistic literature, all the genres of rabbinic literature from all its periods both in aggadah and halacha, ancient liturgical poetry from the land of Israel (*piyyut*), each layer both feeding from the Bible and returning to illuminate it. Israel's culture is like a many-branched tree, heavy with fruit, whose trunk is the Bible and whose roots reach immeasurable depths.

And then one day an axe was raised and the branches lopped off, leaving only the tree's trunk, the Bible. In the late nineteenth and early twentieth centuries, secular Jews in Europe came to associate rabbinic literature with narrow-minded orthodoxy. In particular, secular Zionists in the early twentieth century wished to disassociate themselves from the *shtetl*, from the life of traditional Jews in eastern Europe, which they identified with rabbinic Judaism and rabbinic texts. The Jewish library that had been written since the sealing of the Bible until the modern age was cast away, disregarded like an object of no value. Haim Nahman Bialik mourned the rejection of the Jewish library in his poem "Lifnei Aron Ha-sfarim" (In Front of the Bookcase):

> Do you still remember?—I have not forgotten
> In an attic, inside a deserted *beit midrash*
> I was the last of the last
> on my lips fluttered and died a prayer of the forefathers,
> before my eyes the eternal flame was extinguished.[1]

The hand that severed the Jewish tree of knowledge left a void between the biblical period and our own and built an unsteady bridge across the vast abyss. What moved the axe bearers to forgo the writings of generations and to hold to the Bible alone? The beginnings of an answer can be traced to the time of the Enlightenment, to the aspiration of Jews to establish their culture on the component it shared with the surrounding Christian society,[2] to renounce the old image of the Jew, the world of the *heder* and the yeshiva, and to erect in its place a new Jew who jumped directly through time from the biblical period to the modern day.

The Zionist movement was happy to assume the ideal of this new-old Jew who had returned to the ancestral land to live a healthy and ethical life and who drew sustenance from that land through the sweat of his or her brow. (The Zionist movement was dedicated to reestablishing a Jewish homeland in the biblical land of Israel, from which the Jews had been exiled almost two thousand years previously. It sought to transform Jews from a weak, bookish people and a community of petty merchants to a people who worked the soil and who would have their own national identity in their historical land.) This new-old Jew, who had embraced the Zionist ideology, no longer speaking the languages of other nations or living under foreign rule, had returned to the language of his people and would reclaim sovereignty over the land, unprecedented since biblical times.[3]

This Jewish Zionist aspiration coincided with the romantic Christian view of the Holy Land and its inhabitants and with its longing for the Orient and for days of old. Rabbinic law was viewed as a barrier that stood between the new Jew and his land and was therefore disregarded, its roots in biblical law failing to awaken feelings of affinity. The new Jew in the land of Israel preferred to identify with prophets preaching social justice rather than with Leviticus's laws concerning sacrifices. Indeed, the relationship between the Zionist ideal and Protestant biblical criticism, which differentiated between Israelite and Jew (the Israelite being from the First Temple period, with roots deep in the land, the Jew an exile of a later and lesser era) is fascinating. Christian biblical criticism fed from Christian sources, which exalt prophecy over the Pentateuch's laws.

Socialist, secular Zionism in its extreme form went so far as to demand that the Bible conform to its beliefs and ideology. The confrontation between Saul and Samuel, for instance, was viewed by Moshe Sister of HaShomer HaTzair (an extreme left-wing, if not Marxist, Zionist youth movement) as a struggle between an ideologically progressive, secular leader and a religious reactionary.[4] Here we glimpse the chasm between

Christians and secular Zionists. In Israel, the Bible made its way from the realm of the holy to the temporal, becoming an earthly Bible devoid of heaven. If the Bible is a story of a nonequilateral triangle whose sides represent the people of Israel, the land of Israel, and the God of Israel, the triangle's longest side, God, for the secular Zionists, had faded from the story (similar to God's disappearance at that time from the kibbutz movement's Passover haggadah).

The generations born in the land of Israel sought to "live with the Bible," as in the title of a book by Moshe Dayan (the first child born at Kibbutz Deganya and later a legendary Israeli general and politician),[5] and gazed at its views through biblical lenses, as Yigal Allon (another legendary general and politician in early Israel) poetically did in *My Father's House*:

> Under the influence of the biblical stories, a new dimension was added to my hikes on Mt. Tabor, known to me from the day I first opened my eyes. Of course, nothing was diminished from its concrete reality. The church structures continued to billow on its peak, foreign, not my own, but now when I climbed up, or when I slid down, there rose up before me the great deeds of Deborah and Barak the son of Abinoam; here, I would say to myself, here stood, then, ten thousand men from the tribes of Naphtali and Zebulun . . . ; wandering on the Gilboa or its environs brought to my mind the life, glorious heroism, and death of Saul and Jonathan; and, as if to complete the tragic picture, from the window of my home I could see the Arab village Ein Dor, and before me: the saddened King Saul, most beloved of all Israel's kings, to me. More than once, finding ourselves in Ein Dor, we looked, wordlessly, for the hut of the ghost-consulting woman of En-dor.[6]

The Zionist secularization of the Bible, with its earthly emphasis and the negation of the Diaspora, provided fertile ground for the creation of a movement of secular Israelis in the 1950s who called themselves "the Canaanites." "We are Hebrews and not Jews," claimed the Canaanites, recalling the Christian distinction between Israel and Judaism. It is an amusing paradox that it was Canaanism—which suckled from the Bible's breast—that granted legitimacy to idolatry, the Bible's most hated adversary.[7]

More recently, a dramatic change has occurred in the secular Jewish-Israeli society's culture and in its relation to the Bible. We, Israel's secular Jews, severed the umbilical cord that connected us to the Bible.[8] Many factors have contributed to this change, which has become more and more evident in the past few decades:

a. During the time that the Bible's primacy went unchallenged, the Holocaust was left, awkward and shamefaced, in a dark corner. Gradually, however, the Holocaust emerged from its hiding place, slowly settling into our lives and pushing the Bible off to the side. As we see from the overflowing bookshelves of Holocaust volumes published in Hebrew, the kingdom of the Bible made way for the kingdom of the Holocaust: it would seem that two founding myths cannot dwell together under one roof. The Holocaust, which confronts religious thought with horrendous challenges, was adopted by a secular Israel that desired security in safe borders, not necessarily those promised by God in the Bible. These Israelis believe in the security of nuclear —not divine—power.[9]
b. The *Tanakh*, the pillar of fire for the Zionist immigration movement, no longer illuminates the path among contemporary Israelis, many of whom take for granted living in their own land. The Bible, the model for renewing Jewish sovereignty in the land of Israel, no longer finds listeners among those born into a sovereign state that has already existed more than sixty years. Our generation, which avoids outright calls to aliyah and no longer looks disparagingly at those who leave Israel, now presupposes this lack of interest in the Bible.
c. The ultimate guide for those who cultivate the land and pasture flocks, the *Tanakh* no longer speaks to the hearts of modern Israeli society. Early Zionists exalted the Jew who left the yeshiva to build roads and farm the land. But today the people who work construction in Israel are likely to be Arabs or Romanian guest-workers, and few Israeli live on farms. What has the Bible to do with the antivirus software and microchips for which the Israeli economy has become famous?
d. The Bible is not the story of the individual; rather, it tells the history of a *people*, "the history of Jacob." In our age that worships the individual, there is no room for the voice of nationalism, and not much hope for the literature of the Bible, which is rooted in a sense of communal responsibility, in the notion that all Israel is responsible for one another.
e. Now that the illusion of Israel's unity has grown faint, we no longer need the conception of the romantic Orient, the East of the patriarchs that was supposed to provide a common denominator, a single origin for all Israel. Now that the fire in the melting pot has cooled, ethnic identities of Jews who immigrated to Israel from Yemen, Morocco, Iraq, Poland, Ukraine, and dozens of other places are being

rehabilitated, the tribes taking pride in their diverse origins outside of Israel and not in those inside the Land of the Patriarchs and in the literature of that land, that is, the Bible. Today, authentic Arab-like music has replaced the pseudo-Bedouin melodies that were written by composers who immigrated from Polish villages.

The break between the Bible and secular Judaism was reinforced by the rift between secular and religious Jews over parliamentary coalitions, battles over Sabbath observance and kashruth laws, and military service, especially following the Yom Kippur War of 1973, after the euphoria following the Six-Day War of 1967 settled. An abyss opened between settlers who followed the ideology of reclaiming all of the biblical land of Israel, who believed that the beginning of the Redemption was at hand, and secular Jews, particularly those who supported the peace movement, who do not aspire to the borders of the biblical promise and who fear any manifestation of messianic ideology. The strength of the religious messianic camp, which appears smug with self-confidence, as though it owns a monopoly on Judaism, distanced large portions of the non-Orthodox population from the Bible and Jewish literary sources. The non-Orthodox pulled away from the Jewish library as though proclaiming, "If this is the true Judaism, then we want no part of it. 'To your tents, O Israel.'"[10]

Many among the secular public become anxious in light of those who draw a direct line between the Bible and contemporary life, who interpret the Bible with a new, "current events" interpretation. I will mention only one example, and not the worst: a man who recently phoned in to a radio talk show, offering a "Jewish solution" for dealing with Arab terrorism. The caller emotionally recited three verses from Judges (1:5–7) about the severing of fingers and toes of Adoni-bezek, the king of Bezek, and of his death in Jerusalem.

The Israeli army gives a Bible to each of its soldiers, as it did forty years ago. It is the same Bible, from "In the beginning" to "and let him go up" (2 Chronicles 36:23), but the attached preface has changed, as Yaron Ezrachi has noted. In the 1950s, the chief army rabbi, Shlomo Goren, presented the Bible as a "spring of heroism and salvation," as "the supreme source of inspiration," and "eternal memory," a spiritual message befitting all. In a recent introduction by the chief army rabbi Gad Navon, the Bible has become the "document that grants ownership to our land, the land of our forefathers." To this copy of the Bible has been attached a map "of the Promised Land of the covenant between the pieces."[11] The meaning is clear, if not pleasant, to all who hear it: this Bible belongs to one faction, the faction that has recently claimed exclusive rights not only to the whole biblical land of Israel but also to the Bible.

In spite of all this, a return to the Bible is possible in our generation, but from a place of maturity and lowered expectations. We must recognize that the Bible can no longer serve as the center of an addictive national identification; it cannot provide ready-made answers to questions regarding our existence. Although our relation to the Bible is a familial one, it is a distant relative, an ancient relation that was not written with our generation in mind, and we cannot disregard the thousands of years that separate us in order to embrace it.

What is it that causes us to view the Bible as alien and strange?[12] The Bible is a religious document in which God plays the central role. For many Jews in Israel, God is not present, so that much of the Bible seems meaningless. A Jew for whom God does not fill a central role, or even any role —a Jew who does not believe—remains oblivious to a significant dimension in this literature; participation in religious rituals is likewise not a part of his or her life. Moreover, it is not only the worship of God that is alien to the secular Israeli. The whole notion of a relationship between humanity and God—an elemental feature in biblical literature—is likewise incomprehensible. Like someone blind from birth who knows not what color is, or someone born deaf who has never heard music, thus is the secular Jew precluded from grasping the depth of the religious experience, even if he or she makes a concerted effort to trace its roots.

Many subjects that the Bible addresses are not relevant to secular life: offering sacrifices, dietary laws, the war against idolatry. Quite a few topics may even offend us, such as the fundamental premise that God's rule in the world is a just one or the idea of Israel being the chosen people. What is more, the Bible's value system, as a whole, is not necessarily one in whose light I wish to live my life or educate our youth. Take, for example, the book of Joshua. How are we to identify with the policy of total extermination (*herem*) to which Jericho was condemned? "They exterminated everything in the city with the sword: man and woman, young and old, ox and sheep and ass. . . . They burned down the city and everything in it" (Joshua 6:21–24). Other inhabitants of Canaan did not fare much better, as apparent from the number of dead in the battle at Ai (see Joshua 8:22–29). It is equally difficult to read about Joshua's treatment of the five kings whom he captured in a cave at Makkedah and had impaled on five stakes (Joshua 10:24–26).

To be sure, many of us feel more comfortable reading Judges than Joshua, since Joshua relates the conquest of a land that is inhabited by another people, though it was promised by God to Israel's patriarchs. In Judges, on the other hand, all of Israel's wars constitute their defending the land from enemies who were brought by God to punish Israel for straying after idols (Judges 2:13–16). The book of Judges is the expression of our guilt feelings: each Israelite victory is proof of God's mercy, evidence of God granting another opportunity to Israel to cling to God and follow in His ways.

Turning to the topic of returning to the land, we feel more comfortable with the return to Zion from Babylonian exile than we do with the return from Egyptian servitude, since the return from Babylon was accompanied by many hardships and difficult tests that sprung from the unworthy behavior of Israel's enemies: "When Sanballat and Tobiah, and the Arabs, the Ammonites, and the Ahdodites heard that healing had come to the walls of Jerusalem, that the breached parts had begun to be filled, it angered them very much, and they all conspired together to come and fight against Jerusalem and to throw it into confusion" (Nehemiah 4:1–2). We readily identify with Nehemiah's response, a combination of construction and defense: "From that day on, half my servants did work and half held lances and shields, bows and armor. . . . Those building the wall and the basket-carriers were burdened, doing work with one hand while the other held a weapon" (ibid., vv. 10–11).

It was thus no coincidence that when the minister of education at the time of the founding of the state, Ben-Zion Dinur, sought to shape the observance of erev Yom Ha-Atzmaut (the evening of Israel's Independence Day) as a seder like on Passover eve, a family ritual to be observed around the holiday table that would be set, in this case, with the "Holiday Reader for Independence Day Meal,"[13] the "haggadah" that celebrated the miracle of Israel's resurrection in its land and the establishment of the state contained no references to Joshua. The biblical style of the reader harbors echoes of Nehemiah's language, not Joshua's: "And they have come from all the countries to revive the Land and to inherit it, and our enemies have conspired against us, and they rose against us, together, to fall upon us and to stop us from our work. From that day on half our servants did work and half held weapons and the night was for guarding and the day for work."[14]

The question of which biblical texts we feel more comfortable with is, in the end, irrelevant, since it would be disturbing were a book (or, really, library), written over two thousand years ago, to reflect contemporary beliefs and views. Has the world frozen? Has it ceased changing in the past two thousand years? Have not whole realms of thought developed since the Bible's composition? Have contacts between the culture of Israel and other world cultures not left their marks on our worldview? We live in a dynamic, changing, developing world, and in the light of the transformations in it, we find ourselves reevaluating each day—indeed, every hour—our positions, beliefs, and values. It is unreasonable to expect that we would now make our way by a torch lit on our path some three thousand years ago.

It is imperative for readers to recognize, therefore, that the Bible was not written in order to express *their* values. We are neither the Bible's censors nor its spokespeople. The distance between the Bible and ourselves is vast; if we want to understand what is written in it, we must not engage in apologetics, nor must we ignore those parts that repulse us or try to manipulate or interpret them in ways that do not do them justice. We must study the Bible and try to appreciate it in the context of its time, against the background of the cultural life of its period and the abundance of worldviews it expresses. Written over roughly a thousand years, the Bible does not reflect a monolithic ideology. Over the centuries of its composition, ideological and philosophical changes left their marks. Even in any one generation, not everybody shared a single worldview.

A mindfulness of the historical context in which Joshua was written will explain to us why its writers adhered to ideas that awaken such opposition in us today. The Bible was the manifesto of the monotheistic revolution, which shook the most basic foundations of belief; it was a revolution that required, first of all, persuading the Israelites that they shared nothing with the surrounding people, with the culture or religion of Canaan. It was precisely the close relations between Israel and Canaan—between their language and ours, their literary patterns and ours, and, to a significant extent, also their religion and ours—that required a path that would set out a clear boundary, a high wall between us and them. This, by the way, is the reason why the law was given to Israel not when they already inhabited their land, when they were in close proximity to the Canaanites, but rather in the wilderness, in a cultural vacuum with no other people around—all to teach us that our laws are different and our religion is different from every other people's.[15] It is the fear of idolatry that lies behind the idea of the *herem* —total extermination—as it is described in Deuteronomy:

> When the Lord God brings you to the land that you are about to enter and possess, and He dislodges many nations before you . . . and you defeat

them, you must doom them to destruction: grant them no terms and give them no quarter. You shall not intermarry with them: do not give your daughters to their sons or take their daughters for your sons. For they will turn your children away from Me to worship other gods, and the Lord's anger will blaze forth against you and He will promptly wipe you out. Instead, this is what you shall do to them: you shall tear down their altars, smash their pillars, cut down their sacred posts, and consign their images to the fire. (Deuteronomy 7:1–5)

The book of Joshua carries out the commands set out in Deuteronomy, when it relates how the whole land is conquered and almost all its inhabitants destroyed in order that the people of Israel will not come into contact with idol worshipers and will not, therefore, be tempted.[16] The reader who comprehends the fear of idolatry that created this picture of Israel's complete and utter capture of the land will not identify with that ideology today—the danger of idolatry no longer threatens—and will not shy away from teaching those chapters from Joshua against the backdrop of its time and the crisis that birthed the notion of complete destruction. As it happens, not even all the pages of Joshua are captive to the notion of the complete conquest. Chapters 13–17 express a different notion, as we see from the opening of that literary unit: "Joshua was now old, advanced in years. The Lord said to him, 'You have grown old, you are advanced in years; and very much of the land still remains to be taken possession of'" (13:1).[17]

Paradoxically, anyone brave enough to acknowledge the vast distance that exists between the Bible and ourselves makes him- or herself available to feel closer to it. We must not ignore the religious dimension: the Bible without God is like Hamlet without the Prince of Denmark. That said, by removing the coating of sanctity that has been pressed onto the Bible, the courageous reader is suddenly able to extend his or her arm to touch the human document.

The Torah speaks in human language. It was written by people for the sake of people, and any reader who sits before this human creation can marvel at the artistry, at the clarity and conciseness of a short story in Genesis, the emotional depth of a poem in Song of Songs, and the sophisticated rhetoric and moral profundity of a chapter of prophecy. Indeed, even a prophet who opens his words with "thus sayeth the Lord" frames his message in his own style. Each prophet was a human being, a poet, and a talented and experienced rhetor who gives voice to ideas he wants to impart to his listeners or readers. A reader who is overwhelmed with reverence for the Bible's sanctity, who cannot see the human document, will miss the humor that spills from the pages. The devout reader will fail to notice how the story of the prostitute Rahab (Joshua 2) is mocking Joshua, who, dispatching two inexperienced spies to Jericho, seeks human assistance despite the fact that divine salvation was already promised him (in chapter 1) and who, in the end, learns his lesson only through Rahab, the prostitute who knew enough to quote from the Song of the Sea (Exodus 15:15–16) in her words, "dread of you has fallen upon us, and all the inhabitants of the land are quaking before you" (Joshua 2:9). Joshua should have known to do what was clear to the small-time Jericho prostitute: to rely on God rather than placing his faith in spies.[18]

The story of the origins of the Moabites and Ammonites (Genesis 19:30–38) is, in fact, an Israelite joke that derides those nations as having descended from a union tainted with scandalous incest. It is comparable to the story of Judah and Tamar (Genesis 38), a tale that originated in the kingdom of Ephraim (the Northern Kingdom), which recounts the shameful origins of David from the tribe of Judah and the House of Perez. Genesis 38 traces Perez's conception to an incestuous encounter and intimates even more: by recounting how, during the birth, Perez steals the firstborn status from his twin brother, the story insinuates that, following a "like father like son" pattern, David likewise stole the kingdom from the House of Saul.[19] Examples of parody are not difficult to find in the Bible: the story of the capture of Saul in order to crown him king (1 Samuel 10:20–21) is based on the tale of the capture of the criminal Achan son of Zerah son of Zabdi of the tribe of Judah in Joshua 7:14–18—this, in order to insinuate that Saul is, himself, a criminal.[20]

Acknowledging the human dimension helps readers to detect how the Bible criticizes—sometimes covertly—its own heroes, patriarchs and prophets included. Because of Abraham's decision to descend to Egypt when there was famine (Genesis 12:10–20), his descendants are punished with slavery in Egypt (as pointed out explicitly by Nahmanides in his commentary on Genesis). Likewise, Elijah's insistent condemnation of Israel before God at Horeb (1 Kings 19), the place where Moses had vigorously defended Israel after the sin of the golden calf (Exodus 32–33), explains why God dismissed Elijah from his duties as prophet: he ceased to qualify for the position.[21]

The courage to acknowledge this criticism, to shake off the aura of sanctity that separates the reader from the text, and to recognize the Bible's covert polemics against its heroes rewards the reader with hidden treasures.[22]

One who reads the Bible as a human document will discern the Bible's lack of unity, along with its many layers, the stages in their development, and the growth of ideas that they document. Take, for example, biblical law. The Bible's law code is not monolithic; it was not all handed to Moses on Mt. Sinai but reflects progressive developments and adaptations to the demands of reality. The law of the remission of debts (Deuteronomy 15:1–11), for instance, was created due to the difficulties that were caused by *shmita*, the Sabbatical Year law (Exodus 23:10–13): in a year during which one is forbidden to cultivate the land, there is no source of income to pay debts. The law forbidding the admission of Ammonites and Moabites into the congregation of Israel (Deuteronomy 23:4) also became untenable in the face of widespread marriages to foreign women. In the end, in the Mishnah, the law was amended, following the path taken in the book of Ruth, which legitimized marriage to Ammonite and Moabite women who accepted Israel's God: "The (male) Ammonite or (male) Moabite are forbidden eternally but their women are allowed immediately" (Mishnah Yebamoth 8.3).

Biblical literature grew from a constant, tension-filled dialogue between various social and ideological circles. Many of the Bible's writings interpret other biblical writings that preceded them in order to adapt them and make them acceptable to the contemporary time and religious world.[23] Of the more famous of these cases of inner-biblical interpretation is the book of Chronicles. Written in the days of the return to Zion from Babylonian exile, Chronicles retells the history of the kingship period that was recorded in Samuel and Kings, thereby reshaping the past according to the attitudes of its time. The Bible is therefore a mirror to a vibrant and busy ideological, religious life, to a constant reconsideration of fundamental questions concerning the individual, the nation, and the world. It reveals how adaptation and development of ideas could occur while nonetheless holding on to the essence: that which is beyond time and place.

Readers not fearful of the collapse of the Bible's supposed unity, who are able to grapple with the variety of ideas and worldviews expressed in it, will hear not only the loud rush of the central currents of biblical thought but also the flowing of smaller rivulets that run quietly, the voices of divergent traditions—such as that which tells how the Israelites practiced idolatry up until the land of Israel was conquered (Joshua 24:14) or another that recounts the giving of the Torah in Shechem (ibid., vv. 25–26). Indeed, distance allows us to draw closer, close enough to distinguish the mosaic stones that constitute the enormous picture. Sensitivity to this intellectual wealth, to the dialogue and tensions within the Bible, proves how similar we are to our ancestors. Like those ancient writers, we, too, think, question, cling to ideas, and then abandon them to espouse others. We, too, hold to certain beliefs—eternal truths—that sometimes clash with contemporary challenges. Just as our ancestors devised various ways to reach a compromise between ideal and reality, so, too, do we.

Realizing the similarity between deliberations of the ancient writers and our own draws us closer to the Bible by forming a bridge over the deep fissure that separates us. Suddenly we become aware that many of the weighty questions with which we struggle were a source of concern in biblical times. Just as we find ourselves grappling with questions of our right to the land of Israel, so, too, did the biblical writers: the stories about the purchase of land parcels in Hebron (Genesis 23), Shechem (Genesis 33:18–20), Jerusalem (2 Samuel 24), and Samaria (1 Kings 16:24) were created in order to make clear that we did not take land illegally, nor did we take it forcefully from its legitimate owners. This is made clear in the midrash: "And he bought the parcel of ground, etc." (Genesis 33:18). R. Judan b. R. Simon said, "This is one of the three places regarding which the nations of the world cannot taunt Israel and say, 'Ye have stolen them.' These are they: The cave of Machpelah, the [site of the] Temple, and the sepulcher of Joseph" (Genesis Rabbah 79).[24] Also the story of the Covenant between the Pieces (Genesis 15) justifies the giving of the land into our hands as a response to the transgressions of its previous inhabitants, "for the iniquity of the Amorites is not yet complete" (v. 16). This story contains a bold hint to the Israelites that if they, too, commit transgressions, the same will happen to them (see also Leviticus 18:28).

We are able to identify with some of the values espoused in the Bible such as mercy—a value that the prophet Jonah, who believes that justice rules all, has difficulty accepting—or with the notion of ultimate, executive responsibility that is voiced in the story of Naboth the Jezreelite (1 Kings 21): although King Ahab did not himself act in order to possess Naboth's vineyard, his wife being the one who presented him with the vineyard as a done deal, nevertheless he is the one accused by the prophet: "Have you murdered and also taken possession?" (v. 19). A king, according to this story, cannot hide behind another's shoulders. Ahab represents the ultimate authority, and he is liable for every action carried out under his rule.[25] The ruler is not above the law but is himself subject to it, as is stressed by Deuteronomy's Law of the King (17:18–20).

The joy of discovering that certain of the Bible's values are among those we, too, hold dear does not need to turn to dismay when we acknowledge that many others are utterly foreign to us. Under no circumstances should we busy ourselves with spinning midrash-like interpretations that trample over verses while lending them meanings that they do not convey, only so that we will feel comfortable with them. Such violent acts are never of any help and will never make readers feel less alienated. We must, from the start, forgo any identification with the Bible and its world. This renunciation in no way means that we also renounce knowledge, understanding, appreciation, or even admiration: admiration for the Bible's glorious kaleidoscope of worldviews and for the artistic vessel into which was poured such creative spirit. The humble reader who is prepared to silence his or her own voice in the presence of the Bible's great chorus, who is prepared to learn what the Bible has and not impose onto it what it has not, is the reader for whom I long.

Until now I have spoken about the study of the Bible itself, emphasizing the dimension of *peshat*. That said, the Bible constitutes the foundation of our experience, not its entirety. A boundless universe spreads out and grows from the Bible—a universe of Jewish texts that emanate from and develop out of the Bible. Indeed, every writer is influenced by the books on his or her bookshelves—works that he or she has read and assimilated and that have become integrated into his or her being—and these come to be expressed, either overtly or covertly, in the writer's own work. Each return to an ancient text is a new one; the hundred and first reading of a work is unlike the hundredth. Every generation, indeed, every person, looks at a verse differently. While their interpretative works should not affect our reading of the biblical *peshat*—we cannot impose our ideologies onto the text—these works are legitimate (and even welcome) works of midrash. To what can this be compared? To the taste of the manna the Israelites ate in the wilderness, about which the midrash tells, "He brought down for them the manna, in which all kinds of flavors lodged, so that each Israelite could taste therein anything he particularly liked" (*Exodus Rabbah* 25:3). The midrash is a continually renewed body that revitalizes the Bible's archaic letters, fertilizes leaves that are worn with age, and returns to endow them with freshness, pertinence, and relevance.

This tradition of a thousand and one readings, a thousand and one interpretations that, once written down, become the basis for further interpretations, which will, in turn, be recorded for future generations, began in the library that is the Bible. The Bible is an interbranching network connecting distant texts and binding them one to another. Writings from various historical periods and literary genres call out to and interpret one another, with the interpreted texts then reflecting back, somewhat altered, from a multitude of mirrors. Poets interpret stories, storytellers interpret poetry, prophets interpret the Pentateuch. No literary unit in the Bible stands alone, isolated and independent, with no other text drawing from its reservoir and, in return, illuminating it with new light.[26]

For the reader of the Bible who is unaware or unfamiliar with this web of internal conversations and who has not the tools to search for and reveal them, a shallow and impoverished reading is guaranteed. Of course, he or she might race through chapters. It is not speed readers that we want, however, but those willing to read slowly, to plow the Bible's verses, turning their soil and revealing the deep layers that reach all the way to the very foundations of our culture.

Every literary unit of the Bible, then, responds to numerous readings: one can read it, if only apparently, on its own, in isolation, but one must read it, too, in connection to literary units from which it feeds and which it interprets. It is worthwhile, moreover, to go even further and to read it through the eyes of the literary units that use it as their starting point and that are in dialogue with it. Indeed, each reading will grant the text that is being examined a new dimension of meaning.[27]

What is true for the multiple meanings of each unit in the Bible is true even more for reading each unit in the ever-expanding context of Jewish literature. The Bible is the reservoir for all the genes in our literary makeup. On each layer that is added to the tower of our literature, we find the imprint of previous layers, and so it goes until the modern age—Haim Nachman Bialik and Shmuel Yosef Agnon, Yehudah Amichai, Moshe Shamir, Nathan Zach, and Meir Shalev.

I have referred to genetics, to a cultural-literary heredity, but the use of metaphors loaned from other fields requires great care: heredity is inevitable and passive. The same cannot be said of a cultural ancestry, of the inheritance of knowledge: this requires constant study. Each generation must study the literature of previous generations if it wants to continue the chain, to inherit and to bequeath. Those who do not learn, who do not reach out to sample some of the wealth, will be unable to offer anything to those who follow. The beginning of this chain of giving is manifested in the well-known saying of the sages at the opening of the wisdom tractate of the Mishna, *Pirkei Abot*: "Moses received the Torah on Sinai and passed it to Joshua, and Joshua to the elders, and the elders to the prophets, and the prophets passed it on to the men of the Great Assembly." The links of literary heredity continue from generation to generation, in Israel and in the

Diaspora, in each and every place that "Jewish" is read and taught, in every place "Jewish" is written.

It is incumbent on us to bequeath to the generations to come, too, the spirit of the canon—a great spirit that grows and spreads, both extending its roots and stretching to new heights. The canonical spirit, the divine spirit that floats above our writings, is what will guarantee the existence of Jewish culture and a Jewish people that lives its culture and expands its inheritance. It is the spirit that promises us a historical memory common to all, a network of associations, a shared Jewish language that makes it possible for each individual to communicate with fellow Jews, even when their worldviews are very different. The ability to communicate is essential; it is the glue that will make connections possible between the secular and the religious (even ultraorthodox) Jew and between Israeli Jews and Jews in the Diaspora. Knowledge of the Bible and the literary sources that flow from it will strengthen also the connection to the land of Israel and will supply answers to skeptics who question why we live in that place. Those who study the Bible and Jewish texts will no longer view themselves as Israeli (since what is an identity based on a sixty-year-old country?) but as Jews whose heritage rests on solid foundations of three millennia of Jewish culture. The people of Israel need another giving of the Law, a Law that is not forced onto them but is received willingly, a Law that teaches of a return to the ancient legacy, the Jewish bookcase.

> Receive my greetings, ancient parchments,
> and desire my mouth's kiss, you who sleep in the dust.
> From sailing to foreign islands, my soul has returned,
> and like a wandering dove, weary-winged and worried,
> will flap again on the entryway to the nest of her youth.[28]

First signs of a recognition of the need to combine biblical studies with the study of Jewish literature that is based on it are apparent, for example, in the coursework in the Department of Bible at the Hebrew University of Jerusalem. In the past, a juvenile fear reigned among Israeli biblical scholars that biblical scholarship in Israel will be too "midrashic-like," and they wanted it to be indistinguishable from the study of Bible in European universities (except for the language of instruction, which, of course, would be Hebrew). Jewish sources, such as the apocryphal and pseudepigraphal literature and rabbinic literature, were not included in classroom considerations. To be sure, medieval exegesis was studied, but separately, within a course specifically dedicated to those sources. Today the situation is entirely changed. Now course listings of the department include such courses as "Ancient Jewish Interpretation," "Biblical Interpretation and the *Pesher* Literature of Qumran," "The Sacrifice of Isaac as Reflected in Early Interpretations," "The Stories of the Prophets in the Bible and in Early Jewish Literature," and "The Pentateuchal Books at Qumran—Rewritings, Interpretation, and Textual Criticism." Moreover, in almost every course that is offered and in discussions about almost every text, there is a marked balance between examining Jewish interpretative traditions throughout the ages and in various genres, and the search for the simple meaning of the verse, the *peshat*, using modern, critical approaches to the Bible.

There is yet another welcome sign of change: Israel's first prime minister, David Ben Gurion, established a Bible study group at his home. The group had its ups and downs, disappearing and then being reborn a number of times in the President's Residence, including during the term of the seventh president, Ezer Weitzman. During that time, it was no longer called the Bible Group but rather the Presidential Residence's Group on Bible and the Sources of Israel (*hug beit hanasi letanakh velemekorot yisrael*). The academic advisers of that group (this author included) made certain that at every meeting, which were dedicated to specific subjects or ideas, one lecture would be on the Bible and another would deal with Jewish sources throughout the ages, thereby demonstrating the continuity that exists in Israel's traditions. These initial steps are not enough. Nonetheless, they encourage hope that the Bible and the Jewish bookcase will indeed return to us if we return to them, first.

NOTES

I have written this chapter from a very personal place, as both a professor of Bible and as an Israeli who was born to socialist parents, Zionist pioneers who rebelled against their religious, eastern European way of life and immigrated to the Land of Israel to participate in the building of the new homeland. My secular parents emphasized the importance of Jewish education and sent me to a school in which Jewish studies were highly valued as the foundation of Israeli Jewish culture and as the justification of our existence in our land.

1. All translations are mine. The original poem can be found in Hayyim Nahman Bialik, *Kol Kitvei H. N. Bialik* (Tel Aviv: Dvir, 1960), 54.

2. See Jacobus Schoneveld, *The Bible in Israeli Education: A Study of Approaches*

to the Hebrew Bible and Its Teaching in Israeli Educational Literature (Assen, Netherlands: Van Gorcum, 1976), 243.

3. See Ben-Tzion Mosinzon, "The Bible in School," *Ha-Hinukh* 1 (1910): 23–32, 110–19 [in Hebrew].

4. Moshe Sister, *Mi-Be'ayot ha-sifrut ha-mikrait* (Tel Aviv: Sifriat Poalim, 1956), 231.

5. Mosheh Dayan, *Living with the Bible* (New York: W. Morrow, 1978).

6. Yigal Allon, *Bet Avi* (Tel Aviv: Hakibbutz Hameuchad, 1976), 30–31. Allon refers to stories told in Judges 4–5; 1 Samuel 31; 1 Samuel 28.

7. See also Anita Shapira, *The Bible and Israeli Identity* (Jerusalem: Magnes, 2005), 19 [in Hebrew].

8. See also Uriel Simon, "The Place of the Bible in Israeli Society: From National Midrash to Existential Peshat," in *Yeriot: Essays and Papers in the Jewish Studies Bearing on the Humanities and the Social Sciences*, ed. E. Reiner, I. Ta-Shma, and G. Ofrat (Jerusalem: Orna Hess, 1999), 7 [in Hebrew].

9. See Tom Segev, *The Seventh Million: The Israelis and the Holocaust* (New York: Holt, 2000), 11. See also Simon, "Place of the Bible," 5.

10. Simon, "Place of the Bible," 31; Shapira, *Bible and Israeli Identity*, 24–27.

11. See Yaron Ezrachi, "Tanakh Be-kippah Srugah," *Ha-aretz*, January 22, 1996, B:2.

12. Moshe Greenberg calls this alienation "obsolescence"; M. Greenberg, *On the Bible and Judaism* (Tel Aviv: Am Oved, 1984), 294–97 [in Hebrew].

13. Ben-Zion Dinur, *Mikra-ei Hag Li-se'udat Yom Ha-atzma'ut* (Jerusalem: Ministry of Education and Culture, 1955).

14. Ibid., 3.

15. Yair Zakovitch, *"And You Shall Tell Your Son . . .": The Concept of the Exodus in the Bible* (Jerusalem: Magnes, 1991), 99–133.

16. Moshe Greenberg, "Herem," in *Encyclopaedia Judaic VIII* (1972), col. 349.

17. Shmuel Ahituv, *Joshua*, Mikra Le-Yisrael (Tel Aviv/Jerusalem: Am Oved/Magnes, 1995), 9 [in Hebrew].

18. See Yair Zakovitch, "Humor and Theology or the Successful Failure of Israelite Intelligence: A Literary Folkloric Approach," in *Text and Tradition: The Hebrew Bible and Folklore*, ed. Susan Niditch (Atlanta: Scholars, 1990), 75–98.

19. Avigdor Shinan and Yair Zakovitch, *The Story of Judah and Tamar* (Jerusalem: Institute of Jewish Studies of the Hebrew University of Jerusalem, 1992), 219–20 [in Hebrew].

20. See Yair Zakovitch, *The Pattern of the Numerical Sequence Three-Four in the Bible* (Jerusalem: Makor, 1977), 132–39 [in Hebrew].

21. See Yair Zakovitch, "A Still Small Voice," *Tarbiz* 52 (1983): 329–46 [in Hebrew].

22. See Yair Zakovitch, "Overt and Covert Conflicts in Biblical Literature," in

Migvan De'ot Ve-hashkafot Be-tarbut Yisra'el 1, ed. D. Keren (Jerusalem: Ministry of Education, 1991), 11–29.

23. The pioneering book on inner-biblical interpretation is Michael Fishbane, *Biblical Interpretation in Ancient Israel* (Oxford: Oxford University Press, 1985).

24. See further Yair Zakovitch, "The Aim of Stories Concerning Land Purchase in the Bible," *Bet Mikra* 24 (1979): 17–20 [in Hebrew].

25. See Yair Zakovitch, "The Tale of Naboth's Vineyard," in *The Bible from Within*, by M. Weiss, 379–405 (Jerusalem: Magnes, 1984).

26. A pioneering and important collection of articles on intertextuality in the Bible is Danna Nolan Fewell, ed., *Reading between Texts—Intertextuality and the Hebrew Bible* (Louisville, KY: Westminster/John Knox, 1996).

27. See Yair Zakovitch, "'Go Up, Bald One, Go Up Bald One'—Exegetical Circles in Biblical Narrative," *Jerusalem Studies in Hebrew Literature* 8 (1985): 7–23 [in Hebrew].

28. This is, again, from "In Front of the Bookcase."

Glossary

aggadah: A rabbinic term referring to nonlegal teachings from the Bible or subsequent Jewish literature, especially narrative or didactic material. All rabbinic teachings are classified as either **halakhah** or **aggadah**. In English, one finds the adjective *aggadic*, referring to teachings of the **aggadah**.
amora'im: See **rabbis, classical**
derash: See **peshat and derash**.
derashah (pl.: **derashot**): A rabbinic homily or sermon.
halakhah: A rabbinic term referring to legal teachings from the Bible or subsequent Jewish literature. All rabbinic teachings are classified as either **halakhah** or **aggadah**. In English, one finds the adjective *halakhic*, which means "pertaining to teachings of **halakhah**."
Hebrew Bible: A term used by modern academic scholars to refer to the anthology known to Christians as "the Old Testament" and to Jews as "the Bible" (or, in Hebrew, **Mikra** or **Tanakh**).
Ḥumash: See **Pentateuch**.
kabbalah (or **qabbalah**): Jewish ritual practices and esoteric teachings from the twelfth century CE and later, pertaining especially to ten manifestations of God (or powers emanating from God) that enter into the created world. Each of these ten embodies or reflects a particular aspect of God, such as Wisdom, Justice, Mercy, or Royalty. (Literally, the Hebrew term means "tradition" or, more precisely, "reception, that which is received.")
Karaites (or **Qaraites**): A group of nonrabbinic Jews who emerged beginning in the late ninth century CE. The Karaites reject rabbinic tradition, claiming to base their beliefs and practices exclusively on the Bible itself. Jews who are not Karaite are called **Rabbanites**.
Masoretic Text (often abbreviated **MT**): The received biblical text in Jewish tradition, accepted by both **Karaite** and **Rabbanite** Jews. The MT contains consonants and vowels, as well as cantillation marks (that is,

musical/syntactic symbols for each word of the Bible, which both show how a sentence is structured and provide the musical notes to be used when chanting biblical texts in synagogue). The MT with its vowels and musical notations crystallized in the ninth and tenth centuries CE; the consonantal text used by the MT crystallized in the second century CE, though consonantal texts of the MT type are known from the Dead Sea Scrolls and thus date back to the second century BCE and perhaps further. Biblical scrolls used in synagogue worship are written only with the consonants; printed editions (and, earlier, manuscripts) used for study contain the MT with its vowels and cantillation. The term *Masoretic* comes from the Hebrew word *Masorah* (literally, "tradition").

midrash (pl.: **midrashim**): A rabbinic interpretation of a biblical passage or verse; also, a collection of such interpretations. Classical midrashim were produced by the **classical rabbis** during the first millennium CE and to some degree the beginning of the second millennium CE.

Mikra (or **Miqra**): A standard Hebrew term for the Bible or scripture.

Mishnah: Codification of rabbinic law edited in the third century CE, consisting of six main sections that are further divided into sixty-three tractates, covering civil, criminal, and ritual law. The Mishnah is a centerpiece of rabbinic curriculum and culture to this day. All subsequent discussions of rabbinic law are based on it. See also **Talmud(s)**.

Old Testament: A term used by Christians to refer to the first part of the Christian biblical canon, which for Protestant Christians is identical to the **Tanakh/Mikra** and for Catholic and Orthodox Christians contains all the books found in the **Tanakh/Mikra** as well as several other Second Temple–period Jewish books not accepted as canonical by Jews and Protestants. Only in modern Western culture, with its idolization of youth, would one think that the word "Old" implies some insult to Jewish scripture; in fact "Old" in the term "Old Testament" means "venerable," not "antiquated." Nonetheless, some contemporary Christians avoid the term, instead speaking of a "First Testament" or a "Prime Testament" or using the religiously neutral term "**Hebrew Bible.**"

Pentateuch: A Greek term referring to the first part of the Jewish biblical canon, that is, the Five Books of Moses (known in Hebrew as the **Torah** and also as the Ḥumash).

peshat and derash: Both terms mean "interpretation" (that is, "interpretation of the Bible"). In classical rabbinic texts from the time of the **Talmud** and **midrashim** (i.e., in rabbinic texts dating to the first millennium CE), these terms are generally used as synonyms. Since the twelfth or thirteenth century CE, under the influence of the great French Jewish commentators Rashi and Rashbam, the terms have come to be used to refer to two distinct types of interpretation: **Peshat** refers to interpretations that attend to the immediate textual context of a biblical passage, interpret the Bible using the normal rules of human language, and often focus on questions of style, usage, and Hebrew grammar. **Derash** refers to those rabbinic interpretations that, regarding biblical language as essentially different from normal, human language, find many layers of meaning in biblical texts, focus heavily on single verses (or small groups of verses) rather than larger textual units, often interpret a verse in one book by relating it to verses from other biblical books, and concentrate on practical moral or religious lessons that can be derived from a biblical text. In the sense in which Rashbam uses the terms, **peshat** and **derash** are both legitimate modes of interpretation (though Jewish law is always based on **derash** and does not follow the interpretation one arrives at by using a **peshat** method of reading); they never conflict or contradict each other, because they exist at parallel, nonintersecting linguistic or exegetical planes.

peshat: See **peshat and derash**.
Rabbanite: As opposed to Karaite, a Jew who accepts rabbinic tradition.
rabbinic literature: Usually refers to the literature of the **classical rabbis**: the **Mishnah**, the **Talmuds**, the **midrashim**, and other texts produced in Hebrew and Aramaic by the **classical rabbis** during the first millennium CE. Sometimes the term is also used to refer to later literature that grows out of, interprets, or is based on these first-millennium works, such as commentaries on the Bible and on the **Mishnah, Talmuds**, and **midrashim** (e.g., the commentaries of Rashi or ibn Ezra), codifications of Jewish law, and responses to specific questions of Jewish law written by leading rabbinic authorities.
rabbis, classical: The term "rabbi" continues to be used today, but when scholars of Judaism refer to "the Rabbis" or "the Rabbinic Period," they generally mean what we might call the "classical rabbis," the rabbis whose discussions and teachings are found in the **Mishnah**, the **Talmuds**, and the **midrashim**. The classical rabbis are divided into two main periods: the **tanna'im** (dating to the first through mid-third centuries CE) are the rabbis who produced the **Mishnah**; the **amora'im** (dating from the mid-third through the sixth centuries CE) are the rabbis who produced the **Talmuds**. Both groups are frequently quoted in midrashic collections.
Talmud(s): The central document of rabbinic culture from the mid-first

millennium to this day. There are two Talmuds, one edited into its current form in the Land of Israel in the fifth century CE (usually called the Jerusalem Talmud or the Palestinian Talmud), the other edited into its current form in Mesopotamia in the sixth century CE (the Babylonian Talmud). Both consist of two parts. The earlier part is the **Mishnah**; the later part, known as the Gemara, contains a series of discussions, debates, elaborations, and interpretations of the **Mishnah**. The same **Mishnah** is found in both the Talmuds (minor textual variants notwithstanding); the two Gemaras are completely different works, though some passages appear in both.

Tanakh: A Hebrew term for the Bible. It is an acronym formed from the three parts of the Jewish biblical canon: *Torah* (the Five Books of Moses), *Nevi'im* (Prophets, including both historical books and the writings of the classical prophets), and *Ketuvim* (Writings, consisting of a variety of historical, narrative, and poetic works).

tanna'im: See **rabbis, classical**.

Tetragrammaton: The four-letter personal name of God in the Bible, often transliterated as "YHWH" in English or rendered as "the LORD" in English translations of the Bible. In Jewish tradition for the past two millennium, it is not pronounced aloud, and as a result, scholars are not absolutely positive what the vowels were—but they are almost positive that an *a* came after the *Y* and an *e* after the *w*.

torah: Literally means "teaching" or "guidance" and is often used in the sense of "law." As a proper noun, it can refer to several specific works or bodies of literature:

- **Torah** (especially, "the Torah") refers to the Five Books of Moses or **Pentateuch**, the first part of the Jewish biblical canon.
- **Written Torah** refers in **rabbinic literature** to the whole Bible or **Tanakh**.
- **Oral Torah** refers in **rabbinic literature** to authoritative or sacred teachings not found in the Bible but also revealed to Moses at Mount Sinai, or teachings based on or growing out of that revelation. It includes all the classic works of **rabbinic literature** (the **Mishnah**, the **Talmuds**, the **midrashim**) and also many, but not all, post-Talmudic teachings, many of which were never reduced to writing.
- **Torah** can also refer to the Written and Oral Torahs together—in other words, to all authoritative and sacred Jewish teaching.

YHWH: See **Tetragrammaton**.

About the Contributors

Marc Zvi Brettler is the Dora Golding Professor of Biblical Studies at Brandeis University. He is coeditor of the recently published *The Jewish Annotated New Testament* and of *The Jewish Study Bible*, which won a National Jewish Book Award, and he wrote *How to Read the Jewish Bible*, among other books and articles. He was interviewed by Terry Gross on *Fresh Air*.

Shalom Carmy teaches philosophy and Jewish studies at Yeshiva University, where he is cochair of Jewish Studies Executive of Yeshiva College. He is editor of *Tradition: A Journal of Orthodox Jewish Thought*. He is editor of *Modern Scholarship in the Study of Torah: Contributions and Limitations* (1996), *Jewish Perspectives on the Experience of Suffering* (1999), and *Rabbi Soloveitchik's Worship of the Heart* (2003). His writing focuses on biblical theology, modern Orthodox theology, and the interface of Torah and the liberal arts.

Jonathan Cohen is Associate Professor of Philosophy of Education and Jewish Education at the Hebrew University of Jerusalem. He currently serves as director of the Hebrew University's School of Education. He is the author of *Philosophers and Scholars: Wolfson, Guttmann, and Strauss on the History of Jewish Philosophy*.

James A. Diamond holds the Joseph and Wolf Lebovic Chair of Jewish Studies at the University of Waterloo. He has published widely on Jewish thought, philosophy, and biblical exegesis. His books include *Maimonides and the Hermeneutics of Concealment* and *Converts, Heretics, and Lepers: Maimonides and the Outsider*. He is currently completing an intellectual history of engagements with Maimonides from medieval to modern times.

Yael S. Feldman holds the Abraham I. Katsh Chair of Hebrew Culture and is Professor of Comparative Literature and Gender Studies at New York

University. Her fields of interest include cultural studies and psychoanalytic criticism. She is the author of *Glory and Agony: Isaac's Sacrifice and National Narrative*, a 2010 National Jewish Book Awards Finalist, and is coeditor of *Teaching the Hebrew Bible as Literature* (1989).

Steven D. Fraade is the Mark Taper Professor of the History of Judaism at Yale University, where he teaches in the Department of Religious Studies and the Program in Judaic Studies, the latter of which he chairs. He is the author, most recently, of *Legal Fictions: Studies of Law and Narrative in the Discursive Worlds of Ancient Jewish Sectarians and Sages* (2011).

Robert A. Harris is Associate Professor of Bible at the Jewish Theological Seminary and has served as a visiting faculty member at the Russian State University for Humanities, the Hebrew University of Jerusalem, and the Gregorian University in Rome. The author of *Discerning Parallelism: A Study in Northern French Medieval Jewish Biblical Exegesis*, he has written extensively on the literary hermeneutics of medieval biblical exegesis.

Aaron W. Hughes is the Bernstein Chair of Jewish Studies at the University of Rochester. He is the author of, among other works, *The Texture of the Divine: Imagination in Medieval Islamic and Jewish Thought* (2004), *The Art of Dialogue in Jewish Philosophy* (2007), and *The Invention of Jewish Identity: Bible, Philosophy, and the Art of Translation* (2010).

Moshe Idel, the Max Cooper Professor Emeritus of Jewish Thought at the Hebrew University of Jerusalem and Senior Scholar at the Shalom Hartman Institute, received the Israel Prize in 1999 and the inaugural Emet Prize in 2002. His major interests include the history of Jewish mysticism, the Italian Renaissance, and Hasidism. He is author of, among many works, *Kabbalah: New Perspectives*; *Absorbing Perfections: Kabbalah and Interpretation*; *Kabbalah in Italy*; *Kabbalah and Eros*; and *Saturn's Jews*.

Job Y. Jindo is Director of Academic Programs at New York University's Tikvah Center for Law & Jewish Civilization and an adjunct professor at the New York University School of Law. His publications include *Biblical Metaphor Reconsidered: A Cognitive Approach to Poetic Prophecy in Jeremiah 1–24* (2010). His work-in-progress, titled "Toward a Poetics of the Biblical Mind," explores the inner world of biblical authors as reflected in their writings.

Meira Polliack is Professor of Bible at Tel Aviv University. She has published on medieval Jewish Bible translation and exegesis in the Islamic milieu, Judaeo-Arabic literature, Karaism, and the Cairo Geniza. Among her books are *The Karaite Tradition of Arabic Bible Translation: A Linguistic and Exegetical Study of the Karaite Translations of the Pentateuch from the Tenth to the Eleventh Centuries CE* and *Karaite Judaism: A Guide to Its History and Literary Sources*.

Baruch J. Schwartz teaches in the Department of Biblical Studies at the Hebrew University of Jerusalem. His research centers on the Torah and its composition, on biblical religion and law, on classical prophetic literature, and on medieval biblical exegesis. He is the author of *The Holiness Legislation* and of the commentary on Leviticus in *The Jewish Study Bible*, as well as numerous scholarly articles on biblical topics.

Benjamin D. Sommer is Professor of Bible at the Jewish Theological Seminary. His book *The Bodies of God and the World of Ancient Israel* received the 2009 Award for Excellence in the Study of Religion from the American Academy of Religion as well as the 2009 Jordan Schnitzer Award from the Association for Jewish Studies. His first book, *A Prophet Reads Scripture: Allusion in Isaiah 40–66*, received the 1998 Salo Wittmayer Baron Prize from the American Academy of Jewish Research.

Elsie Stern is Associate Professor of Bible at the Reconstructionist Rabbinical College. She is the author of *From Rebuke to Consolation: Exegesis and Theology in the Liturgical Anthology of the Ninth of Av Season*. Her current research focuses on oral and textual dimensions of scripture in early Judaism.

Azzan Yadin-Israel is Associate Professor of Rabbinic Literature at Rutgers University. He is the author of *Scripture as Logos: Rabbi Ishmael and the Origins of Midrash* (2004) and is currently completing a book on Rabbi Akiva. He is coeditor of the Mohr Siebeck series Texts and Studies in Ancient Judaism.

Yair Zakovitch is the Father Takeji Otsuki Professor of Bible at the Hebrew University of Jerusalem. His main interests are the Bible as literature and the early history of biblical interpretation. He is currently working on a commentary on Psalms. His most recent books include *Inner-biblical and Extra-biblical Midrash and the Relationship between Them* and *The Little Book on the Nature of Angels*.

Index

1 Kings: 18:45, 42; 19, 308
1 Samuel; 1:17, 107; 9:9, 115; 9:18, 115; 10:20–21, 308; 15: 22, 132; 25:9, 146
2 Samuel: 20:19, 145; 22, 186–87

Abram/Abraham (patriarch), 20–22, 47–48, 61n1, 149–50, 153, 308; legacy and teachings, 128–29, 132; as a literary device, 288–89
Abravanel, Don Isaac, 88, 93
Abudarham, 25
Accounts of the Creation and the Chariot, 133
ad litteram reading of biblical texts, 111
After Childhood, 293
aggadah and aggadic interpretations, 42, 44, 65–66, 141. *See also* midrash and midrashic interpretations
Agnon, S. Y., 288
Ahab (king), 310
Ahad Ha'Am, 232–33
Akiva (rabbi), 49, 53, 58–60
"Al hamizbe'ah" (on the altar), 288, 296n21
Allon, Yigal, 301
Alter, Robert, 281–82
Amital, Yehuda, 269–71
'Anan ben David, 95
angels, 161
anthropomorphism, 124, 131, 159–61, 163–67
antirationalism. *See* rationalism and rationalists
Apocrypha, 11n3
"Aqud" (bound), 287–88
Arabic language and culture, 81–83, 86. *See also* Islam and Islamists; Judaeo-Arabic culture
Aramaic translation (*targum*), 27–28, 36–37, 45n7
Aristotle, 125
Aschkenasy, Nehama, 282
atonement and repentance, 22–24. *See also* Yom Kippur (Day of Atonement)

authority, 98, 295. *See also* scripture(s); Talmud(s)
authorship of Torah, 205–6, 268–69. *See also* Moses

Baal Shem Tov, 168–69
Babylonian exile, 305. *See also* Ezra and Nehemiah
Babylonian Talmud (BT), 4, 32, 111; *Avodah Zarah* 36a, 145; *Bava Batra* 14b–15a, 114–15; *Kiddushin* 21b, 272; *Makkot* 24a, 255; *Megillah* 3:10, 29n5; *Sanhedrin* 64b, 137n2; *Shabbat* 31a, 45n4; *Shabbat* 63a, 110; *Shabbat* 88b–89a, 175n4; *Sotah* 16a, 111
The Battle, 290
Ben-Aharon, Yariv, 290
Ben Gurion, David, 281, 314
"the Besht." *See* Baal Shem Tov
Bialik, Haim Nahman, 285, 296n21, 299
Bible/biblical literature, 1–7, 11n4, 13n23, 29n1, 94–96, 257, 260. *See also* scripture(s); Tanakh; approaches and assumptions, 66–69, 77n8, 95, 97, 204, 305–12; canonization of (*see* canon and canonization); as cultural or historical artifact, 96–97, 232, 235, 240, 242; distancing from/drawing close to, 302–3, 307–10; hypertextual qualities, 68–75, 311–12; interpreting, 49–50, 88–89, 110–12, 124, 195–97, 252–53, 311–12 (*see also* biblical exegesis; midrash and midrashic interpretations); language (*see* scriptural language); national development/identity and, 280, 286–95; printing, effect of, 13–14n25, 15; secularization of, 301–3; the synagogue and, 15–27; unity of, 67–75, 309; vocalization of, 77–78n10; Zionism and, 7, 241, 299–301
biblical criticism and critics, 203–29, 248, 300; Breuer/Orthodox movement and, 210–12, 267–69, 273–77; Conservative movement and, 209–10, 217;

biblical criticism and critics (*continued*)
Kaufmann and, 223, 226–27, 230–31;
Reform movement and, 208–9
biblical exegesis, 67–75, 87–88, 132. See also
peshat/derash distinction; approaches to,
204, 260–61; Breuer's view, 272–74, 279n6;
Buber and Rosenzweig's view, 181–82,
185–89, 192, 194–99; Greenberg's view,
258–59; Judaeo-Arabic, 83–88; linguistic
and literary aspects, 86–87; Maimonides's
contribution/role, 124; midrashic, 87 (*see
also* midrash and midrashic interpretations); Nahmanides's view and contribution, 142–45
biblical heroes, 308. See also under individual
names
biblical history. See Jewish history
biblical law, 89, 111–12, 309
biblical narrator. See *mudawwin*
(composer-compiler)
biblical studies (modern), 313–14
binding of Isaac, 67–68, 78n12, 283–90,
289–91
Bloom, Allan, 195–96
Bloom, Orly Castel. See Castel-Bloom, Orly
Blum, Ruth Kartun. See Kartun-Blum, Ruth
Bonfils (Tov-Elem), Joseph ben Eliezer,
228n4
book fairs (Israeli), 47
The Book of [Divine] Unity, 162–63, 165
The Book of Lights and Watchtowers, 97
The Book of Parks and Gardens, 97
Breuer, Isaac, 268–69
Breuer, Mordechai, 267–79; on biblical criticism and exegesis, 267–68, 272–78, 279n6;
on Jewish mysticism, 269
Brisker system of Talmud study, 270–71
Brod, Max, 280
Buber, Martin, 179–202; on Bible, 181–82,
185–89, 192, 194–99; on Christianity, 180;
on God, 183–89, 199; on Jewish law, 180–
81; on revelation, 183; on Zionism, 180
Buber, Solomon, 179
Buddhism, 4
burnt offerings, 49–50. See also sacrificial cult
and sacrifices

camels, 61n1
Canaan, 21–22, 306–7
Canaanism movement, 301
canon and canonization, 9, 11n2, 12n16,
233–34, 246n42, 313; Alter's view, 281–82;
connectivity/unity of, 67–75; Greenberg's

view, 250; normative/formative, 5; Protestant Christian view, 78n11
cantillation marks and traditions, 277, 317–18
Cassuto, Umberto (Moshe David), 218–22
Castel-Bloom, Orly, 292–93
chiddushim (new interpretations), 198–99
Childs, Brevard, 249, 251
Christiani, Pablo, 141
Christians and Christianity, 110, 139, 141, 318.
See also Protestant Christianity
Christian Theologies of Scripture: A Comparative Introduction, 8
Chronicles, 309
Cohen, Hermann, 179–80, 195
commentaries and commentators, 9, 12n17,
85, 97, 258–59. See also biblical exegesis;
under individual names
Commentary on the Rationales of the Commandments, 164–66
composers-compilers. See *mudawwin*
(composer-compiler)
Conservative movement, 209–10, 217
contextual exegesis. See also *peshat* [plain
meaning of text]: historical, 305–7; scriptural (local or surface), 68–69
contraction. See *tzimtzum* (contraction)
Cordovero, Moshe, 177–78n39
covenant between God and Israel, 226
Creation and creation narrative, 116–18, 133,
148–49, 158–59, 191–92. See also Genesis;
Nahmanides's view, 151–53; Soloveitchik
(J. D.)'s view, 271
critical inquiry. See biblical criticism and
critics
crusades and crusaders, 80, 99, 141–42
cultural creativity. See *ruah* and *ruaah le'umi*
(collective spirit [or creative potential])
cultural forms, 235
culture, Israeli secular, 299–316

David (king), 308
Dayan, Moshe, 301
Day of Atonement. See Yom Kippur (Day of
Atonement)
Days of Ziklag, 289
derash, 104, 118. See also *peshat/derash*
distinction
derashot. See homilies
Deuteronomic source, 225–26
Deuteronomy, 234, 306–7; 4:15, 126; 4:29, 104;
4:39, 126; 5, 277; 5:5, 37; 7:1–5, 306–7; 9:10,
38; 11:19, 146; 11:22, 146; 13:5, 146; 15:1–11,
309; 15:12–18, 272–73; 15:17, 53; 17:18–20,

310; 17:19, 40–41; 23:4, 309; 24:1, 53; 27:26, 165; 30:8, 90; 32:2, 41; 32:4, 133; 32:40, 155n11; 33:10, 45n3
devequt (cleaving), 146–47. *See also* God
dialectic idealism, 235
Dilthey, Willhelm, 233, 235
Dinur, Ben-Zion, 305
Diqdūq, 94
discourse analysis, 95
divine, the. *See* God
divine authorship. *See* authorship of Torah
divine names. *See* God
documentary hypothesis, 203–4, 207, 220–22, 225–26, 269
Dolly City, 292–93
Dov Baer, the Great Maggid of Miedzirec, 169–70
Driver, S. R., 257
Duran, Profayt, 88, 93

Ecclesiastes, 40; 1:10, 38; 5:2, 149; 12:9–10, 125
Ehrlich, Arnold B., 217
Ein Sof [infinite; transcendent], 157
Eldad and Medad, 70–71, 73–74
Eleazar (high priest), 158
Eliezer of Beaugency (rabbi), 115–16
Eliezer the son of Shimon (rabbi), 54
elite, intellectual, 82
empirical materialism, 235
empiricism and empiricists, 230–42, 246n40
encounters, dialogical, 184–85, 191, 194–99
Enlightenment period, influence of, 213
Ephrayyim, Moshe Hayyim, 168
epic aspects/stories, 190–91, 193–94
epitomes, 255
Epstein, Jacob, 49
Esau, 192–93
ethics and morality, 23, 129–30, 209, 226, 281, 295. *See also* God
exegesis, biblical. *See* biblical exegesis
exegesis, context-bound. See also *peshat* [plain meaning of text], 93
exegesis, legal. *See* legal rulings and traditions
exegesis, nonlegal, 91–92
exegetes, Christian, 111–12
exegetes, French, 103, 106, 110–16, 121–22n35, 319. *See also* Rashbam (R. Samuel ben Meir); Rashi and School of Rashi
exegetes, Karaite. *See* Karaism/Karaite Judaism
exile. *See* Babylonian exile
Exodus: 1–11, 251; 2:9, 308; 2:22, 74; 3:6, 136; 12:2, 102; 12:6, 49–50; 13:9, 112; 15:15–16, 308; 15:18, 188–89; 15:25, 132; 18:3, 74; 19–20, 277; 20:1, 103; 20:8–11, 117–18; 21:1, 111; 21:2–6, 272–73; 21:17, 50; 22:9, 51; 22:10, 52; 23:10–13, 309; 33:19, 133; 33:21, 134; 34:27, 39; 36–40, 191
Exodus commentaries, 48–49, 221
Exodus Rabbah: §25:3, 311; §47:1, 103
extra-scriptural traditions, 52–53, 58, 60–61
Ezekiel, 216; 1:1–4, 115–16; 5:15, 143; 18, 255; 24:24, 121n31; 38:17, 71–72
Ezekiel (commentaries on), 249–53, 257–58
Ezekiel (prophet), 115–16
Ezra 7:10, 104
Ezra and Nehemiah, 212, 234, 305
Ezra ben Solomon, 160–61

faith. *See* reason and faith
Fathers According to Rabbi Nathan, 34, 42
fetishism, 224, 238
Fishbane, Michael, 197–98
the Five Books of Moses. *See* Pentateuch
the Five Scrolls. *See* Writings (*Ketuvim*)
Fohrer, Georg, 251
Fraade, Steven D., 5, 260–61
Frankfurt school of neo-Orthodoxy. *See* neo-Orthodoxy
Freudianism, 286, 289, 292. *See also* binding of Isaac

Gamliel (Rabban), 54
Geiger, Abraham, 209
Gemarah, 32. *See also* Talmud(s)
Genesis: 1, 116–18, 269–71; 1:1, 111, 116; 1:31, 117, 133, 258; 2, 269–71; 2:1, 153; 3, 270; 3:8, 106; 9:5, 255; 11–12, 270; 11:27–28, 20; 11:29–32, 21; 11:31, 21; 12:1, 20–21; 12:1–4, 21; 12:10–20, 308; 18:1–3, 149; 19:30–38, 308; 22, 285–87, 289; 22:1, 67–68; 22:2, 119n4; 25:22, 104; 27:36, 192–93; 28:15, 151; 29:25, 193; 32:25, 149; 32:31, 149; 37:2, 111, 113–14; 38, 308; 46:2, 150; 46:4, 150
Genesis commentaries, 221, 247
Genesis Rabbah: §1:2, 175n5; §59, 67; §8:2, 175n5
German culture and philosophy, 179
Gershom (son of Moses), 73–74
Gideon, 189
Ginsberg, Asher H. *See* Ahad Ha'Am
Glatzer, Nachum, 184
God, 21–22, 24–26, 79n19, 116–18, 162. *See also* monotheism/monotheistic worldview; theurgy; Yhwh; attributes of, 129–30, 151, 159, 270;

God (*continued*)
Buber and Rosenzweig's view, 183–89, 190; cleaving to, 146, 162, 167; conceptions of, 134, 157, 159–61; contact with through text, 163, 165; governance, 130, 132; knowledge of, 108–10, 127–28; language of, 66; Maimonides's view, 124–30, 133; moral sphere, 224, 226, 236; Nahmanides's view, 143, 145; names, 145, 147, 158–62, 166–70, 177n33, 270

Gog and Magog, 70–72
Goren, Shlomo, 303
Goshen-Gottstein, Moshe, 248
Gouri, Haim, 289
Govrin, Michal, 294
Graham, William A., 3
grammar. *See* linguistics and grammar studies
Greenberg, Moshe, 247–66; on biblical literature/exegesis, 256–59; on canon and canonization, 250; influence of Kaufmann, 247–48
Grimm, Jacob, 188
Grossman, David, 294–95
Guide of the Perplexed, 123–25, 128–35, 137n4, 137n6, 138n18, 140; Intro, 125, 129, 130, 137n6; I:1, 135; I:5, 136; I:16, 134; I:19, 134; I:26, 124; I:45, 132; I:46, 136; I:54, 130, 133; I:55, 127; I:59, 136; I:64, 135; III:25, 133; III:27, 129; III:32, 129, 131, 132; III:47, 135; III:51, 131

Habad (Lubavitch) Hasidism, 170
Ḥadith literature, 89, 96
haftarot, 24–25. *See also* Prophets (*Nevi 'im*)
Ḥaggai, 38–39
ha-katuv (Scripture), 50–52
halakhah and *halakhot*, 42, 44, 88, 256–57. *See also* legal rulings and traditions; extrascriptural traditions, 53; Maimonides's view, 130–31; Midrash and, 58, 60–61; transmission of, 53–54
Halbertal, Moshe, 5
Halivni, David (Weiss), 212
Haran (person), 20–21
Haran (place), 21
Hareven, Shulamith, 292–93
HaShomer HaTzair, 300
Hasidism, 168–74
Hebrew language and grammar, 93–94, 142, 145, 250
Hebrew poetry, 282–84
Hebrew University of Jerusalem, 217–18, 313–14
heikhalot literature and mystics, 157–61

Heimann, Shoshana, 292
hermeneutic markers, 49–50, 54–55, 58, 62n9
hermeneutics. *See* biblical exegesis
Herzog Institute, 271
higher criticism and critics. *See* biblical criticism and critics
Hillel, 34–36
Hinduism, 4
Hirsch, Samson Raphael, 210–11, 214, 268
historical approaches/studies, 235
Hoffmann, David Zvi, 214–17, 225–26
Holcomb, Justin, 8–9
holiness, 135
"holistic interpretation," 252
Holocaust, 285, 288, 302. *See also* binding of Isaac
homilies, 28–29, 92–93, 106
Horowitz, Isaiah, 172–73
Hosea 8:12, 39
Hugh of St. Victor, 120n22
ḥumash. *See* Pentateuch
human nature, 129, 131
human sacrifice. *See* binding of Isaac; national development and identity; national sacrifice
humor in the Bible, 308

ibn Ezra, Abraham, 93, 141–42, 145, 151–53, 274
ibn Ezra, Moses, 87, 92
ibn Gabbai, Meir, 167
ibn Gikatilla, Moses, 87
idolatry, 128–31, 146, 237, 301, 304–7, 309. *See also* monotheism/monotheistic worldview; polytheism/polytheistic worldview
imitatio dei [mimic God's governance], 130, 132
impurity. *See* purity versus impurity
"Isaac," 293–94
Isaac (patriarch). *See* binding of Isaac
Isaac generation, 289–90, 292
Isaiah: 2:3, 119n4; 5:8–10, 109–10; 11:6, 128; 27:1, 143; 29:13, 89, 90; 40–66, 24–25; 40:25, 126–27; 40:26, 145; 42:21, 108; 49:14, 26; 51:12, 25; 54:1, 25; 54:5, 26; 54:11, 25, 26; 55:6, 104; 57:14–58:14, 23–24; 58:5–9, 23; 60:1, 25; 60:10, 25; 62:10, 25
Ishmael (rabbi), 50, 86, 158–59, 161, 175n2. *See also Mekhilta of Rabbi Ishmael* (on Exodus)
Islam and Islamists, 80–82, 93. *See also* Arabic language and culture; Judaeo-Arabic culture; Muhammad

isomorphism, 165–67
Israel (people), 223–26, 234. *See also* national development and identity
Israel Baal Shem Tov. *See* Baal Shem Tov
Israel's Independence Day. *See* Yom Ha-Atzmaut (Israel's Independence Day)
I-Thou experiences. *See* encounters, dialogical
Ivry, Alfred, 138n18

Jacob (patriarch) narrative, 192–93
Jacob ben Sheshet, 160
Jacob's ladder, 150–51
Jacobson, David, 282
James I of Aragon (king), 141
Jephthah's daughter, 286, 291
Jerusalem Talmud. *See* Palestinian (Jerusalem) Talmud
Jewish history, 223–25. *See also* Holocaust; Jewish survival; national development and identity; Zionism and Zionists
Jewish martyrdom. *See* national sacrifice
Jewish mysticism, 139–40, 157–74, 159. *See also sefirot* [manifestations/powers of God]; Zohar; on God, 157, 160–74; Maimonides's view, 138n27; Nahmanides and, 142, 145–47, 161; scriptural language and, 77n9; on Torah, 161–65
Jewish nationalism. *See* national development and identity
Jewish survival, 232–33, 238, 245n30. *See also* national development and identity; national sacrifice
Jews and Judaism, secular, 8–9, 299–316, 304
Jews of Russia, 232
Joseph (rabbi), 125–26
Joseph of Hamadan, 164–66
Josephus, 33
Joshua, 305–7; 2, 308; 6:21–24, 304; 7:14–18, 308; 8:22–29, 304; 10:24–26, 304; 13–17, 307; 13:1, 307
Joshua (person), 70, 71–74
Joshua ben Levi, 38, 40
Josiah's reform, 234
Jubilees, 276–77
Judaeo-Arabic culture, 82–88, 98. *See also* Karaism/Karaite Judaism
Judah [bar R. Simeon] bar Pazzi. *See* Judah ben R. Shimon (Simeon/Simon)
Judah ben R. Shalom, 39
Judah ben R. Shimon (Simeon/Simon), 37–40, 310

Judges: 1:5–7, 303; 2:13–16, 305; 8:22–23, 189; 17–18, 73, 75; 17:1, 73–75; 18:30, 73–75

kabbalah and kabbalists. *See* Jewish mysticism
Kalisch, M. M., 213–14
Kamin, Sarah, 105
Kant, Immanuel, influence of, 246n40, 268–69
Kara, Yosef (rabbi), 107–10, 112, 115
Karaism/Karaite Judaism, 80–83, 85–87, 93–94; approach to halakhah, 88–91; biblical exegesis and, 83–88, 91–92, 98; historical approach, 97; messianism and, 82; narrative and literary approach, 94–96
Karaite-Rabbanite rift. *See* Rabbanite-Karaite rift
Kartun-Blum, Ruth, 282
Katznelson, Berl, 287
Kaufmann, Yehezkel, 218, 223–27, 230–46, 243n5; on biblical criticism, 223–24, 230–31; education, 232–33, 244n10; influence on Moshe Greenberg, 247–48; on monotheism, 231, 233, 236–42; on Torah, 224–26
Ketuvim (Writings). *See* Writings (*Ketuvim*)
Kimhi, David, 92–93, 148
Kings. *See* 1 Kings
kings, Israelite, 40–41. *See also* under individual names
Kitvei Ha-qodesh (sacred texts). *See* Tanakh
Klausner, Margot, 291–92
knowledge, 35, 133, 177n37, 242. *See also* empiricism and empiricists; Jewish mysticism, 82, 134, 237; human, 82, 134, 237; religious, 108–10, 124–25, 127–30
Kohelet. *See* Ecclesiastes
Kohelet Rabbah §1:29, 45n12
Kook, Abraham Isaac, 270
Kreisel, Howard, 137n7
Kristeva, Julia, 293
Kronos, 186
Kugel, James, 67, 77n8, 104

Laban (person), 193
Lamdan, Yitzhak, 287–88
Lamentations, 24
lammah ne'emar (why was this stated?), 49–50
Land of Israel, 80, 82, 99, 300–304, 309–10. *See also* national development and identity
language, human, 66, 75, 124, 127, 135, 307–9
language, scriptural. *See* scriptural language
law, biblical, 112, 216, 222, 225

"leading words," 191–92
lectionaries and lectionary cycles/practices, 15–27
legal rulings and traditions, 57, 59–60, 82, 88–89. See also *halakhah* and *halakhot*
Leibowitz, Yeshayahu, 212
Leon, Moshe ben Shem Tov de, 162
Leviticus: 1:5, 59; 1:10, 57–58; 5:5, 56–57; 11:33, 58–59; 15:2, 56; 16:1–34, 22; 16, 24; 16:29 34, 22; 17:3, 54–55; 17:8, 56; 17:10, 54–55; 17:13, 53, 55–56; 18:6, 56; 22:4, 55; 22:17–20, 55; 23:5–11, 275–76; 23:15, 275–76; 23:16–21, 275–76; 25:39–55, 272–73
Leviticus commentaries, 214–16
Lichtenstein, Aharon, 271
"Lifnei Aron Ha-sfarim," 299
linguistics and grammar studies, 86, 93–94. See also Hebrew language and grammar
listening, biblical, 132
literary devices, 54, 95, 111, 117, 191
literary exegesis, 87. See also biblical exegesis
liturgical poems. See *piyyutim* (liturgical poems)
liturgy, 28–29, 29n9
logic, 81–82. See also rationalism and rationalists
Lonely Man of Faith, 271
Lot (person), 20–21
Luria, Isaac, 169
"lyric" illumination, 190–94

Maggid of Miedzirec. See Dov Baer, the Great Maggid of Miedzirec
magic, 158, 161, 168–70
Magog. See Gog and Magog
Maimonides, Moses (ben Maimon), 9–10, 123–38; on God, 129–30, 133–35; on Hebrew language, 145; on morality, 129–30; on mysticism, 138n27; Nahmanides and, 139–41, 148–50; on scripture and exegesis, 128–36; on Torah, 124–35
Malbim. See Weiser, Meir Leibush
Marah, waters of, 132
markers. See hermeneutic markers
martyrdom. See national sacrifice
Masoretic text (MT), 249–52
Medad. See Eldad and Medad
Meir (rabbi), 43, 108–9
Mekhilta of Rabbi Ishmael (on Exodus), 48–49, 60; *Neziqin* §5, 50; *Neziqin* §16, 51
Mekhilta of Rabbi Shimon bar Yohai (on Exodus), 48–49
memorization and orality in midrash, 78n15

Menahem Nahum of Chernobyl, 174
Mendelssohn, Moses, 208
Men of the Great Assembly, 121n31
Messianic era and messianism, 82, 127–28
metadivine. See polytheism/polytheistic worldview
metaphysics and physics, 130–32, 137n7
midrash and midrashic interpretations, 3, 32, 44, 103–4, 106–7, 109. See also aggadah and aggadic interpretations; biblical exegesis; approaches, 60, 92–93; classical, 84; extra-scriptural traditions and, 58; legal, 48–50, 58; modern, 197, 282; relationships among verses, 67–75; on scripture/scriptural language, 64–76, 197–99; Talmud(s) and, 65
midrash mekhonen (constitutive), 60
midrash somekh (supporting), 60
Mikra Le Yisra'el commentary series, 253
Milcah (person), 21
minayin (whence) legal rulings, 57
Miqra (reading), 80, 170–71. See also Tanakh; Written Torah
miqraot gedolot [Rabbinic Bible], 142
mishem (in the name of) a [sage], 53
Mishnah (*m.*), 3, 32, 90. See also Oral Torah; Avot 1, 42–43; Avot 6, 120n20; Megillah 4:4, 27; Sotah 5:2, 59; Yebamoth 8:3, 309; Yoma 8:9, 30n12
Mishnah Commentary [Maimonides], 131
Mishneh Torah, 123, 126–32, 137n5, 140
monotheism/monotheistic worldview, 245n25, 306–7. See also polytheism/polytheistic worldview; Kaufmann's view, 224–26, 236–40, 242; Maimonides's view, 128
morality. See ethics and morality
Morgenstern, Julian, 217
Moses, 70–74, 97, 134, 206–7; Abraham's legacy and, 129, 132; author/editor of Torah, 103, 117–18, 133–34, 144, 147, 228n4; monotheism/monotheistic worldview and, 238, 242; role in revelation, 38–43, 158, 161, 175n4; Song at the Sea, 143
Moshe Hayyim Ephrayyim of Sudylkov. See Ephrayyim, Moshe Hayyim
Mossinsohn, Yigal, 288–89
Mount Sinai. See revelation; Sinai and Sinai narrative
Mr. Mani, 290
mudawwin (composer-compiler), 95–96
Muhammad, 96
Muslims. See Islam and Islamists

My Father's House, 301
mysticism. *See* Jewish mysticism

Naboth's vineyard, 310
Nahmanides, Moses (ben Nahman), 93, 118, 139–56; on biblical exegesis, 142–43; commentaries, 144, 154; as communal leader, 139–41; on creation, 148–49; on God, 143, 145; on Hebrew language, 145; ibn Ezra, Abraham and, 141–42, 151–53; on idolatry, 146; as intersection and mediator, 139–41; Jewish mysticism and, 142, 145–47; Maimonides and, 139–41, 148–50; Rashi and, 141–42, 151–53
Nahor (person), 20–21
Nakh, 2–3. *See also* Prophets (*Nevi 'im*); Writings (*Ketuvim*)
The Name, 294
narrative, biblical, 190–91. *See also* Bible/biblical literature
narrative technique, 95–96. *See also* literary devices
national development and identity, 39, 223–26, 300; Bible/biblical literature and, 280–81, 286–95; communal, 19, 48; secularization, 282
national sacrifice, 285–95. *See also* Holocaust
Navon, Gad, 303
In the Negev Plains, 288–89
Nehemiah: 4:1–2, 305; 4:10–11, 305; 8:8, 45nn9–10
Nehemiah (person), 305
neo-Orthodoxy, 286
Nevi 'im (Prophets). *See* Prophets (*Nevi 'im*)
Nūḥ, Abū Ya'qūb Yūsuf ibn, 94
Numbers: 11, 75; 11:16, 70; 11:18, 70; 11:26, 70–72; 11:26–29, 70; 11:27, 73–75; 11:28, 70, 72; 28:4, 50; 28:8, 49–50; 29:7–11, 22–23
Numbers Rabbah: §13.15, 275; §15.15 (15.19), 70, 73, 75

oaths, 52, 160
offerings, 57–58. *See also* paschal offerings; sacrificial cult and sacrifices
omnisignificance, 104–7, 274–75, 277
Onkelos, 150–51
Only Yesterday, 288
orality. *See* memorization and orality in midrash
Oral Torah, 5–6, 26–27, 31–44, 81–82, 103, 171–72; authenticity of, 88; Karaites' view,

89–91; *mishnah* [memorization or repetition], 45n10; *sefirot* and, 161
Or Ha-Emet, 170
Orthodox movement, 210–12, 268–69. *See also* neo-Orthodoxy
Oz, Amos, 290

P (Priestly) document, 216, 225–26
paganism, 224. *See also* polytheism/polytheistic worldview
Palestinian (Jerusalem) Talmud, 36–38, 40
parables, 125–26, 128–31
paschal offerings, 49–50
Passover, 275–76
Pentateuch, 2–3, 17–19, 29n5, 203–29. *See also* Written Torah
Pentateuchal criticism and scholarship, 203–10, 224, 227
Perez (person), 308
perfection, quest for, 124
peshat [plain meaning of text], 92–93, 104–14, 145, 274, 311. *See also* peshat/derash distinction
peshat/derash distinction, 105–7, 119–20n13, 271–76
Pharisees, 33–34
philology/philological analysis, 214–15, 223, 225, 259, 276
philosophy and philosophers, 153, 185. *See also* *Guide of the Perplexed*; Jewish mysticism; Karaism/Karaite Judaism; metaphysics and physics; rationalism and rationalists; under individual names
physics. *See* metaphysics and physics
Pirkei Avot, 312
piyyutim (liturgical poems), 28–29
polytheism/polytheistic worldview, 224, 245n27. *See also* fetishism; monotheism/monotheistic worldview; Buber and Rosenzweig's view, 184; Kaufmann's view, 236–40
Presidential Residence's Group on Bible and the Sources of Israel, 314
Prophets (*Nevi 'im*), 2, 4–7, 17–20, 24–26
prophets and prophecy, 78–79n18, 115–16, 132, 135–36, 226. *See also* under individual names
Protestant Christianity, 6, 8, 11n3, 82
Proverbs: 2:4–5, 108; 8:14, 109; 22:17, 110; 25:11, 106
Psalms: 16:3, 145; 19:8, 108; 62:12, 106; 65:2, 136; 73:28, 134; 79:9, 143; 111:6, 102
purity versus impurity, 135, 138n26

Qinyan Torah, 108
al-Qirqisānī, Yūsuf Ya'qub, 91, 97–99
al-Qūmīsī, Daniel, 85

Rabbanism. *See* rabbinic Judaism
Rabbanite-Karaite rift, 81–83, 88–89, 91–93, 99
Rabbi Judah the Patriarch, 32
Rabbinic Bible. *See miqraot gedolot* [Rabbinic Bible]
rabbinic Judaism, 34–35, 44, 107–8, 300. *See also* Rabbanite-Karaite rift; rabbinic literature and texts; *torah lishma* (selfless Torah study); authority of, 115, 256; exegesis and, 110–13; *halakhah* and, 110–11; medieval Islamic period and, 82–83, 92; on revelation, 40, 43; on scripture, 68–69, 78n14; on study, 41–43
rabbinic literature and texts, 3–6, 34, 48, 84. *See also* midrash and midrashic interpretations; Mishnah (*m.*); Oral Torah; rabbinic Judaism; Talmud(s); authority of, 80; rejection of, 299; on repentance and atonement, 23–24; scriptural nature, 13n21
Rachel (poet), 291
Rahab (person), 308
Rambam. *See* Maimonides, Moses (ben Maimon)
Ramban. *See* Nahmanides, Moses (ben Nahman)
Rashbam (R. Samuel ben Meir), 110–18, 258, 272–73, 319
Rashi and School of Rashi, 92, 102–3, 106, 116–17; biblical exegesis and, 112–14, 258; Nahmanides and, 141–42, 151–53
rationalism and rationalists, 81–82, 139–40. *See also* Maimonides, Moses (ben Maimon)
reader, the, 112, 136, 189–90, 192–94, 195–99
reason and faith, 237
Recanati, Menahem, 167
redactor, role of, 115–16, 121–22n35, 251. *See also mudawwin* (composer-compiler)
Reform movement, 208–9
religion, biblical/Israelite, 224–25, 239–40. *See also* monotheism/monotheistic worldview
repentance and atonement. *See* atonement and repentance
revelation, 33, 40, 45n12, 183, 190–94. *See also* God; Moses; Torah
Ricoeur, Paul, 197
Rosenzweig, Adam, 179

Rosenzweig, Franz, 179–202; on Bible, 181–82, 185–99; on Christianity, 180; on God, 183–89, 199; on Jewish law, 180–81; on revelation, 190–94; on Zionism, 180
ruaḥ and *ruaḥ le'umi* (collective spirit [or creative potential]), 232, 235, 238, 240, 246n36

Sa'adiah Gaon, 82, 85–86, 92, 94
Sabbath, 153
sacrificial cult and sacrifices, 49–50, 57–59, 131–32
Sadducees, 275–76
Samuel (prophet), 115
Samuel 1. *See* 1 Samuel
Samuel 2. *See* 2 Samuel
Samuel bar Naḥman, 38
Samuel bar R. Isaac, 36–37
Sarah/Sarai (matriarch), 21, 149–50, 291
Saul (king), 300–301, 308
Schechter, Solomon, 217
Schneerson, Menahem Mendel, 177–78n39
Scholem, Gershom, 159, 198
Schweid, Eliezer, 197–98
science, 125, 137n6, 211, 268–69
scribes, 54. *See also* redactor, role of
scriptural language, 66–69, 78n17, 126; examples, 70–76; Jewish mysticism and, 77n9; Maimonides's view, 124, 135–36; matrices, 68–70, 78n15; parables, 125–26
scripture alone. *See sola scriptura* (scripture alone)
scripture(s), 1–5, 7, 136. *See also* Bible/biblical literature; extra-scriptural traditions; *Miqra* (reading); Tanakh; approaches and assumptions, 64–76, 77n8; authority of, 10–11, 48, 50–51, 131; authorship of, 114–16, 205 (*see also* Moses; Torah); canonization of (*see* canon and canonization); Christian view, 6, 8, 78n11, 82, 110, 120–21n22; conception of, 12n9, 61, 78n11, 112, 135, 157; Greenberg's view, 249, 259 (*see also* biblical exegesis); interpretation and intervention, 50–52; Israeli secular culture and, 299–316; Maimonides's view, 124, 128–31, 135; Nahmanides's view, 141–44, 147–48, 154, 155n11; oral/aural aspect, 6–7, 13n22, 78n15; recitation of, 15–27; theology of, 260–62
secret of divine names, 158, 175n4
secular Jews, 304
seers. *See* prophets and prophecy
Sefer ha-Madda, 140
Sefer Shimmushei Torah, 158, 161
Sefer Yetsira, 153

sefirot [manifestations/powers of God], 157, 159, 161–62, 166, 175–76n13, 177nn36–37
Segal, M. Z., 218
sermons. *See* homilies
Shaked, Gershon, 282
Shaked, Malka, 282–83
Shamir, Moshe, 289
Shammai, 34–36
Shapira, Anita, 281
Shavuot, 275–77
Shazar, Zalman, 233
Shifra, Shin, 293–94
Shi 'ur Qomah literature, 158–59, 161
Shnei Luḥot Ha-Berit (*Ha-Shelah*), 172–73
Shneor Zalman of Liady, 170–71, 177n36
Sibawayhī, 94
Sifra (on Leviticus), 48–49, 53–58; *Aḥarei Mot Parashah* §6.3, 55; *Aḥarei Mot Parashah* §8.1–2, 54; *Aḥarei Mot Pereq* §10.2, 56; *Aḥarei MotPereq* §11.1, 56; *Aḥarei Mot Pereq* §13.1, 56; *Beḥuqqotay Pereq* §8:12, 45n3; *Emor Parashah* §7.1, 55; *Hova Pereq* §1.12, 54; *Hova Pereq* §14.2–3, 57; *Metzora Zavim Parashah* §1.1, 56; *Nedava Parashah* §5.4, 57; *Shemini Parashah* §7.4, 54; *Shemini Parashah* §7.12, 59; *Shemini Parashah* §8.5, 54; *Shemini Pereq* §5.10, 54
Sifre Deuteronomy, 41, 48–49; §122, 53; §351, 45n3
Sifre Numbers, 48–50; §143, 49–50
silence (medium), 136
Simon, Uriel, 107
Sinai and Sinai narrative, 116–18. *See also* revelation
Sister, Moshe, 300
Smith, Anthony D., 281
Smith, Wilfred Cantwell, 4
sod [esoteric meaning of text], 145, 158
sofer. See redactor, role of
sola scriptura (scripture alone), 44, 45n9, 82, 110
Solomon (king), 110, 125–26
Solomon ben Isaac (rabbi). *See* Rashi and School of Rashi
Soloveitchik, Hayyim, 270
Soloveitchik, Joseph Dov, 271
Song at the Sea, 143
Song of Songs (commentary), 106, 160
source criticism and critics. *See* biblical criticism and critics
Speiser, Ephraim Avigdor, 247–48
Stock, Brian, 81, 98
Strauss, Leo, 179–80, 195–96

study of Torah for its own sake. *See torah lishma* (selfless Torah study)
sunna (Islamic oral law or received tradition), 82
survival. *See* Jewish survival
synagogue, the, 15–27, 318. *See also* liturgy

Tabernacle. *See* Tent of Meeting/Tabernacle narrative
talismanics, 168–70
talmud lomar (what is the instruction?), 49–50
Talmud(s), 3–4, 32, 90, 109. *See also* Babylonian Talmud (BT); Palestinian (Jerusalem) Talmud; authority of, 115; Brisker system of study, 270–71; Maimonides's view, 132–33; midrash and, 65; Nahmanides's view, 141
talmud torah lishama. See *torah lishma* (selfless Torah study)
Tanḥum ha-Yerushalmi, 92
Tanakh, 11n1, 18, 44n1. *See also* Bible/biblical literature; Pentateuch; Prophets (*Nevi 'im*); scripture(s); Torah; Writings (*Ketuvim*)
Tannaic period and *tannaim*, 48, 65–66, 319
Tarfon (rabbi), 59–60
targum. See Aramaic translation (*targum*)
Tchernowitz yeshivah, 232, 244n10
tefillin (phylacteries), 112
Temple cult, 24, 29n8
Tent of Meeting/Tabernacle narrative, 191–92
Terah (person), 20–21
Tetragrammaton. *See* Yhwh
textual criticism. *See* biblical criticism and critics; biblical exegesis
ṭhāhir [context-bound exegesis], 93
theologians and theology, 9–10, 183–86, 190–91, 249
theurgy, 166, 170
thirteen articles of faith, 123
Three Days and a Child, 290
Tisha b'Av, 24, 30n13
Torah, 2–3, 12–13n19, 128, 138n14, 204. *See also* anthropomorphism; Oral Torah; Written Torah; authorship of, 205, 268–69 (*see also* Moses); biblical criticism/critics and, 209–12; Breuer's view, 267–68, 272–78; canonical, 19, 207, 233–34 (*see also* canon and canonization); Cassuto's view, 219–20; chanting/translating of, 27–28, 30n17, 37–38, 45n6; conception of, 102–3, 131, 135, 143, 157–65; Greenberg's view, 256–57; Halivni's view, 212–13; Hoffmann's view, 214–17; human language and, 124, 129, 137n2, 307–9;

Torah (*continued*)
    as an intermediary, 157–74, 172–73; interpretations, 99, 113; kabbalistic conceptions of, 161–65; Kaufmann's view, 224–26; Leibowitz's view, 212; letters of, 169–71; Maimonides's view, 128–35; Nahmanides's view, 141–43, 145–47, 154; as name(s) of God/divine body, 159–61; overt (manifest)/hidden (secret) levels, 158, 162–64; Rashi's view, 103; reading of, 22, 29n6, 171; sanctity of, 116–18; science and, 137n6; Segal's view, 218; study of, 108–9, 165, 174 (see also *torah lishma* (selfless Torah study))
Torah Book Week (Israeli book fair), 47
torah lishma (selfless Torah study), 108–9, 174, 256, 265n37
torah she-be'al peh. *See* Oral Torah
torah she-bikhtav. *See* Written Torah
Torat ha-Behinot (theory of aspects), 267–69
Tosafists, 139–40
Tosafot, 4
Tosefta (*t.*), 17; *Megillah* 3(4):21, 45n6
To the End of the Land, 294–95
tradition, traditionalism, and traditionalists, 12n18, 139–40
Twersky, Isadore, 142
tzimtzum (contraction), 169–70

Ugaritic literature, 219
uncleanness. *See* purity versus impurity
Urbach, Ephraim E., 240–41
Ur of the Chaldeans, 20–21

values in the Bible, 253–55, 310–11

waters of Marah, 132
Weiser, Meir Leibush, 274
Weiss, David. *See* Halivni, David (Weiss)
Wellhausen, Julius and Wellhausenian approach, 207, 214, 216–21, 223–24; Breuer's view, 269; Hoffman's view, 214–17; Kaufmann's view, 225–26, 231, 241, 243n6
Wiener, Harold, 217
"Wild Man," 290–91
Wise, I. M., 217
women and national sacrifice, 291–95
women in the Bible, 284
worship. *See* liturgy; sacrificial cult and sacrifices; synagogue, the
Writings (*Ketuvim*), 2, 4. *See also* Ecclesiastes; Lamentations; Proverbs entries; Psalms entries; Song of Songs (commentary)
Written Torah, 5–6, 26–27, 31–44, 118, 176n28; *miqra'*, 45n10, 171–72; *sefirot* and, 161; study of, 40–41

Yefet ben 'Eli, 90–92, 94–99
Yehoshua (rabbi), 59
Yehoshua, A. B., 289–90
yekhol [could mean] legal rulings, 56–57
Yeshivat Har-Etzion, 271
Yhwh, 21–22, 25, 52. *See also* God; monotheism/monotheistic worldview
Yishmael (rabbi). *See* Ishmael (rabbi)
Yizhar, S., 289
Yohanan (rabbi), 38, 40, 50, 59
Yom Ha-Atzmaut (Israel's Independence Day), 305
Yom Kippur (Day of Atonement), 22–24, 50

Zadoq (rabbi), 53–54
Zecheriah 5:5–8, 90
Ze'ev Wolf of Zhitomir, 173
Zionism and Zionists, 232, 282; Bible and, 7–9, 299–301; Buber and Rosenzweig, 180; Hebrew literature and, 285–86; Kaufmann, 241
Zohar, 4, 162; 1:134a–b, 175n5; 3:35b, 175n5
Zohar, Noam, 260
Zunz, Leopold, 208–9